What others are sayin

"*There are a million stories in Key West and June Keith seems to know them all.*"
— **Dave Barry,** Pulitzer Prize-winning columnist. Author.

"*June Keith certainly is an engaging writer. She is a pleasure to read.*"
— **Alan Shearer,** *The Washington Post Writers Group*

"*A June Keith column is like a Key West sunset—once it begins you're hooked until it ends.*"
— **Kenley Jones,** NBC News

"*You'll fall in love with her, and the Keys.*"
— **Captain Tony,** Key West Mayor Emeritus. Saloonkeeper.

"*Her love for the people of Key West makes one wish her type thrived all over small-town America.*"
— **Gene Gabriel Moore,** *Southern Voice,* Atlanta

"*Keith knows first-hand, that Key West has the kind of sweaty, raunchy appeal you either surrender to—gloriously—or you walk away from, shaking your head in disgust. Either way, the town stays under your skin.*"
— **Jeanne Malmgren,** *St. Petersburg Times*

"*The best Keys guide. Current. Opinionated. Poetic. Honest.*"
— **Joel Carmel,** The Book Nook, Key Largo

June Keith's
Key West &

FOURTH EDITION

Palm Island Press
THE FLORIDA PUBLISHERS

Food
Hotels
Beaches
Diving

The Florida Keys

Fishing
History
Writers
Festivals
Attractions
Museums
Wildlife

For Fannie Elizabeth Rogers

Fourth Edition
Fifth printing, revised

Published by
Palm Island Press
411 Truman Avenue, Key West, Florida 33040 U.S.A.
pipress@earthlink.net   SAN 298-4024

Library of Congress Cataloging-in-Publication Data

Keith, June
    June Keith's Key West and the Florida Keys.
       p. cm.
    Includes index
    ISBN-13: 978-0-9743524-0-3
    ISBN-10: 0-9743524-0-3
    1. Florida Keys (Fla.)—Guidebooks. 2. Florida Keys
(Fla.)—History. /. Title. //. Title: Key West and the
Florida Keys.
F317.M7K45 1997   98-67545
917.59'4104'63

Table of Contents

Key West: The Last Resort 1

A Brief History of Key West 5
To Have and Have Not

Architecture 16
The Houses are Gingerbread, the People are Spice

Nuts and Bolts 22
Getting Around…Keys Weather…The Conch Republic

Old Town Walking Tour 28
A Showcase Stroll Through Old Town

Writers 50
18 Pulitzer Prizes…Ernest Hemingway…Tennessee Williams…
Jimmy Buffett…Poetry in Paradise…Bookstores

Art 80
Key West Artists…Galleries

Theater 90
Cinema…Live Theater

Attractions and Museums 95
Where to Go and What to See

Tours by Land, Sea and Air 121
Motor Tours…Water Excursions…Up, Up and Away

Annual Events 137
Paradise Uncovered Month by Month

Little Island, Big Fun 157
Diving…Fishing…Golf…Tennis

Kidstuff 166
Books…Swims…Art

Where's the Beach? 169
A Guide to the Island's Beaches…Gardens and Greenspace

Accommodations 181
Reservations Services…Hotels and Motels…Bed and Breakfasts…
Gay Accommodations

Dining 218
True Stories…It's Not Flipper…Cuban Cuisine

Bars 251
No sniveling

Shops 261
Only in Key West

The Perfect T 269
Shirts by the Pound

Endless Love 272
Weddings Are Us…Weird Science: The Elena Hoyos Story

The Lower Keys:
A Land That's Mostly Water; A Sea That's Mostly Sky 279

A History Stranger Than Fiction 283
Sugarloaf's Weird Past…Trailblazing Lily Bow…The Monkey Keys…
100 Sharks A Day

Key Deer 290
If You Think Bambi was Cute…Spotting Key Deer

Bahia Honda 294
The Florida Keys Biggest and Best Beach. Honest.

Waters of the Lower Keys 297
The Backcountry…Looe Key Sanctuary…Water Excursions

Nature Treats 303
The Blue Hole…Pinewood Nature Trail

Legal Highs 305
Airplane Rides…Sky-Diving…Ultralight Flights

From the Ruins 306
Bahia Honda Bridge…The Bat Tower…The Ferry Ruins

Biking 309
Happy Trails…Bike Rentals

Accommodations 310
Hotels and Motels…Bed and Breakfasts

Dining 319
True Stories

Shops 326
Fish to Nuts

Middle Keys and Marathon: Nothing Succeeds Like True Grit 333

Boom And Bust: A Whistle Stop Town 336
Key Vaca...Zane Grey Was Here...The Eighth Wonder of the World... The Doomed Wives of Henry Flagler...The Old Seven Mile Bridge and Pigeon Key

Nuts and Bolts 350
Information Central...Marathon Airport...Museum of Natural History

Theater 354
Cinema...Live Theatre

Where's the Beach? 355
Coco Plum...Sombrero...Long Key

Nature Hikes 359
Long Key State Park...Layton Nature Trail...Crane Point Hammock

Big Fun 361
Great Biking...Golf...Gyms...Tennis

Fishing 365
Gamefishing on the Hump...15 Tons and Whaddaya Get?

Diving 368
Favorite Dives...Dive Charters

To The Sea 371
Kayak Ecotours...Watercraft Rentals

Accommodations 373
Camping...Marine Resorts...Motels: No Frills, Low Bills

Dining 387
True Stories

Shops 400
Books...Buffett...Velvet Elvis Hot Sauce

The Purple Isles and Their Number One Passion 405

A Bloody History 408
The Indian Key Massacre...The Killer Hurricane of 1935

Historic Landmarks 418
Hurricane Monument...Whale Harbor Tower...Pioneer Cemetery...
Windley Key Fossil Site

Offshore Islands 422
Lonely Indian Key...Lignumvitae Key: What the First Settlers Saw

Beaches 426
Anne's Beach...Library Beach...Plantation Yacht Harbor...The Sandbar

Fishing 428
George Bush Fishes Here...Finding a Guide...Fishing School...Marinas

Diving 434
Favorite Dives...Charters...Instruction

Big Fun 437
Bowling...Tennis...Swings on the Water...Feeding the Tarpon...
Theater of the Sea

Tours by Land, Sea and Air 440

Accommodations 443
Resorts...Motels...Houseboat Rentals

Dining 454
True Stories

Shops 464
Books... Hooks...Treasure Island Village...The Rain Barrel

Sooner or Later Everyone Comes to Key Largo 467

History 473
The First Long Island...Golden Harvests...Just Like Bogie and Bacall...
Key Largo the Movie, the Song

Historic Sites 476
The Albury House...Caribbean Club...The African Queen

John Pennekamp Coral Reef State Park 480
Coral Reef Theater...The Living Reef...Beaching...Camping

Diving 485
Getting a Divers License...Some Famous Dives...Shops and Charter

Dolphins in Paradise 492
A Guide to Where the Keys Dolphins are

Natural Wonders 499
Harry Harris Park...Everglades National Park...Geology Lesson at
MM 103...Wild Bird Center...Key Largo Hammock

Big Fun 506
Biking...Watersports...The Movies

Fishing 508
Where to Go and How to Get There...

Tours By Sea 509
Airboat Tours...Everglades Safaris...Kayak Tours...Sailing...Glass-
Bottomed Boats...A Casino Cruise

Accommodations 514
Hotels and Motels...Camping...Reservation Services

Dining 526
True Stories

Shops 534
Fireworks...Books...Cigars...Art... Secondhand Rows...A Slow
Strip...A Fast one

Without a hint of irony,
everybody calls it Paradise.

– CHARLES KURALT

Paradise Found

THE FLORIDA KEYS ARE LIKE NOWHERE ELSE ON THE PLANET. In a photograph shot from a space shuttle, the Keys appear to be a handful of white pebbles thrown by some giant hand into the shallow, green-blue waters of the Florida Bay. The amazing Overseas Highway and its 42 bridges whipstitch a 130-mile trail from mainland Florida all the way to Key West. The coral islands of the Florida Keys are small, rarely as wide as two miles, usually much narrower. Each has its own attractions, auras, and powerful personalities. There are five regions in the Keys, and you will find wonders worth seeing in each of them.

This book is a guide and a companion designed to answer most often-asked questions about what there is to see and do, as well as where there is to eat and sleep, in the Florida Keys. You'll find descriptions of famous attractions like the free daily sunset celebration, dolphin swims, festivals and annual events, historic bars and renowned restaurants, and America's only living coral reef. You'll also learn the locations of not-so-well-known places, like secret gardens, funky diners, beachfront bistros, and off-the-beaten-path retreats.

In this book you'll meet Jimmy Buffett, and the ghosts of Ernest Hemingway and Tennessee Williams. You'll learn of our spectacular swashbuckling history, and the precious legacy of our early citizens: the world's largest outdoor museum of 19th-century architecture.

With this book you'll reap the benefits from my long-term love affair with Key West and the Florida Keys. I came for a weekend twenty-seven years ago and never left, a common story in Paradise.

Outside of Key West addresses are identified by mile markers, small green signposts with white numbers. Mile markers tell you where you are on the Overseas Highway, the "Main Street" of the Keys. You really can't get lost in the Florida Keys, unless, of course, you want to....

This book is a result of independent research and years of Keys living. Descriptions are based on personal visits and interviews. Prices are always subject to change, of course, as is the management and ownership of businesses.

No one paid to get into this book, and no one paid to get out of it. Welcome to Paradise!

– June Keith

THE
LAST RESORT

Key West

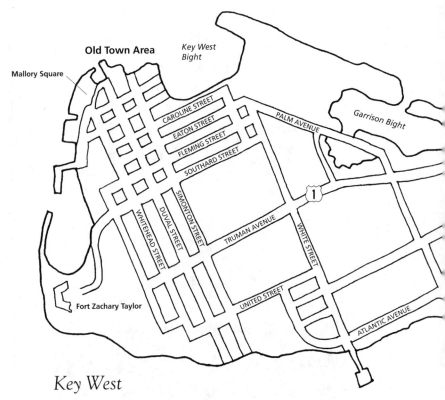

Key West

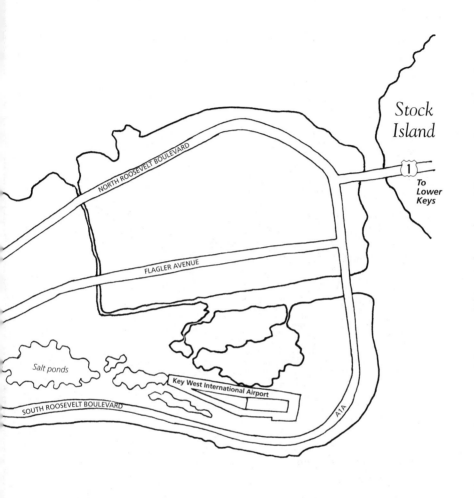

Key West

Frangipani

A Brief History of Key West

S PANISH EXPLORER Ponce de Leon is credited with discovering Florida and claiming it for Spain in 1513. When de Leon's expedition sailed past the southernmost islands of Spain's newest land acquisition, his sailors viewed the dense and twisted mangroves along the islands' shores and called them *Los Martires*, which translates as "the martyrs."

On a later visit to Florida in 1521, Ponce de Leon was killed in a battle with Florida Indians protesting Spain's intentions to turn the savages into Christians. Along with several missionaries, de Leon died after being shot by a poison arrow.

A century later the island of Key West began to appear in charts and maps of the Caribbean with the name *Cayo Hueso* or Bone Key. This, according to legend, was because the bones of dead Indians lay scattered on the beach when the first explorers came ashore.

As European settlers began chasing northern Indians off land along the U.S. east coast, tribes were forced to push farther south. The Calusa Indians of South Florida were forced by stronger, more warlike Indians from northern Florida southward and into the Keys. The Calusas fled from island to island until they reached Key West and could go no farther. Here they fought a final bloody battle that left their sun-bleached bones strewn on the beaches. The hardiest of the Calusas escaped in boats to Cuba, where they eventually spawned a strain of long-legged Cubans.

In 1815, Spain awarded the remote and generally useless island of Key West to Juan Pablo Salas, a St. Augustine native who'd proven himself, in word and in deed, invaluable to his country.

Salas later sold the island, which he'd made no move toward civilizing, to American businessman John Simonton for $2,000. Simonton recognized the potential of the island's deep-water harbor. Convincing others of this, he divided the island into quarters and sold three of them to fellow businessmen Whitehead, Fleming and Greene.

It is unclear exactly why the name Key West replaced *Cayo Hueso*. Perhaps it is the name *Cayo Hueso* twisted on an English-speaking tongue. (Say *Cayo Hueso* five times fast and see what happens.) Perhaps because the name refers so appropriately to Key West's westernmost position in the island chain. In any event, by the time Simonton and his friends took over and started naming island streets after themselves, Key West had become the working name of the place, and eventually it stuck.

After arranging his finances and naming a street after himself, Simonton contacted the U.S. Navy and suggested to them that since Key West is strategically located in the northern Caribbean, it might be a perfect place for them to set up a base of operation.

The USS *Shark*, captained by Lieutenant Matthew C. Perry, sailed into the harbor in 1822 with orders from the Secretary of the Navy to investigate the potential of the island and its harbor, "with a view to further measures for its occupation and for the establishment of a port of rendezvous and for commerce."

Just what Simonton and his pals were hoping for!

Lieutenant Perry's report to his superiors in Washington was very favorable. But the news wasn't all good. Perry reported that there was "among the decent folks on the island tending to their legitimate seafaring interests, a small band of desperados who have paid but little regard to either law or honesty." But the island's God-fearing settlers would keep this wild bunch in line, he suggested.

Lieutenant Perry claimed Key West in the name of the United States in March 1822 and hoisted the U.S. flag. Sailors aboard the *Shark* fired a thirteen-gun salute. Then, their job done, Perry and the USS *Shark* sailed away.

The desperado problem, however, proved to be more unmanageable than Perry had estimated. Pirates of the area continued to plunder, maim and kill in spite of the U.S. presence. In 1823 Captain David Porter was appointed commodore of the West Indies Anti-Pirate Squadron. Porter's mission was to protect American citizens and U.S. commerce from pirates. He was also charged with the duties of suppressing the slave trade and establishing a naval base on Key West.

The island, Porter reported back to his superiors in Washington, was certainly no place for a naval base. There was no fresh water, and the place swarmed with mosquitoes and sandflies. Nonetheless, Porter went ahead and assembled a fleet of shallow draft vessels known as the Mosquito Fleet and, in spite of several outbreaks of yellow fever among his ranks, made fast work of flushing pirates from the area.

Wrecks Ashore

These were pre-lighthouse days, so passage around the Florida Keys, even after the pirates had been chased out of the region, remained a dangerous endeavor. The reef area that lies seven miles to the south of Key West was an extremely hazardous passage when the weather kicked up or when captains unfamiliar with the Keys' tricky, shallow waters sailed up onto the razor-sharp edges of the reef.

Just off Florida Keys shores, the busy trade routes were being used regularly by vessels loaded down with every kind of cargo imaginable. In a few short years, wrecking and salvaging became Key West's primary business. Sharp-eyed citizens stood watch in high towers and searched the horizon for ships foundering on the reef. The first to arrive on the scene and offer assistance, became the captain in charge of salvaging as much of the cargo as possible.

By prior agreement, ship owners and their insurers shared recovered cargo with the salvagers of Key West. Half a recovered cargo, after all, was better than no cargo at all. The wrecking captain, in turn, then divided his share of the proceeds among his assistants. Much of the salvage was finally auctioned off, conveniently, in Key West, since federal legislation forbade any salvaged goods taken from U.S. waters to leave American ports.

Consequently, Key West was quickly becoming quite a prosperous port city. From its incorporation in 1828 until the 1850s, it was considered the richest city, per capita, in the United States. Wharves, shipyards and chandleries soon lined the harbor shore. Buyers from New York, Charleston, and Havana bid on salvaged goods such as fine wines, silks, laces, silverware and furniture from all over the world. Key West grew rich, if not in cash, then at least in fine possessions as wrecking proceeds trickled down into settlers' hands. Mothers and daughters might show up in church wearing new dresses made from a salvaged bolt of silk. The entire citizenry might find itself handsomely shod in fine leather shoes salvaged from a wrecked ship en route to New York. Wealth was everywhere!

But in addition to the profitable wrecking and salvaging industries, fishing, turtling and salt manufacturing had become crucial to the island's economic survival. Between the years of 1830 and 1861 Key West supplied much of the nation's salt, which, before refrigeration, was the chief method of food preservation. It was gleaned not from salt mines but from the sea. Shallow tidal pools on the south side of the island were covered with large, flat evaporating pans which filled with salt water during the wet spring and summer months. When the tidal pools receded during dry winter months, the water evaporated, leaving 340 acres of crystallized salt drying in the pans. Later, during the Civil War, Union soldiers closed down the salt industry when it was discovered that local Confederate sympathizers were smuggling Key West salt into the Confederacy. The salt industry resumed at the war's end, but was wiped out by a hurricane in 1876. By then, salt mines had been discovered on the mainland anyway.

To try to slow down the increasing wrecking that continued into the 1850s, the government began stationing "light boats" and, later, lighthouses, on the dangerous reefs. Sturdier, safer steamships began carrying the valuable cargo that once had been shipped aboard wooden schooners, which were dependent upon the wind and weather.

By 1855 Key West's population had grown to 2,700, and progress had dealt the business of wrecking some serious blows that would ultimately lead to its end.

Southernmost Yankees

Florida seceded from the Union in 1861. Meanwhile, in Key West, Fort Taylor, strategic to the defense of the city's harbor, was quietly commandeered by a troop of Union soldiers in the predawn hours one April morning that same year. It was expected that the townspeople would attack the fort, but that did not happen, and soon more troops arrived, assuring that Key West would be the only southern city to remain in Union hands for the duration of the war. There were, to be sure, plenty of Southern sympathizers in Key West, but with Union soldiers everywhere, they couldn't do much to support the Confederate cause. Key

West was the only place in the country where you had to go north to join the South.

At that same time, the East Coast Blockade Squadron was headquartered in Key West as well. The squadron's mission was to stop blockade runners from sailing contraband to the Confederate troops via the Gulf of Mexico. Nearly three hundred blockade runners were arrested; their ships were impounded and anchored in Key West Harbor. America's most famous blockade runner is the fictional character, Rhett Butler of Margaret Mitchell's *Gone With The Wind*.

The New El Dorado

Because Key West's climate was so much like its nearby neighbor Cuba, only ninety miles away, it did not take long for someone to recognize the area's potential for cigar manufacturing. The first cigar factory was established on Wall Street in 1831. As Key West grew, so did the business of cigar manufacturing.

During the Cuban Revolution that began in 1868, thousands of Cubans emigrated to Key West to find better lives working in the cigar industry which the influx of manpower greatly expanded. Soon the cigar business was bringing over a million dollars into the city annually. By 1871, Cubans employed in the cigar industry were a powerful political force. The original San Carlos Institute, a center of nationalistic politics, was constructed on Duval Street. In the city-wide election of 1876, several Cuban-born men were elected to political offices, including that of mayor.

The devastating fire of 1886, which is believed to have been started in the San Carlos Institute, burned down nearly two thirds of the city, including several important cigar factories and many cigarmakers' houses. But the cigar industry recovered quickly and went on to reach its peak of production in 1890. By then 129 cigar factories operated on the island. Workers produced an amazing 100,000,000 cigars annually.

Cigar factory employees enjoyed excellent salaries and working conditions. Workers often donated up to 10% of their earnings to support Cuba's fight for independence from Spain. Attempting to interrupt the flow of cash to Cuban revolutionaries, however, Spanish agitators sparked conflicts among workers and instigated labor strikes, often based on the flimsiest of excuses. A major strike in 1890 occurred when workers claimed that pay was unfair for making various qualities of cigars. Factory owners paid the same wage for making all cigars, whether cheap ones or very expensive smokes.

To entice cigar manufacturers out of Key West and over to Tampa, incentives such as tax-free land and cheaper labor were offered to Key West factory owners. In Tampa, there were no unions. One by one the cigar manufacturers began to abandon Key West and its strife. So the great shift occurred. By the turn of the century, Key West had lost its position as America's leading producer of hand-rolled Cuban cigars.

Cleaning up with Sponges

Another important industry that started in Key West and moved to a more supportive venue was sponging. An enterprising businessman sailed a shipload of Keys natural sponges to New York City in 1850 and very quickly found a clamoring market for them. By 1890 Key West was the commercial sponging capital of the world.

Natural sponges are soft skeletons of animals that once had lived in the shallow waters surrounding the Keys. Prying them from the ocean floor, drying, cleaning and bleaching them in preparation for the marketplace, was, and still is, a smelly and back-breaking job. Nonetheless, sponging was an important business. At the turn of the century, Key West's sponging fleet was 350 boats strong and employed 1400 men, who harvested up to 165 tons of natural sponges a year.

In time Key West spongers began indiscriminately harvesting sponge beds, ignoring laws designed to preserve the supply. In 1904 several sponge companies were established to take advantage of the rich sponge beds in Tarpon Springs, on Florida's west coast just north of Tampa. Once again Key West's remote location worked against it. Tarpon Springs spongers and merchants had a much easier time getting their wares to the world's shipping routes, and Tarpon Springs soon replaced Key West as the world's prime producer of sponges.

Eventually a weird and deadly sponge fungus destroyed all of the beds in the Florida Keys, and cheap synthetic sponges were invented to take the place of the expensive, natural ones. In the last twenty-five years sponge beds have become healthy and productive again. Several small businesses are harvesting Keys sponges today.

Remember the *Maine*

The battleship USS *Maine* sailed into Key West Harbor in June,1896. Officers and crewmen from the ship were soon incorporated into the community, making many friends and romantic liaisons here.

In late 1897, in a show of America's military strength as well as her support for American business interests in Cuba, President McKinley ordered the USS *Maine* to sail on to Havana. On February 15, 1898, the *Maine* was ripped apart by an explosion in Havana Harbor. Of 354 American crew members aboard, 266 were killed. Those who didn't die were badly burned. Many of the injured were taken by ship to Key West, where they were cared for by nuns at the Mary Immaculate Convent, which had been turned into a temporary hospital. The dead were also returned to Key West, the place where they'd known their last happiness. A special plot in the Key West Cemetery, where many of the victims of the explosion are buried, is a marvelous and moving monument to this bleak chapter in American history.

The cause of the explosion was never determined. Nonetheless, nine weeks later, on April 22, 1898, Spain and the U.S. officially went to war. A short war. It didn't take long for Spain to realize that the Spanish armed forces were no match for America's military might. After a three-month fight on two fronts half a world apart, the U.S. found itself in possession of an empire stretching from the Caribbean to the far Pacific. Not only did Spain grant Cuba its independence; by the time the peace treaty had been signed on August 12, 1898, Spain had also ceded Puerto Rico to the U.S. and cut a deal to sell the Philippine Islands to them for $20 million.

The Missing Link

By the turn of the century, Key West was one of the country's most sophisticated cities, with electricity, streetcars, telegraph cable and regular performances by touring European opera and ballet companies. These performances were frequently mounted in the San Carlos Institute, which was also called, during those palmy days, the San Carlos Opera House.

Moreover, the Overseas Railroad arrived on the island in January of 1912. It connected the entire Florida Keys with the rest of America via a 128-mile railroad to Miami. The railroad also became a link to Cuba. Passengers were able to train to Key West and then board a steamship that would carry them across the Florida Straits to Havana.

The Overseas Railroad, with its remarkable bridges and causeways, was labeled the "Eighth Wonder of the World." When the first train pulled into Trumbo Point in 1912, the event sparked the biggest celebration the island had ever seen.

The railroad that had cost visionary Henry Flagler $25,000,000, and nearly 700 men their lives, was an unfortunately short-lived enterprise. In 1935 the railroad was destroyed by a vicious hurricane that killed nearly 600 people in the Upper Keys. At the time of its demise, the company was deeply in debt, with no hope of recovery in sight. And so the railroad right-of-way and the bridges were sold to the State of Florida, which used them for an overseas highway that eventually opened in 1938.

Smuggling

The jagged coastline of the Florida Keys, with its many inlets, nooks and coves, has long been a perfect entry way for a variety of contraband coming into the country by boat. Nowhere is entry into the U.S. so easy as it is here. To cross the border into the United States, one merely comes ashore. In the 1920s, when the sale and consumption of alcoholic beverages in the U.S. became illegal, the Florida Keys became infamous as a gateway for rumrunning. Havana is only ninety miles from Key West. Beer and rum purchased in Cuba doubled in value when they reached America's shores and doubled again and again as they changed hands, until at last the expensive booze finally trickled down to the consumer. Whiskey, rye and scotch, smuggled from the British Isles via Nassau, followed the same course. Certainly great fortunes were made bootlegging.

When it all ended with the repeal of Prohibition in 1933, hoodlums and syndicates, as well as a surprising number of ostensibly law-abiding citizens, found themselves at the end of a magnificent era of easy money and fortune building. Among the most daring smugglers to accumulate impressive fortunes was Grace Lithgoe of San Francisco. Lithgoe stayed in the Keys for five years, defying capture and finally retiring a rich woman. It is hinted that several of Key West's most famous old families came by their original riches through smuggling.

Aside from the bootleggers, Key West citizens didn't pay much attention to Prohibition. The bar that became Sloppy Joe's, where Hemingway drank both during and after Prohibition, was boldly called "The Blind Pig," a slang term used for anonymous-looking storefronts that hid bars during Prohibition. It seems somewhat like calling a brothel "The Whorehouse," but it's also very typical of the island, where nobody spends much time on subtlety.

Later, marijuana smuggling, which flourished in somewhat the same way as rum smuggling had half a century earlier, reached its glamorous zenith in the early '80s. A new generation of citizens became wealthy, and the restaurants, bars, and trendy shops of Key West prospered. But as the stakes escalated, the game turned dangerous. Finally the once-thriving cottage industry collapsed: some of the players went to jail; others were tricked out of or robbed of their cash; still others blew amazing fortunes on the high life. Only a lucky handful invested in property, businesses and homes.

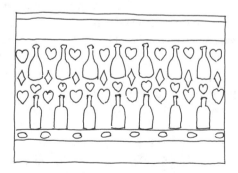

Gingerbread trim from Prohibition days with rum and wine bottles, hearts and spades, for those in the know.

Southernmost Hooverville

By the time the Great Depression had hit in the 1930s, the bootleggers were the only people in Key West making any money. The wrecking, sponging and cigar industries were long gone. By 1934, 80% of the population of 11,000 was on relief. Property owners were unable to pay taxes. The situation seemed hopeless, so city fathers did something that had never been done before in American history: They tore up the city charter and told the federal government that they could no longer survive as a city. At first, the federal government considered evacuating the entire town and moving the citizens to Tampa. But then they came up with a better plan: Turn the city of Key West into a tourist destination!

Julius Stone was sent to do just that. It was his idea to bring Works Projects Administration (WPA) artists to Key West to paint island scenes designed to attract curious travelers. WPA artists also created guidebooks with lists of local tourist attractions for forthcoming visitors. (Ernest Hemingway's house on Whitehead Street was attraction number 18.)

In addition, Stone rallied the townspeople to landscape the streets and beautify the town. He talked Pan American World Airways into resuming service to the city. His efforts led, furthermore, to the resurrection of the Casa Marina and numerous other Key West hotels, motels and guesthouses. It was during Stone's commission, as well, that the Federal Building on Simonton Street and the open-air City Aquarium were both built.

To further promote his vision of Key West as a tourist town, Stone wore pink, yellow or green bermuda shorts and sports shirts. Cubans called him *El Paraquito* (the parakeet) because of his preference for pastel outfits. Stone's success at turning around the helpless town did not go unnoticed. Newspapers around the country carried stories about the lucky workers in Key West who worked in Bermuda shorts. The headline "Workers Go to Work in Shorts," in the mid-1930s, was titillating indeed.

After the hurricane of 1935, Stone was also instrumental in transforming the hurricane-ravaged Overseas Railroad bed into the Overseas Highway, a mammoth project that put hundreds of people to work and brought thousands of people to the Keys. Even President Roosevelt came for the three-day-long celebration of the formal opening of the Overseas Highway in 1938.

Military Town

Meanwhile, the government began work on the Key West submarine base, preparing for the possibility of war, in the late 1930s. The construction and maintenance of the base provided jobs for many citizens who found gainful employment throughout World War II. Just as it did across the rest of America, WW II put the citizens of Key West back on their feet, too.

Key West became a military town during the war and remained so for many decades. The Navy stationed 25,000 personnel on the island and hired many civilians. The backbone of Key West's economy at that time was the Naval presence. Then the island suffered another setback in 1974 when the Navy closed the submarine base and withdrew enormous numbers of its people. Overnight, it seemed, half of the population of Key West was suddenly gone. Businesses collapsed, and the downtown area became a ghost town once more. Stores, bars and restaurants were boarded up. Duval Street buildings were abandoned and left to crumble in the sun.

The Last Resort

This state of desolation did not last long. Once again, it was decided that tourism was the city's only hope for economic recovery. The restoration and preservation of downtown Key West, fully supported by local and state governments, steadily picked up steam. Tourism became everybody's objective for the future. In the early 1980s a county-wide Tourist Development Commission was formed to promote the Keys throughout the world. The TDC collects a "bed tax" which amounts to millions of dollars annually, all funneled into advertising and promotion for the island.

The Key West of today is unmistakably a tourist town indeed, hosting millions of visitors each year. The town's need to attract and satisfy its paying guests colors just about everything that happens here.

Architecture

A s YOU EXPLORE the streets of Old Town Key West, you might feel as if you've time-traveled back to an early New England town. The most fantastic of Key West's wooden houses were built in the 1800s, when the island's wealthiest citizens were making huge fortunes from wrecking, sponging, and cigar manufacturing. In those early days, when the city of Key West was among the wealthiest in the country, homes were lavished with elegant details and elaborate gingerbread trim. But those prosperous times passed, and Key West, by the 1930s, was among the poorest U.S. cities.

Through the years old houses were often allowed to run down by descendants of the once-large families who originally occupied them. Many were divided into ramshackle apartments.

In 1886, while the city's lone fire engine was in New York undergoing repairs, nearly two-thirds of the town burned to the ground. After that fire, federal and municipal buildings were constructed predominantly of brick. Tin roofs on homes replaced wooden shingles because they stopped the spread of fire from one roof to the next; they deflected sunlight and heat, and they also assisted in water collection. Rain ran easily off the roofs into cisterns.

From just after the Civil War until the early 1900s the cigar industry was one of Key West's primary sources of income. To house the workers and their families, factory owners constructed neighborhoods of small cottages. Today, these century-old houses, built predominantly in the "shotgun style," are scattered throughout Old Town Key West.

In much of the rest of America the prosperity of the post WW II-era brought about the construction of suburban homes, created for smaller families. Large wooden houses, difficult to maintain and largely run down by time, were destroyed to make way for modern brick and mortar construction. But fortunately in Key West, few property owners had the money to dismantle their white-elephant houses or to replace them with more modern materials, so here they remain.

Key West is recognized today as a model city of historic preservation. The city's one-hundred block historic district of wooden houses is the largest in the country. These remarkable houses of Old Town Key West, which have survived America's headlong march into progress, will continue to survive. Since the beginning of Key West's preservation movement in the 1960s, city and state preservation laws have been implemented and strictly enforced, insuring that our old houses will continue to provide the world with a glimpse into a magical chapter of America's history.

The pioneering citizens who built these houses of the 19th century speak to us across many generations, from a time when architectural style was dictated by need, and then by culture, and finally, for the lucky few who could afford it, by subjective expression.

The Houses of Old Town

If you find your fundamental knowledge of architecture challenged in Key West, you're not alone. The architecture on this island is difficult for anyone to identify and label specifically. Keeping track of which type of pillar, post or column signifies the stylistic roots of Greek, Roman, or Queen Anne can become a mind-boggling exercise. When someone is bold enough to come out and name the architectural style of a place, you can be sure that someone else will soon come along to disagree. There is no right or wrong to this. The debate can never end.

Most of the wooden homes borrow features from a variety of styles, which were brought to the island from many places, and adapted to withstand weather conditions quite foreign to the rest of America. The people who built them were sometimes legitimate building contractors, sometimes ship carpenters, and sometimes pioneering Americans with enormous enthusiasm and good, old-fashioned common sense.

In describing the wooden architecture of Key West, the word *vernacular* has become interchangeable with *conch* as in "vernacular architecture" or "conch house." Here are the five major classifications of architectural styles represented in Key West's conch houses.

Classic Revival

A popular architectural style in the early 1800s was the classic revival, a style made popular in England. American builders and carpenters adapted the style according to their tastes and needs. The style is identified by well-proportioned rectangular forms, gabled roofs and columned porches. Balance is a determining factor. The majority of the houses in

A Classic Revival style Key West house—"The Gingerbread House"

the historic district are classic revivals. The house many consider to be the fanciest house on the island is the classic revival at 615 Elizabeth Street, "The Gingerbread House."

Eyebrow

The eyebrow house, an offshoot of classic revival, is unique to Key West. There are about 100 of these on the island. Adapted to keep sun and heat out of upstairs rooms, the windows of an eyebrow house are set beneath a heavy roof overhang, supported by corner beams.

Examples of this distinctly conch adaptation are at 816 and 823 Eaton Street. Once you get the hang of recognizing the eyebrow house, you'll spot them frequently.

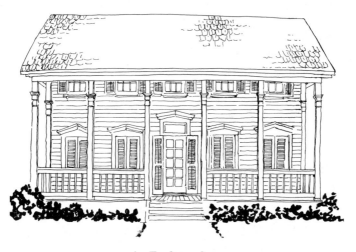

An Eyebrow house

A Bahamian style house

Bahamian

Bahamian style houses are designed to withstand tropical heat and storms. Features are wide, wrap-around porches, and floor to ceiling wooden-shuttered windows, designed to take the best advantage of prevailing breezes. Spacious and rectangular, the no-nonsense styling of the Bahamian house is stunning in its simplicity.

The houses at 730 Eaton and 408 William streets are true Bahamian houses, actually constructed on Green Turtle Cay in the Bahamas and barged to Key West in 1846.

Queen Anne

Queen Anne styled architecture, a category of the broader division of Victorian, was popular in the 1880s, when the residents of Key West were still enjoying a thriving economy. A predominant element of Queen Anne style is a pointed turret on one side of the house. Beyond that single identifying point, just about anything goes. Queen Anne is the most lavish style you'll see here.

Queen Anne-style—"The Southernmost House"

Key West's quintessential Queen Anne house is the very last one on Duval Street, on the ocean at the southern corner of the island. It's called *the* Southernmost House, although there is controversy over whether or not it truly is the southernmost house. There is no question of its authenticity as a perfect example of Queen Anne architecture.

Shotgun

Shotgun houses, also known as cigarmakers' cottages, are the island's smallest homes. Shotguns sit on raised foundations and are recognizable by their very simple design: a hall that runs from the front door to the back, with a parlor and one or two bedrooms leading off it. On the out-

Shotgun houses

side, the little houses feature a door on one side and one or two windows, depending upon the width of the house.

A much-photographed block of shotguns is the 400 block of Truman Avenue, where a row of cigarmakers' cottages have been restored to look much as they did when they were constructed around the turn of the century.

Gingerbread Trim, Conch Architecture's Unifying Trademark

The fancy swirls, designs and forms cut out of wood and used as decorative trims on Key West's wooden houses are known as gingerbread. With a memorable dash of whimsy, gingerbread trim is the unifying trait of conch architecture. It is the memory of gingerbread trim that visitors to America's largest outdoor museum of wooden houses remember most clearly when they recall Old Town Key West.

Some Notes on Getting Around

Key West is a small island, roughly two miles by four miles. The down-town area, where visitors spend most of their time, is smaller still. A hike from one end of Duval Street to the other is less than a mile and will take you from the Atlantic Ocean to the Gulf of Mexico. Those accustomed to walking will find downtown destinations no more than an easy stroll away.

Cars are generally a bother here. If you're bringing a car to Key West, make sure there's parking available at your hotel or guest house. (Many do not have off-street parking.) Metered spaces downtown are $1 per hour; $.25 per hour at Smathers Beach. You'll find private lots, with vary-ing prices, throughout downtown.

At 300 Grinnell St., there is a Park & Ride garage. Park your car all day and ride a shuttle around the island. Parking there is inexpensive, and the shuttles are pretty regular. Park & Ride info: 305-292-8160. To find the garage, follow the signs.

Parking spaces on side streets marked Residential are for locals only! If you don't have local plates, or a residential sticker issued by City Hall, do not use these spots. You will be ticketed. Key West has a large and active fleet of meter readers. Illegally parked cars are often towed, day or night. Don't think the cover of night will save you from a ticket or a tow.

Taxis
The City of Key West sets the fees that cabs can legally charge and those fees are stated on the car or by the driver. Ask if you're unsure. Call 296-6666 for Five Sixes Cab, or 292-0000 for Friendly Cab. Taxi drivers are efficient and personable. Cabby Michael Suib even writes a weekly column in the Miami Herald about his adventures driving a taxi.

Bikes
The island is small and flat, and features near perfect weather year round. Roughly 15% of local residents rely exclusively on bikes for local trans-port. To bike all the way around the island via the bike path, you'll probably need about an hour and a half, so start out early in the morning or later in the afternoon, when the sun is not so high in the sky. Don't try

this trip on a very windy day; if you hit hard wind you'll feel as if you're pedaling your bike under water.

Remember that pedestrians have the right-of-way on sidewalks. If the sidewalk is clear, you're welcome to ride your bike on it. Weaving your bicycle around pedestrians on busy downtown sidewalks is actually illegal! Bicycles move with motor traffic, and follow the same laws as cars. In Key West, you will get a ticket for going through a stop signal, or for riding your bike at night without a light.

Bicycle Rentals

Standard rates for bicycle rentals are $10 a day; $50 a week; $200 a month. Some inns provide bicycle rentals to their guests. Wherever you stay, chances are you're within walking distance of a bicycle rental shop. Be sure to lock up! If you bike after dark, you definitely need a light.

Mopeds and Scooters

Mopeds and scooters a very popular and affordable here. Ambulances respond to an average of 300 moped accidents each year, accounting for nearly half of all traffic accidents. Tourists are involved in most of them. Fortunately, most accidents involving mopeds result in little more than scrapes and bruises. Serious moped accidents involve head injuries— concussions, skull fractures, brain contusions or hemorrhages. Statistics also show that 20% of moped drivers involved in accidents are intoxicated. Moped rentals are usually around $40 a day, or $250 a week. You must be 18 years old and a licensed driver with a credit card to rent one. Use a helmet. Make sure you understand how things work before you leave the moped or scooter rental shop. Be careful. At our house we don't allow our guests to rent mopeds.

Ride the Bone

Ride the Bone Island Shuttle (293-8710) around the island all day (9 a.m. - 11 p.m.) for $8. It's a deal. They loop the island, stopping every 20 minutes or so at hotels and biggest attractions. Park for free at the Welcome Center, 3840 North Roosevelt Blvd., 296-4444, and have a ball. A great deal. Five-day pass is $30.

*The wind blows so hard the ocean gets up on its
hind legs and walks right across the land.*

– E. G. ROBINSON'S SIDEKICK DESCRIBING A HURRICANE
IN THE FILM *Key Largo*.

Frost Free in Paradise—
Keys Weather

THE WEATHER IS DIFFERENT in the Keys. It is temperate year round.
We never, ever have frost. That's why they call it Paradise. Were it
not for the possibility of hurricanes, the Florida Keys would have the
world's most perfect weather. The sun shines here just about every day
of the year. It rains only half as much as it does in the rest of Florida.
The reason has to do with land mass and convection currents. What it
all means is that when skies are dark and wet over Miami and
Ft. Lauderdale, skies in the Keys remain blue and clear.

Afternoon showers in the rest of Florida are common. They happen
when the land heats up and the moist air from the ocean hits it. In the
Keys, the land mass is missing from the equation. Hence, the Keys get
only about thirty-eight inches of rain each year. Key West is the driest
city in Florida.

Highs and Lows

Highest temperature ever recorded in Key West was 97 degrees. Coldest
was 41. On summer's hottest days the Florida Keys have the advantage
of being situated between two very powerful bodies of water, the Gulf of
Mexico and the Atlantic Ocean. The trade winds keep even the hottest
days tolerable.

Usually we have a week or two of cold weather just around Christmas time, which also happens to be the very busiest time of the year down here. When temperatures drop into the 50s outdoors, the temperature is also in the 50s indoors since older Keys homes rarely have insulation or heating systems. So we locals wear many layers of clothes, and even socks beneath our sandals. We probably look mighty peculiar to tourists.

Water temperatures in the Atlantic Ocean are in the lower 70s during the Keys' cooler months. By July and August, the water warms up to the mid-to-upper 80s, and humidity makes it difficult to dry off after a shower.

Weather Forecast: 305-295-1316

Conch, An Endangered Species

THE WORD IS pronounced *konk*. If you pronounce the *ch* in conch, like the *ch* in crunch, everyone will know that you're very new to the island. The regal queen conch is Monroe County's much beloved mascot. A Conch is a native of the Florida Keys; conch refers also to any person, place or thing relating to the Florida Keys, which is known as the Conch Republic. People not born here, but who are dedicated citizens of seven years or more are called Freshwater Conchs.

Conchs suffer conch madness. They live in conch houses. Their sons play for the Fighting Conchs, the name of the high school football team. Their daughters kick up their heels in a girls' drill team known as the Conchettes. Conch Capers is the name of the annual local variety show. Conch cruisers are the cars that work fine here, but you wouldn't dare drive one out of Monroe County. Conched out, AKA Rock Fever, is what you are feeling when you positively, absolutely must get out of the Keys for a couple of days or go nuts.

Eating Conch

Conch chowder comes cream-style or tomato-style like Manhattan clam chowder. Sometimes people order conch chowder, taste it, and tell the waitron there's been a mistake. "I ordered conch chowder," they say, "not clam chowder." The two are close cousins. Order red conch chowder in a Cuban restaurant some time; that's where it's best.

Cracked conch steak is a slab of conch pounded until it's tender or passed through a tenderizer, then batter dipped, and pan or deep fried. Eating this delicacy can be a challenge if it is not properly tenderized. A good place for a conch steak is the Rusty Anchor, out on Stock Island. Somebody in a fish store once told me that the conch tenderizer machine is a real hassle. Not to operate; that part is easy. But cleaning the machine after the conch has been tenderized takes so much time the entire process is not cost efficient.

Conch fritters can be another one of the world's great taste treats—chewy, spicy, crisp on the outside and tender on the inside. They are not difficult to make. Sadly, chefs often skimp on the conch. There should be lots of conch meat in a conch fritter. Otherwise, you're getting what one of my Bahamian Conch neighbors scornfully describes as dough fritters.

Another treat, conch seviche, is seen on menus less frequently. Too bad. Conch meat cooked and tenderized by lime juice is sublime. Don't

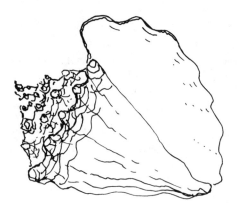

be afraid to try it. Nowadays the conch in stores and restaurants is imported from the Bahamas. The Keys conch population has been nearly annihilated by hungry divers. It is illegal to take them from Keys waters.

The World's Biggest Conch

See the colossal conch, homage to conch spirit, in front of the Key West High School at 2100 Flagler Avenue. Here's a photo opportunity not to be missed. The monument is constructed of metal scraps and built by the metal shop students at Key West High under the direction of former shop teacher and artist George Carey. Carey, a Conch, is descended from a long line of sea-faring Careys including Captain George Carey, who back in 1859 built the Heritage House at 410 Caroline Street.

Blowing Conch

The distinctive sound of a blowing conch travels for distances of over two miles. The shell was used as a musical instrument in Mesopotamia over 4,000 years ago. In some African and island cultures it still serves as a ceremonial trumpet. During Key West's annual Old Island Days, a conch-blowing contest attracts many contestants. It's one of those only-in-Key West activities that draws lots of media attention. Of course, these conch blowers are only required to blow one mighty blast, not recognizable melodies like *The Flight of the Bumblebee* or the *Sabre Dance*.

Rimsky-Korsakov on the conch shell? Impossible you say? Not for Reverend and Mrs. Thurlow Weed. In the mid-70s the accomplished conch shell musicians appeared as guests on television's game show *To Tell The Truth*. Mr. and Mrs. Weed also appear in the 1978 film *The Key West Picture Show*. Reverend Weed was, and remains long after his death, the undisputed king of queen conch playing in Key West.

A Walking Tour of Historic Old Town Key West

THIS WALKING TOUR covers one-and-three-quarter miles of Old Town and one and three-quarter centuries of history. Plan on taking around two leisurely hours to complete it.

The tour begins in Mallory Square, in front of the Key West Chamber of Commerce. A frequently heard question here is "where is the sunset pier?" It's right here. At Mallory Dock. A good time to start the walk is about two hours or so before sunset. That way, you'll be heading into the cool of the evening and arriving back at Mallory Dock in time for the world's coolest sunset.

Here in Mallory Square in 1822, American sailors raised the U.S. flag, symbolizing the purchase of Florida from Spain. The streets of Old Town Key West radiate from this initial settlement, and many of the stately structures you see here were built well over a century ago. These buildings, once warehouses, icehouses and chandleries (stores selling all manner of ships' supplies), are today home to a glittering variety of shops, saloons and bistros.

The Chamber of Commerce is located in a building that was owned in the 1800s by one of the town's wealthiest citizens, wrecking master Asa Tift. The valuable salvaged cargoes from wrecked ships were stored here. The Shell Warehouse next door is in what used to be Tift's Ice House. Before electricity, Key Westers imported ice from New England. Great chunks of pond ice were shipped to Key West, then packed in sawdust and stored in the former ice house you see here.

Mr. Tift was so successful at his various enterprises that he built himself a fine mansion on Whitehead Street, which you can visit today. It's called the Hemingway House and Museum.

In Mallory Square you'll see several crusty characters created out of papier mache. They are more than happy to pose for photographs. In front of the Shell Warehouse, there is a conch fisherman just in from the sea. Out in the square, another fisherman on a bicycle sells fish. And on

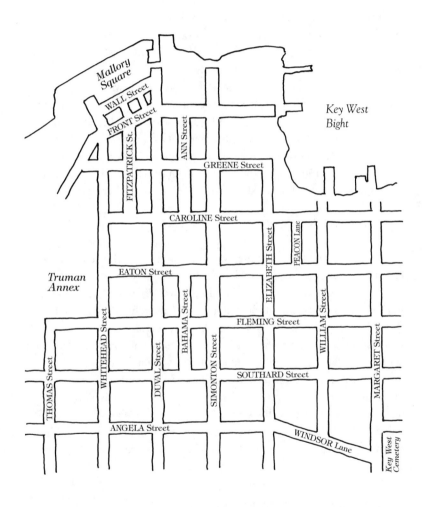

a bench just outside of the Key West Aquarium sits an old sea captain smoking a pipe. Many people particularly enjoy posing with the shark outside the aquarium, which was built by the Works Projects Administration in 1934 and was the island's first tourist attraction.

If you're fascinated by wrecking, the industry that turned this little seaport town into the richest small city in America in the mid-1800s, you'll love the Shipwreck Historeum, where you'll meet Asa Tift, your guide, through exhibits which recreate the shore-side bustle and drama of the wrecking business.

Lined up in front of the Sponge Market are Old Town Trolleys. Trolley tours depart Mallory Square every half hour. Just past the aquarium is the Clinton Market, a large, cream-colored brick building. In its earliest days this was once a coal storehouse. Until the early 1930s it was a naval administration building. Today the building is a complex of shops, air conditioned to near freezing temperatures and full of exactly the kind of merchandise you'd expect to find in a busy tourist center.

Continue on to Front Street.

That great, red brick building, next on the right, with the uncharacteristic chimneys is the Custom House. Built in 1891, it was abandoned in the 1950s and saved from the bulldozers in 1973, when it was added to the National Register of Historic Places. The architectural style is Romanesque Revival. The Key West Art and Historical Society restored this marvelous building which now houses a museum and art and cultural center. Do make time during your stay to visit the museum.

This tiny, nicely tended triangular park just in front of the Custom House is Clinton Square. It contains a monument to the Union soldiers and sailors who lost their lives here during the Civil War. The men didn't die in battle—the only shots fired here were for practice. They died from yellow fever. For the duration of the war, Key West, the southernmost city, was peacefully held in Northern hands.

Whitehead Street, 200 Block

Just ahead on the corner is Mel Fisher's Maritime Heritage Museum. On July 20, 1985, Mel Fisher and his faithful treasure salvors discovered the mother lode of the Spanish galleon *Atocha*, which sank in 1622 with a cargo of gold and silver bars, jewelry, and coins, altogether valued at over $200 million. On exhibit: treasure that lay unclaimed on the ocean floor for more than 360 years.

Cross Whitehead Street.

The Audubon House and Gardens is at 205 Whitehead. The three-story house was home to Captain John Geiger, his wife, and their nine children. When John James Audubon came to the Keys in search of flamingos in 1832, he stayed at the Geiger house. Several original Audubon engravings commemorate the visit.

Just past the Audubon House driveway is a replica of gingerbread trim that was used during Prohibition to indicate the personality or theme of the house on the property. The rum and wine bottles and the hearts and spades advertised to those in the know that gambling, liquor and loose women were available behind a fence like this.

On your right, across the street, still stands an old Navy cistern, one of the biggest cisterns on the island. Before water was brought to the Keys via a pipeline from the mainland during World War II, residents relied upon rainwater, which they collected and stored in cisterns like this. Nearly every home had a cistern of some sort. Key West was the first city of its size to get electricity, in 1887, and the last to get running water, in 1942!

Also on your right you'll find the Presidential Gates. Installed in 1906, these gates were designed to be opened for U.S. Presidents only. The last sitting president to pass through them was John F. Kennedy in 1962, who came here along with the Joint Chiefs of Staff during the Cuban Missile Crisis. Other presidents to pass through the gates were Presidents Dwight Eisenhower and Harry Truman. (To visit Truman's Key West retreat, known today as "The Little White House Museum," go through the Presidential Gates, into Truman Annex, and straight ahead about a block.) President Jimmy Carter visited the Little White House on New Year's Eve, 1997, and President and Mrs. Bill Clinton visited in 2005.

In 1987 a private citizen bought the 103 acres of the non-active Navy base and an offshore island for $17 million. The buyer was Pritham Singh, who once lived a hand-to-mouth existence here in Key West. In the late '60s he sold sea shells by the seashore at sunset. In the '70s, he sold seashore property in Maine and was so good at it that he made a fortune. One day he read in the *New York Times* that the Navy base was to be auctioned off on the following day. Singh hopped a jet, came to town, and sealed the deal twenty-four hours later.

You are welcome to walk through the Presidential Gates and stroll through the remarkably transformed property. Some houses and condominiums are available for sale or rent here. You can't miss the sales office. If you're interested, take lots and lots of money.

Turn left onto Caroline Street.

Caroline Street, 400 Block

Lots of women go crazy in this town, and everyone in Key West has at one time or another wondered which one of them Jimmy Buffett is singing about in "There's a Woman Going Crazy on Caroline Street."

On your right is the garden of Kelly's Caribbean Restaurant and Grill and first home of Pam Am Airlines. The first roundtrip ticket to Havana, Cuba, was sold here in 1927. Kelly is Hollywood actress Kelly McGillis, who starred in movies *Top Gun* and *Witness*.

Next door to Kelly's at the end of the driveway, you can see the green exterior of the Robert Frost Cottage, named for the American poet who spent sixteen winters here. The cottage sits on the property of the Heritage House Museum at 410 Caroline. The house was built by Captain George Carey in 1834—one of the oldest houses in town. Notice the fresh-water well to the left of the front door. Legend has it that Indians, as well as sailors and pirates, came ashore to use this well. The hand-rolled glass windows of the house are original.

At 429 Caroline, at the corner of Duval, you can see the house of Dr. Joseph Yates Porter, Florida's first health officer under whose leadership yellow fever was eradicated. Dr. Porter's bigger claim to fame is, however, the fact that he was born in this house in 1847 and died here, too, in same bedroom in 1927, eighty years later. The entrance, with its double doors, wide staircase, twin Grecian urns, gingerbread trim, and stained glass conch shells, is worth a good look.

The Bull and Whistle Bar, at the corner of Caroline and Duval, is popular for its very laid-back attitude, open air bar, and all-day, live entertainment. The cement-cast bull, charging through the Caroline Street wall of the Bull & Whistle, was created by sculptor June Tvardzik in 1978. We can't quite imagine why.

Cross Duval and continue on Caroline.

Caroline Street, 500 Block

On the left, the historic Fogarty House, now housing a restaurant and bar. In this once proud mansion Dr. and Mrs. John Fogarty entertained Presidents Cleveland and Taft, and railroad baron Henry Flagler. Dr. Fogarty was mayor of Key West and hosted a joyful week-long celebration when the Overseas Railroad arrived in January, 1912.

Next door you'll find the Curry Mansion, built in 1905 by Milton Curry, son of William Curry, Florida's first self-made millionaire. The tour through this many-leveled Victorian mansion is very different from most. In the Curry Mansion you are free to sit at the grand dining room table while a companion shoots your photo. You are invited to spend all the time you like in the library, which is full of goodies, and to poke and peek at will. The Curry Mansion is also a very gracious guesthouse.

You'll next come to Ann Street on the left. At the corner of Ann and Caroline is the building that once housed Pauline Hemingway's interior design shop. After her divorce from Ernest Hemingway in 1940, Pauline became an interior decorator. The building is now actually two houses joined—223 Ann Street and 525 Caroline Street. The Caroline Street address was Pauline's shop.

In the yard at 531 Caroline is a large, East African tulip tree. The tree's tulip-like, orange blossoms appear in the wintertime. There is a jasmine bush and a frangipani tree. Both produce incredibly sweet-smelling flowers. The jasmine has tiny white flowers. Frangipani flowers are waxy with four petals. This house belonged to John Spottswood, a Monroe County Sheriff and state senator. Spottswood was a good friend of President Harry Truman. For many years after leaving office, the Trumans maintained their friendship with the Spottswoods. Mrs. Spottswood recalled that although she'd heard that Truman cursed often, she had never heard him swear. She called the first lady "Mrs. T" and never "Bess."

Straight ahead, on the lefthand corner of Caroline and Simonton, is the Cypress House, a fine exhibit of classic Bahamian architecture. The house that originally stood on this corner really was made of cypress, but it burned, along with two-thirds of the island, in the great fire of 1886. The house you see today was built in 1888 out of Dade County pine. The exterior is painted with a sealant to maintain its natural appearance. The Bahamian features you'll see here are tall, floor-to-ceiling windows, high ceilings, and porches on both levels. Beneath the Cypress House are two cisterns where collected rainwater is used to water the garden and fill the pool. A 40-by-40 foot roof can catch up to 4200 gallons of rainwater in a year!

Turn right here and head up Simonton Street.

Simonton Street, 300 Block

On the left is the old Post Office and Federal Building built in 1934 of petrified coral rock quarried from Windley Key, 80 miles to the north in the Upper Keys. The quarry from which this stone was taken is now home to Theater of the Sea, a theme park.

Now on the right at 314 Simonton we come to the Casa Antigua Apartments, Ernest Hemingway's first stop when he arrived in Key West in 1928. From his second-floor apartment, he must have had a panoramic view—across the tin roofs and treetops, all the way to the Atlantic in one direction and the Gulf of Mexico in the other. It is easy to imagine how Hemingway became instantly enamored of the island.

At the back door of the gift shop, you enter a courtyard and garden full of tropical foliage. Look for a peacock and a very blue tiled pool. Take a camera. If you buy something worth $10 or more, you can visit the garden for free; otherwise, it will cost you $2. But remember, this Eden-like oasis is newly created. In Hemingway's day, this courtyard held an automobile dealership and a repair shop.

As you walk up Simonton, notice the mahogany trees along the sidewalks on both sides of the street. These were planted by the Civilian Conservation Corps (CCC) in the 1930s when young men were taken off relief and given jobs such as beautifying their towns.

Sign of Sandford, at 328 Simonton, is the workshop, studio and show-room of artist Sandford Birdsey. Her storefront windows are a throwback to the days when window shopping was a favorite pastime.

Cross Eaton Street.

Simonton Street, 400 Block

On the corner of Simonton and Eaton sits the First Methodist Old Stone Church. The Indian laurel tree in the front yard is a member of the ficus family, which is well represented on this island. The church is constructed of two-foot-thick coral rock walls quarried from this same property. After the rock had been removed from the earth, the quarried site was used as a cistern. The cistern was so large it supplied water to the church as well as many neighbors and often ships that came into the harbor. The caps of the cisterns are still visible in the side yard.

This stone church replaced an old wooden one. As the new church was slowly constructed of coral rock, the much smaller wooden one remained inside. It took the congregation fifteen years to complete the stone church, and, when it was done, the old wooden church was dismantled and removed, piece by piece, through the newer front doors. In 1892 the first service was held in the Old Stone Church you see today.

At 410 Simonton we now see the William Kerr House. There is no other house quite like this one, built around 1880 by architect William Kerr for his bride. The architectural style is carpenter's gothic. Kerr was an Irishman hired by the government to oversee the construction of the beautiful Custom House in 1891. He also designed the Old City Hall and the Old Stone Church. In front of the Kerr house notice the lush philodendron growing up the massive trunk of a mahogany tree.

At the intersection of Fleming and Simonton, you're standing at the heart of Key West's antique district. The tall brick building on the right is one of the few survivors of the Great Fire of 1886 that destroyed much of the town. After the fire, residents took a hard look at the destruction and realized that buildings of brick and houses with tin roofs were the ones that had survived. These elements were incorporated into the reconstruction of the city. Tin roofs have been popular in Key West ever since.

Cross Fleming Street.

Simonton Street, 500 Block

The elegant Marquesa Hotel and Cafe was once a flophouse, as dark and foreboding twenty years ago as it is bright and inviting today. In the mid 1980s a young woman was murdered here. Her body was discovered the following morning by a passerby who saw her feet, one wearing a sandal, one not, poking out from under the house (shades of *The Wizard of Oz*).

Those pretty silver buttonwood trees that line the block were planted by the Marquesa Hotel. The seeds from these trees resemble the buttons of an earlier day; hence, the name buttonwood.

The name of Dr. Maloney, the original resident of 508 Simonton, is still visible in the stained glass above the door. Today Maloney's former home is a collection of ramshackle apartments.

Free School Alley, home of Nancy's Secret Garden, begins here in the middle of the block on your left. Nancy invites visitors to bring a picnic and to dine at a table beneath the canopy of her spectacular tropical jungle. There is an entry fee of $6 to help pay for the upkeep of this fantastic collection of palms and exotics.

The building at 525 Simonton (Old Island Realty), built in 1890, is an excellent specimen of classic revival architecture, one of the five main styles represented in Key West's historic district. Current owners have received many awards for this restoration. Twin palms in front are particularly healthy Washingtonias, easily identified by their height and tiered grass skirts. There are several other Washingtonia palms on the island, but none so noble as these.

In 1905 the aforementioned Dr. Maloney sold the building at 530 Simonton, now a Sarabeth Restaurant, to the organizers of B'nai Zion. Begun in 1887, it is the oldest organized Jewish congregation in Florida. The island's first Jewish settlers were escaping religious persecution in Russia, heading for new lives in Cuba and South America, when their ships wrecked on the reefs and they found themselves, as many other travelers did, stranded in Key West. Today the congregation has a modern synagogue on United Street.

Before 530 Simonton was a synagogue, it was home to a saloonkeeper who dabbled in wrecking. The captain's walk, from where enterprising seamen searched the horizon for signs of a shipwreck, is still on the roof.

Cross Southard Street.

Simonton Street, 600 Block

Just past the intersection of Southard and Simonton, on the left side, you'll see a good example of a gumbo limbo tree and how the owners of the property have detoured their white picket fence to allow for the tree's thickening trunk. The gumbo limbo is also called the "tourist tree" because of its peeling, red skin.

Coming up on the corner of Simonton and Angela streets, you'll see Key West City Hall. The infamous police station was housed here up until recently, and Fire Station #1 remains. Our police and fire departments were once rife with felonious recruits. In 1976 the fire chief, with the strange but true name of Bum Farto, was charged with two counts of sale and delivery of cocaine. Before his sentencing, he rented a car in Key West and headed out of town. A month later the car was found parked on a side street, but Bum has never been seen or heard from again. Ten years later his wife, who supported herself by baking birthday and wedding cakes, successfully petitioned to have her missing husband declared legally dead so that she could collect his pension. If he is alive, Bum Farto is now in his eighties. Mrs. Farto has passed away, but before she did, she managed to have Bum declared dead so that she could collectwidow's benefits.

In 1984, the assistant police chief was charged with delivering cocaine in fried chicken boxes. He spent ten years in prison.

Turn left onto Angela Street.

Angela Street, 600 Block

This block of Angela has the distinction of having the highest elevation on the island: 18 feet above sea level. When you reach the end of the block, you are at the top of Solares Hill.

The Philip Burton House is at 608 Angela. If Key West historians and tour guides follow true to form, this house will probably become known as the Liz Taylor House because Elizabeth Taylor visited here often. Her host was her father-in-law, Shakespearean scholar Philip Burton. Burton was once headmaster at the Port Talbot School in South Wales, where he met, and adopted, a brilliant student named Richard. The great actor eventually became the fifth and sixth husband of Elizabeth Taylor.

Professor Burton, a great scholar and a kind neighbor, was known for his tireless dedication to local theater and his enjoyment of long, solitary walks. He bought this little house on Solares Hill in 1974 and lived here until his death in 1995.

If you were to continue straight ahead, you would come to the city cemetery, a wonderful place to visit in the cool of the early morning or the late afternoon.

Turn left onto Elizabeth Street.

Elizabeth Street, 600 Block

You'll now see on the right a row of cigarmakers' cottages, or shotgun houses, so called because of their design: a hall begun at the front door and extending back the length of the house. Then a parlor, one or two bedrooms, and finally the kitchen were connected off to the side of the hall. If you were to look through the front door of the house, you would see clear through to the backyard—as if you were looking down the barrel of a shotgun. The open doors at the front and back of the house allowed for a cooling ventilation. Addresses 621, 623, 625, 627 and 629 Elizabeth are all shotgun cottages once lived in by Cuban cigarmakers and their families. Today cottages such as these rent for around $3,000 a month and sell for around $750,000. If you can find one for sale...

The house at 620 Elizabeth is a typically New England-style home, illustrative of the strong ties between New England and the Florida Keys. The gold-colored ceramic star indicates that this house has been restored to its original condition. The pink star, which you see less often, indicates that the residence was once part of an Old Island Restoration Foundation house tour.

Turn right onto Bakers Lane.

Bakers Lane

In the middle of the block, more or less, you'll see a marker for Bakers Lane. Turn here and stroll down this typical Old Town lane for a look at a cozy cluster of cottages whose occupants enjoy the peace and quiet of a nearly car-free neighborhood. However, they do have to put up with ardent fans of writer James Leo Herlihy who make the pilgrimage to his home nearly every day of the year to pay homage to the man who penned the heartbreaking novel *Midnight Cowboy*. Herlihy lived at 709 Bakers. Notice the 1960s-era gingerbread trim on Herlihy's house. Inside, on the door, there is a hinged flap over a peep hole. On the flap Herlihy had written: "God is at the door. Let us see what face he is wearing now."

The Gingerbread House at 615 Elizabeth was a wedding gift from Benjamin Baker to his daughter in 1885. In both corners of this white-picket-fenced yard stand small lignumvitae trees. You can recognize them by their tiny blue flowers and/or red berries, depending upon the time of year. The only tornado ever to hit the island tore this house off its foundation in 1972. Because of the damage, the distressed property sold at a rock-bottom price of $22,500 that same year. Since then, the house has been updated and has changed hands frequently. In May 1998 it sold for $1,125,000! Who knows what it would go for today?

This is perhaps the island's most classic example of gingerbread trim. In the mid 1800s, after the invention of the jigsaw, builders and carpenters identified their work by the fanciful detail of the scroll ornamentation, or gingerbread. It was the the very last thing to be installed on a new house. When the popularity of gingerbread grew nationally, Sears and Roebuck then began selling it in their catalog. Unfortunately, as a result of its mass production, gingerbread trim has lost its individuality.

Moving along to the end of the block, beginning at 608 Elizabeth, we see three new houses built in 1996 and designed to fit in with the historic architecture already present for over 100 years. Here in the historic district, anything new has to be constructed in the style of neighboring houses, built a century earlier.

Cross Southard Street.

Elizabeth Street, 500 Block

The house on the right-hand corner, 701 Southard, has two steep gables for collecting rainwater. The more slanted roof area you have, the more water you collect.

On the left side of Elizabeth Street in the backyard of 631 Southard, is a healthy Key lime tree, which bears fruit year round. In front of Kinky's Construction, at 522 Elizabeth, are two colossal Spanish lime trees. The female of the two produces green fruit in spring and summer months, ripening in August. Next to her, on the right, is a male Spanish lime.

In the yard at 518 Elizabeth there is a pretty flowering tree called poor man's orchid, identifiable by its double-lobed leaves and orchid-shaped flower in the winter. Also, you'll find a fragrant jasmine bush.

Next door at 516 Elizabeth, we see a good example of an eyebrow house, an architectural style unique to Key West. There are roughly one hundred others on the island, each featuring the heavy roof overhang that protects upper-story windows and, thus, the second floor of the house as well, from the direct rays of the sun.

On the roof of 514 Elizabeth, see a roof opening called a scuttle, designed to let hot air flow up and out through the attic, while cooler air flows into the house via doors and windows on the first level. The popular island circulation system is borrowed from ships. When it rains, the scuttle quickly and easily shuts tight. By the way, it rains very infrequently in Key West. Our average rainfall is thirty-eight inches a year, the least amount of any city in Florida.

If you now look toward the right-hand corner of the library parking area, you'll see a huge West Indian almond tree. Around it grow the broad-leaved vines of a prolific philodendron plant. Next to the wheelchair ramp on your left there is a woman's tongue tree, which you can recognize by its long seed pods that rattle incessantly when the wind blows. Hey, what does that have to do with women's tongues?

Turn right onto Fleming Street.

Fleming Street, 700 Block

Now walk to the end of the block and turn right. On your left are the Jerry Herman Houses, at 701 and 703 Fleming Street. Jerry majored in architecture at the University of Miami. While his minor was music, he was such a skilled pianist and composer that his mother encouraged him to pursue music as well as architecture. And so he did, and the rest of the story is Broadway history. Jerry went on to compose music and lyrics for hits such as *Hello Dolly, La Cage Aux Folles* and *Mame*. Thanks, Mrs. Herman!

Jerry's love of architecture and design have not, however, deserted him. Through the years he has restored several Key West properties, none so dramatic as these two fine specimens of Victoriana. The two were identical twins until 703 was fitted with solar generating panels, a modern corruption that knocked it out of the running for several historic preservation awards.

Next, our pink library at 700 Fleming is South Florida's first public library, organized in 1892. For forty-four years the library service was run by the Key West Women's Club. Then in 1959 it moved into this home of its own.

In the library's side yard a palm garden was recently installed. It features twenty-six varieties of palm trees that grow in the Caribbean Basin, from Florida to South America. The garden is open from 9:30 a.m until 5:30 p.m.

At the end of the block, on the left, is the Fleming Street United Methodist Church, erected in 1912. Today a congregation of the Southernmost Church of God in Christ worships here. This church, which replaced an earlier wooden structure destroyed by a 1910 hurricane, is built in a castle style of architecture, alluding to the Kingdom of God.

Turn left onto William Street.

William Street, 400 Block
At 421 William, on the left side of the building, there is a stairway to heaven. The man who was to become my husband lived in the third floor apartment of this house years ago. I climbed that stairway many times.

Another house farther down at 415 William, has been restored to look very much as it did when it was built in 1898. The Key West Bed and Breakfast is the first of a row of beautifully restored historic homes, several of them now used as guesthouses. The Island City House, at

411 William, is one of the largest wooden structures on the island. See
how far back from the street it extends? The Gideon Lowe House, or
Whispers, at 409 William, is another successful restoration. Notice the
yellow elder tree on the left side of the house. This tree flowers three
times a year, so it's nearly always in bloom.

Across the street on the left side we see two houses that were barged
in 1847 to Key West from Green Turtle Cay in the Bahamas. The yellow
house at 408 William was owned by Captain Richard Roberts. The house
next door that fronts on Eaton Street was owned by his brother-in-law,
Captain John Bartlum. In those days, it was easier and cheaper to barge
than to build. The nearest source of hard lumber was 700 miles away in
the Florida Panhandle. And these houses, built by shipbuilders using
wooden pegs, were easily disassembled, transported and then reassembled.

Turn left onto Eaton Street.

Eaton Street, 700 Block
The Calvin Klein house at 712 Eaton was built in the 1890s by a prosperous grocer, Richard Peacon, who lived here with his family for many
years. Locals were shocked in 1980 when fashion baron Calvin Klein
paid $975,000 for the octagon-shaped house after it was spiffed and pol-
ished to pretty perfection by interior designer Angelo Donghia. Donghia
had paid only $45,000 for the place six years earlier. Of course, to Calvin
Klein, a guy who charges $100 for a pair of $20 jeans, the price tag must
have seemed fair enough. Klein's frequent guest, Brooke Shields, seemed
to enjoy visiting Key West more than her host. Klein didn't spend much
time here, and a few years after making the famous deal, he sold the
house at a huge loss. Why didn't Calvin Klein like Key West? One trolley
tour driver says he left because the octagon house didn't have enough
closet space. Nowadays it is not at all unusual to pay millions of bucks for
a pretty property in Paradise.

Turn right onto Peacon Lane.

Peacon Lane or Grunt Bone Alley

Across the street from Calvin's is Peacon Lane, also known by an earlier name, Grunt Bone Alley. Currently there's a sign on this corner, but it may be gone by the time you get to this short thoroughfare only the length of a city block. People seem to love snatching the Grunt Bone Alley sign.

In the first yard on the left side of the lane, you can recognize two travelers palms by the overlapping appearance of their wide, tight stalks near the earth. Each of these fronds, it is said, contains a quart of rainwater—good news for travelers in the tropics in the days before the pipeline delivered fresh water from the mainland.

The Henry Faulkner House is at 328 Peacon. Before he died in a car crash in 1981, Faulkner willed this house to poet Stefan Brecht, son of Bertolt Brecht, with the provision that he never sell it, or dispense with any of the furniture Henry had collected and stored therein. So Brecht, who does not live in Key West, rents the house to a local woman who has lived here for over a decade. She is forbidden to dispose of one stick of Henry Faulkner's termite-infested furniture. Furthermore, she is not permitted to clear out the attic or to alter the premises in any way. So she lives with the gargantuan mirrors in their magnificently carved wooden frames and the art-deco-era chandeliers and lamp treatments that Henry installed thirty years ago. "That's fine," she says. "Imagine all the great energy in here!"

Although Faulkner was a profoundly talented painter whose stylistic flowers, birds, butterflies and slanting houses epitomize the era of the '60s, he longed to be taken seriously also as a poet. He sang jazz in a falsetto voice and claimed to be a large black woman trapped inside a small white man's body. Faulkner's friend, writer James Herlihy, wrote *Midnight Cowboy*, the novel that became the hit movie. It is said that Herlihy modeled the character of Ratso Rizzo after his friend, Henry Faulkner.

Faulkner's Key West house was the setting for several scenes in the film *Criss Cross*, about a go-go dancer's adventures here in the late '60s. The film stars Goldie Hawn and is an excellent physical portrayal of '60s-era Key West. Aside from the fact that the making of the film employed hundreds of Key West people over the slow summer of 1990, and a lot of us got to see Goldie Hawn and Kurt Russell up close, there is little else that is positive to say about it. The film is now on video, but it's understandably difficult to find.

Goldie, by the way, is a true beauty with luminescent skin and a pleasing personality. Kurt's not too bad either.

Now, retrace your steps to the corner of Eaton and William Streets for more historic sights.

Turn left onto William Street.

William Street, 300 Block

On the right corner, look for a huge rubber tree, another member of the ficus family. The rubber tree, popular on the mainland as an indoor plant, grows outdoors year round in this frost-free city. Notice how trees of the ficus family drop thin, aerial branches that return to the earth and take root on their own. Eventually these spindly aerial branches merge to form bigger, sturdier new trunks. Someone has tied a bundle of new branches into a knot, and they have melded quite beautifully, exhibiting the ficus family's strange capabilities.

At 328 William you'll see the "birthday cake" house, so named because of its gingerbread trim in the shape of dripping icing along the roof line and the row of gingerbread flaming candles on the fence around the yard.

Farther down, the little eyebrow house, with the double scuttles, at 309 William, has been in the same Key West family for over 150 years. To the immediate right is Sawyer Lane. Look straight down the lane and you will see, on the left, a massive breadfruit tree. It is the tallest tree in the neighborhood—you can't miss it.

Breadfruit resembles a big, green volleyball and is delicious peeled, baked, and smeared with butter, or cut into chunks and fried in oil. Breadfruit was the cargo on the HMS *Bounty* when a group of mutinous sailors set Captain Bligh adrift at sea in 1789. The breadfruit trees had been loaded onto the ship in Tahiti for delivery to wealthy plantation owners in the West Indies who were to use breadfruit as cheap food for their slaves. Legend has it that Captain Bligh was lavishing the precious supply of fresh water on the breadfruit rather than on the thirsty crew. Another version of the mutiny on the *Bounty* says many members of the crew had fallen in love with Tahitian women, or at least with the

Tahitian women's easy virtue, during a five-month layover and were damned cranky when the ship finally sailed, leaving their lovers behind. It didn't take much to get them mad.

At the end of the block on your right, you'll now see the white building with red trim that fronts on Caroline Street. You're now nearing the Key West Bight, a unique, curving waterfront and seaport area.

Caroline Street, 800 Block

The historic Red Doors Building here is a far cry from its previous incarnation. At the height of Key West's shrimping industry, the Red Doors was a notoriously rough shrimpers bar, nicknamed by locals the "Bucket of Blood." Fights broke out every fifteen minutes downstairs, while upstairs, rooms were rented out by the hour. The first known example of Key West timeshare.

Don't miss all the great food and drink stops here. The first is B.O.'s Fishwagon at 801 Caroline. A bit farther up the street is Pepe's, at 806 Caroline, one of the island's oldest and most beloved eateries. Still farther along, at 920 Caroline is PT's, where pool and pot roast rule. For a sandwich to go, stop in at the Waterfront Market on the Bight and visit the long, inviting deli and sandwich counter. Fresh fruit, veggies, bakery items, fish, and beer and wine are all available here.

Cross Caroline Street and head toward the waterfront.

William Street, 200 Block

On your right you can't miss The Wyland Wall, on the Waterfront Market. It took Wyland a week to paint this reef scene. He paints by airbrush, from the bottom of the wall to the top. In the summer of 1993, Wyland traveled from Maine to Key West, stopping at a new location each week to paint a different mural. He painted thirteen murals, in thirteen stops in thirteen weeks! This is the last one on his expedition. And in 2003, he came back to freshen the original job.

This waterfront area of the Key West Bight includes the seaport and Land's End Marina farther on up Caroline. It is the largest single section of waterfront on the island still free of hotels or condominiums. The City purchased the bight from a shrimp and seafood exporting conglomerate in 1992 for $18.5 million. A red brick harborwalk and wooden pier hugs the waterfront. The City has done a great job of building this recently completed walk. It's a wonderful way to explore the harbor.

This calm, sheltered harbor was once home to Key West's shrimping fleet. After nocturnal shrimp were discovered in the Tortugas in 1949, shrimping flourished. Nearly 400 boats dragged their nets across the ocean's floor each night, pulling up tons of the world's favorite shrimp, Key West Pink Gold, from the nearby waters. During the season, lasting from November through July, shrimpers went to sea for two weeks at a time. They were paid very well, but out at sea there was no place to spend their money. Consequently, when the shrimpers returned to shore, they were rich, randy and ready to party. When things didn't go their way, they fought, often quite viciously. Hence, the notorious Bucket of Blood.

The ever-popular Schooner Wharf Bar is on the waterfront too, on your right. Farther down the brick harborwalk, you'll come to a two-story waterfront building that belongs to Jimmy Buffett. His recording studio is inside.

In the Lazy Way shops farther on, you'll find fortune and tarot card readers, and local artists and craftspeople creating jewelry, hats, painted T-shirts, and gauzy dresses.

Turn right and then make a quick left onto Greene Street.

Greene Street, 600 Block
On your left you'll next see there are two interesting shops: Joseph's Antiques, in the shed at 616 Greene, and the Sea Store at 614 Greene. Bill Ford of the Sea Store is the Audubon spokesman for the Keys. He'll tell you what birds are being spotted, what birds aren't, and where you should go to see the ones that are. (Call 294-3438 for a taped message of the same information.) He'll also give you a bird map and a bird list.

The long, white-painted brick building on the left was built by William Curry in 1878. (You remember William Curry—America's first self-made millionaire who came to town as a penniless youth in the early 1800s. We love this guy!) This was one of his many downtown holdings, an auction hall and tobacco warehouse. Key West Handprint Fabrics is housed here now, but, sadly, handprinting is no longer done. Fabric is printed in Miami instead, but you still can buy fabric by the yard or purchase a dress or shirt made of handprint fabric.

Cross Simonton Street.

Greene Street, 500 Block

A crazy quilt of culture and commerce here. At the Key West Aloe Factory you can view a working laboratory and buy outlet merchandise of perfume and luscious aloe lotions as gifts or tiny, luxurious vacation toiletries.

Watch cigars being hand rolled and buy a souvenir sample of the fragrant Cuban symbol at the Conch Republic Cigar Factory next door to the Kozuchi Japanese Restaurant and Sushi Bar. The Eastern eatery operates inside a very tiny and neatly appointed space across the street from an equally good Thai place. At Kozuchi's, the Japanese beer is very cold, and the sushi bar is the real thing.

Old City Hall, at 510 Greene Street, has undergone a recent restoration, but, in spite of all the thousands of dollars spent, the four clocks on the tower up top still don't agree on the time. The original city hall was built of wood and, consequently, was burned in the fire of 1859. It was rebuilt, again in wood, but it again burned in the fire of 1886. The current brick building was designed by everybody's favorite architect William Kerr in 1891. On the ground-floor level of the building, notice the high archways of an open-air market. The upstairs was used for offices and meeting rooms of the mayor and city commissioners.

The old City Hall building was abandoned in 1962 for the current, much more modern City Hall at Simonton and Angela streets. In 1991, Old City Hall was renovated and brought back to turn-of-the-century splendor. Now that it is considered chic to be 100 years old, City Commission meetings go on here once again.

Thai Cuisine, a restaurant across the street at 513 Greene, is a great restaurant, and, like its name, very unpretentious.

Sloppy Joe's Bar on the corner has been many things to many people, but it's best known as Hemingway's favorite watering hole and home of the annual Hemingway Look-alike Contest that goes on each July 21 on the occasion of the writer's birthday.

Cross Duval Street.

Greene Street, 400 Block

Captain Tony's Saloon is now where the original Sloppy Joe's Bar was founded by Hemingway's good buddy Captain Joe Russell, nicknamed "Sloppy Joe" by the writer. In 1937, in response to a rent hike, Sloppy Joe's Bar moved lock, stock and barrel to its current location. So Captain Tony's is actually the place where Hemingway did his late afternoon drinking.

In December 1936 a writer named Martha Gellhorn came to this bar with the purpose of meeting Hemingway. They met and began a love affair which eventually led to the demise of Hemingway's second marriage. The couple married in October 1940, less than two weeks after his divorce from Pauline. Pauline, wife number two, was the mate with whom he shared his Key West years, considered by most critics to be the most significant time of his writing career.

Captain Tony himself is not around much anymore. He might be at home, visiting with some of his thirteen kids, or being interviewed by some adoring reporter, or on the road with Jimmy Buffett, who likes to pull him up to center stage at his concerts and introduce to his fans the man for whom the song "Last Mango in Paris" was written.

Carved above the stage at Captain Tony's are these words: "Everybody is a star at Captain Tony's." Without the Captain, the place has definitely lost some of its elan. But the beer's still cold.

Cross Greene Street, head into Kino Plaza.

Kino Plaza

Directly across the street from Captain Tony's, walk through a brilliantly colored canopy of bougainvillea into Kino Plaza. Straight ahead you'll see the Kino Sandal Factory, the orginal factory established in 1965. You *have* to buy a pair of leather Kino's that will last you forever, especially if you don't wear them in the snow. The most popular style, the flat thong, is now around $10 for woman, $12 for men.

From Kino Plaza, turn right onto Fitzpatrick Street, which quickly becomes Tift's Alley. And now you're back at Mallory Square once again.

Old Town Walking Tour
· · ·

Writers

The passion we have to create
is all we know of God

– TENNESSEE WILLIAMS

Pulitzer Prize Winners
who live or have lived in Key West
and the years in which they won

Robert Frost	1924, 1931, 1937, 1943
John Hersey	1945
Tennessee Williams	1948, 1955
Ernest Hemingway	1954
Wallace Stevens	1955
Elizabeth Bishop	1956
Richard Wilbur	1957, 1989
Phil Caputo	1972
Joseph Lash	1972
Annie Dillard	1974
James Kirkwood	1976
James Merrill	1977
Alison Lurie	1985

Some Famous Key West Writers

Elizabeth Bishop

Poet Elizabeth Bishop bought a house at 624 White Street in the late 1930s. There she recorded her impressions of Key West and the people she met here in several wonderful essays. For a great view of the island as it was in the 1940s, read *Collected Prose*, which was published posthumously in 1984. While she lived in Key West Bishop took up painting. It wasn't very good, but she did it, and that's what mattered. One of her watercolor images graces the cover of her *Collected Prose*.

Bishop stayed on the island for many years, fishing, swimming and biking. Then, in the '50s, she left and never came back, as if she'd absorbed all she could of the place. She was no longer a Key West resident when she was awarded the Pulitzer Prize in 1956.

Judy Blume

Judy Blume is a hugely successful writer of fabulous books for young people, as well as several adult novels. How I wish this stuff had been around when I was a kid! Blume received a National Book Award for contributions to American letters in 2004. She is pretty, much younger looking in person than her bio claims her to be, and founder of the Kids Fund, a charitable and educational foundation. Here in Key West, she and her husband, writer George Cooper, are important members of the group that rallied around the establishment of the wonderful Tropic Cinema movie theater. Blume is a dedicated member of the National Coalition Against Censorship. Because her writing sometimes deals realistically (and quite beautifully, her fans will tell you) with heavy topics like sex, religion and divorce, her books are sometimes tucked away in dark corners of the library, or banned altogether in some places. All this fame and controversy, of course, make her a perfect Key West citizen.

John Malcolm Brinnin

John Malcolm Brinnin, another Nova Scotia-born poet, died in 1998 at the age of 82. He came to Key West originally to visit with the poet Elizabeth Bishop. He began wintering in Key West in the '40s. Brinnin was a writer of remarkable refinement. His mellifluous speaking voice lives on at the Audubon House where his is the voice of Captain John Geiger, who leads an audio taped tour of the historic house. John Malcolm immortalized his relationship with Truman Capote in the book *Sextet*. Brinnin's most famous work is the fascinating and heartbreaking memoir, *Dylan Thomas in America*.

Philip Burton

Dr. Burton lived at 608 Angela Street from 1974 until his death in 1995. The Shakespearean scholar, actor, writer and director was the step-father of actor Richard Burton. Dr. Burton was sometimes visited here by dear friend and two-time daughter-in-law Elizabeth Taylor. Burton's autobiography is *Early Doors: My Life and the Theater*. His most famous scholarly work is *The Sole Voice: Character Portraits from Shakespeare*.

Phil Caputo

Phil Caputo doesn't live in Key West anymore. But he visits often because he has a passion for fishing, which he describes brilliantly in an 1988 essay called *The Ahab Complex*: "...an obsession to pursue and conquer a monster of the depths regardless of the consequences to one's bank account, career and family life." He shared the 1972 Pulitzer Prize for an investigative series on political corruption in Chicago. Caputo's nonfiction book *A Rumor of War* is said by many to be the quintessential Viet Nam book. It is also the book that put Caputo on the literary map for all time.

Jean Carper

One look at this very youthful and charming author of good news books about nutrition and aging, and you, like many of us here in Key West, will be taking her vitamins, too. You order them on the Internet. Jean's books, with titles like *Miracle Cures*, *Your Miracle Brain*, and *Stop Aging Now* zoom to the top of the New York Times best sellers list as fast as she can research and present them. She also writes on healthy food for U.S. Weekend, a national tabloid. She recently published a healthy cookbook, and a book on maintaining your dog's long life. Yes, Jean has been very successful and she shares her good fortune with the Key West community.

Her money was instrumental in the construction and creation of the fabulous Tropic Cinema, located at 416 Eaton Street.

Tom Corcoran

People who love Key West are crazy for reading Keys writer Tom Corcoran's Alex Rutledge mysteries, set right here in the Lower Keys and full of places we all know and love to recognize in the pages of the fast-paced thrillers. Corcoran can hardly write fast enough to meet the demand for these yummy paperbacks, well suited for the beach, the bathroom or the plane home. Corcoran, a longtime buddy of Jimmy Buffett's, is cowriter on the hit song "Cuban Crime of Passion." Photos by Corcoran have graced seven Buffett album covers. Corcoran has been a disc jockey, screenwriter, navy officer, jouranlist and magazine editor.

Nancy Friday

She's a writer of social commentary and sexy, uncatagorizable stuff like *My Secret Garden*, a collection of women's sexual fantasies (excellent late-night reading). Her many best-selling books including *My Mother/Myself* and *Women on Top* have made her wealthy and famous. Nancy is tall and commanding and always wears a fresh hibiscus tucked behind her ear. In Key West she strides importantly through the places she visits and has been known to set unwary people in her path spinning like tops. But on television talk shows, she's patient and very gracious.

Robert Frost

Frost's elegant poetry won him four Pulitzer Prizes. He wintered in a garden cottage at 410 Caroline Street as a guest of the famous hostess, Jessie Porter Newton. He also stayed at 707 Seminole Street Frost didn't care much for Key West. In letters back home to New England he described it as shabby and dilapidated, which it surely was at the depths of its degradation in 1935. But he found the weather irresistible and spent sixteen winters here, beginning in 1934. Frost wrote no poems about the island. In Key West, he said, he simply enjoyed "barding around." Key West poets celebrate Robert Frost with a festival in his name each April.

James Leo Herlihy
Herlihy lived for three years in what is sometimes referred to as "the hippie house" at 709 Bakers Lane. The house's gingerbread trim features jigcut peace signs. Herlihy's '60s novels *Blue Denim* and *Midnight Cowboy* were made into films. *A Story That Ends With a Scream, and Eight Others* includes several short stories set in Key West. Herlihy's friends in Key West were playwright Tennessee Williams, artist Henry Faulkner, and novelist-playwright Jimmy Kirkwood.

John Hersey
Hersey wintered for many years in a compound on Windsor Lane where his neighbors were Richard Wilbur and John Ciardi. His books include the 1945 Pulitzer Prize winner *Hiroshima*. A final contribution just before his death in 1994, *Key West Tales*, is a collection of odd, sad stories written quite beautifully in Hersey's seductive and seamless prose.

David Kaufelt
As a copywriter in a New York advertising agency, David Kaufelt penned "Choosy mothers choose Jif," the slogan that launched a peanut butter empire. Kaufelt's 1973 novel *Six Months With An Older Woman* was translated into a two-hour movie for TV. Kaufelt and his wife Lynn founded the Key West Literary Arts Seminar in 1982 and, with others, the Tennessee Williams Festival in 2003.

Jimmy Kirkwood
He owned a house at 1023 Catherine Street but wasn't in town often. Kirkwood co-wrote the Pulitzer Prize-winning play *A Chorus Line*. The son of silent screen star Lila Lee, Kirkwood was also an actor as well as a writer. His wonderful books are *Good Times/Bad Times*, *American Grotesque*, *P.S. Your Cat Is Dead!*, *Some Kind of Hero*, *Hit Me With A Rainbow* and *Diary of a Mad Playwright*.

Kirkwood lived between New York, Los Angeles and Key West and sent memorable Christmas cards to a select group of friends. The Christmas postcards featured pictures of Kirkwood and celebrity friends. Scribbled in red ink across the front: "Merry Christmas from the

Kirkwoods." One year the "Kirkwoods" were Jimmy and Elizabeth Taylor. Another time, Jimmy, Mary Martin and Carol Channing.

Alison Lurie

She won a 1985 Pulitzer Prize for *Foreign Affairs*. Her novel *The Truth About Lorin Jones* is partially set in Key West. Lurie's *The Last Resort*, is entirely set in Key West, which is about the only good thing the reviewers have to say about it. Once a professor of English at Cornell University, Lurie now divides her time between Key West, Upstate NY and London. Her book *Familiar Spirits: A Memoir of James Merrill and David Jackson*, covers four decades of friendship with James Merrill and his partner— their wealth, and their preoccupation with the occult. A fascinating read.

John Leslie

The adventures of Key West native and private eye Gideon Lowry are skillfully told by local writer John Leslie. Who-done-it devotees love these mysteries. Lowry loves lazy cats, swaying palms, and reminiscing about the good old days in Paradise. But oh! The troubles he sees! Dig Leslie's sultry titles: *Love For Sale*; *Killing me Softly*; and *Blue Moon*.

Tom McGuane

Jimmy Buffett's great friend lived at 1011 Von Phister and at 123-25 Ann Street before that. His novel, *Ninety-two in the Shade*, was made into a movie which was filmed in Key West in 1975. Locals still talk about the rowdy Hollywood crowd that came to perform in that film. Elizabeth Ashley, Margot Kidder, Peter Fonda, and Warren Oates reportedly adapted easily to the island's free-wheeling ways. Rent the movie if you can find it. It's great. McGuane is currently married to Jimmy Buffett's sister, Laurie. They live in Montana, and often winter here.

James Merrill

Yes, the Merrill Lynch brokerage house Merrill. For the last sixteen years of his life, he spent half the year in a cozy cottage in Key West and the other half in Connecticut. Today Merrill's house is on the Literary Walking Tour, although sadly, many of the folks on the tour confess to never having heard of James Merrill. "Who?" they say. "What did he write?" In the course of his amazingly successful career in poetry, Merrill won the Pulitzer Prize, and he twice won the National Book Award in poetry. His epic poem *The Changing Light at Sandover* is a favorite of Ivy League and Seven Sisters professors. According to Alison Lurie's fascinating memoir, the poem was inspired by Merrill's many sessions with a ouiji board.

Evan Rhodes

For many years the movie star handsome Rhodes lived in the elegant eyebrow house at 621 Catholic Lane. Later he moved up to Sugarloaf Key. Some of his books: *An Army of Children*, *On Wings of Fire*, *Bless This House*, *Forged in Fury*, *Valiant Hearts* and *A Distant Dream*. Rhodes also wrote the libretto for a musical based on his novel *The Prince of Central Park*. The musical went all the way to Broadway in 1985. However, it closed after only eighteen performances. Now, the Prince of Central Park is a film.

Leigh Rutledge

Cat Love Letters. Diary of a Cat. The Gay Book of Lists and *When My Grandmother was a Girl*. Leigh's dedication to hopeless causes, lost souls and sentimentality is becoming legendary. His Key West house is large, *very* large, you might think, for one guy and his partner. The extra space belongs to his cats. There are usually thirty of them wandering around. All of them suffer with heart-breaking injuries or diseases deemed terminal. Leigh performs the miracle of bringing his beloved cats back from death's dark door. Newspaper reporters and *People Magazine* writers ask Leigh questions such as "How many pounds of kitty litter do you use in a week?" "Would you ask someone how many rolls of toilet paper they use in a week?" Leigh huffs.

Laurence Shames

The books: *Florida Straits. Scavenger Reef. Tropical Depression. Sunburn.* Shames's South Florida-based novels are described as comic thrillers and are found on the mystery shelves at the bookstore. Shames came to Key West from New York, where he wrote the "Jake" column for *Glamour Magazine* for several years and an ethics column for *Esquire Magazine* from 1982-1983. Dismayed at how busy Key West was becoming, Shames moved to Southern California in 1998.

Shel Silverstein

He was a Grammy Award-winning songwriter, a cartoonist and the author of the world's best-selling poetry books for children: *A Light in the Attic*, *Where the Sidewalk Ends*, *Falling Up*. Among his hit songs are "The Cover of the Rolling Stone" and "A Boy Named Sue." Silverstein lived on an Old Town street behind a jungle of tropical foliage designed to discourage curiosity seekers. Soft-spoken and earthy, he could be seen walking the sidewalks of Key West in baggy shorts and sandals, poking through the stacks at the public library, dining at local restaurants, and regularly stretching at yoga classes. Silverstein died suddenly, of a heart attack, alone in his little house, in 1999.

Wallace Stevens

One of America's most renowned poets was also an insurance exec from Hartford. Stevens discovered Key West on a business trip to Miami. Throughout the decade of the 1930s, he wintered at the grand Casa Marina Hotel. Although Stevens was here during Hemingway's Key West decade, the two were not friends. Wallace is said to have avoided both Hemingway and John Dos Passos, a writer who lived on the island during the same decade. His one literary buddy was Robert Frost, and even that relationship was a rocky one. When Stevens drank, he grew resentful and confrontative. A fistfight once broke out between Hemingway and Stevens followed by many versions of how the fracas came about and who got the best of whom. By 1940, both Hemingway and Stevens were gone from the island, never to live here again.

Stevens won the National Book Award in 1950 and the Pulitzer Prize in 1955. Because Tennessee Williams enjoyed reading aloud Steven's poem *The Idea of Order at Key West*, it was read at Williams' funeral in 1983.

Thelma Strabel

Following a career as a fashion reporter in Paris, Strabel wintered in Key West in the late 1930s. She loved the place so well that she stayed for several years. In an article about Key West she wrote for the *Saturday Evening Post*, she described the island as "quiet and careless and charming."

Her novel *Reap the Wild Wind* set in 1830s-era Key West, is the story of two wreckers who fall in love with the same local temptress, foxy Loxi Claiborne. The novel was first serialized in the *Saturday Evening Post* and later appeared in book form. A very young, very hunky John Wayne stars in the movie version. In one memorable scene, Miss Claiborne of Key West shocks the gentle folk of Charleston when she sings a naughty song at a genteel party.

Strabel herself became the talk of Key West when she built a house at 400 South Street, designed to rival the original Southernmost House's claim to the title. Strabel's little house has been replaced by a much more elaborate one. The original Southernmost House, one block north, continues to claim the title.

Richard Wilbur

The opposite of riot: A bunch of people being quiet.

Why isn't all poetry this much fun? Wilbur has won a slew of awards, including the 1957 Pulitzer Prize for a collection called *Things of the World* and, in 1989, another Pulitzer for *New and Collected Poems*. Wilbur has twice served as Poet Laureate of the United States. His poems show up all over the place—in the *Atlantic Monthly*, in the *New Yorker*. In 1995, *Moliere's Comedies*, a Broadway hit, was translated from French by Wilbur. Richard Wilbur lives with his wife Charlee in a famous writer's compound on Windsor Lane. Generous with his time and talent, Wilbur performs one or two readings of his poetry every winter in the public library's auditorium. Call the library for a schedule of events, and get there early if you want to get a seat.

William Wright

For a long time he lived on Love Lane, close enough to the public library on Fleming Street to put his portable telephone in his pocket and go next door to work in the icy air conditioned comfort of the chilly archives. Among his biographies are *Lillian Hellman: The Image, the Woman*; *All the Pain that Money Can Buy*; *The Life of Christina Onassis*; *The Von Bulow Affair*; and *Born That Way: Genes, Behavior, Personality*.

Though the subjects of William Wright's biographies are often doomed, the author is upbeat and very dear. Like all of our famous writers' annual library talks, Wright's attract over-flowing crowds.

Great Key West Anthologies

Once Upon An Island, Beyond Paradise and *Mango Summers*, published by the Key West Author's Co-op. Absorbing collections of short fiction, non-fiction, and poetry, from Key West's best up-and-coming writers.

The Key West Reader, the Best of Key West's Writers 1830–1990. Edited by George Murphy. Literature, poems and letters about Key West by John James Audubon, Phil Caputo, Ernest Hemingway, Wallace Stephens, Tennessee Williams and Hunter Thompson.

Bookstores

Key West Island Bookstore
513 Fleming Street ▪ 294-2904
It's the Key West authors' bookshop, hosting signings by people like Jimmy Buffett, James Hall, and Alan Maltz. The best-selling author here is, and has always been, Ernest Hemingway. You can find rare, first-edition and autographed copies of books. If you have a special need or request or question, ask Marshall, the owner, or any one of his well-informed assistants.

Bargain Books & News Stand
1028 Truman Ave. Phone 294-7446
A large, well-stocked bookstore full of books to buy, sell or trade. It also offers local interest books and a well-informed bookseller to answer questions about them. Also hundreds of paperbacks, videos, collectibles, as well as newspapers and magazines are also available. Behind the counter: a bona fide Key West character. In the back room: the Able Body Fitness Center, featuring aerobics, free weights and machines. Work out in air-conditioned comfort, with TV, music and showers, too, for only $5. Open 6 a.m. to 10 p.m. daily.

Borders Express
2212 N. Roosevelt Boulevard ≈ 294-5419
As all local bookstores do, the people at Borders maintain a well-stocked collection of books on local topics, as well as a wall of magazines, a children's section, and lots of bargain tables. There are even occasional book signings, and the bargain counters really do contain bargains.

Valladares and Son
1200 Duval Street ≈ 296-5032
Key West's oldest newspaper stand opened in 1927, when current owner Arthur Valladares was two years old. Today Arthur carries an impressive selection of over 3,500 titles of out-of-town and foreign newspapers, paperbacks and magazines.

Arthur tells the story of the first time he met Ernest Hemingway. The writer, clad in his favorite baggy cut-off shorts and rope belt, reportedly wandered into the recently opened Valladares store in 1932. Arthur said to his father, in Spanish, "Look at the bum." Hemingway introduced himself to the boy, and demonstrated that he spoke excellent Spanish. The store ended up selling Hemingway's books. They got an extra dollar for autographed copies.

Hemingway once asked Arthur's dad to arrange for him to receive the *New York Times* via the Valladares stand. The older Valladares told Hemingway that Arthur was so new to the business, he didn't even know how to order the *New York Times*. So Hemingway made the arrangements himself. Not only did Hemingway have the *Times* delivered from New

York, albeit two days late, but he also ordered *The New York Mirror*, *The World-Telegram* and the *Herald Tribune*, which all came in by train.

Valladares' customers would reserve their Sunday *New York Times* by paying for them in advance. There were always a few extras ordered for tourists, and those went fast. Every week Tennessee Williams wanted a Sunday *Times*, but refused to pay for it up front. Several times he stomped out of the store, enraged, when Valladares was sold out of the *Times* and refused to give him an already-paid-for paper, reserved for another customer.

Poetry In Paradise

Not so long ago, Key West was the scene of a poetry resurgence, with lots of raves and slams happening regularly around town. There was even an award-winning Key West slam team. That particular resurgence is over now, and the raves and slams are fond memories. But the Key West Poetry Guild, founded in 1977, still gathers at 8 p.m., on the first Sunday evening of each month, for a good, old-fashioned poerty read. The event is open to the public; all are welcome to read their work. And where better to stage this traditional gathering than the Robert Frost Cottage, at 410 Caroline Street? It's behind the Heritage House Museum, and yes, it is the very same cottage where Frost wintered for many years.

Will local interest in poetry resurge? Island poet J.T. Eggers says she thinks it will. It's cyclical. To wax and to wane, she explains, is what lyricism is all about.

Hemingway in Key West

(

In 1935, one of Key West's biggest tourist attractions
was a drink called a Papa Doble, which was promoted
as Ernest Hemingway's favorite drink:

Two-and-a-half jiggers of white Bacardi rum,
Juice of two fresh limes,
Juice of ½ grapefruit,
Six drops of maraschino juice.
Mix in an electric blender.

*The better you treat a man and the
more you show him you love him,
the quicker he gets tired of you.*

– FROM *To Have And Have Not*, PUBLISHED IN 1936,
HEMINGWAY'S ONLY NOVEL SET IN KEY WEST

A FEW WEEKS AFTER I arrived in Key West, I begged my new island
boyfriend to accompany me on a tour of the Hemingway House. The
house is magnificent, much more spacious than most on the island,
and in those long ago days of the mid-1970s, not at all crowded the way
it is today. Back then you wandered freely about the place, taking your
time, dreaming your dreams, imagining your imaginings. When I saw
Hemingway's bedroom, I threw myself onto the bed.

"What are you doing?" Miguel asked incredulously.

"I'm lying in his bed," I answered, waving my arms and legs in the king-sized bed. "I'm seeing what he saw, feeling what he felt. I'm going to bed with Hemingway's ghost!"

In the many years that followed that day, I've learned that the great Ernest Hemingway was nothing at all like I imagined he was. (Neither was Miguel, for that matter.)

There's no getting away from Ernest Hemingway in this town. Nothing has promoted our earthy, end-of-the-road machismo image like America's first celebrity writer and Key West's biggest big deal. Stick around for a while and you feel you are sharing the place with his ghost, and indeed, you are. The Hemingway legacy is very much alive and well.

The Key West Years

Hemingway arrived in Key West in April, 1928 after seven years in Paris. He traveled with his newest wife, his second, a small-boned, dark-haired woman named Pauline. Pauline Pfeiffer had befriended Hadley (the first Mrs. Hemingway) and Ernest in Paris. She'd dined with them. Socialized with them. Traveled with them. And somewhere along the way, she'd stolen Mr. Hemingway's heart. A time of terrible suffering followed. Ernest couldn't quite decide how to handle the situation. He sent letters to his guy friends, describing the hell of being involved in a romantic triangle. He loved them both, he said. Finally poor Hadley, who'd stood by her husband through the lean Paris years and donated her small fortune to the family's upkeep, faced the sad reality of the situation and sent Ernest packing, freeing him to marry Pauline.

Pauline was a devout Catholic, the daughter of a wealthy Arkansas family. She was also the cherished niece of perfume king Gus Pfeiffer. As a wedding gift, Uncle Gus bought the Hemingways a new car and later a grand Key West house as well, the first one Ernest had owned. When Hemingway got restless, good old Uncle Gus financed a very expensive African safari, at the height of the Great Depression.

When Ernest and Pauline arrived in Key West, Ernest was 29 years old and as handsome and healthy as he ever would be. He fit right in to Key West's crazy assortment of characters. Mornings he worked on his novel *A Farewell to Arms*. Afternoons he hung around with tough guys who drank, fished and admired Hemingway's worldly bravado. He began wearing a rope around his waist to hold up his cut-off pants. He gave his new friends nicknames and encouraged them to call him Old Master, although he was the newcomer to deep-sea fishing and island living. Hemingway loved fishing excursions that carried him far into the ocean. He liked roughing it—living on Bermuda onion sandwiches (the bio's all say these onions were a staple of his diet), fresh fish, conch salad and booze. Always lots of booze.

Prohibition didn't cramp anyone's drinking style in Key West. Bars continued operating, their liquor and beer supplied by rumrunners who easily and often made the roundtrip between Key West and Havana, located just ninety miles away. Rumrunner Joe Russell, one of Hemingway's buddies, was the original owner of Sloppy Joe's Bar, located today at 201 Duval Street. Charles Thompson was another of Hemingway's Key West friends. Thompson lived for many years after Hemingway died. In the last years of his life Thompson became a favorite interviewee of Hemingway biographers digging for information on Papa's Key West years.

There are many stories of Hemingway's terrible need to out-fish, out-shoot and out-box anyone who challenged him, and even those who did not. His competitiveness sometimes put a damper on things. But mostly, because there was so much about him that was fun, his friends just put up with it. Writer John Dos Passos, a member of Hemingway's Key West mob, wrote: "Hem was the greatest fellow in the world to go around with—when everything went right."

Rich, sporty and devoted, Pauline Hemingway was a dutiful wife who often left their two young sons with nannies or relatives to join her husband on fishing and hunting retreats. The Hemingways summered in Wyoming or Europe and wintered in Key West.

For several winters the Hemingways rented homes on the island. Then in 1931 Uncle Gus bought the house at 907 Whitehead Street for $8,000. The house was designed with a European flair, which greatly pleased Pauline, a former fashion writer for *Vogue* magazine. The Civil War-era house, in the middle of an entire acre of gardens, was one of the grandest estates on the island. It still is.

Once the house was theirs, Pauline hurried to Paris to reclaim her French and Spanish antique furniture out of storage and have it shipped to Key West. (Left from Pauline's dowry—a hand-blown Venetian glass chandelier still hanging in the dining room.) Hemingway designed a writing studio on the second story of a carriage house in the back yard. A catwalk was built to connect the studio to the house. Through the years the Hemingways covered the walls and floors of their home with the skins and heads of beasts they themselves had shot on various hunting trips. Servants cared for the children, cleaned the house, did the laundry and the cooking. They were paid $5 a week each, a good wage for the times.

Hemingway was intrigued with costumes and the impressions they created. Sometimes he was taken for a bum in his favorite Key West garb: a dirty shirt, cutoffs and rope belt. In Wyoming he enjoyed decking himself out in boots, cowboy hat, plaid shirt and leather vest. In Africa he wore a brown felt Stetson and a white shirt with rolled sleeves. Sometimes he wore his hair and beard long and affected a wild-man look. No matter what he was wearing, by the time he was 33 years old, he had begun to tell people: "Call me Papa."

In the 1930s the Hemingways never stayed put for long. Papa was a restless fellow, and Pauline did her best to keep up with him on his travels. Clearly, he was not one to be domesticated. Home, he told a friend, is a place to leave from and come back to. Still, he managed to work well during the '30s, which was the most productive decade of his writing career. In Key West he ate breakfast in bed, wrote all morning in the studio, then napped or walked to the ocean for a swim. Then Papa moseyed down to Sloppy Joe's Bar, located then on Greene Street, where Captain Tony's Saloon is today. Sloppy's was a rough place, where fights were common and the alcohol, as well as the talk, was cheap. Papa's drink of choice was scotch and soda. He paid 25¢ a drink (others paid 35¢ for the same drink) and ran a monthly tab of $25–$30, which means he paid for roughly four drinks a day. Yes, he got plastered from time to time, Joe Russell recalled. But certainly not every day. Mostly, Papa liked to sit, watch, listen and soak up the atmosphere.

When the sun set, Papa headed back to his palatial home, where he enjoyed a hearty dinner accompanied always by plenty of good French wine. If there were guests, and often there were because Pauline loved to entertain, drinks were served on the outdoor patio. Usually he was in bed by 10 p.m., where he read for an hour or two. He was an early riser all of his life.

Papa loved to box, and Key West had several very fine young boxers. Papa set up a ring in his back yard and paid local guys fifty cents a round to spar with him. He also refereed at island boxing matches.

Several Key Westers today remember Hemingway quite well from those days. Jeanne Porter, who grew up on Whitehead Street, played with Hemingway's sons when she was a little girl. She recalls one strange incident. The boys kept several raccoons outside in cages and had named them after movie stars. One day they discovered the raccoon named "Greta Garbo" eating another named "Harold Lloyd," whom she had just killed. Although disturbing Papa when he was in his writing studio was strictly forbidden, the children were so horrified they yelled for him to come. Papa surveyed the scene, went inside and came back out with a shotgun. Then he blew the head off Greta Garbo, in full view of the children. Jeanne says she figures Papa shot the raccoon because he feared she might have rabies.

Key Wester Julia Hoffman, who lived to be quite an old lady, also remembered Papa and told stories about him. She often swam in the water off the Navy base when she was a girl, and Hemingway liked to swim there, too. One day as she was swimming, she felt something suddenly grab her ankle. She was badly startled, fearing that a barracuda had bitten her foot off. "I almost had a heart attack!" she remembers. But it wasn't a fish at all. It was Ernest Hemingway. When they got to the dock, Julia scolded him for frightening her. After that, Hemingway never forgot her; every time the two saw each other, Hemingway would say, "Have you forgiven me yet?"

"He was a very sweet man," Julia always said.

Besides boxing, Hemingway was enthralled with bullfighting, and he traveled to Spain often to hang out with his bullfighting friends. His bullfighting book—*Death in the Afternoon*—was written during his Key West years. He also wrote frequent short stories and grandiose accounts of his fishing expeditions in the Gulf Stream, which he sold to grateful magazine editors in New York.

In 1933, friend Charles Thompson, Papa and Pauline set out for Africa. They bid their children and their home goodbye and did not see

Hemingway's writing studio

them again for nine months. Uncle Gus underwrote the excursion with a gift of $25,000. When they returned to Key West, Hemingway wrote *The Green Hills of Africa* and one of his best-known stories, *The Short Happy Life of Francis Macomber.*

In 1935 a tourist guidebook published by the City of Key West featured a fold-out map highlighting forty-eight local tourist attractions. Number eighteen on the list was Hemingway's home at 907 Whitehead Street. Hemingway was furious. It galled him that he couldn't walk around his own yard without being approached by tourists. So he hired Toby Bruce, a friend of Pauline's from Arkansas, to come to Key West and build the red brick wall that surrounds the house to this day.

Hemingway's Key West was, in many ways, a much wilder place than it is today. The law was lax then. The town was full of rough sailors, northerners on the lam, out-of-work drifters, and other victims of the Depression. Most of the town's people were on relief. Only the bars and the whorehouses flourished, and they were reputedly the best in the country, prompting someone to say, "If you can't get it in Key West, it hasn't been invented yet."

But with the advent of tourism, in 1935, the town began to attract rich Americans who sometimes arrived by yacht and sat in the harbor, insulated from the real world, while Key West citizens were surviving on fish and grits. Papa's reaction to the contrast between the rich and the poor here became fodder for his novel *To Have and Have Not*, the only Hemingway novel set in the United States.

One December day in 1936, Hemingway's third wife showed up at Sloppy Joe's in a black dress, high heels, and pearls, determined to meet Papa. In short order, she did. Her name was Martha Gellhorn, "Marty," and she was a writer, too, but not for a fashion magazine as Pauline had been. Like Hemingway, Marty was an adventurer. She traveled the world, covering wars and disasters for major American magazines and newspapers. Shortly after their first meeting, Papa and Marty traveled together to Spain to cover the Spanish Civil War.

Just as he had done to his first wife, Hemingway demoralized Pauline by carrying on a none-too-secret affair with Martha for a very long time. He prolonged her agony by continually putting off the eventual dissolution of his marriage. Just as he'd done a dozen years earlier, Papa wrote long letters to friends, describing the pain of his romantic triangle. He even wrote letters to Pauline's mother, assuring her that all would turn out well, "no matter what". Pauline hoped the affair would run its course. In desperation, she had a swimming pool installed in the garden of their Key West house, hoping that the novelty would bring her husband back home. It was Key West's first pool, and it cost her an astounding $20,000, which, it is noted on Hemingway House tours, is the equivalent of $250,000 in today's market.

For a while Papa shuttled between Pauline in Key West and Marty in Spain. Being with Marty made him miserable with guilt. Being with Pauline made him miserable with longing for Marty. Finally, at Christmastime in 1939, eight years almost to the day since he'd moved into the elegant house on Whitehead Street, he packed up his clothes and officially moved out.

In October 1940, thirteen days after divorcing Pauline in Miami, he married Martha Gellhorn in Wyoming. His new wife affectionately called her new husband "Pig." Their home, however, was in Cuba at the

Finca Vigia, located in San Francisco de Paula, a town fifteen miles outside of Havana. The marriage to Marty lasted five years. Today Finca Vigia is a museum, into which visitors may look but not enter.

Meanwhile, Pauline continued to live in the house on Whitehead Street with sons Patrick and Gregory until her death in 1951. In March 1963 the house sold for $80,000. The new owner Bernice Dickson soon discovered that tourists and curiosity seekers made it impossible to live in the house that had once been Hemingway's. On January 1, 1964, Bernice Dickson opened the main house as a museum, known as the Hemingway House. Today it is Key West's number-one tourist attraction.

Through the years the Hemingway House tour has been criticized often, even by Patrick Hemingway, who grew up there. Did Picasso really give Papa that ceramic cat in his bedroom? Patrick says no. Is the furniture in the house today Pauline's cherished French and Spanish antiques? No, Patrick says. Did Pauline really have the kitchen fixtures placed on a raised platform to accommodate her tall husband? Ridiculous, Patrick says. Hemingway was six feet tall, and he was not the kind of guy to putter around in the kitchen. Were there six-toed cats all over the place? No, no, no, says Patrick.

Contrary to the story you'll hear from the Hemingway House tour guide, the porcelain urinal in the back yard was brought home by Pauline. She bought it from Joe Russell, owner of Sloppy Joe's Bar, when he renovated the saloon's men's room. Pauline hoped to make a fish pool out of it. Handyman Toby Bruce piped water into the trough and decorated it with Spanish tile. Today it serves as a water trough for the famous Hemingway cats.

As for Henry Faulkner, the artist who painted the Hemingway House portrait that hangs over the Hemingway bed, he is not the brother of writer William Faulkner, as was said on a recent Hemingway House tour. Henry was no relation at all to William.

Does any of this really matter? To most people it doesn't; it's the ambiance that counts. The writing studio is certainly legit, and so are the gardens, the house's wonderful lines, and that long, red brick wall built by Toby Bruce in 1935. Papa has definitely not left the building!

People whose only previous exposure to Hemingway has been a short story in their junior-high American literature book come to Key West, see his elegant home, hear of his four beautiful wives, his six-toed cats, his rugged sportsmanship, and his long-lasting literary success, and fall easy prey to the super-hyped Hemingway myth. And they really don't mind.

At the height of the season the town hums with tourists hungry for fresh information about the long-dead but ever-provocative Hemingway. Historian Tom Hambright, who runs the Florida history department at the public library, says more people come looking for information on Hemingway than on any other subject. At the Key West Island Bookstore, hardly a day goes by, reports the bookstore owner, when he does not sell at least one book written by, or about, the famous Ernest Hemingway.

A Family Tree

Ernest Hemingway married four times. His first wife was Hadley Richardson, whom he married in 1921. The marriage lasted six years and produced one son, John "Jack" Hadley Nicanor Hemingway, born in 1923. Jack Hemingway had three daughters: Joan, born in 1950; Margaux, born in 1955; and Hadley Mariel, born in 1962. Pauline Pfeiffer was wife number two. She married Hemingway in 1927 and had two sons: Patrick, born in 1928, and Gregory Hancock, born in 1931. Patrick's only child is Edwina, born in 1960. Gregory's children are Lorian, born in 1951; John Patrick, born in 1960; Maria Ann, born in 1961; Patrick Edward, born in 1966; Sean, born in 1967; Edward Brian, born in 1968; and Vanessa, born in 1970. There are no children from Ernest Hemingway's third marriage to Martha Gellhorn, 1940–1945. In 1946 Papa married Mary Welsh, who was a devoted companion until the day he died in 1961. They had no children together either.

Vital Statistics

Ernest Hemingway was 6 feet tall. His weighed around 200 pounds, but was capable of gaining his way up to 260. His shoe size was 11½. His eyes and hair were dark brown, in his later years turning white. Ernest Hemingway never went to college. At dawn on July 2, 1961—a Sunday—Ernest Hemingway shot himself in the head with a double-barreled Boss shotgun he'd used for pigeon shooting. He was nineteen days short of his 62nd birthday.

Hemingway Days

> *It's kind of fun.*
> *It's a chance for an old fat man with a*
> *beard to get some attention.*
>
> – RICHARD BARTON,
> WINNER OF THE 1995 HEMINGWAY LOOK-ALIKE CONTEST

Every July the Hemingway legend gives the town an annual infusion of tourist dollars and world-wide publicity when we celebrate his birthday with a week-long festival called Hemingway Days. The Hemingway Look-alike Contest, that goes on for three nights at Sloppy Joe's, attracts the biggest crowds and the most photographers. But there's so much more: sporting and literary competitions; parties and events; contests and playoffs designed to pay homage to different aspects of Hemingway's celebrated life. One year, when stamps were only 25 cents, the U.S. Post Office released a Hemingway stamp, amid much pomp and circumstance, on the steps of the Key West post office. A flock of Hemingway relatives come, too. They help out by judging a couple of contests, presenting the occasional award, and writing memoirs of their hazy memories of Papa. But mostly they just sit around looking Hemingway-ish. With their high cheekbones and rugged all-American good looks they give the festival an air of irrefutable authenticity.

Hemingway Walking Tour 281 Front St. 293-8773

Tour meets at 5 each afternoon on the steps of the Customs House. Information in this walk is officially sanctioned and licensed by the Hemingway family. It covers about a mile of downtown Key Wes, in roughly 90 minutes. The tour does not include a tour of the Hemingway House Museum. That's a separate business. Cost is $25 and you must make reservations on the day you want to go.

Tennessee Williams
In Key West

TENNESSEE WILLIAMS was 30 years old when he arrived in Key West for the first time in 1941. He came to the island to write and to swim. These things he did every day. Throughout his life the restless playwright's choices of locales and lodgings often were based on his need to be near a pool or a good swimming beach.

Thomas Lanier Williams was born on March 26, 1911, in Mississippi. His father was a traveling salesman, and his mother really was a southern belle, like the mother in *The Glass Menagerie*—but a self-styled one. She had been born in Ohio and had arrived in the South only after she had married her southern-born husband. Williams claimed that he adopted the name "Tennessee" because his forefathers helped to found that state.

Following the great success of *The Glass Menagerie* in 1945 and Pulitzer Prize-winner *A Streetcar Named Desire* two years later, Williams was finally able to afford to buy a house in Key West. He bought a modest one-and-a-half story Bahamian house at 1431 Duncan Street, which he decorated in old wicker from Havana. The floors he covered in sisal pago pago, a rope-like plant from Mexico. He eventually added a swimming pool, a writing studio, and a guesthouse resembling a small youth hostel, with two narrow, double-decker bunk beds.

Williams, however, did not spend much time in his Key West house. He lived instead in a series of hotels and rented apartments in the U.S. and in Europe.

In her book *Key West Writers and Their Houses*, Lynn Kaufelt recalls that when she was invited to Williams' home for dinner, a friend in the know warned her that she might arrive at Williams' house "to find no Williams, or Williams in a bathrobe, or fifty people drinking champagne." So were the Williams days in Key West.

In January of 1969 Williams was cajoled by his weird brother Dakin into being baptized at the St. Mary Star of the Sea Catholic Church. Don Pinder, a local photographer who captured a number of significant events in Williams' Key West life, was there for the occasion. "He was crocked," Pinder recalls.

During the last decade of his life Tennessee, now in his sixties, decided to take up painting as a softer, easier way of expressing himself. Painting, he said, did not wear him out the way that writing did. Tennessee's painting instructor was the brilliant and bizarre Henry Faulkner, a Kentucky-born orphan who longed to be a famous poet but had to settle, instead, for being a much lauded painter. Faulkner adored Tennessee Williams and was willing to do just about anything to bask in the playwright's golden glory.

Another friend, Viola Veit, daughter of character actor Conrad Veit, modeled for Williams. When he turned a work over to be sold at the Gingerbread Square Gallery, there was sometimes a note turned in with it. When the painting sold, the note instructed, $500 of the proceeds was to go to Viola for modeling services.

So Williams painted his primitive images in dreamy pastels, giving each painting a dreamy name: *Fairy in a Wicker Chair*; *Great Silence of the Storm*; *Many Moons Ago*; *Recognition of Madness*; *Abandoned Chair Occupied Briefly*.

Nobody ever said that Williams was a great painter, but he was indisputably a literary giant. Some critics believed that Williams' paintings and drawings, with the familiar "TW" scrawled in the right-hand corners, were new expressions of his genius and, therefore, significant treasures. His paintings and sketches sold, too, and brought Williams fresh recognition and respect from new sources: art and collectors magazines.

As talented as he was, the fact remains that Key West has never embraced the world's greatest playwright the way it has Ernest Hemingway. And while Tennessee Williams' works, many believe, outshine those of Hemingway's, it is the charismatic Hemingway who steals the spotlight whenever it turns its hot glare on the writers of Key West.

The reason is simple, says Leigh Rutledge, who writes of Williams in his book, *The Gay Book of Lists*. America cherishes Hemingway because he represents all that is desirable in masculinity: power, aggression, daring and courage. Hemingway, after all, boxed, hunted great, wild beasts, and wrestled giant fish in the Gulf Stream. He wrote of bullfights and war and dangerous thugs.

Williams, though, was a timid man, small of stature and somewhat delicate. As a writer he was profoundly aware of the comedic, tragic ruts and twists of human nature. And this eternal balancing act of man's emotions formed the basis of his work. America is proud of men like Hemingway, Rutledge explains, and sort of embarrassed about men like Williams.

Williams and Hemingway met only once. They were introduced in Cuba, at the Floridita, Hemingway's favorite bar. Williams was uneasy before the meeting, having heard of Hemingway's homophobia. "Hemingway usually kicks people like me in the crotch," he said. As it turned out, the two found common ground in their hypochondria. They discussed Hemingway's plane crash injuries and compared liver problems.

Tennessee Williams lived into his seventies. He died in February, 1983 when he accidentally inhaled and choked to death on an eye drop bottle cap. When word of his death reached Key West, *The Rose Tattoo*, the 1955 locally filmed movie based on Williams' happy-ending play, ran all afternoon and all evening at a chic alternative cinema on Duval Street. The theater was packed for every viewing. Williams died in the Hotel Elysee in New York, a place he called the "Easy Lay." He kept an apartment there that had belonged, up until her death, to Tallulah Bankhead.

The house on Duncan Street remained vacant for many years after Williams' death. A group of Key West writers joined forces to try and have the property made into a sort of shrine to the writer, but the memorial was not to be. The property was sold in 1992 and completely refurbished. The re-do included a high, white fence to keep out curiosity seekers, and a large addition to the back of the house. The gazebo, or Jane Bowles summer house, as Williams called it, was moved back several feet, to behind the fence.

Today there is little to be seen of the house Tennessee Williams called home. But here's a small, odd postscript: Not long into the restoration project, a group of bathroom fixtures—a sink, a bathtub, and a commode—appeared in the grass in a side yard. Propped against the commode was a sign: "Free," it said.

Jimmy Buffett

OR LEGIONS OF HIS FANS, the names Key West and Jimmy Buffett are synonymous. Both conjure images of bright sun, blue skies, sandy beaches, agelessness and fun. If that's how it works for you, Jimmy has accomplished his mission, which is to enjoy his life to the max and to help you enjoy yours. Buffett fans, also known as "Parrot Heads," are of all ages and all walks of life. The theme that unites them is their love of Jimmy Buffett and the songwriter/storyteller's wonderful songs and music. Buffett concerts are famously entertaining, and always packed with thrilled audiences who share Buffett's dedication to the ideal of growing older but not up.

"In concert I try to convince people that if they can't go to Paradise I can bring it to them," Jimmy once said.

A Brief Buffett Bio

Jimmy Buffett was born on Christmas Day in 1946 and grew up in Mobile, Alabama, reading adventure stories by Mark Twain and Robert Louis Stevenson. He remembers being greatly influenced by the novel *Treasure Island* and by the hit musical *South Pacific*. During his childhood, the television series *Adventures in Paradise*, about a guy sailing the South Pacific on a 85-foot schooner named the *Tiki*, further fueled little Jimmy's desire for warm waters, white sand, and the exotic promise of the tropics.

Buffett attended Catholic schools all the way through high school graduation. While attending the University of Southern Mississippi at Hattiesburg, he escaped the genteel world of academia often for the sites and sounds of New Orleans, some 80 miles away. There he began his career in music, playing guitar and singing in clubs on Bourbon Street.

In 1969 Buffett finished his education and married a Mobile beauty queen named Margie Washichek. The couple headed for Nashville, where Buffett planned to continue writing and performing his songs. But jobs were scarce for performer/songwriters, and so he settled for a job as a reporter at *Billboard* magazine, which turned out to be an excellent education in the hard realities of the pop music business. During those two years in Nashville, Buffett was turned down by twenty-three record companies.

"I couldn't get nothing recorded in Nashville," Buffett told a reporter, several years later. "Got depressed, got pissed off, got divorced and left. Best move I ever made."

Musician Jerry Jeff Walker, a frequent visitor and sometimes Keys resident in the '60s, is credited with introducing the downhearted but ever hopeful songwriter to Key West around 1972. Buffett's first stop in town was the Chart Room at the Pier House, a celebrated watering hole where Buffett is still spotted occasionally. Legend has it that Buffett made his Keys debut in the Chart Room that day, where he performed an impromptu concert for the appreciative crowd.

What he couldn't do at all in Nashville, Buffett did well in Key West. The decade of the '70s was one of the island's finest for swashbucklers and poets. Marijuana smuggling was a major cottage industry, and drinking was a favorite sport. The living was easy. Rents were cheap. The island had not yet been re-designated a major tourist destination. On the island of Key West Buffett found the characters and the situations for the songs that laid the foundation for his success. It was at this time and at this place that it all came together, creatively speaking, for Jimmy Buffett.

In 1973 Buffett recorded the first in a string of best-selling albums, A White Sport Coat and a Pink Crustacean. He was 26 years old. By the time he was 30, he was an established rock star. He'd fronted for the Eagles, hung with President Jimmy Carter and Dolly Parton, and become chief executive of his currently multi-million dollar business called "Jimmy Buffett."

In 1977 People Magazine published an article and photographs of Buffett's Aspen, Colorado, wedding to Jane Slagsvol. Buffett called the publicity "the kiss of death"—the end to his relative anonymity. And so it was. When Buffett later bought a house in Aspen, People Magazine reported the fact and accused him of deserting Key West, the place where he'd gotten his start. But he hadn't deserted. He'd merely expanded his range of operations, he explained. Buffett still owns a home in Key West.

In 1985 Key West's Margaritaville, a massive cafe, bar and shop, opened at 500 Duval Street. The house has been packed ever since. Caribbean Soul, Buffett's Florida-based clothing line of Margaritaville-mood tropic wear and T-shirts, nets millions of dollars each year. The *Coconut Telegraph*, a newsletter and catalog of Caribbean Soul clothes published six times a year, is distributed to thousands of adoring—and paying ($5 a year)—Parrot Heads who want to keep up with news of Buffett's latest projects, as well as his current concert schedule.

Buffett's lust for the spotlight seems almost as keen as his sharp business sense. His annual income has been estimated to be around $3.5 million.

The charismatic Buffett frequently contributes to fundraising projects by playing at free concerts. He's an ardent environmentalist and an active Democrat, performing with President Clinton at the 1993 inauguration. The President blew sax.

A Parrot Head Tour of Buffett's Key West

Parrot Heads arriving in Key West are likely to head directly to **Margaritaville**, at 500 Duval Street. There fans will find Buffett's shrine to rock 'n roll and free enterprise—a restaurant serving the quintessential "cheeseburger in paradise," endless music played loud and hard, a city-block-long bar, and a retail shop chock full of T-shirts, books, hats, hot sauce, and other merchandise related to the eternal quest for Margaritaville.

Unfortunately, Jimmy Buffett's concert tour does not come to Key West, but Jimmy Buffett himself does stop into Margaritaville from time to time. When he does, he takes out his guitar and plays a few numbers. When that special event happens is anybody's guess.

For much of the '70s, Buffett lived in a second-story apartment at **704 Waddell Street**. Today the house contains several luxurious condominiums that are rented out to up-scale tourists. To envision 704 Waddell in Jimmy's starving-artist days, push the calendar in your imagination back twenty years. Envision the same house (minus the fresh paint) as it was then, battered by the winds from the sea, baked to silver by the tropic sun. Then, picture Buffett, sitting in a front porch swing, strumming his six-string on the wide, airy veranda.

Louie's Backyard, an eatery next door to Buffett's first Key West home, was not the pretty, manicured, high-priced tourist attraction you see today either. But it is on the beach. To see what Buffett and his friends saw, explore the beach to the right of Louie's. In the '70s a gate separated Louie's and Buffett's backyards. Buffett ate at Louie's, often playing for his supper, often signing for meals that were ultimately never paid for.

Buffet's first haunt, **The Chart Room** at the Pier House Resort, 1 Duval Street, still operates in a small, dark room in a hind corner of the resort. Drinks are now expensive in the Chart Room, and the place is usually frequented by people for whom drinking is a favorite pastime. The place doesn't begin to live up to its mythical, somewhat sinister reputation until very, very late at night.

Upstairs, at an opposite corner of the Pier House Resort you'll find the **Havana Docks Bar**. Bright and spacious, it is very much the opposite in atmosphere of the Chart Room. The video version of Buffett's song "Who's the Blond Stranger" was filmed here in the mid-80s. Florida Senator Bob Graham, who was then Governor of Florida, appears in the video. The blond stranger, by the way, was then-Key West model Susan Pitts, today a Greenville, S.C. photographer and Parrot Head with a really neat video to show her friends and neighbors.

Another Buffett haunt is the **Caroline Street** seaport. Back in the '70s it was home to the island's shrimp fleet. The other side of Caroline Street was lined with shoddy saloons that served the shrimpers who came in from two-week shrimping trips loaded down with plenty of expendable bucks. Mayhem, and sometimes even murder, went on in those bars. Nonetheless, it was not uncommon in the '70s for Buffett and friends to end up down here at the end of a long night of carousing. It was in one of these bars that Buffett reportedly met up with the lady who inspired the song "Woman Going Crazy on Caroline Street."

Today, Jimmy Buffett still owns a recording studio at the Key West Seaport, but the small, two-story building is currently unmarked (see our Old Town Walking Tour). There are rumors that, with the gentrification of the seaport area, Buffett will turn his anonymous building into a snack bar to sell cheeseburgers as well as T-shirts and shorts from Buffett's clothing line, Caribbean Soul. So far, nothing at all has changed at the building he calls "Shrimp Boat Sound."

Dennis Pharmacy Conch Korner at 1229 Simonton Street is still pretty much as it was in Buffett's early island days. Grilled cheese sandwiches. Milk shakes. Cuban toast. Black beans and rice. Beef stew. Basic island cuisine, at easy prices. Lately a plaque has been posted in the '60s-era-decor eatery to let people know that Jimmy Buffett was once a regular.

Blue Heaven Restaurant at 729 Thomas Street is the place immortalized in the song "Blue Heaven Rendezvous." It's a tiny patch of '70s-era, Key West atmosphere, featuring a wonderful collection of zany and unpredictable characters. Even non-Parrot Heads flock to Blue Heaven. It's a trip. And the food is very, very good. Big, morning-after breakfasts are popular for Margaritaville-seeking revelers.

The Scoop via the Coconut Telegraph
800-262-6835
Can't make it to Key West just now? You can still be a Parrot Head. Call the toll free number and the office Parrot Head will put you on the mailing list to receive Jimmy's official newsletter, the Coconut Telegraph.

Trails of Margaritaville Walking Tour
292-2040
If you're still craving more stories about Jimmy Buffett's Key West days, take this two hour (more or less), mile-long tour that includes stops for margaritas in Jimmy's favorite bars. Reservations necessary. A must for Parrot Heads!

Everything in and about Key West is strange, foreign, and interesting. The business houses and public buildings, the dwellings, the gardens, lawns, flowers, trees, soil, and vegetation, the appearance of the people, their costumes, and even their names, all are so un-American and suggestive of a foreign clime, that it is difficult indeed to realize it as one of the busy, enterprising cities of our United States.

– Winslow Homer, 1886

Some Key West Artists

John James Audubon visited the Florida Keys for the first time in the spring of 1832. He arrived at Indian Key on his 47th birthday and soon witnessed a flock of flamingos, which, according to his journal, was exactly what he hoped to find in the Keys.

In Key West, Audubon was a guest at the home of Captain John Geiger, the city's harbormaster. The Geigers were one of the island's leading families, and, since Audubon was an artist of some renown by the time he arrived here, he was invited to stay, as dignitaries were in those days, at the upscale home. The Geiger house at 205 Whitehead Street has since been extensively restored and is known today as the Audubon House Museum. Several Audubon engravings are on exhibit there.

Audubon visited the Keys with the hope of finding many new species of birds to sketch. And he did. When he discovered a specimen new to him, he killed them. Then he ran wires through the dead birds and arranged them in life-like poses. In a personal account of his visit in Audubon's journal, it is chilling to read of how much the naturalist seemed to relish shooting birds! Because he did not have the time to complete his studies of the flamingo, he had one killed and preserved in rum so that it could be shipped to his studio in Charleston, where he finished the job of sketching the bird.

Audubon's 1838 collection, *Birds of America,* is a four volume set containing 435 plates of over a thousand life-sized portraits of birds. The amazing likenesses were first engraved in copper, then printed on handmade drawing paper, and finally painted with watercolors. Often Audubon himself supervised the application of color. In 1841, copies of Audubon's *Birds of America* sold for $1,000.

Audubon's letters, journals and a book entitled *Ornithological Biography,* is a richly detailed account of how the Florida Keys appeared to the naturalist in the early 1800s.

Katherine Proby's book *Audubon in Florida,* is full of surprising revelations about America's premier naturalist artist.

George Carey remembers being in trouble for drawing in the margins of his school papers back in the first grade. Recognizing his potential when he was 12 years old, George's mother scraped together the money for him to study oil painting. Artist Gerald Leak taught painting classes on the grounds of the Hemingway House, where kindly Pauline Hemingway served cool drinks and cookies to the budding artists. Today Carey's magnificent paintings, realistic portrayals of Key West conch houses and store fronts, are strongly evocative of the island's salty, innocent bygone days.

During a stint as metal shop teacher at Key West High, Carey directed his students in the construction of amazing metal sculptures. The first was an 8-foot conch—the school mascot—in front of Key West High School at 2100 Flagler Avenue; a larger-than-life Bengal tiger in the yard of Glynn Archer School at 1302 White Street; and a towering buccaneer wearing an eye patch, a skull-and-crossbones belt buckle, a conch ring, a sword, and a huge, colonial-looking revolver tucked inside his coat, standing in front of Horace O'Bryant Middle School at 1105 Leon Street. George Cary's latest sculpture is a brass manatee, in front of the First State Bank at 3406 North Roosevelt Blvd. The piece is 15 feet long and 10 feet high, and is comprised of three tons of steel covered by brass.

Henry Faulkner was no relation to the writer William Faulkner, though Henry didn't mind if people mistakenly believed he was. Henry was from a poor, disintegrating Kentucky family. He spent most of his childhood in orphanages and foster homes. Thin and delicate and flighty, he epitomized the word "fairy." And yet he eventually found his way to art schools, and into the important galleries of New York City in the 1960s. New York critics called Henry "the American Chagall."

At the height of his success in the '60s Faulkner came to Key West and bought a house, which he shared with pet goats. Henry is still remembered by those who knew him for his penchant for conversing with his favorite goat, Alice, as if she were fully capable of understanding him. With all his odd habits, Henry, nevertheless, fit in quite well. Reveling in every moment of his existence, he considered life itself to be his art: donning a black dress and wailing the blues at Captain Tony's Saloon; reciting poetry at the top of his voice when the mood struck him. As he rode his bicycle through the streets of Key West, he shouted off-color comments to young men along the way. It was not uncommon for him to be physically assaulted for his outrageous antics.

Among Henry Faulkner's Key West friends were Tennessee Williams and James Leo Herlihy, who wrote the novel *Midnight Cowboy*, which was later made into an Academy Award-winning film. *Midnight Cowboy's* central character, Ratso Rizzo, is modeled after Henry Faulkner.

"He seemed always to be running naked through a cannibal village with a sprig of parsley behind his ear, stirring up the natives and somehow, triumphing over them instead of getting eaten," Herlihy once said of Henry.

In the late '70s, Faulkner was commissioned for $3,000 to create a painting of the Hemingway House. Today this painting still hangs over Hemingway's huge bed in the museum at 907 Whitehead Street.

Although thousands of Faulkner's fantastic paintings survive, they are rarely available for sale. People generally hold on tightly to their Faulkners. The Gingerbread Square Gallery in Key West handled Faulkner's and Tennessee Williams' works while they were alive, and still do, whenever they become available.

Winslow Homer spent two winters in Key West—1886 and 1904. He came to paint in watercolors, and to escape the cold, snowy winters of his Maine home. Some of his most famous and often reproduced Key West paintings are *Hauling in Anchor*, *Taking on Provisions*, *Palms in the Storm*, and *Fishing Boat, Key West*. It is clear from these enduring images that Homer loved painting that very-different-from-today, turn-of-the-century-era Key West.

Anne Irvine says, "My life is all about Key West and has been thus far, a fairy tale story."

In the late '60s Anne Irvine, daughter of parents from a middle-class background, found herself married to an Air Force captain in Tallahassee, bored to desperation by her slack existence. So she packed up her kids and her dreams and came to Key West. She began painting, and has been painting and selling her work ever since. What is most characteristic of Anne's work is its bright humor—Anne's joyfulness shines from every painting. "If somebody in Key West wins the lottery," Anne once said, "we'll fly to Paris to celebrate. If somebody up in America wins the lottery, they'll fly to Key West. But if you live here, there's really no better place to be...except maybe Paris for a day or two."

See Anne's work at the Guild Hall Gallery on Duval Street. Anne's often there, too.

John Kiraly's paintings, for many people are simply irresistible. They see them, they want them. The paintings are filled with fantastic plants, columns, statues, archways, waterfalls, and placid pools, all painted in luxurious greens, deep-hued blues, rich purples, pinks and turquoise. Kiraly's works create a sense of deep and restful tranquility—the same sort of serenity that John Kiraly seeks for himself.

Kiraly's images have broad appeal. Often spotted on the walls of television and movie sets, his work is also popular in Japan.

The son of a concert violinist, Kiraly was born in New York of Hungarian descent. He moved to Miami as a teenager in the '60s and studied art at the University of Miami. He lived in Key West for nearly 25 years. Kiraly was the life partner of Richard Heyman (1935-1994), who founded the Gingerbread Square Gallery. Kiraly's work is translated into serigraphs (silk-screened prints) and posters by publishers Chalk and Vermillion, and is available at the Gingerbread Square Gallery.

Stanley Papio established his welding studio and home on a lot in Key Largo. He created a fence with old bedsprings and erected odd renditions of men, women, and animals out of abandoned, often pitifully rusted metal. He encouraged people to leave their old cars, rusted refrigerators, car fenders and kitchen sinks on his property for later use in his art. When authorities complained about the unsightly appearance of Papio's yard, the sculptor replied that the heaps of refuse were future works of art. He fought long and hard with his neighbors, who begged him to clean up his yard and get rid of the odd sculptures.

"A bunch of junk is a welder's glory," he said.

Eventually, in response to the controversy he created in Key Largo, Papio renamed his welding shop "Stanley's Art Museum," and charged 25¢ admission. Tour buses full of awed visitors, folk art collectors, and, eventually, serious critics took notice of Papio's works. Three of his sculptures toured Europe in 1981 as part of a traveling exhibit sponsored by the U.S. State Department.

When Papio died suddenly of a heart attack in 1982, his family donated his work to the Key West Art and Historical Society. The Papio Collection, now on display at the East Martello Museum in Key West, includes nearly 100 three-dimensional constructions, composed of painted or chrome-plated ferrous metal, created by Papio during the final decade of his life. In art circles, Papio's sculpture is internationally praised and is said to display extraordinary visual inventiveness and humor—but you don't have to be a serious art critic to love it.

Mario Sanchez is one of America's most eminent and renowned folk artists. Born in Key West to Cuban immigrants in 1908, Sanchez grew up in Gato Village, an area that gets its name from the Cuban factory that employed many in the neighborhood. Sanchez began carving and painting fish in the 1930s. Later he began illustrating scenes of old Key West, thus documenting the colorful citizens, activities and storefronts of the city's bygone days. The shops, churches, saloons, and neighborhoods in Sanchez's works are all historically accurate. Though many of the buildings are gone now, some, like the East Martello Museum and the San Carlos Theater, still stand. It is fascinating to compare Mario's portraits of old Key West to the Key West of today.

Mario, who has been called a national treasure, in Key West is known for his charm and humor. He worked for four hours every day in an outdoor studio on Catherine Street. Evenings he sat at the corner of Duval and Catherine, with his brother Perucho, to watch the world going by.

Except in a permanent exhibit of his works in the East Martello Gallery, it is unusual to see an original Mario Sanchez carving. The supply cannot possibly meet the demand. And so there are now posters on the market, many of which are signed.

One of his many fans was actor Cary Grant, who came to Key West in 1961 to film the movie *Operation Petticoat*. Grant was so taken with Mario's work that he bought a couple of the carvings for himself as well as one for his friend Spencer Tracy. At Grant's insistence, two Sanchez carvings appear in a hotel lobby scene in his movie *A Touch of Mink*.

Posters of Mario Sanchez's works are sold at the East Martello Museum and Gallery store and at the Gallery on Greene.

Some Art Galleries

There are so many new galleries on the island lately that it's difficult to keep up with them all. Key West has become a wonderful vacation/fine art buying destination. There is truly something here for all tastes. During your visit, keep your eyes on the local papers for news of openings and events. The galleries are busy with a seemingly endless supply of artists and craftsmen, anxious to sell their works. If you fall in love with something, you may find the gallery owner willing to negotiate on price. If you're planning a gallery exploration, a good place to begin is by contacting the Florida Keys Council of the Arts, 305-295-4369, and asking them to send to you their Gallery Guide. It lists galleries throughout the Keys.

Island Arts
1128 Duval Street ✱ 292-9909

Twenty Key West and Lower Keys artists show their work here and take turns minding the store. Prices on prints, paintings, crafts, sculptures and stained glass are very affordable; also, hand-painted greeting cards, boxes, bowls and picture frames; hand-fired tiles and ceramic light-switch covers. All of it has a Caribbean feel. Hours are 10 a.m.–6 p.m. daily. Open later in season.

Gallery on Greene
606 Greene St. ✱ 294-1669

A terrific collection of important area artists, and a great collection of Mario Sanchez reproductions signed by the artist Mario is well past 90 years old as we are going to press with this edition. Also Jeff MacNelly, winner of 3 Pulitzer prizes and creator of the comic strip "Shoe." MacNelly loved Key West, partied here often, and died way too young. Also Geroge Carey and James Kerr.

East Martello Museum and Gallery
3501 South Roosevelt Boulevard ✱ 296-3913

Several locally created or themed art exhibits are shown here each year. All are fascinating and often coordinate with other cultural activities. The gallery is located in a series of arched rooms in a mid-1800s-era brick fort. On permanent exhibit is a collection of wood carvings by native folk artist Mario Sanchez. In the outdoor garden and upstairs in the second and third levels of the citadel are the magnificent and zany metal sculptures of welder and junk sculptor Stanley Papio. When the Key Largo based sculptor died, his family donated over one hundred pieces of Papio's work to the museum.

The gallery at East Martello is part of a wonderful museum featuring exhibits and relics from Florida Keys history. The gallery and museum are open daily from 9:30 a.m.–5 p.m.

Gingerbread Square Gallery
1207 Duval Street • 296-8900

The oldest gallery in Key West, it was founded by Richard Heyman, America's first gay mayor (at least that's what all the headlines said when he was elected by a landslide vote in the fall of 1983).

The most famous of the artists that show here is John Kiraly, represented by publishers Chalk and Vermillion. Original Kiralys are on display here—rare and very expensive—as well as wonderful serigraphs, and posters that evoke dreamy, hopeful images.

The gallery also features rainforest scenes by Key West native and owner Sal Salinero and a whole lot more classically tropic art. Open at 11 a.m. daily and stays open many evenings.

Guild Hall
614 Duval Street • 296-6076

A 25-year-old, two-tiered artists' cooperative, it has been owned since 1985 by seven women members of the gallery's 21 participating artists. The building was constructed in 1919 and restored in 1975. Stairs and railings are from a dismantled Catholic convent. Floor bricks are salvaged from original Key West streets.

"What we bought when we purchased Guild Hall is job security," says Sonia Robinson, a willowy beauty whose original leather bags and painted clothes are inexpensive and sensational. People who work here are the artists who display here. Open 9:30 a.m.–11 p.m. daily.

Haitian Art Gallery
600 Frances Street • 296-8932

The doors of this wonderful place opened for the first time in 1978. Oil paintings, folk art and sculptures are purchased directly from the Hatian artists, allowing them to survive in their native country. Haitian art, by its very nature, is primitive, sometimes very sweet, and sometimes very shocking! Papier-mache fishes and animals painted in bright acrylics are so great fun and very affordable. Open 10 a.m.–6 p.m. daily.

Harrison Gallery
825 White Street ❧ 294-0609

The gallery's owned and operated by wood sculptor Helen Harrison. Harrison turned to woodwork after she and her husband, musician/writer Ben Harrison (*Undying Love*) built the 38-foot sailboat that brought them here from Costa Rica. From scraps of native mahogany, walnut, sea grape and sea hibiscus wood, she creates her richly grained and wood-colored sculptures. Garden metal sculptures are featured as well.

The Harrisons live next door to the gallery in a 100 year-old house. Harrison Gallery is open from noon–5:30 p.m. every day but Sunday.

Key West Art Center
301 Front Street ❧ 294-1241

It was founded originally as an art center by F. Morgan Townsend, who came to Key West to work for President Roosevelt's WPA in 1933. After the Depression, the center became the local Red Cross Building for a while. Then it was abandoned and fell into disrepair.

In 1960 a group of local artists set out to find a place where they wouldn't have to pay rent and therefore could afford to hire a receptionist. Key West Mayor Delio Cobo agreed to let them use the abandoned and condemned Red Cross Building on Front Street, which they then restored and turned into the lovely, little local artist's co-op you see today.

The seventy artists represented here live in the Florida Keys and contribute equally to the upkeep of the building and to the salaries of the staff. Everything you see in the gallery is for sale. Hours are 10 a.m.–5 p.m. daily.

Lucky Street Gallery
1100 White Street ❧ 294-3973

Dianne Zolotow is on the forefront of an important cultural shift for art galleries and non-T-shirt shops. They're pulling up stakes on expensive and busy Duval Street and moving into a cozy old neighborhood on White Street. Dianne shows mostly local artists, and has been doing it very well for many years. Who's hot on White Street lately? Photographer Leo Gullick who does crazy things with color and images.

Lucky Street is one of the galleries participating in the Third Thursday Night on White art strolls. Call for information.

Sign of Sandford
328 Simonton Street ✹ 296-7493

The owner is the artist, usually busy at work in her shop. Sandford Birdsey paints in watercolors, designing the hand-painted fabrics for bags and luggage, and painting silk scarves and furniture and anything else that will hold paint. Her work—bright and very buoyant—reflects her *joie de vivre*. If she's not too busy, have a chat with this world traveler, whose life is art and creativity. This is cottage industry at its most elegant and productive best. Sanford also conducts painting classes and workshops. Usually open 11 a.m.–5 p.m., Monday–Saturday. Closed Sunday.

Studio Alan Maltz
1210 Duval Street ✹ 294-0005

No one captures Key West on film like world-class photographer Alan Maltz. His award-winning coffee table books, *Key West Color* and *Miami, City of Dreams*, are the very finest of their genre. Most recently Alan has completed a book on the entire state and called it *Florida, Beyond the Blue Horizon*. The state of Florida is so happy with the book and the concept they've launched a marketing campaign around the book. Wow. Visit his ultra-chic studio on Duval Street and take home one of his irresistible limited-edition prints. Maltz images in your home keep the Florida Keys alive, and fresh, until you can return again to the real thing. "We're open 8 days a week," Maltz says. If anyone can pull of such magic, it is he. Open at 10 a.m.

Theatre

Cinema

Tropic Cinema
416 Eaton St. ✳ 295-9498

Tropic Cinema features first run movies, foreign films, and films related to Key West's remarkable history. It is also a sparkling venue for community based events, children's theater productions, and concerts. It's a full-time, two-screen theater, with a spacious, art deco lobby serving as a cultural center and gathering place. Key Westers, who enjoy great films and know, through sad experience that the most important films of the day won't make it to the island's mainstream movie theater (the most far-flung theater in a national chain) become members of the Key West Film Society. Their membership dues help to support modern cinema in our town, in this sweet and cozy theater. Box office sales don't begin to cover the costs of having this hip, downtown cinema. Seats are comfy; sound system is top shelf. Even the snack bar is elegant and tended by a beautiful woman. For infomation on what's playing, or on becoming a member of the film society, phone the theater.

Cinema Shores
Atlantic Shores ✳ 510 South Street ✳ 296-2491

Cinema Shores shows art-house and alternative-culture flicks outdoors at the island's most progressive motel. Like a New Age drive-in, only no cars! Lounge chairs are arranged in a corner section of the parking lot, protected from noise and wind. Films run on two projectors: they're shown against a white wall that used to be part of a racquetball court.

Movies are on every Thursday night at 9 p.m. sharp in the summer, 8 p.m. in the autumn and winter. Admission is $5, the popcorn is free, and cocktails are available from waitrons.

The films are the ones that usually don't make it all the way down to Key West, or blockbusters that you might have missed in the big theaters. Call for a schedule.

Cinema 6 Movie Theater
Searstown Shopping Plaza ✱ 294-0000
As you may have guessed from the name, they offer six films, which
change every Friday. During holiday season and peak tourist weeks,
1 p.m. matinees are offered; otherwise, shows begin around 3:30 p.m. or
4 p.m. Is it because we're at the end of the line down here in Key West
that we don't get movies the minute they're released? But we always seem
to get plenty of films that appeal to kids—especially at holiday time. Call
for a complete listing of movies and times.

Key Encounter Theater & Museum
Clinton Square Market, 291 Front Street ✱ 292-2070
Do take the time to see this wonderful, affordable (you make a donation
if you like, or not) and gloriously air conditioned nature treat. If you
can't or don't want to go near the water, this is the very next best thing.
This multi-image movie of the world of the Florida Keys living reef, and
Keys wildlife is projected onto 3 screens, each of them 48-feet wide.
You'll get a very good look at denizens of the deep like scorpion fish,
parrot fish, puffers, eels, stingrays and barracuda. The film is around a
half-hour long, and fascinating enough to entertain folks aged 9 months
to 99 years. Designed by a group of local Creationists, the final moments
of the film feature well-chosen quotes from the Bible. After the film, visit
the nature museum where you'll see the famous 22.5-foot snakeskin of
the anaconda that reportedly once ate a woman. Also on display: art,
shells, stuffed wildlife and merchandise. Hours: Sunday - Friday,
11 a.m. - 5:30 p.m.; Saturday, 2 - 5:30 p.m.

Live Theatre

Eaton Street Theatre
524 Eaton Street ✱
This lovely cabaret theater, located in what was once a Baptist church
attended by President Harry Truman, is still dark as we go to press. But
we won't write it out of the book. We believe in theater, and we are confident the Eaton Street Theatre will revive and survive.

Red Barn Theatre
319 Duval Street (rear) ✻ 296-9911

Before it was used as a theater, the little building that is home to the Red Barn Theatre was a carriage house behind a fine old Key West home. The playhouse was renovated and opened as the Red Barn Theatre in 1980. Since then well over 100 shows have been mounted on the theatre's versatile stage. Cocktails are available at the Chicken Coop bar before the show and during intermissions. Milling with the crowd in the open-air lobby is a mood setting treat.

The Red Barn staff does a great job of advertising upcoming presentations. For an annual seasonal brochure or a schedule of plays and musicals, call or write.

San Carlos Institute
516 Duval Street ✻ 294-3887

The first San Carlos was lost to fire; the second to a hurricane. This current structure was built in 1924 in the architectural style of Cuban baroque, similar in appearance to the presidential building in Havana. The foyer features high ceilings, a crystal chandelier and a rounded marble staircase lined with majolican tiles. In the 1980s the San Carlos was restored to its present nobility. Inside are housed a 400-seat theater, a museum, and a library containing the complete writings of Jose Marti. The museum, where guided pre-arranged tours are available, is open to the public and shows a movie about Cuban-American culture at 1 p.m. and 3 p.m. The San Carlos is open from 11 a.m. to 6 p.m. every day but Monday.

Each January the San Carlos Institute hosts the Key West Literary Seminar. Ballet, opera and theatrical performances are presented here, as well, but no regular program of events is scheduled.

Tennessee Williams Fine Arts Center
5901 W. College Road ✻ 296-1520

Tennessee Williams promised to make an endowment to the Florida Keys Community College for the construction of this lovely theater named for him. When the project was nearly completed, Williams bestowed an audio tape of himself reading his own poetry. He suggested that money might be raised by playing the tape for a paying audience.

The Tennessee Williams Fine Arts Center opened with a production of Williams' play *Will Mr. Merriweather Return From Memphis?* Williams had written the play in 1969, but it premiered in January 1980 at the Arts Center named for him. It was not a memorable show and has rarely been staged again since.

Founders is a group of theater supporters who preview everything presented there on "Founders Night"—the first night of any presentation. The theater seats 300; it's a plush, very modern, high-ceiled auditorium. It is said that there are no bad seats in the Tennessee Williams Fine Arts Center. Believe it. It's a honey of a theater and is, sadly enough, rarely crowded.

Waterfront Playhouse
Mallory Square • 294-5015

The Key West Players, Inc., formed in 1940, moved around for a while, staging shows at various locations around town, until finally settling into the present-day Waterfront Playhouse on Mallory Square in 1960. The theater was an important warehouse during Key West's wrecking days.

In addition to a full season of varied performances, the Waterfront hosts the annual Key West Classics, featuring local celebrities and personalities performing a vaudeville-formatted show.

Live Music

Key West Symphony Orchestra
305-292-1774

Remarkable that Key West has its own symphony orchestra, but we do, and it's grand, thanks to the passion and dedication of conductor and music director Sabrina Maria Alfonso. Alfonso, a Cuban-American with deep roots on the island, founded the Key West Symphony Orcestra in

1997. Alfonso recruits professional symphonic musicians from across the country for each concert. The community, and our many guests, love it! Key West children grow up regularly encountering the glory of live, sym-phonic music. Phone for information on performances or to donate money.

Paradise Big Band
305-745-2118

Since they started just a few years back, the 15-member Paradise Big Band has been wowing locals and tourists alike with their hard swinging sound. They perform all over the Keys. If you get the chance to see them, do. You won't be disappointed. Contact director Joe Dallas for information on booking the band or upcoming performances.

Island Opera Company
305-296-1520

A group of opera lovers who sing their hearts out every chance they get. Some professioinals, most not, and a couple of up and coming students getting their operatic chops in preparation for the world beyond the Keys. Hire them for your next dinner party! Very classy.

Impromtu Concert Series
401 Duval St . St. Paul's Church ✺ 305-745-2283

Lovely classical music in a variety of combinations, featuring American and European touring companies. Seasonal. Each concert more wonder ful than the last $20 for adults. Call for a season schedule.

Attractions and Museums

Key West Aquarium
1 Whitehead Street ✺ 296-2051

In 1934, when Key West set out to turn itself into a tourist town, one of the first things built with the government's Works Projects Administration (WPA) money was this aquarium. Located at the foot of Whitehead Street in Mallory Square on the gulf side of the island, it was the world's first open-air aquarium, and considered to be a modern and fantastic achievement. WPA artists painted several murals of the construction; They are on display in the aquarium still.

The aquarium certainly did what it was supposed to do. Tourists loved the place. The world was much smaller then, and, for many people, this was a first opportunity to see sharks and porcupine fish and sea turtles. For years it was called the City Aquarium and owned by the City of Key West. It's privately owned now, part of the same mega-corporation that owns the Old Town Trolley and the Conch Tour Train. In the early '80s the aquarium was refurbished and enclosed.

In her travel guide for kids, travel writer Susan Moffat rates the aquarium a "3" out of a possible "5." But consider this (you, too, Miss Moffat): there are few great kid-pleasing attractions in the Keys. Among them, the Key West Aquarium is surely at the top of the list. During a 30 minute tour, kids are invited to pet the surprisingly rough hide of a shark, and even watch one eat lunch. Notice how a nurse shark eats a fish: it seems to suck it, like a hungry baby at the nipple, which is how the nurse shark got its name. In a "touch tank," there are conchs, horseshoe crabs, triton's trumpet, and starfish for the curious to pick up and observe.

Marine life on display in the aquarium is caught, tagged and released back into the sea within a year or two. Some specimens have become dependent upon captivity, like Floyd, a giant loggerhead turtle who was found on Smathers Beach after Hurricane Floyd in 1987. In order for Loggerhead Floyd to survive, a substantial part of a rear flipper, gangrenous after an injury, had to be amputated. Floyd's fine now, although he's pretty slow—even for a turtle. He'll probably live at the aquarium for the remainder of his days.

The Key West Aquarium is open from 10 a.m. to 6 p.m. daily. Tours begin at 11, 1, 3, 4:30 p.m., but otherwise you can wander the aquarium on your own. Admission is $10 for adults; $5 for kids 4 - 12. Free for kids 3 and under. Your ticket is good for as many visits as you like on the day you buy it, and on the following day, too.

Audubon House and Garden
205 Whitehead Street ✱ 294-2116

Captain John Geiger's beautifully restored house is a wonderful example of early 19th-century island architecture. The elegant yet utilitarian furniture typifies the period of John Audubon's first visit Key West in 1832. Captain Geiger was a master wrecker and Key West's first harbor pilot. His house was built with the assistance of shipbuilding carpenters and furnished with items salvaged from the cargoes of wrecked ships.

Upon arriving for a visit to the house everyone is given a portable cassette player, headphones and a taped tour. This way, an attendant told us, visitors can pace themselves and linger as long as they like over exhibits particularly interesting to them. The system works well, providing you and your companions are able to keep your tour tapes synchronized. Otherwise, you might turn to one of your pals, your eyes wide with wonder, to remark upon some surprising revelation to find that they are still contemplating some earlier disclosure.

Your hosts, who are only heard and never seen, are the ghosts of the Geigers themselves. Interestingly, the information on the tapes is taken from actual letters and journals kept by the Geigers.

By 1958 the once-elegant home of the prosperous wrecker, Captain John Geiger, was scheduled for the wrecking ball. Mitchell Wolfson, a wealthy businessman and native son, renovated the house where John Audubon slept, and created one of the island's first tourist attractions.

In a garden there are orchids, bromeliads, a lovely herb garden, and papaya, banana and sapodilla trees. The gift shop features bird and garden-themed items. There are canisters of flower seeds and a small collection of books on Keys history. Today, the Audubon House and Gardens is a popular setting for weddings. The Audubon House is open from 9:30 a.m. till 4:30 p.m. Admission is $10 for adults; students $6.50. Kids under 6 go for free.

Key West Butterfly and Nature Conservatory
1316 Duval Street ✆ 294-5349

This steamy biosphere, designed to simulate a humid tropical jungle, is kept at 85 degrees because the 50 - 60 species of butterflies who live here like it that way and so do the plants that share the space. Overhead fly several species of canaries and finches and below a couple of jungle floor frogs. Because the butterflies are so happy here, they often land right on you, particularly if you emit a particularly flowery scent. Before leaving the conservatory you'll pass though an intermediate zone where you examine yourself for any runaways still clinging to your clothes. It's quite an experience being up close and personal with literally hundreds of butterflies. Occasionally you'll spot what appears to be a 4-winged butterfly. In fact, that's two butterflies in an intimate embrace. It's important that they breed often because most butterflies live terribly short lives, on average 10 days only. The lovely Monarch is an exception. Find out how butterflies reproduce, what they eat, and how they warm their muscles in the morning to prepare for a busy day of fluttering about. Personable guides, who apparently have no issues with the heat, wander about and answer your questioins.

The gift shop is full of very cool things, like spectacular butterflies mounted in plexiglass cases, coloring books for kids, jewelry, and lovely, gifty items for the garden. It's a terrific place to shop. The people who founded this place make it available often to local school kids, and donate time and energy to many community projects. They are instrumental in the creation of an open-air butterfly garden in the Bontanical Garden on Stock Island, and are working with the people there to keep it healthy and thriving. So far it's quite amazing.

The Butterfly and Nature Conservatory is open daily from 9 a.m. till 5 p.m. Admission: adults $10, kids 4-12, $7.50, and those under 4, nothing.

City Cemetery
Margaret and Angela Streets ✆ 292-8177

Key West's 150-year-old cemetery covers 15 acres. Because the cemetery's earliest records are long gone, no one knows exactly how many bodies are

Gravestone Symbols

Anchors	*hope*
Calla lily	*majestic beauty*
Clasped hands	*farewell and friendship*
Eye	*divine vision*
Grapes	*fertility and sacrifice*
Ivy	*immortality*
Lamb or cherub	*death of a child*
Laurel	*reward or glory*
Lily of the valley	*bride*
Oak leaves	*strength*
Wreaths	*eternity*
Open book	*divine knowledge*
Pansy	*humility*
Rose	*love*
Shell	*the journey through life*
Lily	*purity, chastity*

buried here, but estimates range as high as 100,000—about four times the city's current population.

The cemetery was created during an era in American history when expansive, landscaped cemeteries were much more popular than grave-yards. They doubled as lush parks, where fanciful tombstones were important expressions of art. It was not uncommon in the 1800s for families to picnic on Sunday afternoons at the tombs of their dead loved ones. The graves of wealthier citizens were marked with elaborate imported stones, into which symbols such as plants, flowers and shells were engraved. Each item has its own meaning. Many graves are marked with brick or tile, representative of the town's Cuban heritage.

Most graves are above ground because during Key West's earlier days there was no mechanical equipment powerful enough to dig into the coral rock that lies just two feet below the island's surface.

Today the City Cemetery remains one of the busy island's most restful and charming retreats. Trees and flowers on this property are some of the most spectacular in town. The cemetery also includes a section for babies and one for pets.

The tiny streets in the cemetery are named. On the corner of Palm and Magnolia Lanes, an ornate wrought iron fence surrounds a number of white stones that commemorate the men who died in the 1898 sinking of the battleship USS *Maine*, in Havana Harbor. A solitary sailor stands on a pedestal above the white marble markers of those who died. Shading his eyes with his left hand, he searches the horizon for his lost comrades.

Also on Magnolia, there is a white, marble-winged angel, placed as a reminder of a child's early death. Between the Angela Street boundary of the cemetery and Palm Avenue, within the cemetery, there is a slightly smaller than life size sculpture of a naked and bound woman. The eerie statue was placed on the grave of the man who lies within. No one knows why he requested this mysterious marker, and he died with the reason.

Key West's most famous hypochondriac, a waitress named Pearl Roberts who died in 1979 at the age of 50, has the best known marker in the entire cemetery. It says: "I told you I was sick," and people come from far and wide to see it. It has been endlessly photographed.

The State of Florida publishes an excellent self-guided cemetery tour, directing visitors to the cemetery's most elaborate, bizarre or sentimental graves, and giving information about the dead who occupy them. The brochure is free and available in the cemetery sexton's office, which is open from 7 a.m. till 4 p.m. daily. The cemetery is open from 7 till 7 daily. Also there are several cemetery tours available. See Tours for more information.

Curry Mansion
511 Caroline Street ☎ 294-5349

Built by Milton Curry, son of William Curry, Florida's first self-made millionaire, the Curry Mansion is one of the town's most stunning architectural landmarks. The five-story, 22-room Victorian style mansion was modeled after a Newport, Rhode Island cottage. When it was built in

1905, replete with Tiffany glass, splendidly carved woodwork, grand verandas and a widow's walk affording a bird's-eye view of the entire city and miles out to sea, it was the most ornate house on the island.

By day tourists are invited to explore the mansion. Only the guest rooms are off limits. The dining room, its elegant table set for a formal dinner, is a good place to take photographs because you are allowed to sit at the table.

In a cozy library you'll see Hemingway's big game gun on display. (No, it's not the gun he used to kill himself. Many people ask if it is.) There are fascinating historical photographs, and a wonderful collection of books which may well keep you entertained for hours. That's just fine. Owner Edith Amsterdam, a consummate hostess, loves it when you find her treasures as glorious as she and her family do.

You will hear a lot about William Curry when you visit Key West's historic downtown area. It was William who built the first house that stood on this property, and his son Milton who tore it down to make way for this stunning mansion. The elder Curry sailed to the Keys from Green Turtle Cay in the Bahamas in 1847. He was a poor boy with a lot of ambition and a pleasing personality when he began working as a clerk in a ship's chandlery. Although he never went near the water, Curry became rich on wrecking. He eventually became owner of the city's largest mercantile business and ship's chandlery. When he died in 1896, seventy carriages accompanied his body to the cemetery.

At the height of his great wealth in 1890, William Curry ordered a set of 18-carat-gold flatware from Tiffany's in New York City. In those tax-free days, a millionaire had more money than he could spend. When the special order was completed, it was displayed in Tiffany's windows before being shipped to Key West. John Jacob Astor, another famous millionaire of the times, happened by Tiffany's, saw the fine flatware, and, not to be outdone, ordered an identical set for himself.

The tour of the Curry Mansion is self-directed. You'll get a brochure highlighting details you shouldn't miss. The house is open daily from 8:30 a.m. - 5 p.m. Admission: $5 for adults; $1 for children.

The Custom House Museum of Art and History
Clinton Square ✆ 295-6616

Lovely and fresh, after a multi-million dollar face lift, this century-old lady is the queen of the harbor. And she always will be. The State of Florida Division of Historic Preservation has designated the Custom House the best example of Romanesque revival architecture and one of the five most important buildings in Florida. Notice the terra cotta faces which adorn the exterior of the Custom House where the arches connect: a lion, a fox, a ram, a human and a demon. So how come the City of Key West allowed the massive Hilton Hotel to dwarf the once stately queen? That's progress for you.

Back in the late 1800s, when Key West was the largest and most important port city in Florida, the U.S. Treasury authorized the construction of the Custom building as a custom house, post office and federal court house. Construction began in 1888 and was completed in 1891, which is where the stunning building gets its local name: "Old '91".

Old '91 was turned over to the Navy in 1932. During World War II it was a center for Naval operations. After the war the building was used for office space and eventually abandoned. For many decades the building was empty, subject to neglect and vandalism. Old '91 went on the National Register of Historic Places in 1973 and was designated a Historic Custom House by the U.S. Custom Service in 1976. That designation saved it from demolition.

Eventually the Key West Art and Historical Society took on the task of restoring the abandoned Custom House and bringing it back into service. A five-million-dollar restoration began in 1992. But it was hard going, all the way. In spite of a multitude of financial problems and iffy benefactors—will he or won't he part with the promised 1.5 million??—the project was finally completed and is now a first-class museum. The modern facility meets all standards for the exhibition of art and historical objects, providing an exciting new venue for traveling displays currently unavailable to Key West due to lack of modern facilities. The displays here are some of the best in the country. Thanks to progress.

Hours: 9 a.m. - 5 p.m. Admission: adults, $7. Students, $5; Kids 6 and under, no charge. Lots of group rates and a museum pass ticket. Call for details.

Cayo Hueso Y Habana
Mallory Square

Providing a fascinating glimpse into Key West's colorful Cuban roots, Historic Tours of America has created a modern interpretation of what our island looked like back in the days when Key West cigar factories manufactured a hundred million Cuban cigars a year. At El Meson de Pepe's Casa Cayo Hueso, you can sample some authentic Cuban cuisine or linger over a Cuba Libre at the bar. Inside, visit old Key West as you stroll past excellently rendered recreations of Gato's Cigar Factory, the San Carlos Institute, Sociedad Cuba, El Anon Ice Cream Parlor, Mariano's Barber Shop, Pepito's Cuban Sandwiches, Mi Abuela's Bodega and other scenes of Key West's Cuban neighborhoods, as remembered in the painted wood carvings of Mario Sanchez, Florida's most beloved folk artist and a Key West native.

Historical photographs on the walls tell the stories of Jose Marti, famed liberator of Cuba who visited the island many times in his quest for freedom in his homeland; Key West's baseball players, many of whom left to play in the minor and major leagues of America; local boxers; showgirls from the Havana Madrid Nightclub; and vicious cock fights encircled by feverish gamblers.

It's a fine exhibit, and also a wonderful opportunity to purchase Cuban cultural icons like freshly rolled cigars, Guayabera shirts, Cuban cuisine cookbooks, a set of dominoes or a real, stuffed fighting rooster. It's free, and divinely air-conditioned. Something for everybody! Admission is free.

East Martello Museum and Gallery
3501 South Roosevelt Boulevard ▪ 296-3913

The red brick fort that houses the museum and gallery is across the street from the ocean, in front of the airport. Plenty of parking is available. You can lose yourself for hours wandering through this incredible collection of Keys artifacts and memorabilia. Exhibits are set along the broad, red-bricked corridors of a Civil War-era fort, created for combat that never happened.

One compelling exhibit is an actual raft built by Cubans who used it to escape from Communist Cuba in 1969. It was found ten miles south of Key West, made from saplings lashed together to form a deck, with a hollow hull containing three innertubes. Attached by wire to the stern was a propeller. A small tree trunk made the mast, which was rigged with burlap sails. It is unknown whether the three Cuban exiles who traveled aboard this handmade vessel ever made it to freedom. No one was aboard the raft when it was found by the Coast Guard. However, identification papers belonging to the three individuals were found.

In another exhibit, a carefully handwritten chart, created after the devastating 1935 hurricane that hit in the Upper Keys contains the names of the dead and the locations of their burials or cremations. According to this meticulous account, 423 bodies were discovered in all. Of those, 164 were local residents; 259 were veterans, working at that time on the Overseas Highway. Many other bodies were washed out to sea and never recovered.

During the Civil War, when Key West remained under Union control, a rebellious Confederate citizen named Caroline Lowe risked her life and her safety in 1861 when she hung a Confederate flag from the window of her home at the corner of Duval and Caroline streets. Posters had been displayed around town warning Key West citizens—most of whom were actually Confederate sympathizers—to show no outward signs of support for Confederate causes. Caroline Lowe disregarded those orders. Local lore has it that when Union troops came to her home to remove the flag, she hid it under her skirt. Or, she might have hidden it in the newell post of her home's staircase. Just where she hid her flag is unclear. Both the skirt and the staircase are on exhibit at the museum. You decide.

Located in an underground wing of the citadel is a gallery featuring a regularly changing exhibit of Keys-related art and, on permanent display, works by woodcarver Mario Sanchez, the island's most famous native artist. The East Martello is also the permanent home of a collection of over 100 metal sculptures by Stanley Papio, most of them on the three levels of the tower.

Plenty of free parking here. Hours: 9:30 a.m. - 4:30 p.m. Self guided tour. Adults, $6. Kids, $4. Ask about group rates and deals on a cost-saving museum pass for several local museums.

Flagler Station
901 Caroline St. Key West Seaport ✳ 295-3562

Historic Tours of America created this replica of a train station as it might have been when the Flagler's Overseas Railroad regularly provided the people of far-flung Key West a train ride to Miami, and then on to all points north. Most people said Flagler was crazy when he decided, in 1905, to build a railroad, with 40 bridges, through tropical wilderness steaming with heat and alive with mosquitoes. But Flagler had the money, the engineers and the resolve, and his railroad proudly chugged into Key West in January, 1912. The railroad functioned until 1935, when much of the track was destroyed by a powerful hurricane. A very well done video tells the story of the construction and destruction of the railroad. Railroad and history buffs will get a big kick out of this museum. Your admission to the Flagler Station historium is free with your Old Town Trolley or Conch Train tour ticket. Otherwise, it's $5 for adults and $2.50 for kids. Hours are 9 a.m. - 5 p.m. daily.

Fort Jefferson
Dry Tortuga National Park ✳ 305-242-7700

As the majestic fort appears on the horizon, alone and mighty, it seems at first to be a magnificent mirage, or perhaps Atlantis rising. Massive and stately, 68 watery miles west of Key West, the red brick hexagonal construction harkens back to a very different time in America's history.

Fort Jefferson, named for President Thomas Jefferson, was designed as part of a coastal defense system built to protect the Gulf and the east coasts. Construction began in 1846 and continued off and on for 30 years. During the Civil War the fort stayed in Union hands and helped enforce the blockade of Confederate shipping. It was also used as a prison for Union deserters, who worked on fort construction. It was a terrible place to be incarcerated; conditions were unsanitary, and, with little hope for escape, prisoners often died from yellow fever.

After the Civil War, Fort Jefferson continued to be a military prison, America's version of Devil's Island. Dr. Samuel Mudd, who set the broken leg of President Lincoln's assassin, John Wilkes Booth, spent four years in a Fort Jefferson dungeon, sometimes tethered in chains and leg irons. Mudd had been sentenced to life imprisonment at hard labor. In 1867 Mudd bravely treated inmates and staff during an outbreak of yellow fever. What did he have to lose? Though the fever killed nearly half the men stationed at the outpost, the other half lived, thanks to Mudd's courage and skill. For his valiant efforts, Mudd was pardoned two years later by President Andrew Johnson. By the time he was pardoned, he was the only prisoner left at the fort.

The federal government declared the area a wildlife refuge in 1908. In 1935 the four islands that make up the Dry Tortugas were named Fort Jefferson National Monument.

Today, after over a century of sun and salt air, the fortress is deteriorating badly. Time has taken its toll on the far-flung structure, created from over 16 million bricks. The National Park Service is patching as fast as it can, restoring the worst spots of crumble but not rebuilding them. A complete restoration would be prohibitively expensive.

Of the four islands that comprise the Dry Tortugas, Garden Key, 16 acres, is the island upon which Fort Jefferson stands. Loggerhead Key supports an 1857 lighthouse that functioned until the 1930s. Bush Key and Long Key are home to rookeries of frigate birds and sooty terns, birds rarely spotted anywhere else in the United States. More than 300 species of birds migrate through the Dry Tortugas. Although the bird islands are within swimming distance of Garden Key, they are sometimes closed during nesting seasons and migrations. Birdwatchers and photographers from around the world flock to the Tortugas, particularly in the spring.

The only concession at the park is a tiny bookstore; there are no snack bars or gift shops, no T-shirts or postcards for sale. Attractions are what nature provides—clear, shallow water, excellent for snorkeling, and balmy park grounds perfect for picnics. The coral here, protected and healthy thanks to the island's inaccessibility, is alive and teaming with fish—and you may well see a precious and endangered sea turtle.

Fort Jefferson is one wild place to pitch a tent. There are 10 campsites, and they include a charcoal grill and picnic table, available on a first-come, first-served basis. You have to take absolutely everything you need with you—including water! You must also take it all back with you when you leave. Park rules say thatthirty days per calerdar year is the maximum time you may spend camping here, but one or two nights will do it for most people. The park has bathrooms but no trash cans. There is no running water or food. Ft. Jefferson campers will tell you that nothing in this world quite compares to the stunning beauty of the endless sky, crowded with stars, on a full-moon night. The silence is magic. Shine a flashlight into the moat waters on a moonless night and see barracudas, eels and lobsters. Fishing is permitted in special areas. Camp for $3 per person, per night.

Nearly 50,000 people visit the Dry Tortugas National Park and Fort Jefferson annually. The park can be reached by daily seaplane service, private boat, or via a ferry service. The biggest crowds are there during bird migration season, roughly February - April, when thousands of sooty terns make a stopover on their migration route.

Fort Taylor
Truman Annex ✆ 292-6713

When the Civil War began in 1861, Captain James Brannon quietly marched his troops into Fort Taylor, placing Key West in Union hands where it remained throughout the war. The fort became an important Union military post. Its cannons were an impressive deterrent to the Confederate Navy—so impressive that the fort was never attacked. None of Fort Taylor's guns or cannons were ever fired.

Construction on the fort began in 1845. Many of the workers who built it were Key West slaves, rented out by their owners for a dollar a day. Workers faced many perils during the building of the brick fort. Mosquitoes, yellow fever, hurricanes and shortages of materials created multiple hardships. In 1850, President Zachary Taylor died in office, and the fort got its name.

In the late 1960s, a backbreaking excavation of the fort turned up not only the discarded, though intact, Civil War guns, cannons and ammunition, but also a number of personal artifacts left behind by soldiers who had occupied the fort during the Civil War and the Spanish-American War. Today, Fort Taylor has the greatest collection of Civil War armament in the United States. Scale models of the big Civil War guns, one-eighth the size of the actual guns, are on exhibit in Fort Taylor's museum. There are some dramatic photo opportunities here, like endless arches and strange nooks and staircases. The top of the fort is an excellent place to view the super powerboat races that loop through the harbor each year in November.

The beach, which locals sometimes call "Elizabeth Taylor Beach" is a favorite for locals, who buy annual passes. For visitors, admission is $1.50

for pedestians or bicyclists. Motor scooters or cars: $3.50 per person, $6 for two people in a car, then $.50 for each additonal person. Park and museum open at 8 am. daily, close at sunset.

Hemingway House and Museum
907 Whitehead Street ✻ 294-1575

Key West's number one tourist attraction, the privately owned Hemingway House and Museum is visited by hundreds of thousands of people each year. The authenticity of the furnishings and the stories of the goings on in the house Hemingway inhabited during the most pro-ductive decade of his life is endlessly disputed. Did he really write his best works here? He wrote *The Old Man and the Sea* in Cuba. Did he create his works on that typewriter on his desk, or did he write them in pencil? Did he really love six-toed cats? Or did they arrive after he'd run off with his third wife? Only Papa knows for sure, and he's gone—though not forgot-ten, by any means. This is another of those Key West tours that is most entertaining when you agree to suspend disbelief. If your guide's version of Hemingway in Key West is convincing and/or entertaining, tip him or her. The guides work very hard for the money. The Hemingway House is

host to a variety of parties, weddings, and during Hemingway Days, annual events. Open 9 a.m.– 5 p.m. daily. Admission $11 for adults. Kids, 6 - 12 years, $6. Under six, free.

Heritage House Museum
410 Caroline Street ✷ 296-3573

Up until she decided to turn the place into a museum, a sixth generation Conch named Jeannie Porter lived in this remarkable house. The Caribbean colonial styled house is chock full of original furnishings, rare antiques and unusual sea-faring artifacts, collected by seven generations of this notable family. Our guide amazed us when he noted the dollar value of many of the treasures. Also, the stories behind them. Famous icons of history, Tallulah Bankhead, Tennessee Williams, fan-dancer Sally Rand, and philosopher, John Dewey, socialized in the quaint parlor. The original chairs in which the famous and infamous once sat are still here. And many of the famous guests sent autographed photographs to commemorate their visits. These are now displayed in the entry hall.

On display are musical instruments from around the world, several grandfather clocks, scrimshaw, a pewter tea set, the guide says was made by Paul Revere (worth thousands!!), and a magnificent shell box, said also by the guide to have been created by Dr. Samuel Mudd during his unfortunate incarceration at Fort Jefferson. Somehow, a toreador's jacket and pants, handmade in Spain and presented to Pauline Hemingway by her wandering husband on the occasion of her birthday, have found their way to this museum. The outfit is so tiny! You wonder if even Pauline, who was small of frame, could have wiggled into it. At the Heritage House, it is exhibited quite simply—laid out on a bed as if waiting for the matador to put it on. Its glittery bugle beads and embroidered seams remind one somehow of a stripper's costume... perhaps a stripper named Carmen. The guide said the costume was, of course, worth thousands.

It's fun to imagine Sally Rand, who really did live for a while in Key West, chatting it up with Tallulah Bankhead, who visited often. Imagine Dr. Mudd sending a shell box to his friends, the Porters, in Key West (and did they think he was innocent?).

When your tour finally arrives in the backyard, you will see the little green cottage where poet Robert Frost often stayed in winter months. Our arrival in the courtyard activated a tape of Frost reading his poem "The Road Not Taken." Frost never wrote a poem about Key West, in

spite of the fact that he and his wife spent many winters here. At one celebrity dinner party here, Robert Frost was seated across the table from Truman Capote. "I don't think I dig that young man," Frost told his hostess. It's all quite fascinating. The Heritage House is open 10 a.m. - 4:30 p.m. Admission is $7 adults; $1 for kids with adults. Monday - Saturday, 10 a.m. - 4:30 p.m.

Jackson Square
Monroe County Court House ● 500 Whitehead Street

You've got to make a stop here and have your picture taken at the "End of the Rainbow" sign. U.S. Highway 1 ends right here, 2,209 miles from where it begins in Fort Kent, Maine.

Behind the sign there is a great kapok tree. The fluffy stuff inside the kapok pods was once used to stuff pillows. Often you will find courthouse employees sitting on the benches here, taking smoke breaks. The county jail used to be located here at Jackson Square, but it has moved into a state-of-the-art facility on nearby Stock Island.

Key West Lighthouse Museum
938 Whitehead Street ● 294-0012

The first thing visitors to the Lighthouse Museum want to know is, "Can we climb to the top of the lighthouse?"

Yes, you can, and, for the ultimate view of the island of Key West, you should if you've got what it takes to conquer the winding, 88-step ascent. Make this one of the first stops on your Key West itinerary to get your bearings. From the top of the lighthouse you'll have a memorable, panoramic view of Key West's harbor. Look out to the Atlantic and see ships steaming across the horizon heading for Europe or South America in the warm waters of the Gulf Stream. Watch cruiseships chugging into Key West Harbor to dock at Mallory Pier. Enjoy the island's visual crazy quilt, formed by hundreds of tin roofs, criss-crossing streets, patches of green yards, and blue swimming pools. See bronzed sun worshipers lounging in the courtyard of a nearby guesthouse. You'll see why Ripley named Duval Street the longest street in the world—because it stretches from the Atlantic Ocean to the Gulf of Mexico (14 blocks in all.)

You guide yourself through the exhibits in the lighthouse keepers cottage. This lighthouse, old though it is, is not Key West's original lighthouse. That one was built in 1825 near the Southernmost Point and operated until it was swept into the sea by a hurricane in 1846. Eight islanders who'd sought shelter in the lighthouse were killed—the only loss of life ever in a hurricane in Key West's history. The new lighthouse was built on higher ground in 1848 at the location where it stands today. Active for 121 years, in 1969 the lighthouse was decommissioned and leased to the Key West Art and Historical Society.

The Little White House

The Lighthouse Museum is open from 9:30 a.m.–5 p.m. daily. Admission: $8 for adults; $6 for kids. Kids under 6 go free.

Little White House Museum
Truman Annex ✸ 294-9911

The two-story, wooden frame residence, built in 1890 to house officers on the Navy base, was vacant in 1946 when President Truman was advised by his doctor to seek a stress-free getaway. The president came to Key West and stayed in the handsome residence. Like so many others before and since, President Truman was instantly smitten with Key West's lazy, tropical splendor and vowed to return as often as possible. Because Truman took such a fancy to Key West and its people, the Navy had the officers' quarters redecorated and modernized in a style described by one reporter of the times as "modest but reliably elegant." In 1948, reporters dubbed the newly restored retreat "Truman's Little White House."

"I've a notion to move the capitol to Key West and just stay," the happy President wrote to his wife after the refurbishing.

During his presidency that spanned the years of 1945–1953, Truman and his staff spent eleven working vacations, a total of 175 days, in Key West. It was during one of these working vacations that Truman reportedly made the decision to fire General Douglas MacArthur over the Korean Conflict. Truman was also in Key West when he decided in favor of the Marshall Plan, whereby America contributed to the rehabilitation of Europe after World War II. When President Truman traveled, his advisors traveled with him. A large press corps regularly followed the popular President to the southernmost city as well. The many photographs and newsreels of President Truman's palm-studded retreat introduced Key West to Americans, many of whom had no idea that an island like Key West, and a place like the Florida Keys, even existed in their country.

President Truman enjoyed strolling through Key West, often visiting Cuban coffee shops and Duval Street restaurants to greet the locals gathered there. Sometimes he dropped in, unannounced, at the Navy mess hall to dine with the enlisted men. Always pleasant, always at ease with the common man, President Truman was named "Truman the Human" by adoring reporters.

After the Truman Naval Base was decommissioned in 1974, the Little White House remained vacant for many years. Much of what could be carried from the house—dishes, linens, artwork, and small furniture—was stolen. In 1990, Henry and Mary Drettmann of Detroit, Michigan restored the Little White House with the help of old photographs and meticulously kept Naval records. When the museum opened in April 1991, it looked very much as it did during Truman's presidency. Nowadays the museum is run by Historic Tours of America. Truman loved to play the piano and poker, take long walks, swim, and drink bourbon when he was on retreat. The original piano remains, where Truman played his beloved Chopin, as well as the original poker table where the President and his cohorts played penny-ante poker. Also on display is an exact replica of Truman's writing desk, upon which is perched a plaque with the President's famous motto, "The Buck Stops Here."

The Little White House has hosted Presidents Eisenhower and Kennedy, and, during WW I, Thomas Edison. Edison lived in the building for six months when he was developing depth charges for the U.S.

Navy. On New Year's Eve, 1997, the Little White House hosted a dinner party for President Jimmy Carter, his wife Rosalyn, their children and grandchildren. Take a 45 - 50 minute guided tour (only) through this historical site for $11, or $5 for kids. Open daily from 9 a.m.–5 p.m.

Mel Fisher Maritime Heritage Society and Museum
200 Greene Street • 294-2633

This former Navy warehouse is now home to sensational treasures found at the site of the wreck of the 17th century Spanish galleon *Atocha*, which sank in 1622. The booty includes Spanish pieces of eight, gold and silver bars, jewel-studded crosses, and chains of 18-carat gold that visitors are invited to touch. All of this is moderately interesting for most, particularly fascinating for sunken treasure enthusiasts.

What is most intriguing at Mel Fisher's museum is the story of Mel Fisher, one of the world's great adventurers and the amazing tale of the treasure of the *Atocha*, that he uncovered on the ocean floor in 1985. The story began when a little boy in California read the book *Treasure Island*. Visions of gold and silver scattered across the ocean floor ignited a passion in little Mel Fisher that fueled his dreams. In the early 1950s Fisher got together the money and the gumption to move his wife to Florida to hunt for treasure. For years, he and his family lived in a run-down houseboat in Key West. They lived off loans and speculative shares, good for a year, that he sold in the classified section of the *Key West Citizen*. If the treasure came in that year, shareholders were rich. If it didn't, they started all over again with new shares for the next year.

The staff of the Treasure Salvors went unpaid for months. They hunted for the *Atocha* by day and lived in low-rent Key West apartments by night, eating fish and drinking cheap Busch beer. They wore T-shirts that said, "Today's the day," the slogan that kept the whole town watching and waiting in wonder at Fisher's tenacity, as well as his ability to sell the dream to others, the shareholders who literally kept the operation afloat.

After a 16-year search Fisher hit paydirt on July 20, 1985. Ironically, it was on the anniversary of the day, ten years earlier, when Fisher's son and daughter-in-law had drowned in a freak boating accident.

Mel Fisher and his treasure salvors operation have been the subject of several *National Geographic* spreads, two made-for-TV movies, and Mel's appearance on Johnny Carson's *Tonight* show. Carson became so intrigued with treasure hunting that he came to Key West and dove with Fisher on the sight of the *Atocha*, to see for himself the remains of the famous galleon.

The actual value of the *Atocha* may not, in reality, be worth the $400 million Fisher said it was. His lawyers say its true monetary value is about half that. And Mel Fisher is gone now. But his search for the treasure, all that it cost him in terms of heartache and money, and his immense enjoyment of the celebrity it brought him, makes for an amazing true story.

In addition to Mel's treasures, there are two floors of exhibits including the richest collection of shipwreck artifacts in the world. On the second floor the story of the Henrietta Marie, an English merchant slave ship that sank off Key West in 1700.

The Mel Fisher Mritime Heritage Sciety and Museum is a not-for-profit organization dedicated to the research, preservation and education for New World history. It claims to be the most visited non-profit history museum in the southeast United States. The society stages a variety of workshops, events and presentations around town throughout the year. If you are a history buff, and see that one of these educational events is going on while you're in town, know it will be well worth your time.

The museum is open daily from 9:30 a.m.–5 p.m. Admission: $10 for adults; $5 for children. Become a member of the society and visit anytime you like for free.

Our Lady of Lourdes Shrine
St. Mary's Star of the Sea Church ⚓ 700 Block of Truman Avenue

Behind and to the right of St. Mary's Star of the Sea Church, stands the Grotto to Our Lady of Lourdes. In 1922, Sister M. Louis Gabriel was inspired to create a grotto as a shrine and outdoor prayer garden. She asked her friends and fellow nuns to help, and together they created the grotto of natural rock gathered on the church grounds.

On the day the shrine was dedicated, Sister Gabriel bestowed this blessing: "For as long as this grotto stands this island will never suffer the full force of a hurricane." The dedication ceremony fell on May 25, 1922, the twenty-fifth anniversary of Sister Gabriel's entry into religious life. Sister Gabriel had come to Key West from Montreal in 1897 to teach music and art at St. Mary's Convent. In 1898, during the Spanish-American War, the convent was turned into a temporary military hospital. Sister Gabriel then worked as a nurse caring for injured soldiers.

At the turn of the century, Sister Gabriel became the convent's bursar, or treasurer. As such, she became acquainted with people throughout the island. The Sister tended to the grotto for the rest of her life. She died in 1948 at the age of 69. Over five hundred people came to the church to see the casket of the beloved Sister buried in the convent's small cemetery, next to the shrine. There is a wrought-iron fence around the Sisters' graves now, but you can still see Sister Gabriel's gravestone.

When hurricanes threaten, it is common to see people paying visits to the shrine where they pray, meditate, and light candles. Sister Gabriel's blessing seems to be protecting us still. Since the dedication of the shrine three quarters of a century ago, Key West has been spared the full fury of a hurricane. There is no charge to visit the shrine.

Ripley's Believe It or Not! Odditorium
108 Duval Street ✱ 293-9939

Every kid who sees this seductive facade wants desperately to go on in. "Odditorium" is a good description of this mostly hokey collection of amazing facts, shocking films, and scary exhibits. One Key West exhibit is a plaque carrying a line from Ripley's cartoon strip. It says: "The longest street in the world. Duval Street, Key West, Florida, runs from the Atlantic to the Gulf of Mexico." And yes, it does. A couple of years ago, someone filched a shrunken head from Ripley's and pawned it at a local shop. The pawnshop owner read an article about the missing artifact in a local paper. Could it be? He called the cops, and, sure enough, the pawned head was Ripley's missing head. Within a week the Ripley's shrunken head was back in its rightful place, with the bug-eating savages exhibit. Open daily 9:30 a.m. - 11 p.m. Admission is $14.95 for everybody older than 12; $11.95 for kids ages 5–12. Kids under 4 free.

Shipwreck Historeum
1 Whitehead Street ✱ 292-8990

The Shipwreck Historeum celebrates Key West's golden era of wrecking, an industry that made this city the richest city per capita in the country during the mid-1800s. Whether or not your kids understand what wrecking was all about and its significance to this island city's history, they'll enjoy this visit to an earlier century where they'll meet master wrecker Asa Tift. Mr. Tift, who, incidentally, built the handsome home on Whitehead Street that went on to become the famous Hemingway House, will try to recruit them as sailors or divers for his next wrecking venture. "How long can you hold your breath, lad?" he asks. "That long? We can use you." This museum, built at a cost of half a million dollars and opened in 1994, is a wonderfully authentic reproduction of a wrecking warehouse. Exhibits feature actual artifacts salvaged from the 1856 wreck of the *Isaac Allerton* and historically accurate films, featuring actors in 1800s-era garb—dig those crazy, side buttoned pants—portraying early Key West citizens. The film characters, portrayed by Key West actors, describe how the phenomenon of wrecking figured into their lives. Asa Tift, portrayed by a live actor, will coach you in the yelling of "Wreck a-shore!!" You yell it again and again until you get it right. "Climb to the top of the tower, if you've got the air," Mr. Tift says. That's the very best part of this adventure, for kids that is. The wrecker's lookout tower is 65 feet high. Once towers like this one were located all over the island, providing bird's-eye views of the harbor and reefs to hopeful wreckers and salvagers. Open 9:45 a.m.–4:45 p.m. daily. $10 for adults; $5 for kids 4–12; kids under 4 free. Shows begin every 20 minutes, and it's a good show. Fun for all ages.

The Southernmost Point in the Continental United States
Whitehead and South Streets, on the ocean

The Kee family has been taking care of business at the corner of Whitehead and South streets since before Key West's most popular tourist stop was officially dubbed, "The Southernmost Point." Generations of Kee have been selling seashells, sponges, conch and other treasures from the sea at the same spot for nearly a century.

The first Kee to the island, a Chinaman, migrated to Cuba in the late 1800's to work in a laundry. There he met his Cuban wife. The couple moved to Key West and made a meager living selling the fish they caught in the waters just beyond the point. They also gathered conch, the tough, tasty mollusk that once served as a staple of the Florida Keys diet. Today, beneath the same cork tree that once provided shade for generations of

Kees men and women as they yanked conch meat from beautiful pink and beige shells, sits a display of straw hats atop an overturned fruit crate.

Before the great cement buoy that marks the site, a little sign was erected that said "Southernmost Point in the USA." It was promptly stolen. Each time the City replaced it, it was again stolen. The Kees regularly reported the pilfering, but City Hall took so long to replace it each time, the late Albert Kee began recreating the sign himself, hand-lettering the words on slabs of driftwood. The theives liked Albert's signs even better! Finally, it became clear that souvenir-crazy tourists would never be able to resist the colorful bit of island art, so in 1983 city fathers installed a massive eight-and-a-half-ton cement monument resembling a giant buoy, encircled in black, red and yellow stripes, to designate the continental USA's southernmost point.

"We call this the conch challenge," says one trolley tour driver to his passengers, as the busy clicks of camera shutters fill the air. "Try taking *that* home." Free.

It will cost you nothing to hang out at the Southernmost Point, and revel in being just 90 miles from Cuba.

St. Paul's Episcopal Church
401 Duval Street ⚲ 296-5142

Key West's first church is named for St. Paul, one of the Bible's most famous shipwreck victims. The original structure was built of coral rock in 1838 and destroyed by a hurricane in 1846. A second wooden frame building was lost to the fire of 1886. A third resurrection was destroyed in the hurricane of 1909. Finally a concrete structure was completed in 1919, and that's the one you see today. But this concrete reincarnation is not without its problems. The cement was apparently mixed with salt water, so the steel beams began to oxidate, requiring a massive project to replace them. Currently, St. Paul's is quite gloriously solid, and visitors are invited to enter the church for a look or a prayer.

John Fleming, one of the town's founding fathers, donated the property for St. Paul's church. He is buried on the grounds, but his tomb is now hidden behind lush foliage. It was once believed that Fleming's ghost regularly wandered the grounds of the church. Then it was discovered that the restless nocturnal wanderer was a white goat, who slept on Fleming's sun-warmed gravestone to stay warm at night.

A heart-breaking scene in the film version of Tennessee William's play *The Rose Tattoo* was filmed at the dramatic exterior of St. Paul's Church.

Wrecker's Museum/Oldest House
322 Duval Street ☎ 294-9502

Here's a real old house, in fact, Key West's oldest. It was built in the late 1820s at the corner of Caroline and Whitehead streets by ship's carpenter and grocer, Richard Coussens. With the aid of mules, logs and manpower, it was moved shortly thereafter to its current location on Duval Street. The city's oldest house was owned and occupied by one of the city's oldest families, the Watlingtons. Captain Frances Watlington, a prominent seaman, wrecker and one-time Key West harbor pilot, spawned nine daughters—all of whom grew up in the little old house. Watlington's descendants occupied the house for many years, thereafter, but were unable to keep up with the maintenance, so in 1973, the century-and-a-half year old house was sold to Rosemary Austin. Austin donated the house to the state for use as an historic landmark.

In a second-story bedroom there is a dollhouse furnished with miniature authentic 19th-century rugs, paintings, and furniture. The dollhouse was created by museum ladies—not the Watlington girls.

In the master bedroom there is an elegantly carved bed, a round mirror inlaid in its elaborate headboard, which stimulates plenty of speculation regarding the marital habits of Captain and Mrs. Watlington and comments like "No wonder they had nine kids." And "Oh! Those kinky Victorians."

The kitchen, or cookhouse, is located in the back yard, as they were in those times, to spare the house and its inhabitants from the heat of the ovens as well as to protect the house in the event of fire. The cooking hearth in the tiny cookhouse is said to be the oldest beehive oven in South Florida. The house is still hot, since there is no air conditioning. Recently the 167-year-old chimney, fireplace and beehive, understandably acrumble, were given a much-needed restoration. Most of the bricks you see are from the original construction.

There's also an outhouse with a drooping crescent moon on its door.

Museum volunteers tell some good stories about the wreckers who inhabited Key West in the 19th-century. You can study a history book to learn of the intricacies of wrecking, or you can take a tour of the Wreckers Museum. It's one of the best deals in town.

Aside from an introductory talk about wrecking, and the role wrecking played in Key West's swashbuckling past, you're on your own in the Wrecker's Museum. However, the volunteer on duty is pleased to answer your questions. Open daily 10 a.m. to 4 p.m. Admission $5 for adults; kids, $1. It gets very, very warm in there in the summertime. Schedule your visit for early in the day.

Sunset Celebration
Mallory Pier

The famous sunset celebration is said to have started back in the 1960s, when a small group of friends gathered daily to share a thermos of martinis and watch the sun slip into the Gulf of Mexico. Folks brought their own lawn chairs. When the show was over, everybody clapped. Then they packed up their chairs and their empty thermos, adios-ed each other, and moved on into the night.

That's how it used to be.

Today, the daily sunset celebration is nothing short of a carnival, featuring every wonderful, and not so wonderful, attraction you would expect to find at a carnival.

The action begins a couple of hours before the sun is actually scheduled to drop when a small army of vendors arrives at the pier to set up their mobile shops. They display their handmade wares on tables or racks, and even on blankets spread on the ground. The open air marketplace is tended by a colorful band of shopkeepers, many of whom appear to be trapped in a 1960s-era time warp. Tourists begin to assemble as the afternoon begins to cool. They buy smoothies, or fresh fruit cups, or popcorn, or slabs of coconut. They fill their cameras with film. They watch as the crowd gets bigger and bigger and bigger.

The carnival acts are many: guitar players, drummers, and bagpipe players in kilts. There are buskers: a mime, a tightrope walker, a sword swallower and a fire-eater. There's a magician and a guy who balances a shopping cart on his nose; trained cats who jump through burning hoops—an act that inflames the sensibilities of animal lovers, who then go home and write angry letters to the mayor of Key West.

The sunset celebration is managed by the Cultural Preservation Society. To become a part of the show,; performers must be sanctioned by the CPS. And there is only so much room on the pier. It is not unheard of for performers and merchants to wrangle over the most desirable locations. Still, you will envy them their simple lives. These people have managed to duck walls, conventions, taxes, shoes, bras and barbers. Who, at some time, doesn't envy that kind of nerve?

Pirate Soul Museum
524 Front St. ● 292-1113

Motivational writer and TV personality Pat Croce, who is also former president and part owner of the Philadelphia 76ers basketball team, decided that Key West, with its strategic position in the Caribbean, was an ideal location for his Pirate Soul Museum. And when this guy devotes himself to a project, he obviously goes all the way, something like the do-or-die characters of the Golden Age of Piracy, portrayed in this museum.

Pirate Soul displays Croce's collection of pirate artifacts and a number of excellent interactive exhibits, one of which scared me half to death when I took it in all by myself. You tuck into a dark room, don earphones, and punch a button to begin. The lights go down and you find yourself in pitch black, with the flutter of bats sweeping past your head. Meanwhile, the sounds of the sea surround you. There is creaking, and moaning, and shrieking, and then...well I don't know what happens then because I ran out of that room and vowed to not return until I had a warm body next to me to cling to. It's that real. And it should be. Museum design firm Gallagher and Associates have created this high-tech adventure that is more modern than anything else going on in the islands. Very fun. And informative. Do you know the difference between a pirate and a buccaneer? Or why captured women pirates were not hung beside their murderous lovers? You will. It will take a curious person a while to get through all this, but it's very entertaining and cool and clean. The recreated Port Royal, Jamaica street is wonderful, with tiny shop fronts displaying swords, guns, medicine kits and bullet removing forceps said to be authentic. In one shop a sign: "We buy from pirates! Thanks to our friends in the seafaring business we offer luxury goods from around the world." In 1690 this English settlement was believed to be the wickedest city in the world! How and why some pirates were knighted, while others hung for doing the very same thing, is all quite fascinating.

The gift shop is full of pirate related booty, perfect for the pirate enthusiast in your life. But I wouldn't think this would be tremendous fun for young kids. And I know one little kid that was a scared as I was when introduced to the virtual vision of Captain Kidd. Open daily, 9 am - 7 pm. $12.95 for adults; $6.95 for children 10 and under. (But I wouldn't recommend this for kids under 10.)

Tours by Land

Key West Nature Bike Tour
Moped Hospital, 601 Truman Avenue ✺ 294-1882 or 296-3344
Don't just see Key West. Smell it and taste it, too. That's what you do on Lloyd Mager's bike tour. A must for nature lovers hearty enough to spend two hours outdoors on a bicycle. Sample native fruits, view local flora and fauna, and meet a true Conch or two on this off-the-beaten path to back lanes and alleys rarely visited by anyone other than locals. Why do we love this place? You'll know better after your environmentalist and long-time island-resident tour guide shows you around. Immensely enjoyable. Very popular. Maybe too popular.

Schedules vary. They're designed around the arrival of the cruise ships. Otherwise, you can go to the Moped Hospital on Truman to begin the tour. But you've got to call and find out when the next one departs.

Cost of the tour is $20 per person. If you don't have bike, you can rent one for $3. "Think of it as an investigative field trip," Magar says.

Conch Tour Train
Mallory Square ✺ 294-5161
The Conch Tour Train is composed of a series of canopied cars pulled by a jeep disguised as a locomotive engine. Your kids are going to beg you to take them for a ride on the Conch Train because, as everybody knows, no kid can resist a train. The train chugs (pretend!) around the island, past the beaches, the airport, and down some of our famous, tropical streets lined with historic houses. Halfway through the tour you stop for a shop-

ping break at the Conch Train gift shop. There's ice cream for sale, too, which makes the kids even happier than they are already! The Conch Train has been pulling happy kids and their parents around Key West for over 35 years. It's open every day of the year, unless there's a hurricane.

Tickets for the hour-and-a-half long tours are $22 for adults; $10 for kids 4-12. Group and charter rates available.

Old Town Trolley
Mallory Square ✺ 296-6688

A good thing to do when you arrive on the island is to jump on an Old Town Trolley. The trolleys are not true trolleys. They're really gussied-up buses, made to resemble old-time San Francisco cable cars by a national corporation called Historic Tours of America. A trolley tour is a good way to get your bearings on your first day on the island. The ride takes about an hour. You can get off at any stop that catches your fancy and climb back on the next trolley that will arrive 30 minutes later. Favorite stops are the East Martello Museum and Art Gallery or the elegant lobby and grounds of the Casa Marina Hotel. Don't forget to ask for a reboarding pass. Before you disembark, ask your driver if you will be likely to encounter any delays in reboarding because of crowds. This has been known to be a problem, particularly at the height of the season. Trolleys depart at 9:30 a.m. and run every half hour until 4:30 p.m., with returns until 6 p.m. Same prices as the Conch Tour Train.

Ghost Tours of Key West
430 Duval Street ✺ 292-3666

Every evening at 8 p.m., as dusk descends over historic downtown Key West, the Ghost Tour departs from the lobby of the La Concha Hotel. The lantern-lit walking tour covers a little less than a mile, and visits places where eerie apparitions have been documented by legend, and sometimes even by photographs. Ghost tour guides drape themselves in black Dracula capes and speak spookily of Old Town legends that have been scaring the pants off locals for years. Ghosts along the way are the scorned wife of a bigamist cigar baron, and, at the Audubon House ("Most of my guests say this place is for the birds," David cracks) a haunted doll, thought to be a replica of a young girl who died of yellow

fever 150 years ago. There are several ghost tours operating downtown
these days. This one is the original, as conceived of and designed by
David Sloan. David is author of the best selling book *Quit Your Job and
Move to Key West*. Sure, it's a good idea - if you're as smart and innovative as David Sloan. $18 for adults; $10 for kids aged 12 and under.

Island City Strolls
305-294-0566
Historian Sharon Wells, creator of the annual *Walking and Biking Guide
to Historic Key West*, offers a number of wonderful and enlightening treks
or bike tours of Old town Key West. Whether your interest is history, literature, or architecture, there is a tour for you. Even gay and lesbian
themed tours. Group tours especially geared to your special interests
available, too. Just call and tell her what you're looking for. She's been in
Key West for a long time and she knows her stuff.

Tennessee Williams' house

Tours By Sea

Key West Express
Key West Seaport ✆ 800-273-4496

Sail to or from Ft. Meyer's Beach (year 'round service) or Marco Island (seasonal service only) on high-speed passenger ferries featuring comfortable seating, with air conditioning, a fully stocked bar and snack bar, and even TV. The trip takes around 3 hours. These are popular for day trippers, but a number of Key West hotels offer special rates to people arriving in town on them. Call for information. Keep in mind that weather conditions can cancel or delay these trips. So long as the weather is mellow, so is the ride. Boats dock at the fabulous new ferry terminal in the Historic Seaport in downtown Key West. Same day roundtrip $135 for adults; $125 for seniors over 62; $115 for kids aged 6 - 12; kids 5 and under ride for free. Reservations recommended. Check for promotions. And remember, Homeland Security guidelines for travel apply. You must have a valid photo ID proving citizenship or a passport.

Fast Cat Fort Jefferson Tour
201 Elizabeth ✆ 296-5556

The 62-foot power catamaran called the Fast Cat makes a roundtrip excursion to Fort Jefferson every day. The boat leaves shore at 8 a.m. for the two-and-a-half hour cruise to Fort Jefferson. On board there's a continental breakfast. It docks before noon, and stays at Ft. Jefferson for four hours—plenty of time to tour the fort and enjoy the buffet lunch on the beach prepared by the Fast Cat crew. You get back to the dock in Key West by 5 p.m. In addition to the lunch, snorkel gear and unlimited soft drinks are included in the $110 fee. There is also a national park entrance fee of $5 for adults only. Kids 2 - 17 go for $80. Kids under two go for free, but you really wouldn't want to take such a little kid on this long, sunny trip. Students, seniors and active military with IDs get $5 off their fares. No alcoholic beverages served.

The Yankee Fleet Cruise to Fort Jefferson
294-7009 ✱ 800-634-0939

The 100-foot Yankee Freedom II ferry departs the Key West Seaport at the foot of Margaret Street at 8 a.m. daily for Ft. Jefferson and the Dry Tortugas. On the way, a complimentary breakfast of coffee and muffins is served, and a naturalist guide lectures on marine wildlife and maritime history. He or she will point out the place where Mel Fisher found the wreck of the Spanish ship *Atocha*. You may see dolphins or sea turtles. On board there's a air-conditioned cabin with gallery and bar. And then, the fort appears on the horizon. There is an other-worldliness to this moment, a sense of indescribable awe. *How can this be?* your senses scream.

Your guide takes you on an informative tour of Fort Jefferson and introduces visitors to the fort's intriguing features, the history of its on-again, off-again construction, and its status as an obsolete, though fascinating, monument to national ambition and determination. You'll see where Dr. Samuel Mudd was imprisoned, sometimes in chains, for being part of the conspiracy to kill President Abraham Lincoln…or was he part of the conspiracy? Following the tour, passengers have four hours to explore, picnic (they'll serve your lunch, too) and snorkel (the boat provides the snorkel gear, free) before the ferry heads back to Key West. This is a long day, and not particularly exciting for children.

A roundtrip to Ft. Jefferson is $95 for adults; $85 for senior citizens, $60 for kids 16 and under. This is a long trip for a kid. Ft. Jefferson's historic charms are definitely limited for them.

Parasailing

Parawest Parasailing
700 Front Street, A & B Lobster House Marina ✱ 292-5199

Fly through the air with the greatest of ease, strapped into a seat suspended beneath a parachute connected by cable to a fast boat. The boat takes off and as it gains speed, the chute inflates and, like magic, you are lifted high into the air! Very thrilling. You get a panoramic view of up to 25 miles in several directions. But the ride never lasts long enough—only 12 - 15 minutes. Parasail for one person is $45. Parasail with a friend, in tandem, for $80, but you can't weigh more than 500 pounds. If you are interested in parasail thrills like free-falls and dips, tell them. They charge more. But they'll do it. Parawest is open daily from 10 a.m. Boats leave every hour on the hour. Reservations are suggested.

Fury Flyer Parasailing
Hilton Marina ❧ 245 Front Street ❧ 294-8899 ❧ 800-994-8898
You don't even have to get your feet wet to soar above the Key West Harbor with the Fury Flyer. Their platform wench boats pull you right into the sky, dry. You can wear whatever you want. In some ads for operations like this, couples in tuxedo and white bridal gown are seen sailing in tandem above the harbor just to show you how easy it is to fly high. And if the rest of the wedding party wants to come along, that's certainly possible, too. They'll pay $10 each to sit on the boat and watch.

Parasails for one are $40. Tandem sails (two people) are $75 and a bit tricker to set up. Tandem sails stay in the air longer.

Girl Guides

Venus Charters
292-9403 or 305-304-1181
Venus Charters is lesbian owned and operated by Captain Karen Luknis and/or Captain Debra Butler. The women will take up to six people (of any sexual orientation) snorkeling, lobster diving, fishing, nature touring, dolphin watching. Clothing optional. Snorkeling and fishing gear on board. Fully licensed and insured. Excursions can be from 4 - 7 hours. Two is the minimum number on an excursion. A great way to see the wonders of the local waters. Rates are compeitive.

Mosquito Coast Wildlife Tours
Hurricane Joe's Marina ❧ 294-7178
When partners Sue Cooper and Robin Roth visited Key West back in 1998 they had a great time doing every outdoor activity they could find.They sailed and snorkeled and glided and toured. Then, on their last day in town, they took the Mosquito Coast Wildlife Kayak Tour, founded and run for many years by Dan McConnell. They decided that the kayak tour was the very best part of their vacation. Back home in Darian,

Connecticut they found themselevs talking often of the islands and imagining what it would be like to live and work on the water in Key West.

"We figured we're young, we can do this now," said Sue. And so they did. They packed up and moved to the southernmost point where Sue landed a job as a kayak tour guide for Mosquito Coast and Robin worked for the Sebago. After a year or so Dan told the women that he'd had enough of kayak touring and was ready to retire. He offered to sell them the business. They bought it and added an outfitters shop located at Hurricane Joe's on Stock Island. They'll pick you up for the tour there, or at the original location, at Flamingo Crossing Ice Cream shop on Duval Street.

The Mosquito Coast kayak tours take you into a wonderland of unique and beautiful mangrove islands and crystal-clear water, as you silently glide across the water in the comfort of advance-design sea kayaks. Before heading out into the backcountry, you study a map which shows exactly where you're going, as well as listen to an enlightening talk on how the various elements of the backcountry's fragile ecosystem are interdependent. The mangroves, the trees that anchor the small islands of the Keys to the shallow bottom, are a fascinatingly complex system of natural checks and balances.

On the journey you'll learn to handle, and love, sea kayaks designed precisely for this environment. The water is shallow here, inches deep in some places. It is sad to see the great, yellow slash scars in the sea grass meadows created by powerboat propellers; it can take up to ten years for these wounds to heal.

In the backcountry you can see wading birds, birds on wing, lemon sharks, stingrays, and horseshoe crabs as well as remarkably clear water where the kayak tour anchors for some underwater exploration. With snorkeling equipment, participants see the natural world of the back-country from beneath the surface of the calm, clear waters.

It's a long, hot day but a rewarding one. The kayaks are not difficult to maneuver, but it does take some muscle power, and you may well feel the effects later that night. But you'll also understand how the delicate environs of the backcountry, so near and yet so far from civilization, are in such peril.

Waverunner Tour
Key West Boat Rental and Watersports Center
617 Front Street ☛ 294-2628

Ride alone or with a friend on a waverunner tour of the island of Key West. You'll cover 28 miles in 90 minutes and see the island city from a whole new perspective. There are four quick stops. You'll find out just what your Waverunner can do: it's a wet and wild ride! Ziplock valuables that you simply must carry along into plastic baggies. Stuff them into the waterproof compartment under your seat And don't forget waterproof sunscreen. You'll don a full-torso life vest and be fully instructed on the operation of the Waverunner. Maneuvering a Waverunner is very simple, but just to be sure you know what you're doing. Most rental agents will ask you to sign a form that says you are willing to take responsibility for the vehicle and agree to respect nature and others on the water.

You have to be 22 years of age to rent a Waverunner; People aged 18 - 21 may rent one if they can show that they've completed a boaters safety course from the U.S. Coast Guard. Tours leave at 10 a.m., noon, 2 p.m., 4 p.m. and 6 p.m. Cost is $100 for one person on a Waverunner; $110 for two sharing the same one.

To simply rent a Waverunner you'll pay $95 for an hour; $60 for a half hour. You must agree to stay in a designated area, within view of the rental center.

Glass-bottomed Boats

Discovery
Lands End Village Marina ☛ 293-0099 ☛ 800-262-0099

A 78-foot, three-level boat, with plexiglass windows along the lower deck providing passengers with a close-up view of the underwater world. On the upper deck are seats in the open for sun lovers. Three viewing wells are on the main deck, as well as an air-conditioned seating area where you can enjoy wine, beer, soft drinks and snacks. The two-hour trip is a nice alternative to snorkeling and a way to show the wonders of the reef to very young children, the elderly, and anyone who doesn't want to get wet. Most of the two hours are spent getting out and back from the Eastern Dry Rocks, located about 6.5 miles offshore.

On the first trip of the day kids under 6 years of age, accompanied by an adult, go free. Call ahead to make sure. Regular fares are $35 for adults, $16 for kids under 12, and kids 4 and under always go free. There are several trips each day, concluding with the sunset cruise. On that, champagne is served as the ship sails back into the harbor.

Champagne Sunset Cruise: $35.

The Appledore

Schooners

Schooner Appledore
201 William Street ✦ 296-9992

The 86-foot windjammer sailing ship *Appledore* winters in Key West and summers in Maine. The *Appledore* is a working ship, with a live-aboard crew. The tall wooden schooner has sailed around the world. The attraction here is all American authenticity. Now this is a mighty vessel. You'll probably want to join the crew and sail away. Seriously away.

The *Appledore* makes two trips to the reef daily. The buffet lunch is fresh fruits, veggies and sandwich fixings. The sunset cruise is very elegant, with hors d'oeuvres, drinks, and plenty of champagne for around $40. Their snorkel trip is $65. Weddings are frequent on the Appledore. Also, an all-day island adventure. Call for details.

Schooner Liberty and the Schooner Liberty Clipper
Hilton Marina, 245 Front St. ✦ 292-0332

The 80-foot traditional tall ship Schooner Liberty makes three two-hour sails daily, at 11 a.m., 2:30 p.m., and sunset. Day sails are around $38 for adults, $27 for kids 12 and under. Beer and wine, but no food, is available for sale on day cruises. Sunset cruise features all the beer, wine or champagne you can drink for $53 per person. If you want a snack, bring it along. No problem.

The 125-foot Schooner Liberty Clipper makes several evening dinner sails, hosted by the Hard Rock Cafe. Watch as your Caribbean-themed menu is grilled and prepared. Food is sumptuous and plentiful. Jerk chicken. Conch salad. Black beans and rice. Fried plantains. Cheese and fruit. Dine buffett style. Full cash bar. Dinner sails are two-and-a-half hours long, and cost adults $65 and kids $45, on Tuesday, Thursday and Sunday nights.

In May the Liberty Clipper sails back to its home port of Boston. You can take that cruise, even if you're not a sailor. You can also take the cruise from Boston to Key West in October. Phone 305-295-0095 for more information on these trips. Private charters available on both Liberty Schooners. Yes, they'll fire the canon, but only if some other ship sails too close . . .

Schooner Western Union
202 William Street ☞ 292-1766

The schooner *Western Union* was built here and launched from Key West Harbor nearly 65 years ago. The classic frigate is 130 feet long and features 4,800 feet of sail, and Spanish mahogany deck and ribs. The wood was imported from the Cayman Islands. Cayman Islanders and Key Westers worked together to craft this marvelous beauty. Each rib of the hull is fashioned of wood from the same tree to strengthen the curve of the hull, adding flex, and avoiding breaks at the joints on particularly rough seas. It was the last tall ship built in Key West.

After a maiden voyage to Nova Scotia in 1939, the *Western Union*, sailed by Captain Dick Steadman, spent the next 35 years laying and maintaining more than 30,000 miles of cable stretching from Key West to Mexico to Venezuela. When cable lines were retired, so was the *Western Union* and her proud captain. Captain Steadman, who died in 1997, enjoyed visiting the *Western Union*. She's as sleek and sturdy today as when she was brand new, he said.

After several misadventures by other owners, the *Western Union* sailed back into Key West, where she is lovingly maintained by Paul and Evalena Worthington.

The *Western Union* is available for Day Sails, Sunset and Starlight Cruises, private charters, weddings and other seafaring adventures. Call for dates and times of full moon sails and other scheduled special events. All sails feature live music, beer, wine champagne and soft drinks. And, they shoot off a cannon! Make reservations for the daily sunset cruise. A stunning adventure.

In the last few years a new tour: the after-dark Star-gazing tour with your guide to the stars, Joe Universe. Astronomer Joe points out various constellations, star formations, and seasonal planets. The cruise goes out every night as long as Mother Nature cooperates. Drink all the soda, beer or wine you like, and there's even conch chowder, which is a great treat on a breezy night at sea. Call for prices and schedules.

Tours By Air

Key West International Airport
South Roosevelt Boulevard

The funky terminal, built in the 1950s to accommodate two airlines and 35,000 passengers a year, is currently among the busiest small-town airports in America. A couple of years ago it was decided by the powers that be that the time had come to bring Key West International Airport into the twentieth century. That fueled a great, fiery controversy. After several years of bickering between politicians who wanted modernization and air-conditioning, and citizens, who thought the funky old airport should remain funky and hot, it has been decided by a majority of the people to simply restore the funky old terminal rather than flatten it entirely to make way for an all-new one. And that's what you see today, the updated and restored old building, which works, and works well.

In spite of the upgrade, people arriving in Key West for the first time are still quite tickled by our airports lack of pretension.

In the 1950s, flights on the Cuban airline Aerovias Q flew passengers between Key West and Havana for $18 roundtrip. Twenty years ago a little airline known as Air Sunshine, or "Air Sometimes" as locals jokingly called it, was the only game in town. Air Sunshine flew DC 3's on hour-long flights to Miami for around $50 roundtrip. In the last twenty years big airlines like Delta, American, and US Air have tripled the number of flights in and out of Key West; ticket prices have tripled too.

In spite of its tiny size and funky old-fashionedness, Key West International Airport does a splendid job of handling thousands of visitors annually. And since there's only one gate for all arrivals or departures, you never have to worry about missing your friend's arrival.

Some folks like to joke that Key West International Airport's name is longer than its runway. Actually the 5,000-foot runway is long enough to handle large jets. For a few years in the early '80s commercial jets did fly into Key West, and they were fast! Seventeen minutes in the air between Key West and Miami. But they made so much noise that citizens complained, and the jets then were banned.

Something new: City buses now service the airport. Take the Blue or the Green route bus which swings by the airport hourly.

Little Airlines

Cape Air
800-352-0714 or 293-0603
Tiny 9-passenger, twin-engine Cessnas fly between Key West, Ft. Lauderdale, Naples and Ft. Meyers. Best part of this trip is the painted planes, riotous colors of island themes.

Gulfstream International Airlines
800-523-3273
Gulfstream services Florida and the Bahamas and is a co-carrier with Continental Airlines and some other big guys, too. Rates for travel within Florida are usually a bargain compared with to big airlines.

Seacoast Airlines
866-302-6278
We've flown with Seacoast and we love it. The planes are tiny but the pilots are a hoot. They'll tell you all about what's going on below so it's not only transportation, it's also a tour of the Florida's lovely west coast when you fly from St. Petersburg Airport to Key West, or to Marathon. Your luggage can't weigh much. The people who run Seacoast are sweet and resourceful. They'll work with you to find the flight you need, and a way to get you where you want to go on time. They got me to a funeral on short notice a year or so ago and I'm forever grateful for their kindness. They've also worked some great deals with hotels and sights in town. Ask for their recommendations.

Island Aeroplane Tours
Key West International Airport
294-8687
Conch pilot Freddy Cabanas started Island Aeroplane Tours in 1987. In March 1991 Cabanas intercepted a Cuban MIG jet while flying over Key West in his Pitts Special, while the Navy failed to spot the Cuban jet in U.S. airspace. Cabanas says he averages 5,000 tours a year in his Waco planes and has accumulated over 10,000 air hours in his career. Of 600 Wacos built, only about 100 are still flying. The Waco biplanes carry two passengers each and feature open cockpits. The Pitts biplane is strictly for

aerobatic rides and instruction. Pilots looking to learn the delicate art of the loop-to-loop learn how at Island Aeroplane. Occasionally, Freddy Cabanas takes the Pitts up just before sunset to perform a dazzling demonstration for astonished tourists. He climbs, he falls, he loops, he spins as gracefully as a bird. The dare-devilish Cabanas clearly loves flying.

Island tours for two people, of around eight to fifteen minutes, cost $50–$110. There are three combination reef and island tours, twenty minutes to an hour long, costing $150–$225. And if you're very brave, ask about Freddy's daredevil aerobatic flights, guaranteed to turn your belly upside down. One person at a time.

Seaplanes of Key West
Key West Airport ✱ 294-0709 ✱ 800-950-2359
Daily flights to Fort Jefferson, and magnificent Dry Tortugas National Park, 68 sea miles west of Key West. (Read about Ft. Jefferson on page 104). Two amphibious planes carry 5 passengers and another carries nine. Amphhibious planes can take off and land on land, or on water. They leave Key West by land and land on the water at Fort Jefferson. Spend half a day there or go for the whole day. Reduced rates for kids. Seaplanes provide you with snorkel gear (to borrow) and a cooler of soft drinks, which you'll need. It's hot out there. And dry. Half-day trip is around$200 for adults and $140 for kids twelve and under. Six and under pay $110. Full-day, which is over six hours at Ft. Jefferson, is $325, $245, and $190. Don't forget $5 park entrance fee for adults.

Air Key West
305-923-4033
FAA licensed charter airline. Professional. Reliable.Affordable. No lines. No waiting. No hassles. You set the schedule. They service many cities that offer no scheduled air service. Think you can't afford a charter? Depends on how many people are travelling. If you can fill the plane you'll get the best rate of all. Local residents use this plane to fly to Miami malls for Christmas shopping. It's fun having your plane waiting for you back at the airport. . .

How to get from Miami Airport to the Keys

Greyhound Bus Airport Shuttle
Key West Airport ☏ 800-410-5397

Direct bus shuttle from Miami International Airport to Key West, or vice versa, is available on a 43-seat Greyhound bus leaving from Miami three times daily; early morning, noon, and late afternoon. One-way to Miami takes around five hours and costs around $32 one way, or $60 round trip. What's annoying about taking the bus is that it stops frequently along the Keys. Greyhound Bus Terminal is now located at the Key West Airport. your gang or wedding party, leave your cars home, call ahead and make arrangements. Competitive rates. Seat belts. Baby seats available.

Keys Shuttle Airport Shuttle
289-9997 ☏ 888-415-9997

Full-sized passenger vans deliver you from Miami or Ft. Lauderdale airports to the Keys. Six trips daily. They travel from Key West to the airports, too, leaving five times daily. Key West to Miami Airport is around $70. To Ft. Lauderdale $80. Kids aged 4 - 12 travel for half price; kids 3 and under travel free. It would be far easier to book your flight right into Key West—both cost and time-wise. If you can't do that, call the shuttle.

Ambiance Sun Big Purple Bus Service
877-246-4786

New to the Florida Keys in 2005 is the Big Purple Bus, offering regular daily departures from Key West to Miami, Ft. Lauderdale, and Orlando aboard a very nice and plush purple bus. Amenities include wireless Internet access, meal and beverage services, a lavatory, and on-board attendants, like on a plane. Travel executive class and get free beer and wine, a DVD player with choice of movies, and a bigger, better seat. Only 30 seats on the whole bus. Alternative is a seat in the main cabin.. The price is right, too. Doesn't this sound like fun? And there are lots of specials. Phone them and ask how they can make your visit to South Florida even better.

Annual Events
Paradise Uncovered Month by Month

January

Average temperature: 70°
Average rainfall: 1.9 inches
Sunset: 5:50 p.m.

Old Island Restoration Foundation Old Island Days & House and Garden Tours ✽ 294-9501

A series of events scheduled from mid-January till late March, designed to celebrate Key West's island roots.Food festivals featuring island cuisine, and a nationally renowned, juried sidewalk art show. In the midst of all these celebrations is the Conch Shell Blowing Contest, which garners the most attention. Journalists come from all over to meet the strong-lipped competitors of the contest, which, as far as anybody knows, is the world's one and only competition of its kind. a ticket, board a Conch Also a series of house tours through five private residences. Ride the trolley or take a self-guided tour and find your own way around with a map. This is the OIRF's big fundraiser of the year, and it's popular indeed. You want to go into the homes of Key West's rich and famous? Here's your chance.

Island Food & Music Festival
Bayview Park, Key West ✽ 294-2587

Sponsored by the Key West Rotary Club for a weekend in mid-January, the fundraiser offers rides for the kids and good food for everybody. Lots of performances by local celebrities, which makes the admission fee worth your while. A great opportunity to experience a sampling of what Key West has to offer musically. Some rumblings were heard, after the 1996 festival, about high prices on kids' rides. If you've got a big family, you might find this afternoon kind of pricey. Remember, it's a fundraiser, and the Rotary raises a lot of funds for a lot of good causes.

Race Week in Key West
781-639-9545
Sailboat races sponsored by *Nautica*. Up to 3,000 sailing enthusiasts people sail or or haul 300 yachts to Key West and compete for class championships in this international sailboat regatta. Usually held the second half of January. All kinds of fun for the yachting set and boater groupies.

Key West Craft Show
Key West Players ‣ 294-5015
Nearly 100 crafters and artists display their works for sale on Whitehead Street between Greene and Caroline streets. Sponsored by the Key West Players.

Key West Literary Seminar
419 Petronia Street ‣ 800-293-9291
Second week in January. Stands with America's greatest literary fests. Themes like poetry, travel writing, journalism, and literary superstars like Hemingway and Tennessee Williams discussed by world famous writers, scholars and critics. Social events mix attendees with presenters, real writers with wannabes, but the really famous people are often disappointingly shy or last-minute no-shows. Like Augusten Burroughs in 2005.

Sculpture Key West
Ft. Taylor Historic State Park ‣ 295-3800
Wonderful, engaging and unique exhibit of contemporary outdoor sculpture January through March. The exhibit, which is much appreciated by locals as well as tourists, is the brainchild of Jim Racchi, an important sculptor in his own right, who works as a ranger at the park. Jim has been exhibiting his own brilliant works there for years. Jim formed Art in the Park, which has grown into Sculpture Key West, an international fine arts event. See it. Brilliant, Jim!

February
Average temperature: 71°
Average rainfall: 1.6 inches
Sunset: 6:16 p.m.

Wesley House Valentine's Party
The Curry Mansion • 511 Caroline Street • 296-8964

Held every year at Edith Amsterdam's house, the regal Curry Mansion. Up to 1,000 people dress in romantic red in honor of the day of hearts and love. Magnificent trays of food are donated by local restaurants. A busy bar. Always there is a hot band and a fabulous raffle. Prizes are get-aways, bicycles, jewelry, sailing trips and meals at area restaurants. It's a great party. Admission is around $20 per person or $35 for a couple. If you don't have a sweetheart on Valentine's Day, this would be a good place to find one. Proceeds from this big bash benefit Wesley House Daycare Center.

Gordon Ross and Friends
296-6196

A stellar cast of local singers, musicians and other performers put together an evening of truly great entertainment. All proceeds from ticket sales benefit local people with AIDS. If you're in town for this, don't miss this annual February production.

Annual Kelly McGillis Classic/Women's Flag Football
800-465-9332

The largest women's flag football tournament in the United States goes on at Wickers Field in mid to late February. The actress, a big fan, is here to lend support, enthusiam, and her name!! She's a big fan and a player, too.

Old Island Days Art Festival
Key West Art Center ✱ 294-0431

Last weekend in February (or first in March). The juried fine art show is
sponsored and organized by the Key West Art Center. At least 100
artists, representing all mediums and all regions of the country, are
selected from several hundred applicants. The exhibits sprawl from the
corner of Whitehead and Caroline Streets, the Presidential Gates, on
into the Truman Annex. Show hours are 10 a.m.–5 p.m. Although an
estimated crowd of 20,000 people wander through the booths of art, artist
friends who have appeared in the show a few times say very little actual
selling goes on.

Heritage Festival
Fort Zachary Taylor ✱ 292-6850

A weekend, usually toward the end of February, of living history at this
authentic fort, now a National Historic Landmark. The celebration of
Key West's fortunately under-utilized military might feature re-
enactments, skills demonstrations and a sea skirmish. Participants are
invited to wear 1800s-era costumes, just like the actors do. Every year at
least one couple marries in antique wedding finery. See what life was like
in 1861 when Union troops occupied the fort. Highlight of the affair is a
dinner party on Saturday night followed by the firing of the cannon that
was never fired in wartime.

Sponsored by the Florida Park Service and the Friends of Fort Taylor.

March

Average temperature: 73°
Average rainfall: 1.5 inches
Sunset: 6:31 p.m.

Spring Break

Although some downtown merchants welcome spring breakers, many locals don't like it at all when the town fills up with students hell-bent on having a good time. Spring breakers rent mopeds and drive through the streets at all hours, beeping their horns and yelling to each other. They're noisy, and that seems to be everyone's chief complaint. It's not the kids individually, it's their number. Too many!

Because many hotels and reservations services have discouraged the breakers from finding accommodations in Key West, and there are other communities that do welcome the kids and their money, we are no longer seeing the numbers we once did. Nobody likes being where they're not wanted. New spring break destinations like Pensacola Beach, which is more easily accessible to many students, and Mexico, which is much cheaper than Key West, are coming into vogue. Also, cruises are cheap and safe spring breaks.

At this time of the year it's spring break for many Americans, not just rowdy students. It seems that March up north is when many people cannot, will not, put up with one more day of dreary winter weather. So they fly or drive or crawl to the Florida Keys. That means March is a very, very crowded time of year to be here. If you can make it at any other time, you should.

Key West Fishing Tournament ✴ 800-970-9056

Designed to promote sport fishing and release of game fish, season-long competition kicks off in March and runs through November. Sixty Keys guides and captains register to make their fishing customers eligible for prizes at the end of the season. Visitors can also report notable catches directly to the official tournament station and receive a certificate noting the specifics of the catch. Fishing events included in the tourney are a shallow water Team Flats SLAM in June and an overnight Southernmost Swordfish Tournament in July. Call for all the details.

Conch Shell Blowing Contest
Ocean Key House Sunset Pier ✻ 294-9501
Usually held on the last weekend in March, on the waterfront. A funny little contest that has grown into a world famous annual event. Once contestants tried merely to blow a suspended honk on the conch shell. Now, melodies and all sorts of amazing feats are performed by people of all ages. Something free and fun to watch.

April

Average temperature: 77°
Average rainfall: 1.7 inches
Sunset: 7:44 p.m.

Seven Mile Bridge Run
PO Box 500110, Marathon, FL 33050 ✻ 305-743-2969
On a Saturday morning, mid to late April. The bridge closes and the starting gun fires at 7 a.m. Two hours later, traffic is backed up many miles in both directions as a bus drives over the bridge to pick up anyone who hasn't made it to the finish line. Then, the bridge reopens while contestants are massaged by volunteer therapists set up at the finish line. Free de-kinking mini-massages are for bridge runners only! Only 1500 runners allowed. Many more runners attempt to participate in the run than the bridge can actually handle. If you think you're ready for the challenge, here's how to get in: Send a self-addressed, stamped envelope and request an application. They're sent out about a month before the event. The minute you get yours, fill it out, write the check, and mail it back in. Immediately! Competition to just get in is vicious!

Conch Republic Independence Days & Celebration

The Conch Republic was born on April 23, 1982, in response to a United States Border Patrol blockade of the road where the Florida Keys meet the mainland near Florida City. Border guards searched every car entering or exiting the Keys for illegal aliens and drugs, as if the Keys were another country. They created a border where there was none. Traffic was backed up for nineteen miles, and many hours. Word got out quickly, and would-be visitors headed away from the Keys. Tourism is the lifeblood of the Keys economy. It was a very bad scene all around. Furious over the intrusion, and stung by being treated by the federal government as a separate country rather than part of the United States, Key West Mayor Dennis Wardlow and a group of businessmen staged a secession ceremony at Mallory Square, the center of Old Town Key West. A single shot was fired, and heard by media around the world. Key West and the Florida Keys seceded from the union, declared war, surrendered, and then demanded foreign aid. The border blockade was abandoned, and a stream of reporters swarmed into the Conch Republic to witness the coup. Small fortunes were made in Conch Republic T-shirts, arm bands and hats. Uncle Sam was embarrassed internationally while the rowdy denizens of the Conch Republic celebrated one of their most glorious chapters.

There are Conch Republic passports that have reportedly been recognized by immigration officers in thirteen Caribbean countries, Sweden, Russia, France, Spain, Ireland, and Germany. In 1994, I witnessed my husband convincing a very nice, and moderately suspicious, Canadian border guard in St. Stephen, New Brunswick, to stamp his Conch Republic passport, but not until after he'd run our names through an Interpol computer, and we'd suffered a half hour of incredulous stares.

There is an official Conch Republic flag, too. We have ministers, ambassadors, commodores and secretaries. Each April there is a parade. There are parties, drag races (people in drag, racing down Duval, not car races.) A Pirates' Ball. A pig roast. All designed to celebrate our independence. 10th Annual Taste of Key West

To order your passport contact the office of the Secretary General, Peter Anderson, 296-0213. Long live the Conch Republic!

Taste of Key West

AIDS Help, Inc. ✆ 305-296-6196

Key West's answer to spring fever. An annual round up of the very best local restaurants have to offer. Small, one or two-bite samples of their best dishes are sold from booths and tables. Wine, too. Everybody turns out and it's a big, fabulous party of food and drink. A wonderful way to work your way through Key West's gustatory offerings. A benefit for AIDS Help Inc., . The event has gone on in several different venues, most recently at the Truman Waterfront overlooking Key West Harbor. Location for future Tastes may be up in the air, but the event will go on in April. It's a winner.

May

Average temperature: 80°
Average rainfall: 2.7 inches
Sunset: 7:58 p.m.

Harry S Truman's Legacy Symposium
Little White House Museum ✱ 294-9911
Scheduled for the week after America's 33rd president's May 8th birthday
is the Truman Legacy Symposium, a gathering of Truman scholars, historians, fans, and even a few surviving members of Truman's staff. Also
several grandsons. Symposium themes are topics such as national security, civil rights, and the quest for peace in the Middle East. Truman was
opposed to segregation and prejudice in any form and that made him way
ahead of his time. In 1946 he proposed the formation of America's first
civil rights commission. Congress told him to get lost. The symposium,
co-sponsored by the Truman Library in Indepedence, Missouri, often sells
out the entire Tennessee Williams Fine Arts Center. What better place
for this stuff than Key West, the town that President Truman much preferred to Washington, D.C. Make your reservations now if you want in.

Key West Songwriters Festival.
305-296-4222
A little old get together for country songwriters has turned into a whole
lot more in the decade since it started. Festival is headquartered at the
Hog's Breath Saloon. Each year some some of America's foremost performing songwriters are showcased in a number of informal venues
around town. A few years back I watched and listened to songwriter Tia
Sillers perform her hit song "I Hope You Dance" which was absolutely
memorable! She's written a whole lot of other stuff you'd know and recognize, but that song just knocked everybody out. If you're into country
music, this is definitely your week! Call for a schedule but usually around
second week in May.

Survivors Party
La Te Da ✻ 296-6706

Memorial Day Weekend—usually held at La Te Da on Duval Street. The first Survivors Party went on in the now defunct Monster Bar on Memorial Day, 1975. Conceived and produced by Key Wester John "Ma" Evans, the annual costume (if you like) party celebrates late May's traditional tourist lull, a time when locals take back the town. Always a fundraiser, for the last eight years for AIDS Help, the party features a glorious buffet contributed by the island's restaurants; local comedy; musical and variety acts; drag queens; performance art; and a campy survivors award ceremony. Admittance is usually around $20, which, considering the food and the entertainment, is a real value. The people at Survivors Parties are the island's creative core, the movers and the shakers united for two common goals: good times and AIDS Help. T-shirts from this party are collector's items. A heartfelt party: fun for locals and visitors, straights and gays.

Queen Mother Pageant
David Thomas ✻ 296-0079

A mid-May spoof on beauty pageants featuring a line-up of island boys dressed like girls in a hilariously funny, and eminently campy affair that sells out each year. The costumes and performances make this a spectacularly entertaining event, and money raised (over $100,000!) goes to various helping agencies - like Hospice of the Florida Keys or AIDS Help. Key West's most inventive performers like Rikki Regretto and Patticakes, and Hellen Bed model gowns, bathing suits and the participate in the all-important talent program. One year Hellen Bed played "Lady of Spain" on an accordion with a wicker headboard strapped to her back, wearing a red sequined dress, with a rose between her teeth. The Queen Mother gets to wear the crown for one year. During her reign she sponsors at least two fundraisers, usually many more. The pageant is always held at LaTeDa, which is magically transformed into themes like Egyptian Nights. The producer is a truly marvelous and remarkably imaginative drag queen and performer named DDT, who says "the Queen Mother Pageant is an R-rated event. No one under 21 without parent or guardian is allowed." But it's not dirty. It's naughty and nice.

June

Average temperature: 82°
Average rainfall: 4.4 inches
Sunset: 8:15 p.m.

Pridefest Key West ✱ 292-3223

Annual celebration honoring diversity, openness and freedom in the city that has, as its official slogan, "One Human Family". One year a rainbow flag that covered the entire width of the island was carried by a thousand volunteers. The flag stretched from the Atlantic to the Gulf of Mexico. A truly fabulous event. Also part of this event is Pride Follies at the Tennessee Williams Fine Arts Center, featuring performances by every remarkably talented person we can get up on the stage in one evening. And there are lots and lots of them here.

Cuban American Heritage Festival
5570 Third Ave. ✱ 295-9665

Around mid-June, an event growing in popularity. Coast to coast conga line beginning at the Atlantic Ocean, shimmying down Duval Street, all the way to the Gulf of Mexico. Don't know how to Conga? You will. It's easy and once you start you'll have trouble stopping. Also salsa parties celebrating the Cuban cigar industry of Key West's bygone days, Cuban cuisine, and lots of music and partying. Party headquarters is El Meson de Pepe's at Mallory Square.

Chicken Fest Key West American Heritage Festival
305-707-5088

Across American there are lots of festivals devoted to chickens, that is the cooking of chickens. Here, they are a protected bird. We even honor and celebrate our chickens with parties, contests, 5K runs and chicken dances. I'm waiting for the Perdue guy to show up for this.

July
Average temperature: 84.5°
Average rainfall: 3.6 inches
Sunset: 8:22 p.m.

Annual Swim Around the Island
745-2860

Sometimes in June, according to tide schedules. Anna Fugina started this tradition on July 4, 1977, when she swam around the island, a 12.5 mile trip, in eight hours flat. In 1978, after she'd learned to use the tides to her advantage, she made the swim in six and a half hours. The following year, a couple of Anna's friends went along on the swim to keep Anna company. The next year swimmers began bringing along coaches in boats to row along beside them. One boat for each swimmer. Lately the swim has been taken over by the Keys Evangelistic Ministries and proceeds from the event benefit their work.

Underwater Music Festival
Looe Key Reef ✴ 872-9100

Usually held on the first Saturday in July. One of America's most unusual musical events, and one of the Keys most publicized happenings. The spin-doctors love this story! The scenic coral reefs of the Looe Key National Marine Sanctuary, six miles off Big Pine Key, is the setting for this underwater concert, founded by WWUS Radio News Director Bill Becker many years ago. Music is blasted over the coral reef for an underwater audience of up to 800 snorkelers and divers. For six hours, music—reggae, new age, and jazz—is played over eight Lubell underwater speakers suspended from dive boats. The broadcast features a commercial-free program designed to highlight and augment the underwater experience. The event is for fun, but also to reinforce reef conservation.

To participate in the festival, divers and snorkelers book rides aboard area dive and charter boats in the Lower Keys.

In 1995, the hit of the festival was a group from the local Elvis fan club. The Snorkeling Elvises (yes, that's really the name of the club!), descended 25 feet, in scuba gear, white jumpsuits and black Elvis wigs, with guitars, to entertain fellow divers. The music festival is followed by a seafood festival (on land) in the little town of Big Pine Key.

Big Pine Seafood Festival
872-2411 ✺ 800-872-3722
Follows the Underwater Music Festival. Visitors are invited to sample conch fritters and chowders, and visit arts and crafts booths.

Minimal Regatta
Schooner Wharf Bar ✺ 292-9520
July 4th weekend. Any excuse for a party, this one is "the only boat race you can view from start to finish from shore." A major challenge is staying afloat for the length of the race. Schooner Wharf Bar, at the foot of William Street, sponsors this annual, all-day party event. Competing vessels are built of:
- one sheet of 4x8' ¼" plywood
- two 2x4x8' lumber
- one pound of fasteners
- one roll of 2"x60 yard duct tape
- no caulking or adhesives

Painting of boat is optional. The winning vessel becomes the property of Schooner Wharf, where it goes on display.

July 4th Hospice Picnic
Casa Marina Resort ✺ 294-8812
Staged on the lawn and beach of the historic Casa Marina Resort, this is the fundraiser of the year for Monroe County's Hospice program. A beachside picnic with an endless supply of hot dogs, hamburgers, salads and watermelon. An afternoon of entertainment provided by local celebrities. Lots of activities for kids. Hot fun. A raffle with great, donated prizes, like a framed serigraph by world-famous artist John Kiraly, who lives and paints in South Florida. The entire town turns out for this.

July 4th Fireworks

They set them off from the White Street Pier but you can see them all over the island. Best view is from the top of the La Concha Hotel, at 430 Duval Street.

Hemingway Days Festival

P.O. Box 4045, Key West, FL 33041 ✺ 294-4440

Sixteen major events celebrated during the week of July 21, which is the date of Ernest Hemingway's birthday (born in 1899). Members of the Hemingway family, scholars, and thousands of participants make it to this annual event, Key West's very hottest. Begun in 1981 as tribute to Hemingway, the week-long celebration includes a short-story contest, story-telling competition, and macho sporting challenges like a 5K run and arm wrestling championship and golf and fishing tourneys. Also walking tours of Hemingway's Key West, and poetry readings. A Writers' Workshop and Conference opens with a gala on the lush grounds of the Hemingway House. The Hemingway Look-alike contest, which attracts over 100 big-bellied, white-bearded men, goes on for three nights at Sloppy Joe's Bar.

In 1997 the festival was nearly canceled due to a dispute with Hemingway's sons over the licensing of Papa's image. The issue was resolved, the festival goes on, and anytime anybody buys a Hemingway T-shirt or anything else evoking the image or name of Ernest Hemingway, his heirs get a cut of the action.

Reef Awareness Week

Contact: DeeVon Quirolo ✺ 294-3100

Week-long event, usually second half of July, to increase awareness and support for the world's third longest coral barrier reef. On Children's Day kids are led on guided tours and free excursions to the coral reef on a glass bottomed boat. Local television airs a Reef Awareness Film Fest. Speakers, poetry readings, an art auction and reception, annual membership meeting, diver first aid courses, a mooring buoy splicing party and lots more activities all relating to the reef go on throughout the week.

Reef Relief is a grassroots organization founded in 1986, to protect the endangered Florida reef.

Mini-Lobster Season

The two-day Sport Lobster Season is always the last consecutive Wednesday and Thursday in July, beginning at 12:01 A.M. on Wednesday and ending at 12:00 midnight on Thursday. The rules have been somewhat altered in the last few years. Bag Limit: Six (6) per licensed harvester (you must have a saltwater fishing license with a lobster stamp) per day in Monroe County; twelve (12) per licensed harvester per day throughout the rest of Florida where the harvest of lobster is permitted. The two-day total of twelve lobster per licensed harvester in Monroe County can only be possessed when transporting your catch by car on, or after, the second day. The Florida Marine Patrol hands out information and pays close attention to make sure the divers don't violate the rules or bring home illegal lobsters. No night diving for lobster allowed. John Pennekamp Coral Reef State Park in Key Largo is closed to lobster harvest during the mini-season.

Many hotels and guesthouses jack up prices and require two or three-day minimum stays during the two-day event.

August

Average temperature: 84°
Average rainfall: 4.6 inches
Sunset: 8:11 p.m.

Coral Reef Spawning

America's newest and perhaps weirdest spectator sport is a night dive with the hope of showing up on the reef in time to watch the annual, simultaneous release of eggs and sperm by billions of coral polyps. The egg bundles look like bb's or pearls. Those who have seen this other-worldly event say the sight is spectacular and worth all the trouble it takes to get there at the very instant it all begins. Spawning has gone on forever, of course, but it is a recently discovered phenomenon on U.S. reefs. It was first observed in 1990, at the Flower Gardens Reef Bank, 100 miles off the Texas coast. The phenomenon occurs each year, usually five to eight days after the August full moon, and every dive shop and promoter in the Florida Keys knows all about it. Just ask them for details.

Call the Florida Keys National Marine Sanctuary, 305-743-2437 for more information.

September

Average temperature: 83°
Average rainfall: 6.4 inches
Sunset: 7:45 p.m.

Womenfest Key West
296-4238 ✴ 800-535-7797

Usually right at the beginning of September. A week of wine tasting, tea dancing, gallery browsing, sunset cruising, and a sisters-for-brothers blood drive, empowerment seminars, guided bike tours, film festival, theater, lesbian comedy, street fair, tennis tournament, golf tournament, and backcountry kayak tours. Wet T-shirt contest is infamous! Promoters say they expect to host over 4,000 women. September is a nice, quiet time in the Keys, and this is a terrific get-together.

Florida Keys Poker Run
Matt Cochran ✴ 295-3286

Third weekend in September. Motorcyclists drive down the Keys in a charity event for children. Yes, their bikes make big noise, but those bikers raise a lot of money for good causes. The run starts in Miami and includes five stops throughout the Keys. At each stop participants draw a card. At the end of the route, which is Key West, the highest hand wins a cash prize and often other other great awards. Each year 13,000–20,000 motorcycle enthusiasts thunder into downtown Key West to congregate outside Sloppy Joe's Bar on Duval for one wild Saturday night. Call for details and a schedule.

October

Average temperature: 79°
Average rainfall: 5.4 inches
Sunset: 7:13 p.m.

Fantasy Fest
296-1817
Key West's answer to Mardi Gras. An annual ten-day island-wide festival climaxing in the famous Twilight Fantasy Parade held on the last Saturday in October. Theme of the fest, which changes from year to year, is reflected all over town—in costumes, shop window displays, and restaurant decors. 50,000 people from all over the world converge on the island for this party.

Make your plans early. Visitors who come for the Fest year after year book the best rooms, months or even a year in advance, in spite of the prices. Hotels and guesthouses hike their prices to the max. The airlines are packed—make reservations as soon as you possibly can.

The Fantasy Fest party moves from neighborhood to street block, from restaurant to bar, from club to hotel. The fun, glitz and glitter never stop. It simply changes locations, adjusts attitude, and moves to a new scene from time to time. Follow the crowds and you won't miss any of the action.

Fantasy Fest launches with the Goombay Festival, a traditional street fair in Bahama Village. This is a locals' favorite. Everyone turns out to dance with their neighbors, eat something authentically African or Cuban, and wander among the pretty displays of African-American fashions.

The Pet Masquerade and Parade on the great lawn of the Marriott's Casa Marina Hotel is always a crowd pleaser and attracts some pretty bizarre pet/owner look-alikes.

The Pier House Pretenders in Paradise, also known as the World's Most Outrageous Costume Contest, is a gala centerpiece to the Fantasy Fest celebration. Prizes, including cash prizes worth $10,000, are awarded in various categories appropriate to the theme.

One of the rowdier events of Fantasy Fest, Sloppy's Toga Party, is fueled by live, smoking rock 'n roll. There are plenty of prizes for the best togas.

At sunset, on the Friday before the big parade, party animals don Caribbean marching clothes and costumes (What kind of costume? Let your your conscience be your guide) and join the Masquerade March through Old Town. The group gathers at the City Cemetery. The merry band is led by fifes and drums through the winding streets of downtown Key West, picking up many more carousers along the way. The crowd finally spills into the Tea Dance in the street, at the 801 Bar at 801 Duval.

And then, the climax: the Twilight Fantasy Parade. The streets are packed. The mood is frenzied! This is the parade the whole world watches. Floats, imprecision marching groups, all kinds of bands playing all kinds of music, and thousands of masqueraders from every corner of the world come to Key West for the parade.

On the morning after, Children's Day at Bayview Park is on from noon to 5 p.m. (information: 292-8611). Families turn out for Children's Day, and that's why this event attracts local political candidates. They're out glad-handing, kissing babies and supporting Moms and apple pie. Great fun, particularly if you don't have to vote for one of these shame-less panderers.

Call for a brochure and schedule of events.

November

Average temperature: 74°
Average rainfall: 2.45 inches
Sunset: 5:47 p.m.
Hurricane season ends November 30

Key West Offshore World Championships

Early to-mid-November more than 50,000 powerboat fans arrive for the Indianapolis 500 of powerboat racing. Annually it's the biggest collection of high-performance ocean racing boats assembled anywhere in the world. Powerboats with four 1,000-plus horsepower engines cost over a million bucks! The powerboat racers follow a circuit of national races. The powerboat race season ends each year with this week-long event—where the world's champs are crowned in the Triple Crown of powerboat racing. Catamarans, or twin-hulled powerboats, reach speeds of 125–150 mph! Best viewing spots are just about anywhere on the Historic Seaport as well as harbor-front hotels—the Hilton, Hyatt, Pier House, and Ocean Key House. And oh! The parties!

Pirates in Paradise
Contact: 296-9694
One of Key West's newer events, this celebration also marks the happy end of another hurricane season. A celebration of Key West's swashbuckling past, the festival where would-be pirates and wenches get to live a pirate's life in a real thieves' market and encampment in the woods along the beach at Fort Taylor State Park and do the sorts of things that pirates did, drink and plunder, in ruffley costumes.

Parrot Heads Meeting of the Minds Convention
500 Duval Street ✹ 292-1435
According to Meeting of the Minds organizers, the first Parrot Heads in Paradise Club was formed in 1989 in Atlanta. There are now almost 160 clubs in the United States, Australia and Canada with more than 18,000 total members. As well as promoting Buffett's music and its associated laid-back lifestyle, Parrot Heads follow the motto, "Party with a Purpose." Lately the group's local charity has been the Cancer Foundation of the Florida Keys. Parrotheads party nicely, spend lots of money, and are usually rewarded for their dedication to all things Jimmy with an appearance by the party man who started it all, Jimmy Buffett.

December
Average temperature: 71°
Average rainfall: 1.8 inches
Sunset: 5:38 p.m.

Key West Women's Club Christmas Party
319 Duval Street ✺ 294-2039

It has become a local tradition for the Women's Club to kick off the
Christmas season with this annual tree-lighting party on the first Sunday
in December. This is a free party, open to all. Always lots to eat and
drink. Entertainment, too.

St Paul's Christmas Concert
401 Duval Street ✺ 296-5142

Make a joyful noise unto the Lord! This seasonal high point is our
island's bright Christmas star. It's performed only once each year and goes
on in stately and venerable St. Paul's Church. Stained glass, seasonal
decorations, and a musical program featuring a parade of the island's most
creative performers. Buy your tickets early—or you'll have to sit on the
steps of the church.

Little Island, Big Fun

Snorkel

If you can swim you can probably snorkel. A snorkel trip to the reef aboard a catamaran, schooner or power boat will cost anywhere from $40 to $50 per person. On some boats the snorkeling equipment rental fee is included in ticket price. Most snorkel trips out of Key West will take you to the area of the Sand Key Lighthouse reef. When shopping for a trip you should ask how many others will be going on the same trip and how many crew members will be along to assist. It's kind of like the teacher-student ratio. You don't want to find yourself in a huge group.

Certain Keys weather plays havoc with the reef, limiting visibility beneath the water, and creating some serious chop on the surface. If it is possible, avoid going to the reef when the weather is lousy. Don't expect the booking agent to discourage you from going out, however. On the contrary. They want you on that boat! No matter how choppy the sea.

Most snorkel boats offer a daily sunset cruise as their last trip of the day, sometimes in combination with a snorkel trip. The "combo" is a good way to squeeze all the gusto you can out of one afternoon on the water.

Dive Charters

The Fury
Hilton Marina ✻ 245 Front Street ✻ 294-8899 ✻ 800-994-8898
Three-hour snorkeling trips leave twice a day at 9:30 a.m. and 1:00 p.m. The *Fury* is a 65-foot catamaran with a shaded lounge and spacious sun decks. The reef trip includes snorkeling equipment and professional instruction, as well as free beer, wine and sodas. There is also a combo snorkeling/sunset sail that leaves at 4:00 p.m. in the winter and 5:00 p.m. in the summer. On this trip free champagne is also offered. All snorkel trips are $40. Kids ages 7–12 are half-price. Kids 6 and under go free.

The Sebago
201 William Street • 294-5687

Three-and-a-half hour snorkel trips to the living reef, all equipment and instruction included, are at 9 a.m. and 1 p.m. daily aboard the Sebago Marquesa, a 68-foot catamaran featurning a full bar. The bar opens on the way back into port. The *Sebago* and the *Sebago 2* are 60-foot catamarans with freshwater showers, and free soft drinks. The *Sebago* also offers a combo snorkel and sunset cruise, featuring all of the above plus a magnificent view of the sunset on the way back into port on the last trip in the afternoon. Snorkel trips are $45. The two-hour sunset cruise with unlimited beer, wine and champagne is $37. Children go on all *Sebago* trips for half price. Check out the Snorkel Power Adventure, an all-day package of fun on the water. Cost: around $150. Very cool.

SCUBA

If you have a PADI Certification card, the universal diver's license, be sure to bring it with you to the Keys. There are several charter dive boats catering exclusively to scuba divers, and many boats that take both snorkel and SCUBA divers to the reef. But they will all require you to show your certification card.

A 3-day PADI Certification course is available locally, as well as the popular resort course, so called because it is designed to give vacationers with limited time the chance to dive the reef with a minimum of on shore instruction. Resort course divers learn about scuba equipment in the morning and dive at two coral reef locations in the afternoon, all for a set price. They are accompanied constantly, on the reef, by a dive instructor, and are not qualified to dive alone. Nor are they certified to SCUBA dive.

Dive Schools and Charters

Captain's Corner
0 Duval Street • Ocean Key House • 296-8865

Scuba divers interested in dives on less frequented reefs will appreciate the *Sea Eagle*'s daily dive trips designed for advanced SCUBA divers.

Advanced dives are $65 for two-tank, two-location trips. Equipment rental is $30. Combination SCUBA and snorkel dive trips are offered twice daily. Cost is $35 for scuba; $30 for snorkel. Snorkel equipment is included; scuba gear is an additional $30.

The Captain's Corner is a five star rated facility, offering PADI accredited instruction up to Assistant Instructor and the popular Resort Course for beginners. The three or four day PADI accreditation course is $350 plus tax. The Resort Course is $100. And—in the summertime there are twilight wreck and night (SCUBA) dives. All instruction is available in Spanish, Czech.

Southpoint Divers
500 Truman Ave.
292-9778 or 800-891-DIVE
Southpoint Divers caters to SCUBA divers. Wrreck or Reef trips depart twice daily aboard 46-foot dive boats that comfortably accommodate 20 divers. All crew members are PADI instructors. Certified divers using their own gear pay $65 for a two tank dive. The same dive with all equipment is $80. If room permits, snorkelers accompanying scuba diving companions are welcome, but the dive destinations are suited to scuba, and not snorkel, diving.

The Resort Course at Southpoint Divers is $135. The three day certification course is $450.

Fishing

The waters of the Florida Keys contain over 600 varieties of edible fish, and plenty of them. A day of fishing off Key West is one of America's great tourist bargains. When you are in Key West, you are 130 miles out to sea already, mere minutes from the world's greatest fishing.

Who Needs A Fishing License?

Non-Florida residents must have saltwater fishing licenses when fishing from either a boat or land. Licenses are available at the County Court House, 500 Whitehead Street, and also from tackle shops and marinas. A seven day license for non-Florida residents costs under $20; an annual license is around $32. On most charter fishing boats the license is provided by the boat.

Call the Florida Marine Patrol at 800-342-5367 for further information, but don't be surprised if they take a while to answer.

Charter Boat Row
Garrison Bight Marina ✦ Palm Avenue and U.S. 1

Thirty-five members of Key West's charter fishing boats are docked at the Garrison Bight on the Amberjack Pier. A visit to charter boat row is lots of fun, particularly in the afternoon when boats are returning to port. Sometimes there are fish being made ready for the frying pan on cleaning stations along the wharf. Huge, hungry sea birds hover over the pier, waiting for their share of the feast. On a visit to the bight you'll see the fishing boats and meet the captains and crews who run them.

Party Boats

To experience the salty thrills of offshore fishing, without spending a fortune to hire a private charter, sign on for a fishing trip aboard a party boat, where up to 50 anglers share the fun of dropping lines and waiting for the bottom fish to bite. You'll pay around $25–$30 for a trip out to

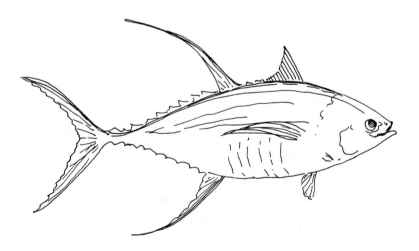

Yellowfin tuna

the deep blue sea, and that price includes your license, tackle and bait. They'll even give you a pill to ward off seasickness. On party boats there are mates to teach you the intricacies of offshore fishing. You'll find party boats from Key Largo to Key West at commercial piers.

Charter Sport Fishing

Sportfishing boats carry up to six anglers 15 or 20 miles out to sea to do battle with leaping monster fish like marlin and sailfish. It costs plenty to fish with a knowledgeable captain who knows where the fish are. A day

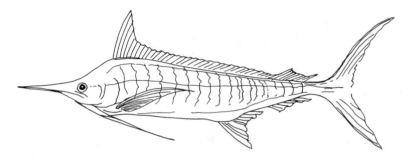

Blue marlin

on a charterboat can cost up to $625, but that fee can be split between passengers, if you don't mind sharing the boat. Arrange your trip directly with the captain. Ticket booth vendors on the sidewalks promise to arrange for anything, and they will—it's just that the arrangements they're making are often hit and miss. Usually the charter boat captain supplies everything but your food and drinks.

To find a private charter visit charter boat row, any marina, or call ahead to the Chamber of Commerce for a list of all types of fishing charters. Phone 800-FLA-KEYS.

Flats Fishing

Flats or shallow-bottom fishing is nothing like charter boat and party boat fishing. Flats fisherman must have sharp eyes, good instincts, lots of patience and sunscreen. Shallow fishing excursions travel on open skiffs, with shallow draughts and nothing above the deck to interfere with fly casting. They reach the mangrove islands at dawn. There are frigate birds, and great white herons swooping low as fish become visible in the clear shallow water. Here are tarpon, bonefish and permit, the wily creatures flats anglers are looking to hook. None of them are edible. The trick to fly-fishing is to convince the feeding fish that your hook is a tasty morsel of crab. But it's hard to fool these fish. They are wary, and very cautious. After you catch them, you measure them, photograph them and deliver them back into their crystalline world. Fishing in the backcountry is as much about enjoying the surroundings as it is about catching fish.

Saltwater Angler
243 Front Street • 294-3248 • 800-223-1629
Located in Hilton Hotel complex. Complete booking service for back-country guides as well as offshore guides available at the Saltwater Angler store. Also, equipment and supplies for fishing enthusiasts.

Golf

Key West Resort Golf Course
Junior College Road, Stock Island • 294-5232
A Rees Jones designed 18-hole championship golf course with a full house of dog-legs, water hazards and mangroves, located on one of the largest areas of greenery in Key West. A lake behind hole number ten is a sanctuary for rare birds. Three teaching professionals year 'round.

Pro shop is open from 6:30 a.m. till 6:30 p.m. daily. Play till sundown. Pay $150 for 18 holes in season, $85 summertime. Includes cart. Callaway clubs rent for $40 a day.

Tennis

Bayview Park
Truman Avenue, 1300 block
Recently refurbished courts at Bayview Park are looking pretty spiffy lately. Here are the rules: Time limit for play is 45 minutes or one set, whichever

comes first. There is no system for reserving court time, and you can't reserve a court if your partner is not yet present. The park is open from 7 a.m. till 11 p.m. No dogs allowed. No charge to use these public courts.

Casa Marina Court
Reynolds Street at the Beach ✆ 294-4436
These are also city-owned courts, free to the public. A small parking lot is for tennis players only. To schedule call ahead. Time limit here is 30 minutes or one set, whichever comes first.

Swimming

Florida Keys Community College Pool
College Rd. Stock Island ✆ 296-9081 Ext.565
If you simply must swim, and the water at the community pool is too cold for you, come here, where they'll only charge you $3 to swim your heart out in a very nice, nearly new, heated pool. Call for hours.

The Martin Luther King Jr. Community Pool
300 Catherine Street ✆ 292-8248
One of the island's best kept secrets is this big, beautiful pool in Bahama Village. Also, there's a baby pool, picnic tables, and basketball courts. The pool is open from 9 a.m.–6 p.m. Lap swimming hours, summer months, but those lap swimming times are subject to change around quite a bit. Call for the current schedule. Free to all.

Bocce Ball

Southernmost Bocce Ball
Bocce ball is serious fun for the local crowd that gathers at the six red clay courts at Sonny McCoy Indigenous Park, White Street and Atlantic Boulevard. You'll find here a crowd of Key West professionals: journalists, historians, politicians, executives, attorneys, and even judges, all very friendly. Tag along to the bar scene after and make some new friends. Games begin just as the sun is fading and the cool breezes of the Gulf Stream begin to blow over the land. There's even an annual bocce ball ball.

Gyms & Fitness Clubs

Bargain Books & News Stand Able Body Fitness Center
1028 Truman Ave. ✺ 294-7446
This basic gym is located in a room behind the books and news. Gym features free weights and machines. Air conditioned, TV, music and showers, too, for only $5. Open 6 a.m. to 10 p.m. daily.

Caribbean Spa
Pier House Resort, 1 Duval Street ✺ 296-4600
Free to guests of the Pier House, it's also open to hard-bodies with the money to buy a day at this a chi chi gym. In addition to state-of-the-art fitness equipment, jacuzzi, steam room, sauna, there is a full service beauty spa. The gym is small but rarely crowded. Appointments are necessary for services at this stunningly pristine spa.

Club Body Tech
1075 Duval Street, Duval Square ✺ 292-9683
Air-conditioned, very modern gym with pounding, high-tech music to match. Hours are 6 a.m.–10 p.m. weekdays; 8 a.m.–9 p.m. Saturday; 9 a.m.–9 p.m. Sunday. Join for a day, or a week, or a month, or a year. Lots of modern equipment. Showers. Steam room. Trainers for hire.

Shape U. Family Fitness Center
2740 N. Roosevelt Boulevard in Overseas Market ✺ 294-9193
Tourists welcome. Treadmills. Nautilus. When you do the Stairmaster, you can watch TV at the same time! You might hear arguments over what TV programs to watch, when the talk show crowd clashes with soap opera devotees.

Paradise Health and Fitness
1706 N. Roosevelt Blvd. ☎ 294-4120

A full circuit weight room. Join short or long term. Nutritional and fitness counseling. Kick-boxing—which is *very* popular among Key West professional women—and 35 other classes every week. Personal trainers available. A wholesome, clean, bright place.

Pro Fitness Center
1111 12th Street ☎ 294-1865

Memberships not as expensive as the others, maybe because of its weird location in the basement of the Professional Plaza, a building full of mostly doctors' offices, behind K-Mart. This place smells more like a gym than any other gym on the island. The owner and trainer is Mr. Fitness, of the Sunday column in the *Key West Citizen*.

Yoga College of India (Bikram Yoga)
927 White St. ☎ 292-1854

Hot yoga. Bikram Yoga devotees spotted in this school include Terrance McNally and George Stephanopoulus. Several 90-minute classes daily, beginning at 8 a.m. Last class at 6 p.m. Sunday, 10 a.m. only. Call for more. A very challenging workout, an amazing body shaper and confidence booster. Bikram Yoga will make you bullet-proof! Newcomers welcome. If you can't take big heat—stay away.

Coffee Mill Cultural Center
916 Polhaski Street ☎ 296-9982

Stop by and pick up a schedule or ask them to FAX you one. Aerobics, stretch and relaxation classes, karate, African dance. Newcomers always welcome. Sweat and shape up on a great, bouncy floor.

Curves of Key West
1101 Key Plaza ☎ 293-8777

If you belong to Curves back home, you know the routine. You're welcome here with a Curves Travel Pass. No day rates. Curves Key West T-shirts are very popular. Wear yours back home and show your shapely friends that you get around! Hours: Weekdays 6:30 am - 1 pm, 3:30 to 7 pm. Saturday mornings. Closed Sundays.

Kidstuff

Children's Animal Farm Monroe, County Detention Center
College Road, Stock Island ✽ 293-7331
Take the kids to jail! On alternate Sunday afternoons the Sheriff opens
the doors to the little farm-like zoo beneath the detention center. There
is no charge for you and your kids to visit with tropical birds, snakes, fer-
rets, rabbits, horses, ponies, pigs, sheep, chickens, ducks, cows, llamas and
whatever else happens to be boarding there at the time. Last spring a
sloth spent a couple of weeks at the farm and created quite a stir with
local kids who'd never seen such a creature before. Groups can make special arrangements to visit. There is no charge. Call ahead to see if the
farm is open during your visit. It's pretty much hit and miss as one volunteer is in charge and she has a busy life outside her animal tending duties.

Discovery Underseas Tours
Lands End Marina/Foot of Margaret Street
293-0099 ✽ 800-262-0099
A great trip out to the reef where kids get a big kick out of the huge,
slanted plexiglass windows on the bottom of the boat that open up for
viewing the mysteries of the reef seven miles off shore.

Kids three and under go free on all trips. Kids under twelve go for free
on the first trip of the day, providing there are seats left over after the
paying customers are aboard. First trip is around noon. Kids must be
accompanied by an adult. Call for information and reservations.

Key Encounter Theater & Museum
Clinton Square Market, 291 Front St. ✽ 292-2070
A very inexpensive and entertaining film appealing to adults and their
kids. Take a break in this air-conditioned mini-theater, and watch a
multi-image movie of the world of the Florida Keys living reef, and Keys
wildlife projected onto 3 screens. The film is about a half-hour long, and
is the very next best thing to actually being in the water, at the reef,

yourself. Only it's a lot cheaper and a lot drier this way. There is a very noisy parrot, and other interesting nature treats, too. Free, but you can give a donation if you like.

Mom's Baby Stuff Rentals
296-7113 or 305-923-5092
Everything you need for baby is for rent here. Cribs, portable cribs, strollers, highchairs, Swing-o-matics, and jogging strollers. Walkers, backpacks, baby gates, and umbrella strollers. Rent a rocking chair for a day or a week. If you call ahead and put in your order, your baby stuff will be at your hotel or guesthouse when you arrive. Business hours. Plan ahead!

Monroe County Library
700 Fleming Street ✺ 292-3595
Every Saturday the county library hosts a children's hour at 10:30 a.m. Kids do arts and crafts and watch a movie. During the summer months, children's librarian Karen Jensen hosts children's hours four days a week. For a schedule of programs tailored to specific age groups, phone the library and ask for the children's events schedule. Children of all ages are welcome throughout the year.

Martin Luther King Memorial Pool
Catherine Street ✺ 292-8248
A terrific pool beside a shallow kiddie pool around which local mothers congregate on hot days to put their babies and their feet in the water. Older kids are kicked out of the pool for lane swimming hour and water aerobic classes, but these activities are usually scheduled for very early in the morning, and later in the afternoon. The pool is open from 11 a.m. until 6 p.m. daily. There is no admission charge.

Charter Boat Row
Garrison Bight Marina ✺ Palm and North Roosevelt Boulevard
Around 4 p.m. the charter fishing boats come back to port after a day of deep sea fishing, usually with fish to be cleaned. As the captains or mates clean the fish, they toss scraps to a flock of very appreciative pelicans

who gobble them quick as lightening. Kids love watching this. It's truly amazing how much a pelican can swallow, and how flexible are the throats of long-necked sea birds.

Some kids, at least five and up, love going out to sea and fishing with their parents on a party boat. Deep-sea fishing on a party boat is a surprisingly inexpensive and wonderfully entertaining way to enjoy the Keys. On party boats, kids ages 5–12 go for half price, which is around $20.

Beaches

P EOPLE PROBABLY ASSUME that Key West must have some pretty amazing beaches, being at the end of a string of tropical islands and all. Well, our beaches are amazing, but not for their looks. Our beaches are not the extra-fine sanded, coffee ice cream colored stretches people imagine when they think "Florida beach." Like many things southernmost, the beaches here are rough, battered and kind of seedy. Lots of character, but not all that pretty—not in the traditional sense anyway.

The locals' favorite beach is at **Fort Taylor,** an 87-acre state park with a pre-Civil-War-era brick fort, several acres of Australian pine trees, spacious parking areas, a scattering of picnic tables, and a few grimy charcoal grills for whoever claims them at the beginning of each new day.

The track of pine-needle forest that separates the parking lot from the bluff and the beach below it is always a few degrees cooler than the rest of the island. The forest floor is sheltered from the sun by the pines and cooled by breezes from the deep, rough channel where the Atlantic Ocean and the Gulf of Mexico collide in an endless tumult.

Bring along a beach chair, or a tough hide, to lie on the rocky (you can hardly call it sand) Fort Taylor Beach. Swimmers will find water deep enough here for a good workout not too far from the stony shore, but those stones are really hard on the feet. In fact, they're downright obnoxious. For playing, wear rubber sandals or sneakers into the water.

For swimming, wade out into the water with your sneakers on, then toss them back onto the beach until you get back from your swim.

Walk the beach all the way to the right toward a jetty of rocks. They're steep-sided, slippery and dangerous, just as the sign says. Climb up onto the path that winds along the bluff above the beach and continue on around the point. You'll come to another long string of huge gray, sharply planed boulders. The water beyond the rocks is very rough, full of currents, and absolutely no good for swimming. Find a perch on the rocks and wait for sunset. It is glorious from this location.

This is the sunset setting for many windy weddings. Sometimes you will see two or more wedding ceremonies going on at once. And a funeral. By now, so many of the ashes of former Key West people have been tossed into the wild winds that blow into a fury as the day draws to a close, that the locals have named this part of the shoreline **Ash Beach**.

The Park has a few rules to remember. Thong-style bathing suits are not allowed on this beach, nor is topless sunbathing. Rangers will give you a plastic bag when you enter the park so you can take your trash back out with you. Few garbage cans are available in this area, to cut back on costs. The park recycles aluminum cans and makes compost. Cigarette butts go into ashtrays donated by the R.J. Reynolds Tobacco Company. Warning: get out of Fort Taylor Park by dusk or risk being locked behind its very high, barbed-wire laced security fence. This really did happen to people I know, and they had a hellish time climbing over the gate in the dark.

You enter Fort Taylor through Truman Annex, at Southard Street. Follow the signs to the ticket booth where you'll pay $2.50 for a car with one person, $5 for a car with two and fifty cents for each additional person. Buy an annual State Park pass. It's for up to eight people in a car and works at all Florida state parks.

South Beach is located at the very end of Duval Street, on the Atlantic Ocean. A concrete pier extending fifty feet beyond the last block of Duval Street provides a good sunning and people-watching area, as well as entry via a ladder into water deep enough for a swim. A recently constructed black wrought-iron fence closes off the pier to the public from 11 p.m. until 7 a.m. each day. The beach, and the beach restaurant, are closed during those hours, too.

A thin layer of pebbly sand covers South Beach. There are plenty of sheltering palms for shade. This was for many years very much a locals' beach. Tennessee Williams sunned here, as well as a number of other local celebrities who appreciated the relative peace and calm of this often-overlooked public beach.

Today, South Beach is frequented by locals and tourists alike who gather here to take in the sun and the Key West color, in a place with easy access to refreshments and bathrooms. Because the water is relatively shallow, and almost the entire area is enclosed by fences, it's a particularly user-friendly beach for small children and babies still innocent enough to get amusement from a plastic bucket and shovel at the edge of water so calm it barely moves.

On South Beach, dedicated explorers will find the occasional nature treat stranded in the shallow pools on the craggy surfaces of the long, slippery, green, sea-slime covered rocks along the shoreline. They might see a hermit crab, no bigger than a thumbnail, or tiny, wiggling shrimp, barely discernible to the naked eye, or a rare, delicately whorled sea shell.

You swim at your own risk off South Beach because there are no lifeguards. Dogs, alcohol and glass containers are all prohibited. You use the bathrooms, rustic but clean, in the city-owned restaurant.

When you've had enough of the great outdoors, you can go inside and order breakfast, lunch, or dinner, while you watch the beach and the sky from a canopied deck, built of rough square beams painted blue and, somehow, evocative of a funky New England beachside resort. There is a full bar inside the restaurant.

Another public beach downtown is **Simonton Street Beach,** where Simonton Street ends at the Gulf of Mexico. Tucked between two giant resorts, the Pier House and the Hyatt, you'll find a tiny, gritty square of beach with public bathrooms and a few metered parking places.

The crowd that tends to congregate here is pretty rough as are the waters beyond the pier. Many nicer places are available on the island to go for a swim or to sunbathe.

To take your dog for a dip, or to view another local beach scene, take South Street over to Vernon Avenue, turn right, and head to the end of the block. **Dog Beach** is straight ahead. This tiny, public beach is next to Louie's Backyard, a restaurant at the corner of Vernon and Waddell. The beach is sandy with tiny waves here, but the shoreline is rocky and slippery.

Jimmy Buffett's first Key West home is next door to Louie's, at 711 Waddell Street. Like the others on this side of the block, the house was recently restored to its original seaside splendor by the Coconut Beach Resort. Today it is a much spiffier place indeed than the shabby, salt-and-wind-battered rental house where Buffet composed "Margaritaville"—*Strumming my six-string, on my front porch swing…*

Another beach dear to locals for its off-the-beaten-path charm is located below the white concrete pier at the corner of Vernon and Seminole streets. On either side of the pier, you can swim at the tiny, sandy strips of beach.

Twenty years ago it was called **Broken Glass Beach**. My neighbor, an artist named George Lee, once created a beautiful mosaic fish on his backyard fence with glue and bits of sea-worn colored glass he had collected during daily swims off the tiny beach. People also take their dogs swimming here. It is also called "Casa Marina Beach," although it is public and not part of the Casa Marina Resort on the same block.

The waters here are perfect for beginning snorkelers. The scenery beneath the calm surface is good, and the water is shallow. I have spotted quite large stingrays gliding along the sandy bottom in this area and plenty of fish hanging around the aging Casa Marina pier, just to the left of the beach.

Monroe County Beach, at the foot of Reynolds Street, is a wide sandy cove beside a long, wooden pier officially named the Reynolds Street Pier, but known locally by a variety of names like the Dick Dock, the Queer Pier, or Gay Bay. You get the picture. Not so many years ago this wooden pier was a favorite sunning place for bronzed beauties from the island's gay population. Gay tourists, perhaps having heard about the Queer Pier from an older brother—or sister—or returning to the island for the first time in many years with fond memories of sun-baked afternoons on the Queer Pier in the pre-AIDS era, will still find their way to this popular sunbathing wharf. But the "Dick Dock" is no longer what it used to be. By now, many of the local beauties have moved on or decided to take better care of their skin and sworn off sun-bathing, or found new roosts on the more cosmopolitan Fort Taylor Beach. Today, the Queer Pier is pretty hetero.

Monroe County Beach is broad and sandy, studded with palms and a few Australian pines. A series of concrete-surfaced pathways converge at a spacious gazebo, right in the center of the beach. There is plenty of parking here, a very funky concrete bathhouse, sheltered picnic tables, swings, a jungle gym, and a snack bar. Astro City is a small, usually busy playground, featuring a whirly-gig, a great jungle gym, swings, monkey bars, and a sandbox. At the back of the playground you can eat at a couple of picnic tables beneath a roof; this is a favorite birthday spot for kiddies. The Italian restaurant here is fabulous and the bar is a wonderful place to sip and beach.

On the opposite side of the beach from the Reynolds Street Pier sits the West Martello Tower, surrounded by a high, curving wall of red brick. For a cozy hideout from the wind on blustery, cool days, settle yourself down in the soft sand at the foot of the West Martello Tower's sheltering brick wall. Recently restored and renamed is the **C.B. Harvey Rest Beach Park**. Cornelius Bradford Harvey, nicknamed C.B., served two years as a city commissioner and eight years as mayor of Key West. The park is accessible to the handicapped, with wheelchair pathways that lead to the water's edge. There are erosion-fighting dunes, sea oats and other vegetation, foot bridges, and a bike path. The brand-new picnic tables are rarely in use.

Across the street, at the corner of White Street and Atlantic Blvd., the **Higgs Beach Dog Park**, created with private contributions. There are two sections, one for little dogs weighing 25 pounds or less, and one for the others. Both sides have bi-level water fountains for dogs and their owners. The area is fenced and lighted and there are 12 stations with bags for picking up dog doo doo. The first rule of the park is that you must pick up after your dog.

Smathers Beach, on the southern side of the island, is a half-mile-long stretch of quite wide, man-made beach. Because of the reef, there is no pounding surf on any of Key West's beaches. The natural process of erosion that grinds giant boulders down into tiny grains of sand does not occur here (there's no surfing here). The sand on this beach is imported from the Bahamas in huge barges. Last time they re-sanded the beach it cost the city $350,000 for two barges of Caribbean sand. It all blows away eventually, so every few years, the renourishment process beings all over again.

It is now illegal to park your car, van or camper along the curb of South Roosevelt Boulevard, which winds along the side of the beach, or across the street on a very bumpy, very dusty strip of earth with the unlikely name of the "Bridle Path." Unlikely, because no one rides horses around Key West. Parking meters, at a quarter an hour, are new, and here to stay in spite of the outcry from local citizenry. There are bathhouses and a few picnic tables but no lifeguards.

The crowd at this beach is active. It's a good place for fun-seeking, sun-loving tourists to find each other. There are beachcombers wandering along the water's edge, spirited volleyball games, frisbee tosses, and watersport rental concerns. For a fee, you can try parasailing, windsurfing or jet skiing. Unfortunately, the seaweed can get very heavy, and pretty stinky here. Swimming is not always lovely.

Burgers, snowcones, soft drinks, smoothies and all manner of refreshments are offered from the many snack trucks which arrive bright and early each morning to claim a spot in the heart of the action. Be prepared to pay for the cup if you ask for ice or water.

A wide, flat concrete promenade/bicycle/skate path begins at the foot of the beach at the corner of Bertha and South Roosevelt and continues for the entire length of Smathers and well beyond. The parade of bodies in motion on the bike path goes on all day long. Dogs are not allowed on this beach. It is also illegal for women to sunbathe topless here.

At Atlantic Blvd. and Thompson Street you'll see a sign for a **Nature Preserve**. It would be a bad idea to take anything other than a mountain bike down this path, and a sign even says no bikes. The going is kind of rough due to crab holes and ficus tree roots, but the path is short and you come out on a pretty cool, and usually secluded, strip of **Rest Beach**. There are signs along the way to tell you what you're seeing. And if you look inside a crab hole, you'll often see a big, scary looking crab in there.

Gardens and Green Space

Key West Botanical Garden
College Road, Stock Island • 296-1504

This beautifully tended piece of paradise is home to more than 50 species of butterflies, the recently discovered Cuban fig-eating bat, and 7,000 plants. There are more kinds of trees on these 7.5 acres of tropical humid forest than there are in all of Western Europe. Further, this remarkable place is a layover for many migratory birds, and the only forest of its kind in America that you can actually drive to. Popular with bird-watchers and tropical plant lovers, the garden would still be a mostly abandoned relic of an earlier time, were it not for the efforts of Key West Botanical Garden Society members, who rallied hard to bring the garden back from near extinction. They've done an admirable job.

The Botanical Garden was originally established back in 1935, as a project of the Federal Emergency Relief Administration, designed to put locals to work and attract tourists to the area. The Botanical Garden was planted with eighty different species of plants and covered 55 acres of land. Opened to the public in 1936, it became a major South Florida attraction, featuring an exhibition center, aviary, amphitheater, greenhouses, walkways, and hand-built stone walls. All went well until World War II, when part of the garden was claimed by the federal government as the site for an emergency war hospital. Once the government moved in they continued to expand, placing water tanks and county civil service buildings on the property. Then the tiny Key West golf course expanded beyond it's original boundries and before long the Botanical Garden that had been so important to Key West's suvival in the 1930's was reduced to a few acres of neglected gardens. The fine old exhibit house and ampitheater fell into disrepair and although the Botanical Gardens appeared on tourist guides, it was difficult to find. No one spent much time there except for a handful of squatters who camped among the ruins. And the place that had attracted biology students from all over the country was declared unsafe for students.

In 1988 the Key West Botanical Society was formed, and in 1991 management of the gardens was turned over to them. Since 2000 the Society has secured several important grants, enabling them to re-estabish the tropical forest in all of its earlier grandeur. And they've only just begun! Today there are benches and resting places, tables and path-ways, and brochures that lead visitors on self-guided tours. It is a wonderful place to visit, picnic, meditate, wander. Students from the

Hibiscus

local high school are learning about native flora and fauna, and the botany students, from many colleges, are back. The ampitheater is used for a vareity of presentations and the butterfly garden is alive with activ-ity. The gardens feature both native and exotic plants, and the last remaining specimens of the Stock Island tree snail. Environmentalists warn that prospects are pretty grim for the snail. It is hoped that the restoration of this forest may prolong their existance and that of 30 more endangered species. The garden is operated on a non-profit basis. Admission is around $5, less for seniors and children. Join the Key West

Botanical Garden Society and your admission is free. Group tours available. Call for information on the garden and the Society.

Bayview Park
1400 Truman Avenue

In the past year a lovely lush carpet of fresh green grass has been installed in Bayview Park, and dogs have been banned from the place. The Bayview's bathrooms, ball fields and tennis courts have been refurbished. Even the old bandstand, that has showcased hundreds of concerts and events since the park was created in 1923, has undergone repairs and received a fresh coat of white paint. Today the park looks as inviting as it did back in the 1920s.

The tract of land that is Bayview Park was once the yard and garden of a wealthy cigar manufacturer, Eduardo Gato. The millionaire's mansion stood in the middle. When Gato sold the property to the City, his house was moved to 1206 Virginia Street and turned into a charity hospital known as Casa del Pobre. Today Gato's house is an upscale complex of condominiums. According to local legend, Casa del Pobre has long been haunted by the ghost of a nurse who occasionally materializes to take midnight pulses.

In the fall, the Key West High School's cheerleading squad practices in one corner of the park. On weekends there are picnics and birthday parties. The park is studded with magnificent tropical hardwood trees. On either side of the bandstand there are lignumvitae trees. You'll recognize them from their stature, they're shorter than other trees, and more shrub-like. In the spring they are covered with delicate blue blossoms.

In the area behind the bandstand there are several important monuments that memorialize Key West boys who served in Viet Nam, a local man killed at Desert Storm, soldiers of the Confederacy, and Jose Marti, a Cuban poet and leader of the Cuban Revolution.

Nancy Forrester's Secret Garden
1 Free School Lane (off the 500 block of Simonton Street)
294-0015

It has taken Nancy Forrester thirty years to bring this magnificent mini-rainforest to its current state of grandeur, and now she's sharing her marvelous 16,000-square-foot gallery of tropical plants and fruit trees with the world. Commune with a spectacular collection of sumptuous tropical flowers, fruit trees, giant hardwood trees, and butterflies. This garden of flora is located in an unlikely place, and though it's in the very heart of Old Town Key West, it's difficult to find. And there's no parking area. But none of that will matter once you enter the place. You're welcome to stay in the garden for as long as you like. Picnic. Or rest.

In the middle of the property there is screened conch-style cottage, available for rent. It is a favorite honeymoon retreat for couples staging their weddings in the garden. When you marry here, an orchid will be named and dedicated to mark the event. Then you can come back every time you're in town and see how it's doing.

Open 10 a.m. to 5 p.m. Admission $6; off the 500 block of Simonton Street.

Little Hamaca Park and the Salt Ponds
Government Road (off 1500 block of Flagler Avenue) ✒ 294-2116
When you turn onto Government Road on your way to the boardwalk and trail through Little Hamaca Park ⅔ mile away, you'll pass Key West's Salt Ponds. Look to your right to see these shallow tidal pools that are home to many species of fish, and a variety of birds, including the rare roseate spoonbill.

These tidal pools were once part of an important island industry, salt gathering. Large, flat, evaporating pans were laid out in the very shallow pools. Salt water flowed into them during the spring and summer months. When the tidal pools receded during the dry months, the moisture evaporated, leaving 340 acres of crystallized salt dried on the pans.

Also on your right is the runway of the Key West International Airport. Watching planes arriving and departing is fun, and enormously entertaining for kids.

Little Hamaca City Park has a picnic area, a parking area, a bicycle stand (this whole trip is best experienced on a bike), and a boardwalk. Information plaques tell the story of these transitional wetlands. The three main species of mangroves are well-represented here. The red mangroves grow up, and then bend back into the water to plant new roots. Black mangroves shoot straight up out of the mud. Buttonwood trees grow along the shoreline—they line the sides of the Overseas Highway in some areas of the Keys—and emit salt on the underside of their leaves. Taste one and see for yourself.

The trail through Little Hamaca Park is ⅕ mile long. Two boardwalks lead through the marshes and lowlands. Between the two is an area of hardwood hammock. There are endangered species of animals living here: the Key West raccoon, the red rat snake, and the white crowned pigeon—so named by John Audubon in 1832. The discovery of these special inhabitants on this property saved it from being turned into a concrete suburb of Key West.

Little Hamaca Park is open from daylight until sundown, daily. There is no admission fee.

Charles "Sonny" McCoy Indigenous Park
Atlantic Boulevard at White Street ✦ 292-8157

The Indigenous Park is named after the Key West mayor who served the longest time in office: five two-year terms. Mayor McCoy, who was an architect and a world-class water-skier, went down in the history books when he water-skied to Cuba in the early '70s.

The native tree park is planted with a great sampling of indigenous trees including several endangered species. There is no charge to explore the grounds. Many trees are marked with their common as well as Latin names. You'll see lots of island trees like silver buttonwood, gumbo limbo, geiger tree, wild dilly, autograph tree and satinwood. Also an amazing ficus tree. Sometimes there is a printed guide to the trees available at the entrance. Often there is not.

Doves, mockingbirds, butterflies, as well as a multitude of chickens, are in evidence. It's very quiet. There's rarely a crowd. Every summer, a small army of boy scouts spend a weekend camping on the grounds.

The park is open Monday through Friday from 7 a.m. till 4 p.m. There is parking and rest rooms. Also a pavilion for picnicking.

Wellspring Medicine Garden
800 Amelia Street ✦ 292-2022

A jungle garden sanctuary dedicated to spirituality, higher consciousness, and healing. Peaceful folks are invited to commune with nature, join a meditation circle or put in some solitary time at the koi pond. The goldfish are large and happy. Everywhere you look you'll see something wonderful—small snakes curled around thin tree trunks, a grassy walk, Buddhas smiling benevolently from odd perches, and thick chunks of crystal. The garden is shaded with exotic hardwoods. No special training is required and all are welcome to attend meditation circles. Chi-netics, a special form of Tai Chi, is practiced in the garden. Healing massage available. The garden is open during daylight hours. There is no fee to enter. Check in for a schedule of events.

West Martello Towers
Atlantic Boulevard and White Street ✳ 294-3210

The Joe Allen Garden Center (named after beloved local son, Joe Allen, who served as state representative in Tallahassee) is housed here. The West Martello is one of a trio of forts built on the islands' coasts in the 1800's. Both the East and West Martello Towers were built mostly by slaves, and completed in 1862, just one year before the Emancipation Proclamation outlawed slavery. In 1890, the U.S. Navy used the West Martello Tower for target practice, which is why it looks as if it barely survived the Civil War. In fact, none of Key West's three forts ever was involved in battle.

The Key West Garden Club maintains this lovely ruin turned flourishing tropical garden. Admission is free, but you must be wearing shoes and a shirt, not a bathing suit. Children are to be accompanied by adults, and no dogs are allowed. When you enter you will be greeted and told all about the fort's marvelous history. There is much to see, and long lists of plants to search out. There are marvelous photo opportunities against the backdrop of cool, red bricks, crumbling fireplaces and 135-year-old arches. You'll find the base of a tower that was blown away by gunfire, as well as many well-placed benches for peaceful times. On a jungly knoll there is a gazebo, popular for weddings.

The Garden Club sponsors frequent lectures and discussions on growing their beloved orchids—the more exotic, the better. Club members bring their own orchids into the garden on a Saturday in mid-May and compete for prizes for best species and best hybrid. At an annual plant ramble, plants are offered for sale, and refreshments are served. The event, a local favorite, is open to everyone, and everyone comes. Magic! Call for a schedule of events.

Accommodations

WHILE I WAS DOING RESEARCH for this guide, I was driving through the Keys with my (then) 17-year-old son. I was pointing out various hotels and guesthouses, telling him what I knew about them, how popular they were and so forth. Then I asked him where he would choose to stay were he a tourist coming to the Keys for a visit. Funky and old-fashioned? Or sleek and new?

"It would depend on who I was traveling with," my wise Capricorn said.

It really does depend on who you're with. Kids, for example, will be happiest staying in a motel or hotel with a pool. Their parents will, no doubt, appreciate this feature as well. Some properties have hot tubs but no pools. If you tell a reservationist that you want to be near a beach, and the answer is that the beach is nearby, ask how nearby?—how many blocks? And then check a map. But the island is, after all, a small place and easily negotiated.

It is important to check on features such as telephones and televisions in rooms. In many guesthouses, the main phones are not answered after business hours. If you need to be accessible, you should check on this point. You can count on air conditioning and, in most places, islandy ceiling fans. Breakfast isn't always part of the deal in a guesthouse, and so-called cocktail hours often feature no cocktails at all, but wine or punch instead.

Parking is at a premium here. An inn, especially a downtown inn, won't necessarily have a parking lot. And though most places in Key West are within walking distance of downtown, several fine, family-oriented places are located on the south side, also considered to be the quiet side of the island, and definitely a car ride from Duval Street and the tourist attractions.

Pets are usually not welcome, and when they are, they'll cost up to $25 per day extra. Many guesthouses discourage children, and some prohibit children all together.

Gay guesthouses are sometimes exclusively for gay men. Or gay men and gay women. Or gay women only. If you're timid around the subject or the presence of homosexuality, state that to the reservationist. If you're extremely sensitive, you should know that Key West is a gay-friendly destination, and up to 20% of our population is gay.

It is difficult to nail down rates in the thumbnail sketches that follow. This list is merely a sample, an overview, of what is available. Often a hotel has four seasonal rates. During Fantasy Fest week, the week that ends on the last Saturday night of October, rates are the highest of all. The other peak week is the one between Christmas and New Year's Day. You will also probably be asked to commit to a minimum number of nights during these times. Rates also shoot up on 3-day-holiday and special-events weekends. The Lobster mini-season in July, for example, is a local event that hikes prices. Check our chapter called "Annual Events" for a schedule of some long established events most likely to continue.

Some summer weekends offer low rates, and fall is also a time when great values can be found. Early December has traditionally been a grindingly slow time for tourism—which makes it a wonderful time to visit. No lines and no humidity. Many folks enjoy Key West at this time of the year; many come annually to Christmas shop and enjoy a pre-holiday R & R in Paradise.

Key West's hotel rates are some of the highest in the country. You will find better deals thirty or fifty or one hundred miles up the Keys, but, if you definitely want to stay in Key West, you'll pay plenty. And don't forget to add in the local, state, and tourist taxes, for a total of 11.5% on all accommodations.

Renting a house of your own for a week or two is a popular alternative to staying in hotels and inns. If you have a good-sized family or group, you might investigate this possibility. Many wonderful houses can be rented for short terms, and usually the amenities include a pool, a washing machine and dryer and a telephone—everything exactly as if you were in your own home. Maid service is usually available, also.

Lately a number of hotels or apartment houses are being turned into condominiums and going on the market at prices like $750,000 for a two bedroom, 1.5 bath, 650 square foot nook in Paradise. And, of course, time shares. Sales people find you on the street and take you for a talk about the possibilities of timeshare ownership.

Reservations Services

Once you've scheduled your visit, you can call ahead to a reservation service. They'll find you what you want and make the reservation for you. They collect their fee from the place, not from you. Reservation services are highly competitive in the Keys. The ones listed here have free 800 numbers. Call around and chat with various reservationists until you find one you really like. Then, get down to business. A good reservation service can save you a lot of time and hassles—particularly if you are the mad-cap, spur-of-the-moment type.

The website Fla-keys.com maintains a list of hotels, motels and guest houses and details about them. Check out this resource for the bottom line on prices.

WWW.Fla-keys.com

Florida Keys Visitors Bureau
800-648-6269 ● 800-352-5397

Key West Innkeepers Association
800-492-1911

At Home in Key West
888-459-9378

Destination Paradise
800-403-2154

Information Services

Key West Chamber of Commerce
800-648-6269

Gay Chamber of Commerce
Key West Business Guild ● 800-535-7797

Hotels and Motels

Almond Tree Inn
323 Whitehead Street ✸ 296-7786 ✸ 800-225-0639

Thanks to innovative use of a cement wall that separates the inn from
the busy streeet, the Almond Tree Inn is remarkably mellow and private.
Located just a half-block from the crossroads of old Town Key West,
Truman Avenue (US 1) and Duval Street, it features 22 very nicely
appointed rooms. Stay here and you'll sleep well, any time you want to,
and be ready to head back out to the party any time you want to also.
There's even a place to park your car, because you definitely won't need it
when you stay at this location. Amenities like neat brick walkways, tropical plants, heated pool and jacuzzi, complimentary continental breakfast
and daily happy hours are nice to come home to. Several queen suites
and a king suite with a sitting area are fairly priced. Remember: Location.
Location. Location. No pets. Very nice, helpful staff. Still fresh and neat
after it's recent restoration from a very funky motel into a modern and
spiffy inn.

Banyan Resort
323 Whitehead Street ✸ 296-7786 ✸ 800-225-0639

The Banyan Resort features thirty-eight individually designed timeshare
units (available for rent to the public), in eight renovated Victorian
houses, five of which are on the National Register of Historic Places. The
entire compound takes up roughly half a city block, with lush gardens,
swimming pools, a jacuzzi, a bar, and a fish pond. There is no ocean view,
but Fort Taylor State Park beach is nearby, and it's a good one.

The place gets its name from the spectacular banyan trees in the front
yards of the Cosgrove house, at 321 Whitehead Street, and the Delaney
house, at 323. Here are fine examples of how one banyan tree can cover
literally acres of ground. In India, several families can live in the thick
roots and branches of one banyan tree. The banyan's aerial roots drop
from the upper part of the tree and take root in the ground beneath,
forming new trunks wherever they may land. The banyans on this property are some of the finest anywhere. Unit number #702 is the most
spectacular one, with three stories of windows overlooking the garden

and the majestic banyan tree that gives the place its name. All units have full kitchens and private patios.

Best Western Key Ambassador Resort Inn
3755 S. Roosevelt Boulevard ✱ 296-3500 ✱ 800-432-4315

One hundred rooms on seven nicely landscaped acres, directly across the street from the Atlantic ocean. From the pool deck, elevated to take advantage of ocean breezes, you look out across the blue sea. Located on what employees like to call "the quiet side of the island," the Key Ambassador makes the most of its location with large, clean, quiet rooms, ocean views, and a congenial atmosphere.

The employees here are particularly gracious and seem genuinely concerned with your happiness. The resort has been owned and operated by the same family that built it in 1958. Every two years, the family says, the property gets a face-lift. And, sure enough, the place looks brand-new, and even smells new.

A substantial complimentary continental breakfast is served in a bright breakfast room from 7 a.m. till 10 a.m. daily, and coffee is always available in the lobby. The guest laundry is a great convenience. And though it's difficult to imagine why you might need one of these on vacation in the Florida Keys, there are ironing boards in every room! Also screen-enclosed balconies come with every room. Outdoors, in a chickee hut, there is a fitness center challenging enough for a real workout; a poolside bar and burger grill; and several nice picnic-table groupings and barbeque grills are available to guests.

It's a great place to stay when you want to be away from the downtown tourist crowd, although downtown is only ten minutes away by taxi. Or bring a car; there is plenty of parking. The airport is close, but since large jets are prohibited from landing on the island, the noise is not offensive. There are several restaurants within a mile radius, and a spectacular oceanside promenade that runs for a two-mile strip along the beach on the southern edge of the island.

Rooms are oceanview, poolview, harborview or gardenview. "The harbor," by the way, probably refers to the salt ponds, or mud flats, behind the motel. The ocean is the Atlantic Ocean, and it's a fabulous sight.

Casa Marina Resort (Wyndam)
Reynolds Street on the Ocean ❧ 296-3535 ❧ 800-874-4118

Although he did not live to see it completed, railroad baron Henry Flagler planned the Casa Marina, a glittering southernmost layover for his affluent Overseas Railroad customers traveling to Cuba. (Passengers trained to Key West, then steamshipped to Cuba, ninety miles away.) The hotel opened on New Year's Eve, 1921. In the pre-Depression splendor of the 1920s, Casa Marina guests fished, sailed, shot traps, played tennis and croquet, and danced beneath the stars on a seaside courtyard.

To imagine how glamorous an evening at the Casa might have been back then, read the party scenes in F. Scott Fitzgerald's *The Great Gatsby*. Sit in a wicker chair on the hotel's veranda and sip something cool. Time this reverie for one of those magical evenings when the full moon is on the rise even before the sun has set.

The Casa Marina started out with two hundred small guest rooms. Each contained a sink with running water; half had private baths. When it opened, the Casa's rates were very high for that time, from $8–$12 a day, and $84 a week on the American Plan—all meals included. During the Casa Marina's reign as the island's premier luxury hotel, the Astors and the Vanderbilts were frequent guests, as well as showbiz notables like Gregory Peck, Gene Tierney, Rita Hayworth, Ethel Merman, and Al Jolson. Guy Lombardo's band played, and Sally Rand, the fan dancer who lived for a while on the island, taught local kids tap dancing on the grand ballroom's polished hardwood floor.

In spite of its glittering clientele, the Casa Marina, like Flagler's railroad, was apparently ahead of its time—or perhaps in the wrong place at the wrong time. The hotel's elegance stood out conspicuously in an otherwise shabby town. By the end of the '30s, the hotel, unable to fill its 200 guest rooms, shut down.

The completely restored Marriott's Casa Marina reopened in 1979. Today the hotel has over 300 rooms of varying degrees of quality and dimensions. Loft suites contain two bedrooms, full kitchens, and spectacular views of the Atlantic. The grounds of the Casa are meticulously maintained, terraced, and dotted with the same coconut palms, Bermuda grass and 500-foot long beachfront enjoyed by America's most "rich and famous" back in the Gatsby days. You don't have to stay at the Casa to marvel at its Spanish Renaissance architecture, giant arched doorways, and polished hardwood floors. Stop in to the lobby for a look. Or go out to the beach for a drink.

Ask about the many vacation packages offered here. Nightly rates during season are extreme; not so crazy in the off seasons. Call for rates, and don't say I didn't warn you.

DoubleTree Grand Key Resort
3990 South Roosevelt Blvd. ● 293-1818

Way on the other side of the island, a mile or so from the airport. Newest hotel in town, and very nicely done. Excellent pool area, and when you feel energetic, take a walk out on the South Roosevelt promenade that hugs the south side of the island. The seaside walk way is busy all day with walkers, bikers, roller bladers. No need to bring your car. To further discourage you, there is a parking fee! Rooms are very thoughtfully arranged. Bring a family, or a pal, or a lover, and in all cases you'll find exactly the correct combination of roommating. Hotel offers regular, complimentary shuttles to the airport, Old Town area, and the golf course. Food is fine. Service is lovely. A true getaway with the DoubleTree guarantee.

Eden House
1015 Fleming Street ● 296-6868 ● 800-533-KEYS

There once was a starving artist, a friend of mine, here in the tropics. About ten years ago he got a break and moved to New York City. (I hear you saying "That's a break?") There he became a big success. Nowadays, when he comes to Key West with his wife of the moment (he's had a couple), where does he stay? That's right: the Eden House. Nowadays, of course, he demands a room with a private bath.

And there you are. The Eden House has the kind of character that appeals to writers, like my old friend. Europeans particularly like it, too. There's an interesting ambiance, a history; and iron beds just like in your grandparents' house.

In 1990, the Eden House was roughed up for a filming to look like it did back in the 1960s. In real life it looked like a movie set. But in the resulting film, a stinker called *Criss Cross*, which must be Goldie Hawn's only bomb, the hotel looked legitimately funky. Before they left, the movie people put the place back together again, just as it had been before they arrived. This hotel has been through some changes!

The Eden House opened as the Gibson Hotel in 1924. Local legend has it that gangster Al Capone liked staying here, where he spent his days rocking in a favorite chair on the veranda. The rooms are small and efficient, clean and affordable. With some rooms you hang out near the pool, or on the sun deck or the veranda, or in a hammock beneath the cool shade of an enormous ficus tree in the backyard.

The pool is nice, with lots of decking, and a nearby private sun deck allows topless sunbathing. Breakfast and lunch are sometimes served, sometimes not. It depends on how rattled the German chef is that season. But you can always count on a very good dinner, served in the outdoor dining area, where authentic German food is served, as well as the standard American stuff—all of it outstanding.

Suites are the most expensive. You can also rent a private room with a bath, or, most cost-saving choice of all, rent a semi-private room and share a bathroom with one other room. During weekdays, in the summertime, you can get an even better deal. Ask about a European room and you might just find the very best deal in town.

Hilton Resort and Marina
245 Front Street ✺ 294-4000 ✺ 800-HILTONS

Brand-spanking-new hotel that developers claim they designed with an "historic flavor." In fact, it feels futuristic. Before the Hilton, it used to be that the best part of cruising out of Key West Harbor was the postcard-perfect view of the harborfront with its grand centerpiece, the 1891 red brick Custom House. Now, from the water, you've got to search the horizon for a tiny tip of red brick to know it's still there. The Hilton Resort has wrapped its 178 rooms around the poor little Custom House and nearly hidden it entirely. There's also a 400-car parking garage where nothing used to be.

The Harborside Hilton offers plenty of amenities: a private gym; private balconies in all rooms; a marina filled with plenty of charter boats for cruising or diving; and a free boat shuttle from the marina to Sunset Key, a tiny offshore island upon which an astonishing number of condominiums are being erected. On a spot of sandy shore the Hilton has set up a private beach for their guests.

Harbor-front dining is lovely, but not at lunchtime because of the heat. On the second floor, the deck bar has a sunset happy hour with live music.

But wait, there's more: a couple of yacht slips, and a harborwalk that connects the hotel to Mallory Square, the very heart of the downtown tourist area. The resort hopes to attract important business people with plenty of executive meeting rooms with computers and high-tech communication gadgets that business people need, even when they're getting away from it all. Rooms have big beds, wall safes, two phones, hair dryers, and ironing boards for really, really fastidious guests. Oceanfront rooms start at $300 a night. Kids stay free with their rich parents.

Otherwise, a variety of rooms, views, minimum stay requirements, and local holiday and events price-hikes must all be figured into the formula to find what rate you'll pay for a room. Too many variations and possibilities to list here. Use the 800 number and check for yourself. Happy hunting.

Island City House Hotel
411 William Street ✹ 294-5702 ✹ 800-634-8230

It's actually three guesthouses—circa 1889—in one compound, with private tropical gardens, a huge deck, jacuzzi and pool, all connected by a meandering red brick path. You can get lost in the Island City House's lush grounds and gardens. That is, I can, and I have. The Arch house, one of Key West's only remaining carriage houses, built in the 1880s, contains six suites, all with full kitchens, private baths, air conditioning and phones. All of the buildings have three-story wraparound porches that guests adore.

Nice features are hammocks on small porches of some units, many cats, and an excellent pool, nearly invisible because of the proliferation of lush plants.

Continental breakfast is served in the courtyard patio. Heavenly! Kids under 12 stay free. Make sure you know how to find your way to breakfast before you go to bed. No pets, no Spring Breakers, no parking available on premises. Rates are standard Key West rates.

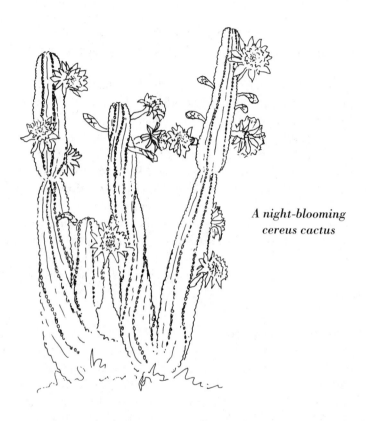

*A night-blooming
cereus cactus*

Key Lime Inn
725 Truman Avenue ▪ 800-642-4753

Key West's first motel. They called them motor courts in the 1930s, when
a retired circus performer, gruff but lovable Joe Zorsky, cleared away most
of the trees that remained of Key West Mayor Walter C. Maloney's one-
time tropical fruit grove. The grove covered an entire square block, and
right in the middle of it was the mayor's house. After Maloney's death
the house stood abandoned, and appeared so foreboding it was rumored
among neighborhood kids to be haunted.

Joe Zorsky built 18 tiny cottages on his cleared land and founded the
Cactus Terrace Motor Court. Zorsky, perhaps more tolerant of freaks than
most due to his background in the circus, befriended necrophiliac Dr.
Count von Cosel after he was arrested and charged with "not burying a
body." (See von Cosel's story on page 276). When an army of reporters

arrived on the island, Zorsky helped set up von Cosel's interview on the grounds of the Cactus Terrace.

In the 1950s Zorsky, who sometimes juggled for his guests, bought one of the island's very first televisions and set it up outdoors for community viewing. Zorsky's neighbors were invited to join his guests in watching the amazing invention. In 1971 Zorsky was shot to death in a burglary. New owners bought the place, installed air conditioning, a pool, and renamed it Key Lime Village.

A reconfigured and reorganized Key Lime Inn re-opened in January, 1999, by the historical property's newest owner Julia Fondriest. Fondriest has done a masterful restoration of the original Maloney house and has rearranged the property to provide for plenty of parking. There are still 37 rooms, cottages and bungalows, but they've been substantially upgraded. The gardens, once a lush grove of fruit trees, is being restored also.

The ambitious Fondriest's latest aquisition is the Lighthouse Court, which follows.

Lighthouse Court
902 Whitehead Street ✹ 294-9588

For many, many years this was Key West's largest exclusively for men hotel. But a new owner took over not so long ago and not the place welcomes all comers, which is great because it is a terrifice property, with forty-two suites, rooms and cottages. The compound, surrounded by very high privacy walls, is directly across the street from the Hemingway House and next door to the Key West Lighthouse, a 92-foot tower from where nosy tourists strong enough to climb to the top can see right into the grounds as you sip your morning coffee on the poolside deck. Full breakfast and lunch are served daily from 8 a.m. till 4 p.m. in a courtyard cafe and bar. The bar stays open into the evening. The gym is much more than adequate. All rooms are newly redecorated and have phones, televisions, and mini-refrigerators. Many have private baths; some rooms share baths.

La Concha Hotel
430 Duval Street ▪ 296-2991 ▪ 800-745-2191

The San Sebastian Troubadours of Spain performed at the grand opening when the seven-story La Concha Hotel opened in January, 1926. Advertised as "the only absolute fireproof hotel in Key West," the La Concha was patronized by high society until the Depression years. The demise of the Overseas Railroad in 1935 spelled disaster for this one, and the Casa Marina hotel. Like many downtown buildings, the La Concha, located right in the center of Duval Street, was closed for several years. On the hotel's roof, the Top, a seedy bar with tall windows offering its customers panoramic views of the island, continued to do business. Customers reached the Top via two ancient elevators that carried them through the decaying hotel, up to the roof.

The Holiday Inn gave the place a $20 million renovation in 1987 and ran it until 1996, when the Remington Hotel Corporation took over, then Crowne Plaza. Today the La Concha is very elegant indeed; the lobby and dining room are ultra-chic, cool, and subdued. Rooms are small but sweet, decorated with Victorian-era furniture and ceiling fans. The swimming pool is disappointing—very shallow, and the pool area is kind of crowded—but it's up a few stories, which means it gets a good breeze and uninterrupted sunshine.

The elevator still transports folks to the roof for one of the best bird's-eye views of the island. (The other great view is from the top of the Key West Lighthouse—but that's 88 steps up, with no elevator. And it costs $5 to get in.)

Over the years several people have made suicidal leaps from the top of the La Concha. The most famous suicide was local attorney Fred Butner, one-time president of the Monroe County Democratic Committee, who set up an elaborate scheme to make his suicide look like a murder. He jumped early on a clear, autumn morning. When he was found, several of his pockets were stuffed with cash, and in another pocket, a tape recorder that had apparently continued recording while he jumped. In his last minutes, Fred spoke as if he were defending himself against his black-mailer, ostensibly in conversation with his former secretary. "Hello, Susan. I got your note. Here's the hush money you demanded in your letter. What do you mean, this isn't enough? You've upped the price? I don't have that kind of money!! Wait! No! NO!" Then, the thud, as he landed on a carport roof, six stories down. In his office, investigators found copies of blackmail notes supposedly signed by the secretary, obviously forged by Butner. Within hours, the lawyer's evil plot unraveled when it was learned that the former secretary had been nowhere near the La Concha that morning and that Butner was in some trouble so sinister he chose to kill himself rather than face the scandal that was sure to follow. What was it? No one knows—except his psychiatrist. And he's not talking.

The news crews from *Hard Copy*, and the writers from the *National Enquirer* are all gone now, so all's quiet and subdued once again at the La Concha Hotel. Cocktail time at sunset at the Top is still glorious. Don't miss the view; And take advantage of the lovely photo opportunities on top of Key West's highest building; Pose on the western side of the roof with the Key West Harbor in the background, and possibly a cruise ship or two behind you. A strange anachronism, indeed.

The La Concha has 160 rooms and suites. The Hemingway and the Tennessee are two-bedroom suites, with king-sized beds. Now in the lobby, Starbucks Coffee!

Paradise Inn
819 Simonton Street ✹ 293-8007 ✹ 800-888-9648

If your idea of a vacation in paradise is simply luxuriating in the balmy, bright atmosphere of the southernmost islands, this is the place for you. Built in 1995 in classic Bahamian style, this luxurious inn includes two renovated cigarmakers' cottages, a newly constructed guest cottage and 15 guests suites housed in two-story buildings with traditional tin roofs and blue Bahamian shutters and porches. Gardens are exquisite, featuring fruit-bearing Spanish lime trees, fragrant night-blooming jasmine and ylang-ylang tree. Brick walkways are lined with sculptures by local artist John Martini, as well as Latan palms and Barbados cherry trees. These gardens have earned for the Paradise Inn an Award of Merit from the Florida Chapter of the American Society of Landscape Architects.

There's a heated pool, whirlpool spa, and a lotus pond, home to Japanese koi, and lots of decks, verandas, and balconies. It's difficult to believe that this cleverly designed oasis takes up a little less than one acre of land. Space is so well utilized that you never feel crowded.

Free off-street parking is a plus, if you insist on using a car on the island. More likely you'll park it and leave it parked. You're within walking distance of everything.

This is a premium inn, with premium prices ranging from $175-$355 in the off-season to $270-$545 at the height of season.

Pier House
1 Duval Street ☛ 296-4600 ☛ 800-327-8340

When it was built in 1965, the Pier House Resort, gulfside at the foot of Duval Street, was the first of the modern, upscale resorts on the island, and for many years enjoyed a reputation of being the place to stay. (Now there are literally dozens of choices.) The complex of low-rise, box-like buildings is greatly enhanced by spectacular gardens and maze-like tile walkways. There are several bars and bistros, all of them quite pricey, but also top-shelf quality. You might expect the rooms to be much more extravagant then they are. But guests are treated well at the Pier House, and that's part of what they come here for. Employees, beautiful and haughty, appear to have been are hired for their looks and their attitudes.

An army of rich and famous have stayed here, or at least hung out at the bars or eaten in the restaurant. John Travolta. Liz Taylor. Margaux Hemingway. Jimmy Buffett. Truman Capote. Tennessee Williams. Big-time drug smugglers. And lots of Miami *nouveau riche*.

The tiny beach feels very European. Women take their tops off. Guys with big bellies talk on cellular phones and puff cigars. Children play at the water's edge. The pool is pristine and still inviting, in spite of its advanced age. The Caribbean Health and Beauty Spa on the property is a great plus, too. You'll think you're in Switzerland! At night, huge tarpon swarm around an underwater spotlight beneath the pier—a oddly hypnotizing sight. Late in the evening the after-theater crowd gathers at the Wine Galley where Bobby Nesbitt is the piano man at the piano bar. Sunset at the Havana Docks, where One World performs, is memorable, too.

A brand-spanking-new, five-story building with suites as well as rooms opened in recently. Rooms are available at a variety of rates, from $200 to $300 in the off season; $300 to $400 in season. Rooms in the new building with views of the Gulf of Mexico are considerably more expensive.

The Reach Hotel (Wyndam)
1435 Simonton Street ✹ 296-5000 ✹ 800-874-4118

The last time I lunched at the Reach Hotel, the waiter told my companions and me that Maria Shriver was scheduled to arrive a half hour hence with a party of eight. We ate slowly and were having our coffee when Maria arrived with her entourage: her three children, one of whom was a brand-new baby; the baby's nurse; the other children's nanny; and two bodyguards. Maria looked our way and flashed us a somewhat beleaguered, though friendly, smile.

"She's incredibly nice," the waiter confirmed a few minutes later, somewhat disappointed.

That happened before the Marriott Corporation took over the Reach Resort and sucked the character out of the place—just when it was beginning to have some. The Reach is still quite beautiful in its own way. But a shabbiness and a pedestrian atmosphere have crept into a property that was, in its day, quite spectacular. Gone are the little things that made it special, like the spiffy little gourmet deli, the superb croissants and desserts created by the house baker, and The Library Bar, where retired editor and movie producer Frank Taylor held court in a bar created just for him. The lobby bathrooms, however, are still some of the most spectacular on the island.

The dining room looks a lot better after dark than it does by day, when sunlight pours through French doors. The once-tiled floors are now covered with a nondescript-colored carpet. In summertime, the oceanside dining room and deck open only for dinner, and, until sunset, the only bar open is the beachside bar.

The Reach beach, a white, natural-sand bay, is one of the nicest on the island. That's why it's so crowded. Not everyone you see sunning here is staying here. Reach guests share the pool, and the waterfront, and a small third-floor gym with guests from nearby guesthouses and B & Bs, who all receive passes to the Reach facilities. The crowds can get pretty thick. And forget about swimming laps in the pool; it's small and always busy!

Rates on rooms with ocean views cost the most. Call the Marriott Reservation Center at 800-228-9290, or call the hotel directly for rates.

The Marquesa Hotel
600 Fleming Street ☞ 292-1919 ☞ 800-869-4631

Here's the extra feature that makes the Marquesa Hotel just a tad different, some might say finer, than every other resort in town: in every closet, next to the fluffy, white waffle-weave cotton guest robes, there is an umbrella, emblazoned with the Marquesa's elegant emblem. The umbrellas don't get much use. It rarely rains in Key West. But the fact that they're there, at the ready in every room, is an indication of how the Marquesa pampers its guests.

The Marquesa has been showered with awards since opening its magnificently renovated doors in 1988. Of particular note is the Zagat Survey, which recently named the Marquesa 17th best hotel in the U.S.! The management works hard to keep the accolades coming with charming features like live orchids in every room, twice-daily maid service, Godiva chocolates at turndown, and room service available for breakfast and dinner. Parking is plentiful and free. All rooms have telephones, voice mail, TV, AC, and security safes. Grounds feature two pools in a meticulously tended split level garden.

The Marquesa, located on a block in the center of old town, is well over 100 years old. The main building was built in 1884 as a single family home. Later the house was converted to commercial use and was, at different times, a haberdashery, the original Fausto's Food Palace, and a bicycle shop. In 1901, the rear of the house was partitioned into 21 sleeping spaces with two decrepit bathrooms. The house was inherited by a daughter, who was a Catholic nun. For many years the place was owned and operated from afar by an order of nuns in New York. Current owners bought the building from them in 1987, did a massive 9-month-long restoration, and opened the first version of the Marquesa Hotel, 15 elegant units. In 1993, they purchased two neighboring historic buildings transformed them into 12 additional guest rooms.

In the Marquesa's cool, bright lobby there are amazing photographs of the Conch-Victorian buildings that are the Marquesa, as they were many years ago, as they are today, and as they appeared throughout the multimillion dollar restoration, for which the Marquesa has also garnered awards.

Like everywhere on the island, room rates are highest in winter and holiday weekends. Choose a standard room or a junior suite. No kids under 12; no pets.

Sheraton Suites

2001 South Roosevelt Boulevard • 292-9800 • 800-45BEACH

This gigantic complex of nearly identical suites, all 184 of them decorated in turquoise, gray, pink and peach, is a frightening glimpse of the
future of Key West and the Florida Keys—if the developers and hotel
chains have their way with the islands. If you're looking for a homoge-
nized version of coral island-architecture and ambiance, you'll like it
here. The hotel is not ten years old yet, so it is still glowing with new-
ness.

Bathrooms here are elaborate. Each commode is in its own private
little room; king bed suites have jacuzzi bathtubs; twin double-bed suites
don't. That's the only difference. Every suite has many mirrors and drawers to tuck away your stuff (everybody brings too much), an ironing
board, a wet bar, a microwave oven and a coffeemaker. The refrigerator
is stocked with items like Evian Water, the 8-ounce size, for $3.25.
Sunglasses with the Sheraton logo cost guests $12. Coffee, which you
make with hot water and instant granules, is free.

The food in the Sheaton dining room is very, very good. Every time
I've had the good fortune to eat there, I've been impressed with the quality. Prices are reasonable, too. It's definitely an attraction for me.

Across Highway A1A is Smathers Beach. Some rooms have an ocean
view; others overlook the pool and garden courtyard. Less expensive
rooms face other hotel buildings. All come with different rates. In the
brochure, the Sheraton calls this location "on the sunrise side of the
island," which is apt: there is a majestic sunrise here, and a lovely oceanside walking and bicycling path. A couple of good restaurants—Martha's
and Benihana—are a very pleasant mile walk from the Sheraton. This is
a favorite promenade for locals, and a very busy beach during the height
of tourist season. You don't want to be here during Spring Break, when
college kids turn the place into a modern-day *Where The Boys Are*.

There is parking, and the hotel offers transportation to the downtown
area. The historic district and Old Town Key West are just a little too far
to walk to and from each day, even if you do get up with the sunrise. The
free trolley shuttle service is convenient, but you'll need a taxi if you're
staying downtown to party till the wee hours.

The Sheraton offers many packages and deals throughout the year.
The national reservation desk is open 24 hours a day at 800-325-3535.

Southernmost Motel
1319 Duval Street ✺ 296-6577 ✺ 800-354-4455

Aside from the standard amenities, there's nothing out of the ordinary here. This is a garden variety resort destination motel. At a desk in the motel lobby you can rent bikes or mopeds or hook up with tours, snorkeling trips, and sunset cruises. Location is dandy, right on Duval—but what location in downtown Key West isn't great? You'll find a parking place in the Southernmost's big lot, although you won't need your car, just some comfortable walking shoes.

There's a nice pool, and if you want sand, a beach. South Beach, owned by the City of Key West and frequented by a motley group of locals and tourists, is about a block from the motel. There's an eatery, a bar and a raw bar on the beach. Waitresses come around and take your drink orders so you can sun and imbibe at once. It's a good beach for kids, too—sandy and shallow. Guests of the Southernmost are also invited to enjoy the pool and sun pier at Southernmost Motel's nearby cousin, the South Beach Oceanfront Motel.

Summer rates are lowest. Children under 18 stay free with parents. You'll pay $10 for an extra person in the same room. Call for rates.

South Beach Oceanfront Motel
508 South Street ✺ 296-5611 ✺ 800-354-4455

This oceanside motel's most important feature is its proximity to the Atlantic. You'll find the standard amenities here, as well as a gate that leads you to South Beach, the public beach right next to the motel. There is also an olympic-sized pool and a sun pier.

Parallel to the South Beach Motel pier is the Atlantic Shores, and their wild and wonderful pool and sun pier where guests are invited to bare their souls, and their bodies. The area is the daytime hangout of bartenders, dancers, and other beautiful people of the night. The G-string crowd is clearly visible there, and clearly unbothered by it.

Prices here are jumpy, but fair. They rise and fall according to what traffic will allow. Lowest rates are between May and early December. Just like everywhere.

Traveler's Palm Garden Cottages
815 Catherine Street ☛ 294-9560

Seven cottages surrounding a communal pool and garden, all secluded behind a high, flower-covered fence, and connected by red brick walkways, this private compound takes up nearly a full city block. This is the place Charles Kuralt rhapsodized about in his best seller *Charles Kuralt's America*. His bungalow was the very best one in the place—two bedrooms and a private pool with a fence of its own inside the compound fence.

"Is this the pool where Charles Kuralt swam naked?" I asked.

"So he says," laughed a personable young lady with an English accent. "Everyone wants to know about that! Yes, this is where he stayed. But we don't know what he did here, of course. There's a privacy fence."

The Charles Kuralt Cottage, as it has come to be known, is $375 a night during season, and $300 in the off season.

The Old Town neighborhood is kind of iffy in an overgrown, many-cats sort of way, but it's well on its way to gentrification. It's certainly safe, and it's colorful. The busy downtown area, Duval Street and all its thrills, is a short hike away—maybe farther than out-of-shape folks, or people not accustomed to the humidity, might want to walk. A nearby Cuban restaurant, El Siboney, is considered by many islanders to be the best one in town. (If Charles Kuralt dined at El Siboney, he didn't mention it in his book.)

The Traveler's has off-street parking, kitchens in most units, jacuzzis, barbecues, and, thanks to that high wall and many palms and flowers, a wonderful sense of separation from the rest of the busy world. Studios, one-bedroom apartments and private rooms have various prices, are very fairly priced.

The inn's owners, Clyde Hensley and wife Brigit, confessed to Kuralt that, though they'd enjoyed creating the Travelers Palm, they were growing restless and anxious to rid themselves of all their earthly possessions. But when Kuralt's book came out, with its glowing description of the Hensley's, their kids, and their dog, people began flocking to the place for a Kuralt kind of experience.

"We're having too much fun to leave now," Hensley says.

Bed and Breakfasts

Avalon Bed and Breakfast
1317 Duval Street ✦ 294-8233-✦ 800-848-1317

This fine house has had a long and colorful past. Listed on the national Historic Register, it was built in 1902 by a Cuban physician and named the Cuban Club Hotel. It was a meeting place for the local Cuban Club. Later it was converted by the same doctor into St. Joseph's Hospital. During the golden years of the middle 1920s it was the elegant Oceanview Hotel. It closed during the Depression, and reopened as the Casa Blanca Boarding House in 1952. The cheap, comfortable house was a beloved winter retreat for many, some of whom returned year after year to soak up a month or two of soft winter sun.

The house was restored and transformed into a more upscale bed and breakfast in 1992. New owners in 1998 are steadily fine-tuning. All 10 rooms have phones, voice mail, private baths, queen-sized beds, TV, AC, and a fridge. On-site managers run the place with intelligence and charm. They know the island. Breakfast is served European cafe style, on a wide deck with a view of the Atlantic. It's on the quiet end of Duval Street, across the street from the amazing new Butterfly Museum. Some parking. Prices are quite reasonable and the inn is very comfortable.

Center Court Historic Inn and Cottages
916 Center Street ✦ 296-9292 ✦ 800-797-8787

Just a half block from Duval Street, Center Court is a compound of cigar-maker's cottages nicely renovated by beautiful and bright Naomi Van Steelandt. After its completion in 1994, Center Court received several awards for historic preservation. Center Court features tropical gardens surrounding a small but lovely pool and jacuzzi. There's an exercise pavilion and a private European sun deck where you may sunbathe naked, but you've got to put your suit back on to venture into the common area for a swim in the pool. Breakfast is expanded continental, which means muffins, fruit juices, coffees and teas. Center Court has become a favorite stay for models working on location for one of many international fashion catalogs shot in Key West during balmy winter months. They love that exercise room. And because it's fairly new, everything in the place is in good working order, and very clean.

Almost everything you'll want to see in Key West is within walking distance, or rent a bike at the bicycle rental shop on the corner. Center Court is located on two-block-long Center Street, that runs through an old Key West neighborhood. Bordering blocks are a marginal blend of old and new. The guesthouse property, however, seems blissfully private and separate from the neighborhoods that surround it. The area is very safe as well as convenient, too.

Center Court has four double rooms in a main guesthouse, several efficiency cottages, one and two two-bedroom cottages scattered in the neighborhood. Children are welcome in cottages, and so are small pets. All rooms have private baths, phones, TVs, air conditioning and ceiling fans. You can put your jewelry in a safe, and every unit gets its own hair dryer. Rates are Key West standard and well worth it.

Banana tree

Courtney's Place
720 Whitmarsh Lane ✦ **294-3480** ✦ **800-869-4639**

Kid friendly. Pet friendly. Baby boomer friendly. Hey, it's friendly! Courtney's is named after the daughter of Nashville songwriter Chuck Krumel and his designer wife Linda. Linda passed away in 2005 and Courtney herself is mostly in charge of things nowadays. Courtney's Place is a tiny enclave of renovated conch cottages located between Simonton and Elizabeth streets on Whitmarsh Lane. The first time you wind your way through Old Town neighborhoods to find this little corner of the world, you'll wonder if you'll ever find your way back out again! You will, but you won't necessarily want to. Much of the island once looked like this—innocent and slow; now, it's a vanishing scene. No two units are alike at Courtney's. Cottages have three, two or one bedroom, all with complete kitchens. Linda Krumel was the architect/designer. Her work is clever and spirited. And durable. You'll probably take some of her ideas on utilizing small spaces home with you.

When the Krumel's good friend, the late Shel Silverstein, moved to Key West, he gave Linda the key to his newly purchased little old Conch house and asked her to renovate and design the outside and the interior exactly as she liked. Whatever she liked, he promised, he would like, too. And he did. I like to imagine the two of them in Heaven right now, renaming and rearranging, drinking and dining at God's sushi bar and having a ball.

Courtney's offers standard amenities, big breakfasts, and an informal ambiance. Park your car in Courtney's free lot. Courtney's rates don't rise and fall all over the calendar. There are winter rates. There are summer rates. Period. Courtney's is booked way in advance by people who come year after year. Rooms; suites; cottages. All rates are for two-person occupancy only. Extra people: $20. Kids under 12 stay free. If you have a pet you'll be asked to pay an extra $25, which covers the length of your visit.

Curry Mansion Inn
511 Caroline Street ✦ **294-5349** ✦ **800-253-3466**

An astute travel writer once described the experience of staying at the Curry Mansion as being much like visiting a rich, eccentric aunt. You might compare it to time-traveling back 100 years and staying in the home of one of Key West's wealthiest families.

Amenities are standard—private baths, phones, mini-refrigerators, TVs, and breakfast by the pool. But the hospitality here, like this century-old mansion, is polished and old-world. Guests are welcome to roam the mansion as they please. Favorite activities include snapping photos in the formal 19th-century-era dining room, whiling away an afternoon in the well-stocked library, and chatting with hosts Al and Edith Amsterdam at cocktail hour by the pool, sometimes with live entertainment.

Several older types of rooms and suites are available in the house, while some newer rooms were added on more recently. You may well prefer staying in one of the exterior units. Since the Curry Mansion is a museum, too, (see the Museums chapter of this book for details) paying sight-seers wander in and out of the museum all day. They won't enter your room, of course, but you will hear them milling in the halls. If privacy is of prime importance to you, if your ideal vacation is lying on a chaise and reading trashy novels by a quiet pool, this probably is not the right place for you.

Rates are Key West standard. Higher in season and during special events and holidays. Some parking is available, but from this location you really don't need a car to get to the best places on the island.

Duval Gardens
1012 Duval Street ☎ 292-3379 ☎ 800-867-1234

There's no pool at this recently renovated wooden house, and the style is more Florida house than conch house, but there is a jacuzzi. The location of Duval Gardens, at the corner of Duval Street and Truman Avenue, is super. Not everybody wants to be this close to the coursing river of humanity ever-surging up and down this famous tropical thoroughfare, but if you're one to stay up all night, this is definitely the place for you.

Rooms are light, bright, airy and private, each with its own private entrance. Hosts Andrea and Bryan lay out a big, hot breakfast, featuring bracing main courses like a sausage-and-cheese casserole, or French toast. The place accommodates up to twelve guests at a time. An hour before sunset, a spiked tropical punch and snacks are served on the front balcony. Rooms are equipped with usual amenities, including refrigerators and telephone answering machines.

Guests get discounts on bicycle rentals at the Moped Hospital less than a block away, and there's a safe bicycle storage locker at the inn. Off street parking. Room rates are fairly priced.

Duval House
815 Duval Street ✺ 294-1666 ✺ 800-223-8825

Considering Duval House's location on the island's busiest street, it should encourage you to know that the place has been named "one of the ten special, secluded, romantic inns in the USA" by *Vacations Magazine*. In September, 2000, Ft. Lauderdale's *Sun Sentinal Newspaper* readers chose Duval house as their favorite Key West guest house.

Many of the town's B & B's and guesthouses are new, but not this one. This is an old, long-established inn, with no unnecessary pretense. It's weathered, but in the very best sense. And within walking distance of everything you want to do and see.

Twenty-nine rooms, all different. Rooms, suites, efficiencies. Far from the hubbub, a spacious garden, pool, and gazebo. Hibiscus is the house flower; they're everywhere. Many rooms have skylights, and some have balconies or terraces. Parking is plentiful. And here's a new twist on the morning news: in the breakfast room each morning all current guests' hometown temperatures are posted.

Children over 12 are welcome. Manager Renner James is a sweetie, and knows absolutely everything there is to know about Key West. If you dare, call on the day you wish to arrive for a chance to find a bargain. The rare, un-booked room goes on sale in the afternoon.

Duval House guests are regulars. One family—cousins, aunts, in-laws and cousins—comes every December, for Christmas week. They party and shop all over town, and on Christmas morning gather in the gazebo to open their gifts. After gifts and the house (complimentary) continental breakfast by the pool, they gather their things together, bid each other fond farewells till next year, and hustle out to the airport for their flights home. Good prices, and well worth it.

Eaton Lodge
511 Eaton Street ✱ **292-2170** ✱ **800-294-2170**

Carolyn West's great-grandfather, Harry M. Stevens, invented the baseball scorecard as well as the drinking straw, an item originally used in
baseball parks. Today, his innovative spirit lives on in his enthusiastic
and capable granddaughter—proprietress of the Eaton Lodge.

Carolyn says she has found what she describes as "liberty in tranquility" in Key West. She's mad about the island, and her passion shows in
everything she says and does. Carolyn and her husband Steve bought the
house at the foot of Eaton Street a couple of years ago. Built in 1832, the
Eaton Lodge is one of the oldest wooden structures on the island. The
Wests lovingly restored the house and brought it up to its current state of
authentic, 19th-century wooden-house magnificence. The place is full of
nooks, unexpected pockets of serenity that particularly appeal to writers
and artists and other reflective souls. All rooms have private baths, televisions, telephones for free local calls, four-poster, carved-mahogany or
brass beds. And many antiques.

Throughout their numerous travels, Carolyn and Steve have been
collecting curious antiques, beautiful foreign objects like a mirrored Thai
spirit house, and countless other pieces of fine art. Now they have a
showplace for their unusual treasures. The living room is so full of things
to see it feels like a museum. Carolyn calls it "a feast for the eyes."

Carolyn bakes lots of breads and other treats for her guests, and
invites them to feel at home in her spacious kitchen. Breakfast is served
out in the garden, a lush tropical oasis planted with palms and a jungle of
bougainvillea encircling a plunge pool, jacuzzi and spa. Each evening,
seven chatty parrots oversee the sunset cocktail hour, with a complete,
self-serve bar in the garden as well. The garden is a popular setting for
weddings. Other amenities include bicycle rentals, and a library of books
that Carolyn keeps current. Room rates here begin at $95 and go up to
$260. But this is more than an inn. It's an experience. A vacation. A trip.

"Some people don't get this lifestyle at all," Carolyn says. "But for the
rest of us, it's Paradise."

Frances Street Bottle Inn
535 Frances Street ❧ 294-8530 ❧ 800-294-8530

The owner and host, a former Philadelphia insurance salesman, gets around in a wheel chair. So this inn is truly wheel chair accessible. The Bottle inn is a Historical Preservation Society winner and favorite Key West guesthouse in *Travel & Leisure* magazine; high ceilings, hardwood floors, wooden doors and roomy porches in a lovely Old Town neighborhood; very Southern ambiance and laid-back atmosphere; breakfast on the porch. And your kids and well-behaved pets are welcome.

The Frances Street Bottle Inn was completely restored in 1987 by Bob Elkins. When he bought it, it was a notch away from being a bona fide flophouse. Located on the corner of Frances and Southard streets, it is a nice walk away from Duval Street. Before it was a boarding house it was a corner grocery. Just before it's renovation, it was used as the set of the *Meteor* newspaper office in the short-lived Fox TV series *Key West*.

Seven air-conditioned rooms with private baths are furnished with queen or king sized beds. A jacuzzi is in the brick backyard. Expanded continental breakfast and evening social hour. No phones in the rooms. No off-street parking.

Gardens Hotel
526 Angela Street ❧ 294-2661 ❧ 800-526-2664

The extensive gardens that cover nearly a quarter of a city block were designed in the 1930s by a wealthy botanical enthusiast named Peggy Mills. Peggy devoted years to collecting the exotic flora you see here and created this jungle-like garden of palms, sub-tropical plants and flowers. She paved the grounds with red bricks. The brick walkways are still intact, as are many of the fountains and wrought iron furniture groupings. Peggy Mills' famous tinajones, huge earthenware jars for rain collecting designed in Cuba in the 1800s, weigh over a ton each! Peggy Mills is gone now to that great garden in the sky, but her splendorous earthly garden still thrives. Current Gardens Hotel owners consider this soft, green haven in the center of Old Town as one of the island's greatest treasures. It is a private place, however. To wander these palatial grounds, you've got to rent a room.

The house, built in the 1870s, was restored to its present state of opulence and opened as a hotel in 1993.

The Gardens Hotel was resold for $7 million in 2004. It has been named among the best hotels in the world by Conde nast Traveler, and has hosted such luminaries as George Clooney and Cher. There's a pool, a full private bar, and white marble bathrooms. Each of the 17 rooms and suites are different from each other. The newest owner has installed new lamps, duvets, curtains, and paintings by local artists in every room. Guests enjoy their lovely continental breakfast in the bright, white breakfast porch. Even the people who work here are particularly good-looking.

The Gardens aims for high end, and the prices match. When people ask me where I would stay if I were a visitor to the island I tell them I'd choose the Gardens Hotel. No question.

Key West Bed and Breakfast
415 William Street • 296-7274 • 800-438-6155
Built in 1898, this attractive guesthouse is full of works by many of the island's most fantastic artists—some of them still living, many of them not. Works of artists like sculptor Jim Rache, and painters Craig Biondi, Ron Clemons, Van Eno, and hostess Jodie Carlson are represented here.

Throughout the house you'll find high ceilings, hardwood floors and natural Dade County pine walls. Eight guest rooms are all fitted with queen-sized beds, but have no televisions or telephones in the rooms, and air conditioning is in guest rooms only. Four rooms on the second floor share two bathrooms. If you must share bathrooms, these—with lots of tile and high-gloss-painted surfaces, are as nice as they can be. A porch at one end of the second-floor hallway is very comfortable, with a large hammock and an old-fashioned porch swing. In the downstairs common areas there is a piano for anyone who can play it, a good library, and more great porches. The kitchen is spacious, utilitarian, and unstoppably cheery.

Breakfast is fresh fruit. There's a juicer and lots of oranges, so if you want fresh-squeezed, go for it. Baked goods are cooked on the premises each evening, in time for breakfast the next morning.

In the back you'll find a dry sauna, an outdoor shower, and a large jacuzzi. Orchids are everywhere because Jodie loves them.

La Mer Hotel and Dewey House
504 and 506 South Street ✺ 296-5611

Surprisingly, in Key West there is only one guesthouse with an ocean view, and this duo of turn-of-the-century houses is it. The Dewey House, one of the places where philosopher John Dewey stayed on some of his many visits to the island, has recently been redesigned and incorporated into the La Mer complex. These are upgraded guesthouses, appealing to honeymooners and others seeking the upscale romance of an oceanside retreat. The rooms, all with private baths and several with ocean views, are decorated in an elegant, contemporary motif.

An extended continental breakfast, featuring hot and cold dishes, fruit, and fresh pastries, adds to the drama, and so does the palm-strewn beach located just behind the houses. Bathrooms in the Dewey House feature bathtub jacuzzis; all rooms have televisions and telephones. The Dewey House is a totally smoke-free environment. Kids under 18 are unwelcome at both houses.

The La Mer, with eleven rooms, and Dewey House, with eight rooms, are part of the Old Town Resort complex that includes South Beach Oceanfront Motel and the Southernmost Motel, located in the same neighborhood. Guests at all facilities are welcome to use pools at the motels, parking, and a guest reservation office at the Southernmost. The South Beach Motel's breezy sunning pier that juts out into the Atlantic is a favorite place.

On South Beach behind both guesthouses, actress Kelly McGillis and her husband Fred recently opened yet another Key West restaurant. The Duval Beach Club is open from 8 a.m. till 11 p.m. daily, serving meals and cocktails indoors, or on the beach.

La Pensione Inn
809 Truman Avenue ✺ 292-9923 ✺ 800-893-1193

A renovated Victorian mansion built in 1891 and restored a hundred years later, La Pensione is listed on the National Historic Register. It has only seven rooms, all of them spacious, with private baths, furnished with king-sized beds. No television, no telephones. Breakfast waffles, muffins, fresh fruit, and endless coffee are served on a massive, carved-mahogany dining-room table. There's a private pool, lovely trees and, very nearby, the elegant, double-steepled St. Mary's Star of the Sea

Catholic Church. There's off-street parking and one wheelchair-accessible room. Rates are on a par with comparable properties. Management is always on the premises. The location is sensational—a few blocks from all the best restaurants and museums. No pets. No kids. This is a place to luxuriate. Relax, for heaven's sake!

Merlinn Inn
811 Simonton Street • 296-3336 • 800-642-4753
Since taking the place over in 1997, the Merlinn Inn's newest owner has made plenty of changes and upgrades. It used to be that you couldn't see the Merlinn Inn for the thick hedge of aurelia that marked the front boundary. That's gone now, so from the street you see the building's wide veranda and the inviting rocking chairs on it. You can also look in to see a sea hibiscus tree, coconut palms, mango and sapodilla trees, and a pool in a central courtyard.

Property pets are two parrots and a cat. Yours are not welcome. One room is handicapped accessible. All units are non-smoking. There are 10 standard rooms, 5 king suites, and 5 cottages with separate bedrooms and living rooms. All are fitted with bathrooms, air conditioning, TV. No phones, but there is a phone booth outside. Six off-street parking places. Children in cottages only. Breakfast is a nice expanded continental (*i.e.* fresh baked goods; there are a number of fine bakers on the island these days) and served by the lily pond.

The Mermaid and the Alligator
729 Truman Avenue • 294-1894 • 800-773-1894
The classic Queen Anne-style building that is now home to the Mermaid and the Alligator guesthouse was built in 1904, a year before the stunning St. Mary's Star of the Sea Catholic Church, directly across the street. The Mermaid is owned, operated and occupied since January, 1997, by Dean Carlson and Paul Hayes. The team lived in Hawaii for five years, prior to arriving in Key West. They live here now, they say, because in addition to a fabulous tropical climate, our island has a wonderful, cozy sense of community that works well with their sense of tradition.

"We consider our place to be a traditional bed and breakfast," explains Dean, "because we live here, too. It's our home and we share it with our guests."

Wine and beer is served at happy hour. A grand breakfast is served in the gardens, in view of the elegant pool and Wilbur Thomas' sculpture of the mermaid and the alligator. (The sculpture, by the way, inspired the original developers to name the place after the piece, rather than the other way around.)

There are no TVs or phones in the island-elegant rooms, but there are private baths. Five rooms in all, each very different from the other. The Caribbean Queen Room, featuring a gargantuan Roman soaking tub, is most dramatic of all. The living room is cushiony and inviting. Dean says he's delighted when he finds a guest asleep on the couch in front of the TV, because then he knows he's accomplished his goal of providing an intimate and comfortable getaway for his clients.

Off-street parking! No smoking indoors. No pets. No children under 16.

Papa's Hideaway
309 Louisa Street ✺ 294-7709 ✺ 800-714-7709

Papa's is a small, homey operation, just two blocks from the Southern-most Point, and one block from Duval Street. Papa's offers small, adequate studios, 4 in all, each with a king-sized bed and pullout futon. Units have private baths, kitchenettes, patios and porch. A shared pool and jacuzzi are within the enclosed compound. Bread and muffin continental breakfast daily. Rent on these units is very affordable. Owner Ellen Nowlin, who has been running the house since 1994 with partner Pat McGee, says: "Our guests never feel crowded. We have plenty of room here." No pets. Well-behaved kids welcome. Off-street parking!

Bed and Breakfasts
• • •

Some Gay Guesthouses and Hotels

Alexanders
1118 Fleming Street ✴ 294-9919 ✴ 800-654-9919

The three houses that make up Alexanders contain sixteen rooms, and because these are turn-of-the century buildings adapted in 1981 to guest-house style, no two rooms are alike. In fact, each room or suite is very different from the next, all appointed in a casual, tropical island style. Third floor treehouse rooms with skylights and stained glass windows are particularly appealing. Some rooms have private decks and verandas.

Although this is a predominantly gay guesthouse, everyone is welcome—except children and pets; 70% of guests are men: 30% women. The swimming pool is open 24 hours a day. The grounds are private, and nude sunbathing is permitted on two of the decks. Items on the expanded continental breakfast change daily as does a daily cocktail hour, each day with a different theme, and featuring hors d'oeuvres and spirits. All rooms and suites are equipped with telephones, TVs, and refrigerators; several have wet bars.

Coconut Grove
817 Fleming Street ✴ 296-5107 ✴ 800-262-6055

This isn't the fanciest guesthouse, but it's the friendliest. There are twenty-two units here in three buildings, two on one side, and one on the other, of Fleming Street. The Coconut Grove has an interesting feature—a sun deck located above the third story of the main building, affording guests a beautiful and private panoramic view of the island.

Another feature at Coconut Grove is six complete apartments, with living rooms, bedrooms, kitchens, and decks. The apartments are fully equipped and are an excellent value.

The pool and jacuzzi (clothing optional) are open 24 hours a day. A full continental breakfast is served daily, and there's a happy hour in the common room every day but Sunday. Every room has a television and all but two have private baths; these two rooms share one bath.

Women are welcome, but 99% of the guests are men. Many of them are regulars. No pets, no off-street parking.

Heartbreak Hotel
716 Duval Street ✱ 296-5558

The owners say their simple, elegant and utilitarian hotel is located on the gayest block in downtown Key West. There's no phone and no pool at the Heartbreak Hotel but it's still a fun place to dwell. Sun at the Bourbon Street pool, and when you've had enough of that enjoy discovering the many great clubs, restaurants, and coffee shops just outside your door. Rooms are very clean and quite a deal. Guests share a community kitchen. Rates get better the longer you stay. And you won't need your car. Leave it at home. You can dwell here for a week or a month. The rates are great. But you can't park a car here. So leave it home.

The Equator Resort
818 Fleming Street ✱ 294-7775 ✱ 800-278-4552

The Equator is a meticulous restoration of an ancient enclave of dilapidated buildings. Men only. Very upscale. Back in the 1970's Bill Galchutt, of Miami, and John Kosik and Steve Bass, of Chattanooga, vacationed frequently in the balmy, friendly, old-fashioned laid-back town that was once Key West. Twenty-five years later, older, wiser, and with lots more resources, the trio decided to open their own gay guesthouse in tribute to those wonderful, carefree days of old.

"The Equator is a guesthouse for yesterday, today and tomorrow," explains Galchutt. "We try to capture what was wonderful about Key West then, and we try to make it what we feel a modern guesthouse should be today."

Toward that end, the Equator features data ports on every phone so that guests can plug in laptop computers. There's voice mail on room phones, a definite step into the new millennium. (Many guesthouses don't answer their phones 24 hours a day, so if you need to contact someone in them, you may well be out of luck.)

Every newly created room features a private bath, TV, complimentary robes and snacks. Pocket kitchens in some; just a fridge in others. The rooms are painted and tiled in Mediterranean tones; light and bright. Queen or king-sized beds. A couple of extra-long full beds. Also one handicapped accessible suite. All rooms are non-smoking.

Full, hot breakfast. Happy hour. Clothing optional around the heated pool and whirlpool. There's always somebody around on concierge duty. Like many guesthouses on Fleming Street, this one has no off-street parking. But why bother to bring a car? You can easily walk to wherever you need to go, or cab.

Curry House
806 Fleming Street ✺ 294-6777 ✺ 800-633-7439

This is the oldest, exclusively male guesthouse in the city. The atmosphere is subdued and rather reserved, which works well in this grand 1890 Victorian house. The house's nine rooms—seven of which have private baths and two share a bath—are furnished with period antiques. Rooms are also equipped with phones, refrigerators, clock radios, and French doors that open out onto long, wraparound verandas. (There's a communal television in the communal area.) Located in the center of Old Town, the Curry House is convenient to all the great restaurants, saloons and attractions. A pool and jacuzzi in the clothing-optional patio area make it unnecessary for guests to leave the premises if sun and relaxation is all they're looking for. A hot breakfast and afternoon wine are served daily. No off-street parking, but you'll find parking on the street, although you don't really need a car.

Oasis Guest House
823 Fleming Street ✺ 296-2131 ✺ 800-362-7477

and

The Coral Tree Inn
822 Fleming Street ✺ 296-2131

This is actually one property on two sides of the street, each house with its own name. Your host Victor manages to be in both places at once. This is an upscale property; the Coral Tree Inn was recently totally refurbished and is particularly new and shiny.

Both houses have large heated pools and, at the Oasis a 24-man jacuzzi! Clothing is optional around pools and decks. The daily continental breakfast is sumptuous and, in addition to a standard 6 o'clock wine and hors d'oeuvres, Victor serves afternoon pina coladas at the pool.

Although this is an exclusively gay-men operation, the sexual temperature here is tepid, Victor told me. You'll find much hotter houses nearby. The Coral Tree is more couple-oriented.

Guests in each house have keys to the other, since the houses share amenities. All rooms have televisions, VCRs, phones, refrigerators and private baths. Bicycles are available for rent. A comprehensive library gives information on the sights and restaurants on the island. Parking is available on the street.

At the Oasis there are two rooms that share one bath and these are the least expensive rooms on the property.

Pearl's Rainbow
525 United Street ✸ 292-1450 ✸ 800-749-6696

Formerly the Rainbow House, and before that, the Pines. This lovely inn has become the world's largest hotel exclusively for women, and added a new page to its distinctively unique history. Not only was the original building the Keys' first gay guest house, it was also the first inn to offer private baths in every room. Built originally as a boarding house for Cuban cigar factory workers, it was an apartment house before finally being converted into a guest house reserved exclusively for gay men and women. Now the men have been 86'ed altogether, and Pearl's Rainbow features 38 rooms and suites, every last one of them with a private bathroom. With the new expansion comes another chi chi pool, an additional deck, and a second hot tub. Continental breakfast is served in a pavilion in the garden area, between the pool areas.

Units are also outfitted with telephones, televisions, and sometimes, refrigerators. All rooms, from standard to deluxe, have queen beds, tropical decor, air conditioning and Bahama fans.

Location is wonderful. At the Rainbow House you won't need a car at all, since you're in the heart of the downtown, just off Duval Street, and yet on a quiet, safe street that's easy to wander back to late at night. The beach is a 5-minute walk away and the area is studded with great saloons and bistros.

Pearl's Rainbow is a well-managed operation, with a growing reputation. Newest owners are Heather Curruthers, and Leslie Leonelli, who met in New York City when they both performed in the Stonewall Chorale, the country's oldest mixed gay and lesbian chorus. Now they live in Key West exclusively, and run Pearl's Rainbow. Women—of any sexual orientation—preferring a women-only place to stay, are very welcome here. No men, children or pets.

Sea Isle Resort
915 Windsor Lane ✹ 294-5188 ✹ 800-995-4786

Sun-worshippers will be happy to know that this small resort boasts more sun decks and more sun per room than any other guesthouse in Key West. And you can take your sun on any one of three levels, or, work your way to the very top, where clothing is optional and sunbathing is very serious business. There's a hot tub on the third-level deck, too. If you've had enough sun, wait for nightfall—the hot tub is open 'round the clock.

Rooms at the Sea Isle feature queen-size beds, mini-fridges, and private baths. You'll find a good little gym to work out in, with lots of free weights and Nautilus machines. Off-street parking is plentiful. Pets are welcome—for an extra $10 per day. The resort is well-located on a relatively quiet street, yet well within easy walking distance of the best restaurants and shops. Rates are moderate.

Travel Information for Gay Tourists

Key West Business Guild
513 Truman Avenue ✻ 294-4603 ✻ 800-GAY-9759

Travelers considering Key West can write or call for specific information as well as a free guide to the city. The Key West Map & Directory is a complete listing of gay accommodations, businesses and attractions. Information packets are sent to all callers. Tourists are invited to visit the office and browse through literature supplied by guild members.

The guild was formed in 1978 by a group of business leaders from the gay community to promote Key West to the gay market. Members represent gay-owned and gay-friendly businesses.

The travel industry publication *Recommend Magazine* estimates that more than 20% of all tourists visiting Key West annually are gay or lesbian. The gay consumer usually spends more on the average than other tourists.

Gay and Lesbian Community Center
513 Truman Avenue ✻ 292-3223

Stop in for a chat with a local, for information, or to check out displays on local gay living and history. Nice, friendly people, mostly volunteers.

Gay Trolley Tours
294-4603

You'll know it's a gay tour from the rainbow festoons on the trolley. It's an excellent and informative tour of Key West highlighting the island's rich gay and lesbian history. For example, did you know that Key West was the first city in America to have an openly gay mayor? It was in 1982. He was Richard Heyman, of Grand Rapids, Ohio, and he was glorious. He was elected by a landslide, and served for two terms.

Saturdays at 11 a.m. only. Call for information on group rates.

Dining

WHERE SHOULD YOU EAT? The possibilities are staggering. Is it atmosphere you're looking for? Impeccable service? A good view? Ethnic cuisine? Gourmet food? It's all here—somewhere. The fun part is finding it. Investigate carefully; there are dozens of eateries to choose from, and you probably don't have dozens of evenings for experimentation.

In Key West, a tropical island with an ever-changing population and work force, few things remain the same for long. That's especially true in the restaurant business. The eatery your friends loved when they vacationed here last fall may have undergone some changes since then—perhaps a new chef is training or new management has taken over or the place is completely gone. That is not to say, if it's still there, that it won't be just as good as your friends remember it, maybe even better. That's what makes Key West dining, and life, such an adventure: nothing is ever the same way twice.

Keep in mind, too, that Key West's newspapers publish many glowing restaurant reviews throughout the year. The restaurant reviewers who write them, encouraged by free meals and spirits and royal treatment, can make even mundane places sound fantastic. Don't be fooled! No authentic restaurant critics work in this town. The reviews depend on advertising dollars: the bigger the ad, the more spectacular the kudos.

Remember, when making dinner reservations, that the height of the dinner rush in island restaurants is 8 p.m. Therefore, it's unwise to make reservations for dinner at eight, although, certainly, no one will say you can't. Even fifteen minutes earlier or later can make your dining experience a whole lot nicer.

All that said, be assured that fine dining and great food await you here. Try the seafood: dolphin and yellowtail, conch steaks and fritters; they're all unlike anything you'll find elsewhere.Cuban food is unique, and addictive, and very affordable. That's why, at the height of tourist season, Cuban restaurants are packed to capacity. This is the cuisine you'll find yourself craving when you get back home—it's that good. (Don't forget to pick up a cook book while you're on the island.)

Something else to consider: not all restaurants have children's menus, while some have very good ones. In a few restaurants you will be asked to go elsewhere if there are children in your party. If you have special needs for highchairs or children's seats, or handicap access, it is wise to call ahead and make arrangements, instead of simply showing up, fussy kids in tow, for dinner at eight (not eight!)

The following restaurants are some of the island's most popular, the ones that people will send you to when you ask them for a recommendation for a good place to eat. These brief descriptions will hopefully answer the most frequently asked questions about food, service, ambiance, and prices. Generally parking is a hassle. If there is ample parking, I will tell you. Otherwise, think about walking to the restaurant, or taking a cab.

Some Restaurants

Nine One Five
915 Duval Street ❦ 296-0669

From time to time the New York Times people come to our island for a quick look around and subsequent travel article. They do a mostly good job of heading away with a good overview of what's new and hot in the city. For the past few years the consistant topper on that list has been Nine One Five, a place as unpretentious as its name. The building, right on Duval, is Victorian featuring a gracious wraparound porch, perfect for people watching. Tasting, sharing, and ordering a bit at a time is encouraged. Excellent service. Lunch or dinner. Beer and wine.

The Cafe
509 Southard St. ❦ 296-5515

There is a sense of place, an aroma of steamed veggies and incense, a glint in the eyes of the young, healthy people who work them, that infuses every great vegetarian restaurant in which I've been. That same, comforting atmosphere has been created right here in Key West by the people at the Cafe and it is truly wonderful! The head chef, a lady I met in a yoga class, sports some lovely tattoos and knows her way around tofu, ginger and a whole lot more wholeseome goodies that make the food here absolutely delicious in addition to absolutely healthy. Since the doors opened, it's been packed. And deservedly so. They even deliver! Ask about daily specials, always glorious. Prices are good. Beer and wine.

Antonia's
615 Duval Street ✺ 294-6565

Sicilian and classical Italian cuisine. Two beautiful Italian women founded this place, Antonia and her childhood best friend, Claudia, who grew up in Rome together. Later Antonia came to Key West to start a restaurant with her husband, Chef Phillip Smith. Claudia, working for TWA in New York City, came for a weekend visit just around the time that Antonia and Phillip were running perilously low on set-up funds. Claudia invested her nest egg and became a partner. The partners are often the hostesses, while a tall, all-American blond named Tiffany tends the beer and wine bar.

Service is elegant but not fast. The tone is European, very laid back. If you're in a hurry, dine elsewhere. Same advice if you don't have lots of money. If, on the other hand, money and time are both plentiful, and you're looking for a romantic dinner that unfolds like a long-awaited love letter, make reservations at Antonia's. Menu is a la carte. Servings are small, but the food is so rich, you'll find your appetite satisfied very quickly. Save room for desserts, though; they're delicate and truly memorable. No parking, but municipal parking is located behind the restaurant off Simonton Street, next door to City Hall. Dinner only, from 6 p.m. Note: Antonia's contributes to AIDS Help with an annual and always well attended $125 a plate annual banquet. If you're in town for one of these, go. You'll meet some of the best people on the island, enjoy a fantastic meal, and contribute to AIDS Help!

Ambrosia Japanese Restaurant
1100 Packer Street ✺ 293-0304

Ambrosia is located in a tiny building that once housed a Cuban coffee shop and restaurant on the corner of Packer and Virginia streets. The conversion has been quite marvelous as every square inch of space is utilized with Eastern charm and wisdom. Ambrosia is often packed at the height of the dinner hour, and there are always lots of locals in the mix. The head chef, Masa, is also the owner. Before opening Ambrosia, Masa worked in several other Japanese restaurants on the island. He's been entertaining his ardent fans and followers, and satisfying the palates of sushi lovers both local and visiting, for a long, long time. There's tempura, too. Everything you order in this lovely Japanese restaurant is fresh, tasty, and beautiful to look at. Try black bean or ginger ice cream. Amazing! Wine and beer.

Bagatelle Restaurant
115 Duval Street ✻ 296-6609

Remember when Jackie Gleason on *The Honeymooners*, used to say "a mere bag of shells...," which was Ralph Kramden's bastardization of the phrase, "a mere bagatelle"? Well here you are: A mere bagatelle, Key West style. The big draw here is the wrap-around veranda. It's so damned inviting, although the view has been much compromised by new construction on a parking lot directly across the street. Not only did they pave Paradise, they put a brick addition onto the bank and blocked what was once a pretty view. Too bad.

Dining on the veranda is still lots of fun, though. The flow of humanity down at this end of Duval is thick and colorful. Bagatelle has good food, but not great food. Servers are efficient and will happily answer all your questions about the menu. One of the best things you'll eat at Bagatelle is the seafood chowder - thick, creamy and memorable. Lunchtime sandwiches and salads are imaginative. Look for portebello mushroom with polenta, and Jamaican chicken. Lobster and stone crab dinners are the most expensive, like everywhere. Bagatelle opens for lunch at 11:30 daily. Dinner from 6 p.m.–10 p.m.

Bahama Mama's
324 Petronia Street ✻ 294-3355

Southernmost soul food. Owner Cory Sweeting is a 4th generation Bahamian. The restaurant's logo is Cory's grandmother wielding a wooden spoon. Most of the recipes are hers, too. Feast on conch chowder, conch salad, and conch fritters, chicken wings, black bean chili, plantains, pigeon peas and rice, collard greens, crab and rice, cheese grits, and don't miss the shrimp hash cakes, a pancake-like delicacy. Excellent fish, curried ginger chicken, served in a charming Caribbean-spirited courtyard, located in Key West's own Bahama Village.

Don't be in a hurry here. Come for an adventure with your dinner. Enjoy the pots of flowers, bright murals, noisy roosters, languid cats, bicyclists and pedestrians. Beer and wine only. Schedule is by mood, but they aim to open for breakfast by 9 a.m. Monday through Friday, and for lunch by 11. They close by 10 most nights. Walk or cab. There's little parking in this area.

Banana Cafe
1211 Duval Street ✎ 294-7227
Mario Sanchez, woodcarver whose folkish images of old Key West are nationally renowned, was born in this house in 1907. (See a collection of Sanchez works at East Martello Tower Gallery.) Danielle Dahon and her son Christopher Collect came to Key West for a short vacation in June of 1992, and ended up signing the lease for the Banana Cafe two weeks later. They've been here ever since, serving fine food, beer and wine with a French street-cafe flair. Bacon, lettuce and tomato sandwiches are slathered with homemade mayonnaise on fresh-baked French bread; crepes are stuffed with goat cheese and walnuts, or Norwegian salmon and sour cream and onions. Service is good. Eggs with toast and bacon cost twice as much as you'd pay in a diner for the same thing—and they don't butter the toast! But hey, that's the French way. Several dinners nightly at prix-fixe price. Also, live jazz at dinnertime. No off-street parking, but parking is usually available on side streets in the neighborhood. Hours: around 7 a.m. to 11 p.m.

Blue Heaven
729 Thomas Street ✎ 296-8666
The Blue Heaven is is a terrific place for breakfast, lunch or dinner, but the word is out and tourists have made the restaurant a must-see stop on their Key West itineraries. The lines have become legendary. Come early. Sundays are impossible. Summertime is a good time, if you can bear the heat. No reservations. No off-street parking. Lots of shade from huge, ancient trees. Chickens, dogs and cats are commonplace, but usually well-behaved. The food is wonderful.

But it's not just a restaurant; it's art galleries and shops, too. The building has wonderful history: There used to be a boxing ring that was used by several local sparring partners of Ernest Hemingway. And cockfights were there, too. Even a rooster graveyard, complete with tiny tombstones, remains in one corner of the property. Ask to see the gambling wall, once a blackboard listing scores and odds of various sports. Also a water tower that once stood on Little Torch Key and provided water for the crews building the Overseas Railroad in the early 1900s. The tower was later taken down and reassembled at Blue Heaven where it stands today. In little shops and galleries in the compound, paintings, carvings, jewelry, photography, painted rocks and coconuts are for sale. There's even a a bead business with a plucky entrepreneur who will braid a bead strand into your hair that will last up to six months and guarantee to turn heads back home.

In his best selling book, *Charles Kuralt's America,* Kuralt says "Their sauce could make cardboard taste good!" A remark that will forever be included in ad copy promoting the Blue Heaven. But it's true! Somehow, the informality of the outdoor dining room stretches back into the kitchen as well as into the attitudes of the waitrons.

The Blue Heaven is open from 8 a.m.–3 p.m., and from 6 p.m.–10 p.m. Closes for a summer vacation, but vacation dates vary. Parking is on the street, and sometimes difficult to find. You must dine at Blue Heaven at least once during your visit to Key West. Their motto: You don't have to die to come here!

B.O.'s Fish Wagon
801 Caroline Street ✎ 294-9272

Home of the Square Grouper Sandwich. After a long battle over zoning, B.O. (Conch Buddy Owen) moved his tiny, old-fashioned take-out fish wagon from Duval Street to its current location at the corner of William and Caroline streets. B.O.'s is always crowded with happy customers. They sip beer and wine and chow down on fried fish sandwiches, terrific hand-cut French fries, conch fritters and chowder. Lunch specials feature generous helpings of picadillo with rice or meatloaf and mashed potatoes, with prices starting at $7. Real funky. Real fun. Picnic tables and friendly fellow diners. B.O. says his place is "the only native Key West restaurant on the island." Friday evening happy hour from 6 p.m. till 9 p.m., features live music and a good party. Parking in the near-by lot will cost you more than your grouper sandwich.

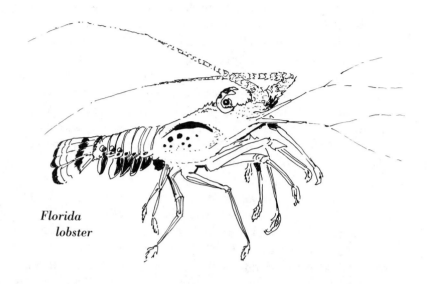

*Florida
lobster*

Pisces
1007 Simonton Street ✒ 294-7100

Reservations are a good idea. Award-winning French/Caribbean cuisine
served in an outdoor garden or indoor dining room, as elegant as it gets
downtown. The elegance is established in a big way by the haughty
attitude of the servers. They do a hell of a job. In spite of the big prices,
fancy dishes, and imperious ambiance, people show up in T-shirts and
shorts and nobody at Pisces minds, as long as they have the $100 or so
per person it will cost them to wine and dine here on excellent, but
small, portions of beautifully prepared gourmet food. Wine list is
extensive. Lobster Tango Mango is the most amazing lobster dish I've
ever had, and I'm from Nova Scotia where lobster rules. Duck is famous,
too. Fish is prepared with reverence. Everything tastes wonderful! A
locals' special occasion place. Many say this is Key West's finest
restaurant. A couple of lawyer friends, visiting from DC, told me that
Pisces was the very best food they'd had anywhere in the Keys. Dinner
only 6 p.m.–11 p.m. No off-street parking.

Cafe Marquesa
600 Fleming Street ✆ 292-1244

Make reservations. You will definitely need them. "Food of the Americas" theme lends itself to a terrific variety of interpretations by celebrity chef, Susan Ferry, a protege of even bigger celebrity chef Norman Van Aken. Seafood intensive with Caribbean flair, of course. Signature dishes include grilled sea scallops with roasted red pepper coulis and pineapple salsa, and rack of lamb with roasted bananas and papaya compote. Post-modern dining room, with white columns, trompe l'oeil murals and an open kitchen, seats only fifty diners at a time, so service is uniformly exceptional. Cost of a meal here averages about $50. But absolutely everything is beautifully sublime. Dinner only, 6 p.m.–11 p.m. A very chic wine bar, too.

Café Solé
1029 Southard Street ✆ 294-0230

Chef and owner John Correa is the son of a restaurateur and has worked in the business all of his young life. John has trained in the culinary arts in the Provence, Normandy, and Bordeaux regions of France, as well as in Venice, Italy. Ads for Café Solé describe the experience as "a meal in Provence" and that's a very fair description. Exquisitely fresh ingredients and sumptuous sauces make the food here quite remarkable. Chef John, though interestingly innovative, never wanders too far from tried and true tradition. His Italian and Caribbean-inspired flourishes are right on target.

Fresh seafood dominates the menu. Duck, chicken, lamb, pork, beef, also available most nights. Check out the fixed price dinners. Otherwise, prices are upscale: Appetizers from $7–$10. Entrees $22–$27, with a good selection of wines fitting the same price range. The food is very special, the atmosphere understatedly elegant, the service impeccable. But don't take any of it all too seriously. It's a fun place. Charming Chef John enjoys journeying out of the kitchen to visit with his appreciative guests. Dine indoors or in the garden beneath a lush breadfruit tree. There's even a highchair for your baby. Lunch and Dinner daily. Lunch prices are less than dinner, so if you can make one great meal a day, one day make it at least lunch here. Make reservations. Some side street parking available.

Camille's
1202 Simonton Street ✴ 296-4811

When Camille's was located in their original digs on Duval Street, it was not unusual to see the line stretching around the corner. Camille fans were willing to wait because they knew they'd get consistently great food. Now Camille's is in a new location, with enough room to seat every one of her clamoring fans. Camille's also has a new, full liquor license and lots more parking.

Camille's serves the heartiest breakfast in town—thick homemade bread and toast, banana and fruit muffins, three-egg omelettes full of lusty goodies like cream cheese, asparagus, and salmon, and coffee any way you like; every herbal tea known to man—hot or iced. Lunch fare is stick-to-your-ribs stuff like thick soups, stuffed sandwiches you can barely fit your mouth around, and the best grilled cheese-and-tomato sandwich you've ever imagined. Dinners are superb. Everything is kind of pricey, but well worth the extra dollar or two. Young, trendy-looking waitrons wear island casual fashions—short shorts, backless shirts, clogs or sandals. The boys are very cute and the girls will remind you of a Key West version of Frank Zappa valley girls. But don't be fooled, these servers know their business and keep Camille's running smooth as a clock.

Owners Michael and Denise Chelekis have owned and operated the restaurant since 1991. Michael used to be an entertainment director at a casino in Atlantic City. Denise was Donald Trump's director of catering. When she left him, Trump said: "I know you will succeed because you've watched and learned from me." You don't want to believe a guy with that kind of an ego, but you've got to admit, he was right. Denise and Michael have done an excellent job. Camille's is an island favorite. You'll *never* get a bad meal at Camille's. Open seven days.

Captain Bob's Grill
2200 N. Roosevelt Boulevard ✴ 294-6433

Steak and seafood. House speciality, and it's a good one, is surf and turf: prime rib and Maine lobster for $16.95. Look for daily specials like fresh-caught dolphin, or snapper dinners for around $17. Order from the lunch or dinner menu any time. Food is hearty and crowd-pleasing. Big, funky nautical-themed dining room. Highchairs are available.

This is one of the places frequented by busloads of tourists on sight-seeing tours. When that happens, you get a dining room full of hungry diners all at once. The service is good, nonetheless, if you see a bus parked in its big parking lot, you'd best move on and save this dining experience for a quieter time. Kid's and senior citizens' menus. Open 11 to 11 daily.

Chico's Cantina
5230 Overseas Highway Stock Island 296-4714

About five miles from downtown Key West, Chico's is a favorite stop for Mexican food—not that the food is so spectacular, though it is just fine—but because the whole operation is spectacular. Dad's in the kitchen, Mom and the kids wait on tables. They're always nice and efficient. Choose standard Mexican fare from the menu, like tacos and burritos, fajitas, quesadilla and guacamole, or from the huge blackboard of specials that change nightly. Usually there's one or two fishes, steak, and chicken, all enhanced with chipotle sauce or green chilies. Prices are reasonable—and there is a parking lot! When you leave downtown, you find these perks. Combination platters are served with beans and rice. The salsa is fantastic and you can get it to go. Chico's sells gallons of this stuff to locals. If you sit by the door, you'll watch them coming in and out all evening for pints of salsa.

Chico's opens for lunch and dinner; from 11:30 a.m. till 9:30 p.m. Wine and beer only. No reservations. Lines do form during the season. Closed Mondays.

Conch Republic Seafood Company
631 Greene St. on the Key West Harbor 294-4403

Hi-tech meets Old Key West in this mammoth, open-air restaurant and bar located on the Key West Harbor Walk. The giant bar specializes in rum, the brew of the tropics, hosting over 80 different brands from all over the world. Sample your favorite cocktail mixed with premium rum, or try one of the house specials, like a Conch-a-pore Sting, or the Bight Me, or the Big Easy Conch Colada. There's a stage for live music, and splendid overflowing raw bar. Also lunch or dinner on stainless steel-topped tables.

Entrees are good, seaside treats like fish and chips, fish sandwich, salads and burgers. Also daily specials, like twin lobster tails. Prices are fair enough—remember, this is waterfront dining, and nothing on the waterfront comes cheap—not anymore, anyway.

Kids love big, busy fish aquariums. If you're lucky, you can get a booth next to the aquarium—better than TV! Bathrooms are painted by local artist Holly Blandeaux—trust me, you haven't seen a bathroom like this before. Also, gift shop features a nice array of nautical-themed goodies and an excellent book department. Check it out. Pay to park.

The Deli Restaurant
531 Truman Avenue ⚑ 294-1464

Family owned and operated since 1950, this funky and old-timey restaurant is a locals' favorite. Fried chicken (served with your choice of two home-cooked veggies, $8.95) is the best in town. Veggie platter is four vegetables for $6. Our teenaged son recommends the open-faced roast beef sandwich, French fries and gravy, $6.95. Order breakfast all day. Yummy home made cakes and pies are on display. This is where cops and ambulance drivers eat, and it's packed during the season. Good service. Smoking and non-smoking areas. Air-conditioned. A few parking places out front and in a tiny lot at the back.

Dennis Pharmacy Conch Korner
Simonton and United Streets ⚑ 294-1890

Since 1962. Jimmy Buffett ate here in the mid '70s when he was a starving rock-and-roller. Locals know that when they need a grilled cheese sandwich like Mom used to make, or chili with lots of ground beef, or a bowl of white bean soup and toasted Cuban bread, there's only one place to go: the Conch Korner at Dennis Pharmacy. It's great for breakfast, best for lunch, closes way too early for dinner. Prices are very fair. Wander through the drugstore while you wait for your lunch. This is one of the Florida Keys' last remaining independent pharmacies. Celebrate with an old-fashioned milkshake. The Conch Korner is open every day but Sunday, 7:30 a.m. till 6:30 p.m.

Duffy's Steak and Lobster House
Simonton Street at Truman Avenue ✆ 296-4900

Duffy's no-nonsense lunch and dinner menus attract many locals as well as visitors to the island looking for great seafood. The dining room is a bright, split-level room lined with lacquered, blond wood booths. Seafood here is very fresh and nicely, not fussily, prepared. No fancy names or descriptions. Straight food. Beef is top quality. An artist friend of ours says that Duffy's prime rib is the best on the island and a visiting Italian gourmet we know goes to Duffy's when he wants a great steak. Prices are fair. Dinner entrees prices start at $12.99 for a 10 oz. prime rib and top out at $26 for surf and turf. Portions are satisfyingly robust and come with salad, fresh baked bread, potatoes or vegetables. Service is fast and friendly.

Lunchtime fish sandwich ($8.99) is one of the best on the island. Bet you can't eat the whole thing! Duffy's cold seafood salad is $13.99 and a great island lunch. Steaks and seafood available all day. Duffy's is a consistently fine family restaurant with the ambiance of a bustling tourist town favorite, which is exactly what it very competently is. Full bar. Highchairs. Excellent kid's menu. Open daily from noon till 11 p.m. They won't take reservations, so you might find yourself waiting a bit on really busy nights. Wait if you must. It's worth it.

Finnegan's Wake
Corner Green and James Streets ✆ 293-0222

Key West's only Irish pub and restaurant with live, real live Irish entertainment. Guinness, Harp, Bass and Murphy's Stout are on tap. Save this place for when you're tired of seafood. Entrees run between starters like potato leek soup, Irish brown bread, and potato pancakes, and main courses like Irish stew, corned beef and cabbage, and a wonderful shepherd's pie, just like your Irish waitress' Mommy used to make. Opens at 11 a.m. for lunch, daily. Late-night menu after midnight. Full, busy bar. Happy hour 4 p.m.–7 p.m., Monday thru Friday; it's always packed.

Goldman's Bagel and Deli
Winn Dixie Overseas Market Place ✆ 294-3354

Breakfast and lunch only. One of the things misplaced New Yorkers used to love to gripe about in Key West is the island's lack of a decent deli.

And it was not uncommon to see misplaced northerners climbing off the plane after a visit to Manhattan with a bag of bagels. Mark and Alison Bailey arrived from Philadelphia in 1998 and set out to change all that. Goldman's now boils and bakes over 120 dozen bagels a day, and delivers them still hot and fragrant to places like the Pier House, the Casa Marina, and the Gardens Hotel. Goldman's bagels are served aboard the Yankee Freedom, and sold at the Waterfront Market. So you never have to go without an authentic bagel again.

Beatle Sundays, that's every Sunday, feature Beatles music and the usual menu of deli goodies like hot corned beef, pastrami, grilled reubens, kosher franks, smoked salmon, and whitefish, herring in wine or cream. Kippered salmon is creamy and perfect. This is not a kosher deli, although some kosher meats are available.

Lots of parking, mid-range prices, and excellent service make Goldman's a popular stop. To-go counter is busy, too. Breakfast and lunch only.

Half Shell Raw Bar
Land's End Village, foot of Margaret Street • 294-7496
Famous "Eat it Raw" T-shirts. It doesn't get any fresher than this. Raw bar items like oysters, clams and shrimp are popular at the bar, which is always packed with characters from near and far. Real spicy conch chowder and fried fish with potato and corn-on-the-cob are popular choices at tables. Everybody loves the fried squid rings and the close-up view of the harbor. Everything is served on paper and plastic. Even plastic utensils! Fast, friendly and efficient servers hustle and bustle endlessly in this busy, friendly place. You share long picnic tables with backless benches, and might find yourself comparing tourist notes with folks from Cleveland or San Diego. The bar is fun, especially if you're working on your clam-and-oyster-shucking technique: These guys are the best. In May there's an annual shucking contest.

Hard Rock Cafe
313 Duval Street • 293-0230
Hamburgers, T-shirts and celebrity guitars in an 11,000-square-foot, 3-story Victorian mansion that was once a shell shop, then a restaurant

and club, now the 57th link on the Hard Rock Cafe chain. Dine indoors or out. Visit the gift shop for T-shirts and hats.

Kelly's Restaurant
303 Whitehead Street ✎ 293-8484
Many people want to eat here simply because it belongs to film star Kelly McGillis. But this building is interesting for other reasons too. The building, home of the first office of AeroMarine Airways, once stood on the waterfront, a couple of blocks away. It was later moved to its present location and Aero Marine Airways became Pan American Airlines. That's why the sign out front claims this to be the company's birthplace. Pan Am started the first passenger service to Havana from this building in 1927. Flights were twice weekly between Havana and Key West, on a tiny fleet of three planes called the Nina, the Pinta and the Santa Maria.

Along with a much-needed facelift to the exterior of this very old and historically significant building, Kelly has added a brewery, an aeronautical museum and a local writers library. The bar is an airplane wing. In a brick-floored garden in the back, Kelly has built an outdoor stage that is quite dramatic on full moon nights. A variety of events, from poetry under the stars to jazz singer Melody Cooper's stunning one woman shows, go on here.

Lunches are good, servers are nice. The thing is, nothing ever tastes the same twice, and you get the feeling that this place is only a front or an excuse for something really big going on elsewhere, behind the scenes. Maybe it's a micro brewery. But prices are fair, so have a mound of fried onions; great! Full bar, happy hour 4 p.m.–7 p.m. Buffalo wings. Cheap drink prices. No parking.

La Te Da
1125 Duval Street ✎ 296-6706
La Te Da has come and gone and come again since it opened in the early 1980s in a house where, a century earlier, Cuban revolutionary poet Jose Marti is said to have enraptured crowd with his stirring, balcony speeches. Today you can sip a cocktail on that same balcony. Dining at LaTeDa isn't as fabulous as it used to be. With friends I dined there on New Year's Eve, 2004. Food was unmemorable, but the staff was excel-

lent! Service was wonderful, our host was charmming, and when it began to pour (we ate outside) management was concerned that we might get wet and melt. We didn't. LaTeDa is an institution in this town. When you're here, you always feel as if you're at a party.

La Trattoria Venezia
524 Duval Street ✶ 296-1075

"La Trat" as it is called locally, is one of the island's most often recommended eateries. Cream-colored stucco walls, dark wooden beams, white lace curtains and tablecloths and tiny, faintly flickering candles create a dreamy, romantic atmosphere that most people find irresistible. A little slice of Europe in the heart of Old Town Key West. La Trattoria is a family operation, founded over 20 years ago by Sicilian brothers Carmelo and Costantino Vitale. The brothers speak English, French and Italian, which attracts an international crowd.

The menu features traditional dishes from Southern, Middle and Northern Italy. The Vitales are also influenced by classic French cuisine. The steak au poivre at La Trat is legendary, and so are the crepes and pastas. There's a full bar and lovely wine list.

Around mid-December La Trat begins opening for lunch, which is a great value—after-dark sauces at lunchtime prices. Off season, the place opens for dinner only, from 6 p.m.–11 p.m. daily.

Louie's Backyard
700 Waddell Avenue ✶ 294-1061

Name any restaurant award given in South Florida and chances are you'll find it on the trophy shelf at Louie's Backyard. Long considered to be Key West's very finest restaurant, noted for it's ambiance as well as it's unique menu, Louie's is an island tradition, and a perennial favorite of tourists and locals alike.

Louie's is first and foremost a visual extravaganza. You enter the 1909 classic revival building through a broad, wide-board floored veranda, equipped with several inviting rocking chairs reminiscent of Key West's slow-moving, bygone days. Immediately to the left of the entrance, a tiny, elegant bar is tucked away, almost out of sight. Decorated with rows of chic cocktail glasses and every imaginable variety of spirits, Louie's cozy inside bar is usually peopled by at least two or three shy souls.

Up several steps into the indoor dining room, through wide French doors into the outdoors again, you'll see several tiers of tables. You descend, a few steps at a time, until finally you arrive at the Afterdeck Bar, a chic little cocktail den beneath a canvas awning, as lovely and alluring as any you'll find on the French Riviera.

Jimmy Buffett once lived in the house right next door to Louie's Backyard and even penned his big hit "Margaritaville" there. From his front porch swing, where he claims to have composed his ode to wasting away, Buffett would have been able to view patrons coming and going in and out of Louie's on their way to the Afterdeck.

Louie's is perched on the Atlantic Ocean on the south side of the island, so you'll hear and see the tiniest waves lapping at the beach. On full-moon nights, you won't find a more breathtaking view of the ocean anywhere.

The food can be some of the best you've ever tasted. Then again, it can be so mundane the price will seem well beyond the value. Who knows why? That's just the way it goes. It's a hit or miss place, but when they hit —and more often than not they do hit–oh! Lunch is served from 11:30 a.m. to 3 p.m. every day. Dinner is from 6 p.m. to 10:30 p.m. Dress is casual to dressy, and most people dress a bit when spending $50 on lunch or $100 on dinner. You absolutely must make reservations. You're going to ask for a table on the outside terrace, right? So is everyone else, so be prepared to be disappointed. No highchairs for babies, and no children's menu. Walk or cab. Parking is difficult because Louie's is in a residential neighborhood.

Mangoes
700 Duval Street • 292-4606

Dining in a brick courtyard overlooking the wild and wonderful scene that is Duval Street is the kind of experience people come to the Florida Keys to have for themselves. Entrees feature plenty of Caribbean island goodies like coconut, passion fruit, mangoes, yucca, mojo and jerk spices.

Lunchtime features somewhat exotic sandwiches and salads. I've never come away from Mangoes impressed with the service. But the food, though a bit pricey, is interesting, and it's a it's a fun and comfortable spot as long as it's not too hot and you sit under an umbrella to protect yourself from the sun. The open-air bar is a favorite watering hole.

Margaritaville Cafe (Jimmy Buffett's)
500 Duval Street ✺ 292-1435

Open 11 a.m. for lunch and dinner. Food is tasty, simple and well-spiced, 'cause that's the way Jimmy likes it. Pretty good fish sandwich. Yummy beans and rice. Blackened hot dog. Conch chowder and fritters. Nice veggies. A terrific "Cheeseburger in Paradise," served just like the song says "with lettuce and tomato, Heinz 57 and French fried potatoes." A dish called Couch Potatoes is fantastic: twice-cooked French fries smothered in chili, cheddar cheese, and sour cream. To die for! Come to think of it, you could die from eating too much of this, it's soooo bad for you. Desserts unremarkable. Young, valley girl and boy servers. Funky, oilcloth covered tables and straight-back chairs. At lunchtime, this place is flooded with locals—lots of judges, politicians, and civil servants, since it's located halfway between City Hall and the County Courthouse. Afternoons are busy, as Duval Street shoppers duck in for happy hour margaritas, and at night, Parrot Head tourists keep the place jumping. After 10:30 p.m. loud music is provided by a wide assortment of road bands who appear for a week or two at a time. A long, fully stocked bar. No off-street parking. Air conditioned. Yes, Jimmy does make surprise visits!

Martha's Steak and Seafood
S. Roosevelt Boulevard (A1A) ✺ 294-3466

Right on the Atlantic Ocean on the quiet side of the island, Martha's is a long-time favorite of tourists who like to stay on this softer side of Key West. An ocean view from just about every table; piano music every night from 6:30 p.m. till 10 p.m. Dinner only from 5:30 p.m. till 10 p.m. Fine, leisurely dining. Service is wonderful. Fresh, nicely prepared seafood and grilled entrees. House specialties are roast prime rib with baked stuffed shrimp. Also filet mignon with lobster tail.

Show up in time for the early-bird special from 5:30 to 6 p.m. and take $5 off every entree. Same deal next door, at **Benihana Steaks and Seafood (294-6400)**, owned by the same people and located in the same building. Customers are generally waiting outside for the door to open at 5:30 p.m. No lunch. Lots of parking. Large, nicely dim dining room. Open seven days. Make reservations for large parties.

Martin's Cafe Restaurant
416 Appelrouth Lane ✺ 296-1183

Yes, this is the same place that used to be located behind the Eden House Hotel. Owner is German native Martin Busam, a classically trained chef. Busam prepares German and island cuisine and serves it in a quaint, open-air dining area. You can sit inside, too. Martin's food is wonderful, and the German dishes, wiener schnitzel, jaegar schnitzel, and potato soup, are authentic and delicious. Desserts are great. Breads are home-made. Martin's has what he decribes as an "eclectic' wine list and several popular German draft beers. Dinners only. Famous Sunday brunch from 10 a.m. till 3 p.m.is still one of the best in town. Parties of six or more should definitely make reservations

Meteor Smokehouse
404 Southard Street ✺ 294-5602

The Meteor was the name given to a fictitious Key West newspaper, so named when Hollywood decided to make a weekly, one hour show featuring our quirky island. It was about a frustrated, would-be author who drives to the end of the road to seek fame and fortune as a writer for a homey little newspaper called "The Meteor." Each plot of the Fox Network show began and ended in the office of the Meteor. Our son Miguel was an extra in the show. He was a newspaper boy, but not for long. Unfortunately, the show wasn't well received and after a few horrific episodes it disappeared, never to be heard of again. All that Hollywood left behind was a big sign that hung in front of the supposed Meteor Newspaper newsroom. When somebody showed up to create a smokehouse restaurant and BBQ right next door to one of America's favorite bars, the Green Parrot, that Meteor sign was there for the taking. And they hung the sign in their place, and the Meteor began a new flight. Large booths and knotty-pine walls hung with old black and white photos of other famous barbecue restaurants. The Meteor's smoker cooks food at 225 degrees and it takes 22 hours of smoking to cook the pulled pork, and six hours to smoke ribs. Fueled by buttonwood, a keys mangrove tree. Salads, vegetarian dishes, and excellent desserts, worth a visit if you've already had dinner. Free parking.

Old Town Mexican Cafe
609 Duval St. ✸ **296-7500**
In nearly three decades, Gail Brockway has started up some of Key West's
most successful and memorable restaurants. The Old Town Mexican
Cafe, inspired by a two-year sabbatical in New Mexico, is Gail's latest
venture. As always, Gail is in the kitchen, preparing her spectacular
dishes herself, her way. Everything is authentic, simple and luscious. Most
tables are on a deck, beneath a pair of very grand mahogany and
poinciana trees. Some tables inside, if you like, but you'll miss all the fun.
This is informal dining, but the service is excellent. Gail demands that of
her staff. Latin music keeps the tempo hot, and the chili-scented aroma
from the kitchen will keep your mouth watering. Thank God for those
fresh chips and salsa on every table! You think Mexican food is heavy,
right? Not here. Try spinach salad, or deep fried fish taco with shredded
cabbage, or the grilled fish with fried kale. Vegetable dishes are very
satisfying. Exotic desserts with peppers and chocolate. Prices are low on
the Key West scale. Beer and wine. Try it once and be assured, you will
be back! Right in the heart of the action on Duval Street, and probably
Duval Street's best value.

Pepe's Cafe
806 Caroline Street ✸ **294-7192**
Founded in 1909, a year when a thousand or so local citizens were
employed in cigar making, several terrible hurricanes hit the Keys, and
out in the Southwest, Geronimo, the famous Indian chief, died as a prisoner of war. Read about these and other fascinating historical tidbits
while you wait for your food. The menu is pure entertainment, and it
includes recipes, too. Like Pepe's red beans? Copy the recipe right off the
menu. Thursday is Thanksgiving dinner day—roasted turkey with all the
trimmings for $15.50. Get there early before they run out of bird, or stuff-
ing. Barbecue dinners on Sundays. The grilled cheese sandwich at lunch
is the best in the world. Meatloaf is very good, too. Breakfasts are very
hearty. Go early to get a seat beneath the world's biggest ceiling fan, built
of a washing machine motor and five-foot-long wooden blades. Booths
are very private. Sit in a corner and no one will find you. Free pickles for
pregnant women. Busy locals' bar out back. Pepe's is a little pricey, but
hey, this kind of authentic, Old Town Key West atmosphere doesn't
come cheap.

Pier House Bars & Restaurants
1 Duval Street ✱ 296-4600

The Pier House is one of the oldest resorts on the island and still one of the most glamorous, in spite of lots of new competition. In addition to the main dining room, which is the fanciest and most expensive of all the dining and drinking places in the Pier House Resort complex, there is a Harbour View Cafe for outdoor, gulfside dining, and the Pier House Market and Bistro on busy Front Street. The Chart Room Bar, tiny, dark and chic, and a popular spot for dedicated drinkers, serves the least expensive cocktails in the complex.

The Pier House is a venerable institution. Everything you buy here—a drink, a room, or a basket of conch fritters—will cost more than anywhere else. But it won't necessarily be better . . . Bring money, throw caution to the wind, be demanding—they expect it.

PT's Late Night Bar and Grill
902 Caroline Street ✱ 296-4245

PT's claim to fame is his hours. You can eat here anytime from 11a.m. until 4 a.m. Daily, affordable specials. Sandwiches, fish and chips, burgers, jerk chicken, and home-style meatloaf or roast beef with mashed potatoes. Seafood. Eight TVs! Satellite sports all day and all night. Busy pool table. Icy air conditioning. No windows, so you never know what time it is. Usually packed because it's good. You'll find a metered parking place on the street.

Rusty Anchor
Fifth Avenue, Stock Island ✱ 294-5369

"Where can we get fresh local seafood?" Right here. This is the place. The Rusty Anchor wholesale business delivers fresh fish to most of the restaurants of Key West every day. So the fish you'll eat in this restaurant is the freshest of all, just off the boat. Fabulous fish and chips for $8. The most tender fried conch in the world. Great local art and photography in a very spacious, cement-floored, two-leveled place, with lots of fast waitresses, thick chowders and fried fish. You'll usually find a few gritty fishermen sitting around the bar in their white rubber boots. The photographs on the walls are black-and-white studies of famous Key West people and scenes, so naturally Ernest Hemingway is in evidence.

That huge, abandoned building 50 yards or so across the street and to the left is the old dog track. Across the street to the right is a brand new public park and playground. The Rusty Anchor is open 11 a.m. till 10 p.m., closed Sundays. Lunchtime is always packed with local workers who know they can get in and out in a hurry. Plenty of parking. Big fun!

Seven Fish
632 Olivia Street ✻ 296-2777

This very conchy neighborhood at the corner of Olivia and Elizabeth has such heart and charm it has the power to lift your spirits. It's the real thing, and so is this charming and very popular bistro. From the moment the doors opened to this tiny, beautifully stark cafe, it has been jumping, and jumping quite elegantly. Service is excellent. Food is wonderful. There's more than fish here, but the fish really is the star of this show. Sauces are perfect. Also stonecrab cakes. Vegetable egg foo yung. Even a traditional meatloaf. Don't skip dessert! A little pricey but the food is so good you don't mind. Open 7 nights from 6 p.m.–11 p.m. Make reservations! Or, drop in later in the evening for dessert and coffee.

Shula's On the Beach
Reach Resort, Ocean end of Simonton Street ✻ 296-6144

Supercoach Don Shula and his partners established the Key West location of their chain of 20 award-winning steak houses in February, 2001. Shula's is very pricey, but steak aficionados say its worth the money. At most Shula's restaurants waiters wear tuxedos, but here, in famously laid-back Key West, they wear khaki pants and polo shirts. A valet will park your car, and every table features magnificent ocean views. Specialties are steaks and seafood. Lunch is less expensive than dinner, so check it out and if you're impressed and intrigued with the quality and the presentation (both sterling) come back for a $35 steak. Everything is ala carte. Full bar and well planned wine list. Do you get that big testosterone boost from the beef? Or from knowing you've got what it takes to pay the big bill? Either way, Coach Shula's counting on you.

Square One Restaurant
Duval Square ✴ 296-4300

The bartender at this popular with locals bar is Patrick Hayes, who stars in the restaurant's hilarious television ads and enters drink-design contests, which he often wins. A couple of Hayes's award-winning cocktails are *Monkey Nuts* and *Godiva Mint Mist*. Hayes's happy hour customers are a wonderful mix of locally colorful characters. He keeps them entertained with wacky antics and skillful barkeeping. You want some local color? Here it is. American cuisine, with plenty of seafood dishes. Service is the best. Michael Stuart, the handsome and gracious host, is also Square One's owner. Ambiance and tradition make this place great.

Sands Seafood Bar & Grill
1420 Simonton St. & Ocean ✴ 294-2000

This is one of my favorite places to take people from out of town. Why? One reason. At the Sands it is possible, and advisable, to get a table on the beach, take off your shoes, and wiggle your toes in the sand while you sip your favorite cocktail and/or eat your seafood lunch or dinner. I mean, why do you come to an island anyway? This is it! The Sands people aim to please, and offer a number of enticements like daily all-you-can-eat specials, a wicked salad bar with the usual offerings, plus a few more like peel-and-eat shrimp. A bar. Music. Private areas available for your own event. And that ocean . . . Lots of free parking in the Reach parking area across the street. Come for lunch or dinner.

Thai Cuisine
513 Greene Street ✴ 294-9424

A favorite place to call for to-go. Fast, free delivery in the downtown area. The food is terrific, authentic, and inexpensive, and all portions are generous. The restaurant occupies half of a refurbished auto body shop, but in the other half of the building, there still is an auto body shop. Across the street is Key West's handsome Old City Hall, which makes this an important neighborhood, historically. Also, right down the street on the corner of Duval and Greene, is Sloppy Joe's Bar. When you dine here, inside or out, you won't lose sight of the fact that you're in downtown Old Town Key West. Prices are very affordable, nevertheless.

Damn Good Food To Go
294-0011

If one day you find that vacationing has worn you ragged and you simply cannot budge from your bed, even to eat, call these folks. Let someone else do the schlepping. Order in from these guys. They're standing by from 7 a.m. till midnight, and create overflowing sandwiches, a half-pound burger and fries, tuna with jalapeno, and excellent salads. Also, for breakfast, biscuits and gravy, or lox and cream cheese on New York bagels. Call and ask for what you want. They'll get it to you with lightening speed.

✖
Captain Cliff's
Fool-proof Boiled Shrimp

Select a pot large enough so that the shrimp will be
under water. Add estimated amount of water to cover
the shrimp. Put pot and water on burner. Add
Louisiana Shrimp Boil to water (1 oz per pound of
shrimp). Bring to a rolling boil. Add shrimp. Water
will stop boiling. It will take a few minutes to boil
again. Watch pot closely and at the first bubble that
comes from the bottom of the pot, or the very first
indication of starting to boil, remove the shrimp from
the burner and pour enough water off to leave the
shrimp barely covered. Add 6 to 10 ice cubes (not to
chill; just to stop the cooking). Shrimp will be crunchy
and not tough.

Grunts & Grits

Split fresh-caught, cleaned grunts and dip in flour
seasoned with salt and pepper. Fry well on both sides.
Serve with hot buttered grits.

Fresh Seafood Available on Keys Menus

Conch—Imported from the Bahamas, but they are the same as conch in local waters. There are just plenty more available there. Ours are endangered. Be warned that conch is tough but interestingly different from anything else you've tasted.

Dolphin or Mahi Mahi—The fish, not the mammal! Throughout the tourist season, many restaurants will offer dolphin fish as their catch of the day. It's plentiful and easy to clean, to cook, and to serve. With very little fuss, dolphin fish can easily be turned into an elegant and tasty dish. In some places dolphin fish is referred to as mahi mahi, so as to avoid confusing it with the aquatic mammal thought by some scientists to be more intelligent than man.

"I wish I had a nickel for every time one of my customers accused me of killing Flipper and serving him up for dinner," a veteran Duval Street waiter once said.

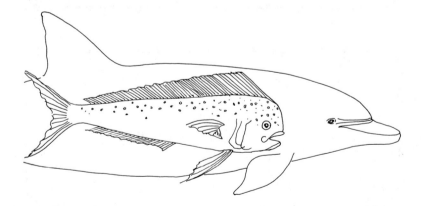

Dolphin comparisons: the fish (foreground) and the mammal (porpoise, background)

Florida or Spiny lobster—Although the lobsters, or bugs, you get from Florida waters are quite different from their northern cousins—they're tougher, and they're clawless—a skillful cook can make a nice bug sing. The trick is to cook them very briefly. Lobster season runs from August through the end of March. If you order lobster at other times of the year, you'll eat frozen.

Grouper—If you like cod or haddock or scrod, you'll love grouper. It's lean, chunky, firmer and flakier than dolphin and, most people believe, has more flavor.

Grunts—A staple and longtime local favorite feast, good for breakfast, lunch or dinner. You will rarely see grunt fish listed on any restaurant's daily special board, however. In Depression-era Key West, grunts and grits was a regular meal for Conch families. It combined resourcefulness (anyone can catch a grunt!) with inexpensive grits. The grits were handed out, free of charge, along with flour, sugar, butter and milk at the WPA project office on Whitehead Street, where the Green Parrot Bar stands today. An average-sized grunt weighs about a pound and is easily caught off any bridge or pier. Grunts are a staple catch on party boats, and yes, they're called grunts because of the noise they make when you catch them.

Maybe the Tourist Development Council should come up with a new name for them to bring them back into vogue.

Scallops—They're not indigenous to the Keys but in such demand that you will see them offered on many menus. They're imported, most likely frozen, but they are certainly not objectionable, since they freeze well. But fishes from local waters are delicious, and as fresh as you could ever hope for. Therefore, we recommend that you pass up the scallops and go for the local fishes.

Shark—You will see shark on "specials" menus, but not often. Some people like it just fine and say it tastes similar to swordfish. Some folks deal with it by squeezing lots of fresh lemon on it. An old South Florida trick for preparing shark for eating is to soak it in salt water in the refrigerator for a few hours. Then, generally, shark is grilled. Some adventurous types do order shark when it's offered, and they'll probably tell you it tastes pretty good. But a shark is a huge, oily muscle of a fish. So many others are so much sweeter, in disposition and in flavor.

Snapper—Yellowtail, red, mangrove or grey. There are many kinds in the Keys, and any one of them is as good as the next. Snapper would probably be most people's choice for the most delicious fish caught in local waters. Snapper is so delicious that once you are initiated, you will find yourself searching and hoping for more. Yellowtail is the snapper you see most often on menus.

Shrimp—In 1984, one windy winter evening, my husband threw his cast net off the end of the White Street pier. Minutes later he pulled in a half pound of pink shrimp. Again and again he tossed the net into the water, filling it each time with shrimp. He caught around 30 pounds! Now, every time we walk or drive near the White Street pier, Michael retells the story of that magical night when the wind was just right and 30 pounds of pink gold swam into his net.

There are countless ways to enjoy fresh shrimp. Our favorite is boiled, in Old Bay Seasoning, then peeled and dipped in cocktail sauce laced with lots of horseradish and key lime juice. Very simple to prepare!

Shrimp is America's most widely eaten seafood, and certainly a staple of most Keys restaurants. Shrimp is a huge local harvest. Although there are many varieties of shrimp available on the market, Tortuga pink shrimp, taken from the shrimp beds located some 70 miles west of Key West, are considered superior to all.

Stone Crab—Of the thousands of edible species of crab in the world, the heavenly stone crab is the main one indigenous to this area. Stone crab legs are harvested from October 15 through May 15. Only'one leg is taken from a single crab. The creature, returned to the water, regenerates another. Compare the taste of a stone crab to that of a Maine lobster claw. Very delicate, and many shellfish connoisseurs believe it's the finest-tasting crab on the planet.

Tuna—A grilled tuna steak tastes something like the very best steak you ever had. Odd, huh? There's nothing better than fresh tuna. There's nothing worse than not fresh tuna. You may be offered black fin, blue fin, or yellow fin. Have it. Eat it rare! Eat it raw! Tuna is a favorite of sushi chefs.

Wahoo—O.K., so they have parasitic worms called wahoo worms in their guts. The worms won't hurt you! If I hadn't told you, you would never have known. Unless, of course, you pulled one out of the water and prepared it for supper. In that case, you'd be glad I told you.

Wahoo is the largest member of the mackerel family. Mackerel is a somewhat oiler fish. November and December are Wahoo months here. Wahoo is a very tough guy to catch and is usually caught by anglers looking for a fight with marlin, dolphin or tuna.

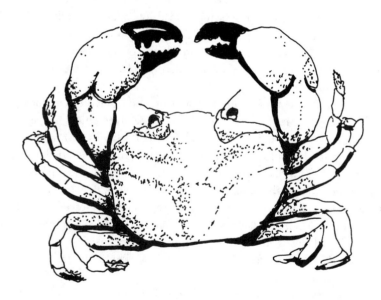

Stone crab

Conch Cuban Cuisine

THE BEST DINING-OUT or taking-out deals in Key West are found in the Cuban restaurants, but beware: Cuban cuisine is addictive. Dining in a Cuban eatery is an adventure unique to Southern Florida. The people who work in Cuban restaurants don't take themselves, or their customers, too seriously. Cuban servers, often an entire family in each restaurant, are warm, easy-going and friendly. They won't mind if you practice your Spanish when you order, so go ahead.

What makes Cuban food taste so good is the heavy-handed use of fat. Lard is the first ingredient listed on the Cuban bread wrapper, followed by white flour, sugar, and salt. Cafe con leche (coffee with milk) is sometimes made with evaporated milk and sugar. Flan, a sweet custard dessert served floating in golden sugar syrup, is made of condensed milk and many eggs. The low-fat revolution hasn't caught up with Keys Cubans yet. Cuban bean soups are studded with chunks of pork, stewed to mouth-watering tenderness. Only black beans, a Cuban staple, are cooked meat-free.

Some of the mouthwatering and quirky sounding favorites on most Cuban menus are Italian style liver: strips of beef liver, onion, peppers and garlic, seasoned and sauteed in oil; fried pork chunks: first roasted, then deep-fried chunks of fatty pork; piccadillo: ground beef fried with onions, peppers, tomato sauce, cumin, olives and raisins; and ropa vieha (translation: old clothes): shredded flank steak boiled, then stewed in tomato sauce. With every Cuban meal, local restaurants serve buttered and toasted Cuban bread, a substantial scoop of rice, fried plantains, and a cup of black beans. You dump the beans on the rice.

"White or yellow rice?" the waitress will ask. This is an aesthetic call; either color tastes the same.

French fries and salads are served as an alternate choice to beans and rice. But go for the beans and rice. You can eat French fries and iceberg lettuce salad anytime.

A bowl of white bean or lima bean or chicken soup, with a side of toasted bread, makes a substantial meal. Rice and beans, with a side order of plantains, makes a meal, too.

Service in a Cuban restaurant is fast, efficient and never fussy. You can ask for your waitrons to describe a dish, and they will—if they speak English.

Cafe Con Leche

Visiting any Cuban coffee stand takes me back to my earliest days on the island when I fell into the habit of visiting the nearest shop first thing every morning for a large cafe con leche and Cuban toast. At Cuban coffee shops, girls like me—and there were lots of us—were called "hippas," the feminine version of hippies, long after the decade of love was over.

It is not unusual for newcomers to find themselves hooked on Cuban coffee. The island's sultry, balmy calm induces most people to start nodding around mid-afternoon. That's when a blast of sweet, Cuban coffee works magic.

Cuban coffee, which isn't actually Cuban at all—there are no Cuban food products in America, there's an embargo on—is rumored to be considerably stronger than the regular Colombian or Peruvian stuff Americans are used to. But actually, it probably isn't stronger at all. It's espresso coffee, so the beans are roasted longer, and darker, but that doesn't necessarily mean it's any higher in caffeine than what you've been drinking at home. What hooks you, what kicks you in the head every time, is that jolt of concentrated caffeine along with two teaspoons of sugar. Ask them to cut down on the sugar.

Cubans are an earthy people and very big on charm. Visiting the Cuban coffee stand is guaranteed to hike your enthusiasm—no matter what you drink there.

Some Cuban Restaurants and Coffee Stands

Cuban Mix Deli
3840 N. Roosevelt Blvd. ☛ 292-3999

For a taste of old Key West, visit Fred Salinero's Cuban Mix Deli and sample some mango or guava ice cream, made from his grandfather Jesus Caromona's recipes. Senior Carmona founded El Anon, a famous Cuban ice cream parlor here on the island in the 1940s. Other ice cream flavors are sour sop, tamarind, fresh strawberry, vanilla, and chocolate with nuts. Other Cuban standards are the Cuban sandwich, Cuban toast, and Cuban coffee. Also flan, bread pudding and Key lime pie—all of it made the old fashioned way, just like it was done in the late 1800s when Key West was the cigar making capital of the world. Located right next door to the Welcome Center, Fred wants people to find out, as soon as they arrive in town, about Cuban cuisine. 7 a.m. - 6 p.m. daily.

El Siboney Restaurant
900 Catherine Street ☛ 296-4184

In Key West, the people's choice of the best Cuban restaurant is an ever-changing thing. Every place seems to have its years of glory, its turn at the top. Today, many people will tell you El Siboney is the best.

El Siboney serves lunch and dinner. The waitresses wear red shirts and black pants. El Siboney takes no credit cards—cash only. During season people wait on line to get in. There's a counter, and plenty of tables. Photographs of Cuban scenes are on the walls. Open 11 a.m. - 9 p.m., every day.

Five Brothers
930 Southard Street ☛ 296-5205

The ony place in town for bollos (pronounced "boy-ohs"), ground black-eyed peas, seasoned with garlic, salt and pepper, deep-fried and served in greasy, little brown bags. Also Cuban-style sandwiches and cheeseburgers on Cuban bread are memorable, and coffee made to order. Everything is made to go—outside you can sit and eat on a couple of benches. It's a small store, packed with nifty coffee-making gadgets like the ones you need to make authentic cafe con leche, canned chorizo sausages packed in lard, and castille soap. Busy at lunchtime. A scene from old Key West! Open 6 a.m. till 6 p.m.. Closed Sundays.

El Meson de Pepe on the Boulevard
3800 N. Roosevelt Blvd. ☎ 295-9448
El Meson de Pepe on Mallory Square,
410 Wall St., Mallory Square ☎ 295-2620
Pepe Diaz started out in a tiny coffee shop and Cuban grocery on upper Duval. My co-workers and I bought many cups of sweet con leche and cuban toast there while employed at the Miami Herald's Key West bureau office. That was more than 20 years ago and it's been a treat watching Pepe's kids grow and prosper. Pepe and his wife have also enjoyed great success in those years between then and now. I love it that Pepe says, whenever he sees me, "you haven't changed a bit!" So eat at Pepe's restaurants. There is great food. Live music. You WILL dance to the Caribe band. Guaranteed. Pepe is dedicated to great food and the preservation of Cuban conch heritage in Key West.

Jose's Cantina
800 White Street ☎ 296-4366
Jose's is generally nowhere nearly as hectic as El Siboney, Old Town's busiest Cuban restaurant, possibly because the prices are a bit higher at Jose's. Sometimes, folks hungry for Cuban head over to Jose's when the line is too long at El Siboney. Jose's food is every bit as good as you can get anywhere. Jose does a big take-out business; it's fun to order a paella or roast pork dinner to go.

La Dichosa
1206 White Street ☎ 296-6188
La Dichosa. La Dichosa in Spanish means "the chosen." The bakers at La Dichosa begin their work in the wee hours of the morning, way before dawn. They bake 3,000 loaves of Cuban bread in two styles. One is deluxe, identified by a decorative cord that runs right down the middle of the loaf; that one will cost you a quarter more than the bread without the middle cord. At dawn, bread is being delivered all over town. Five Brothers is La Dichosa's biggest customer, buying 75 loaves of the good stuff every day. La Dichosa opens before dawn and shuts around 2 p.m. As we are going to press, this business is for sale. Uh oh...

Bars

EOPLE WHO LOVE HANGING IN BARS will be thrilled to discover Key West. The list that follows highlights a few old favorites and/or famous reputations. As wild as these islands are, we still abide by a law that says no booze shall be sold before noon on Sundays, presumably so that no one will get too oiled up to go to church. Some restaurants feature champagne brunches where they offer complimentary spirits, thus staying legal. No selling, you see.

Key West Pub Crawl Walking Tour
Reservations: 744-9804
Lots of great stories about who drank where, when, and did what then. Tour price of $35 includes five drinks and a martini t-shirt souvenir. Tour meets on Duval Street, weaves around the Historic Seaport, and back to Duval. You must phone first to reserve your spot. Ask about group rates. Tours are Tuesday, at 8 p.m. and Saturdays at 7 p.m.

Some Bars

Afterdeck Bar at Louie's Backyard
700 Waddell Street ☞ 294-1061
Careful now, this is a very treacherous place. Very charming, very seductive. The full moon never looked more brilliant than it does from the Afterdeck. After a few hours and a few drinks, you might find yourself thinking things like "Hey…why don't I just wrap things up at home, move back, and stay for good? I could tend bar. Or wait on tables. Or work in construction. Why not?"

You've been warned…

Atlantic Shores
510 South Street ❧ 296-2491

Not a family place! Not a place for the easily shocked. Certainly not a place for homophobes. (Actually, all of Key West is a bad destination for homophobes!) If you love picnics and cookouts, you'll love having your lunch—tuna sandwich, hot dogs or burgers—at this seaside bar and eatery. A pool and an ocean are here for swimming and sunbathing. Clothing is optional, so count on seeing nudity, as well as near-nudity. Food is ample and cheap. A bar, good service, and the $2 rental on all-day deck chairs make this a great place for uninhibited hedonists. They're here, too. But oh! In the summertime it is so hot, even on cool days—no wonder everybody is stripped down to near or complete nudity. Limited off-street parking.

Bull & Whistle
280 Duval Street

You can't miss the bull charging through the cinder block wall. I know several couples who met for the first time at "The Bull," as it is known locally, a long-time institution. You don't have to enter the premises to decide whether or not you want to drink here and listen to the live music; get a sneak preview on the sidewalk right outside. It's a good resting spot on Duval Street: Open air. Funky. Live. Relax over a beer, some great, live local music, and consider your next move. Upstairs, a clothing optional bar. Really? Really!

Captain Tony's Saloon
428 Greene Street ❧ 294-1838.

Yes, Hemingway really did hang out here in the '30s, when the place was called the Blind Pig, and then Sloppy Joe's. It was operated by Hemingway's good fishing buddy, Joe Russell, who was given the nickname "Sloppy" by Papa himself. (Hemingway was fond of nicknaming.) Martha Gellhorn, who was to become the third Mrs. Hemingway, came to Sloppy Joe's in 1936 looking for Hemingway, and she quickly found him.

Key West's own swashbuckler, Captain Tony, bought the place in 1958 and owned it for several decades. Mayor Emeritus Tarracino (he was mayor from 1989 to 1991) came to Key West from Elizabeth, New

Jersey, after a sinister-sounding misunderstanding with a bookie. In Key West he became a charter boat captain, and eventually a barkeep at Captain Tony's, where his craggy fame has grown by leaps and bounds. Charisma is this guy's middle name, and if you haven't read about him in some newspaper, magazine or book somewhere, where have you been? Members of the press love Captain Tony for the free beers he happily dispensed to them at his saloon, and for his outrageous philosophies and opinions.

Captain Tony has thirteen children, born to a half dozen beautiful women. The last son showed up in 1995, having just been told by his mother of his father's identity. Imagine your mom pulling out the latest edition of *People Magazine* and saying, "Son, this man—Captain Tony—is your father." The son journeyed to Key West and showed up just in time for a tear-jerky Christmas reunion with his brothers and sisters, who report that he fit right in with the clan. A few years later, the same guy turned up as a contestant on the TV show "Survivor." Sadly, he didn't last long . . .

Captain Tony sold Sloppy Joe's in the early '90s, and retired. In 2005, the Captain celebrated his 89th birthday.

Conch Flyer Restaurant & Lounge
Key West Airport ✶ 296-6333
This place is pretty much like dated airport lounges everywhere—kind of dark and gloomy, no matter how brilliantly sunny the day, and filled with desperate looking characters: drab waitresses, people afraid of flying, people hoping for happy reunions, or mourning the departure of lovers, or celebrating the departure of relatives and friends. Through the years this place has been unable to shake its seediness. In fact, they haven't even tried. Opens at 5 a.m. for breakfast and closes by midnight. The menu is sandwiches only, until 7 p.m.

Aqua
711 Duval Street ✶ 294-0555
Drag shows. Music. Dancing. Karaoke nights. TV and sports. A mixed bag of music, live entertainment, wild bartenders doing zany things, fundraiders for local charities and organizations, and, of course, booze.

Happy hour 2 p.m. till 8, when the evening's events unfold. Lots of events and contest like a talent contest for the best looking guy or gal in the house. How much will you take off to win? Big fun. Everybody welcome. Go when my favorite drag queen, Goddess, is on duty and I promise you'll have a ball.

KWest
705 Duval Street ✺ 292-8500
Fine looking Go-Go boys perform every night from 10 till closing. Happy hour daily from 3 - 9 features jazz and showtunes. Live showtunes, piano and a whole lot more on Wednesdays and Saturdays, with Bobby Nesbit, or Joe Lowe. A quintessentially Key West pub. The staff and crowd is mixed and fun. No attitude, so everyone, gay or straight, feels comfortable here. KWest and Aqua have taken the place of the infamous Copa, the island's most raucous late night club, until it burned to the ground in August 1995. Kwest, and Aqua next door, are different from that. A little more modern. Friendlier. Brighter. More mixed and more fun. You'll see some of the same faces from the old days here, just a little more settled down.

Flagler's at the Casa Marina
1500 Reynolds Street ✺ 296-3535
Coffee Butler plays piano here, and he's a local celebrity you must not miss. Old-time visitors might remember him and his ensemble—Coffee Butler and his Cups. These days, it's just Coffee, from 8 p.m. till 12 p.m., a couple nights a week. Everything at the oceanside Casa Marina is particularly romantic at night.

Irish Kevin's
211 Duval Street ✺ 292-1262
A great place to get smashed with your best friends and family. A totally riotous scene with live music, lots of profanity, and non-stop drinking. Don't stop in for a drink. Stop in for a slosh on a night when you don't have anything to do, or anyone to answer to, the next morning. Guinness chugging contest puts this bar on the map!

Sun Sun Beachside Pavilion at the Casa Marina Resort
1500 Reynolds Street ⚬ 296-3535

Live entertainment and refreshing tropical drinks add to the flavor of this favorite island retreat. The scenery is unbeatable. Beach. Sky. Sand. Water. Bikinis.

Full Moon Saloon

It's gone now, but you're probably looking for it anyway. Once it was the local, late-night bar that was home away from home for infamous drug dealers, smugglers, island entrepreneurs, champagne dolls and cocaine whores. That scene is all over now—fodder for the history books. Too bad you missed it. Actually, it's probably better that you did.

Green Parrot
601 Whitehead Street ⚬ 294-6133

The first and the last bar on US 1. A longtime locals' bar, busy from the time it opens at 10 a.m. to the seedy wind-down at 4 a.m. Open air, no glass in the windows, just spidery wrought iron to keep out thieves when the place is closed. Unusual artwork and slogans are pasted on the walls. Once this place was called the Brown Derby, and before that it was a morgue, and in the 1930s, it was the place where the WPA handed out food and clothes to broke natives. The building is now listed in the National Register of Historic Places.

You'll find friendly bartenders, pool tables, pinball, darts, and the best jukebox in town. Never a cover; never a minimum. Great live entertainment on weekends. Open-mike poetry slams are raucous and renowned as are best tattoo contests. Plenty of advertising in local papers let you know what's going on. You'll make friends fast in this bar. The sign above the bar says it all: "No Sniveling."

Havana Docks
Pier House (Upstairs) ⚬ 296-4600

Everything at the Pier House is done with as much flair as the all-American staff can muster. The bar that stretches across the width of the building facing the sunset is an elegant place to watch the sun go down.

The place opens an hour before sunset, and closes an hour later. A bar devoted to sunset!

Hog's Breath Saloon
400 Front Street ♥ 296-4222

A bar inside. A bar outside. Three bars in all, and seven televisions. The great live music starts every afternoon at 1 p.m. sharp. It was originally founded in Fort Walton Beach, Florida, in 1976 by Jerry Dorminy, a native of Birmingham, Alabama, who views drinking as a sport just as important as sailing or fishing. Additional Hog's Breath Saloons are located in the French Quarter of New Orleans and in Cancun, Mexico. The cult of world travelers faithful to the Hog's Breath Saloons are called Hog Heads, a kind of Yuppie Dead Head cult, they say.

Key West's Hog's Breath features a daily happy hour from 5 p.m.– 7 p.m., with live entertainment all afternoon and evening, and a busy raw bar and a world-famous T-shirt concession that sells a truly amazing number of shirts. Enjoy light cuisine like sandwiches, conch fritters, raw seafood, Caesar salad and burgers. Their ads claim their drink prices are the lowest on Duval and urge you to remember: "Hog's Breath is better than no breath at all." Open 11:30 a.m.–1:30 a.m. daily.

Rick's/Durty Harry's/Rumrunners
202-208 Duval Street ♥ 296-5513

This is a rocking entertainment complex: Big screen TV's. Satellite dishes. Sports forever. Live entertainment. Rock 'N Roll. Late-night karaoke daily, 11 p.m. till closing. Nine bars! Big party spot, noisy, frantic and young. A full bar and live entertainment nightly. Open from 10:30 a.m. to 4 a.m. Monday through Saturday; noon till 4 a.m. Sunday. Happy hour daily. "Bogey says the best live entertainment and lowest drink prices in the islands...Rick's."

Behind Rick's: Durty Harry's. Live hard rock six nights a week and televised sports delivered via two satellite dishes. Raucous. Young.

Rumrunners, where reggae rules. Upstairs, there is a topless bar.

Schooner Wharf
202 William Street ✹ 292-9520

A salty, dockside bar with a raucous, swashbuckling atmosphere, it's unmatched anywhere in downtown Key West. A big-time favorite, with happy hours, parties, fundraisers. Music begins late afternoon (sixish)

Schooner Wharf Bar
Filet Mignon Recipe

Take four filets and cook quickly over high heat until medium rare. In a large bowl mix

1 pint Jack Daniel's
1 pint Courvoisier
1 pint vodka
2 tsp. bitters
2 tsp. lemon rind
1 qt. Perrier

Dip filets quickly into the liquid mix.
Remove and pat dry.
Slice filets into small chunks.
Throw to the dogs.
Drink the gravy.

and goes on till two. Michael McCloud, king of the island crooners, rules. It's an institution!

Sloppy Joe's Bar
201 Duval Street ✹ 294-5717

There's a whole book about Sloppy Joe's illustrious 60-year history, written by local historian Sharon Wells, and you can buy it in the Sloppy Joe's gift shop. Latest news from Sloppy's: air conditioning! Installed in

February '96, just in time for the steamy summer months and the Hemingway Look-alike Contest. Bless them. The coolest place of all is at the door, very inviting. Also, world-famous Hemingway shirts in every color of the rainbow: you'll spot them everywhere—from Paris to Halifax to Laguna Beach. Did Hemingway really drink here? Yes!

Live music all day and all night.

Turtle Kraals
Lands End Village ✆ 294-2640

You can wear this T-shirt as a sort of trophy after you prove yourself worthy by drinking your way around the world. From the large selection of beers, drink 21 brands and you get your own "Drink Your Way Around the World" T-shirt. Happy-hour oysters are a quarter apiece; live music nightly. Open-mike nights attract some grueling amateurs, and some great local color—you never know.

Blu Room
422 Appelrouth ✆ 296-6667

This is the place our son, now in his twenties and living far away, hangs out on his rare visits back home. He's sure to meet up with former classmates and neighbors there and the club rocks for as late as is legally possible. The Blu Room features an extreme and excellent sound system, hip DJs, a busy dance floor, plush couches, and a back yard bar for more intimate conversation. Late-night, laid-back Key West.

Wine Galley at the Pier House
1 Duval Street ✆ 296-4600

The Pier House is simply the most elegant resort on the island, and this flair shows in this chic but cozy piano bar where nightly entertainers include guest talent—some pro's, some amateurs—all having a ball making music with piano man Larry Smith. Smith's wide-ranging repertoire is astonishing and crowd pleasing. His guests are sometimes well-known performers, sometimes people who toil at other jobs like Stacy Rodriguez, business editor at the Key West Citizen by day, sultry singer by night.

Names of Your Favorite Pubs Here

Shops

Besame Mucho
315 Petronia St. ☎ 294-1928

Dearest one . . . shop here once and life will become a joy forever. Strangely enough, the store's motto is true. You will feel happy in the store and when you leave the store, with your bag of goodies. Wonderful, interesting stuff you won't see anywhere else. Kiehl's products. Odd and touching art. Good, sincere Mexican jewelry. Scents for your home. Rhinestone hair clips. Pillows and bedclothes and candles. Shopkeeper Meredith grew up right here in Key West, raised by parents who encouraged her to believe in magic. Wear a Besame Mucho, cap-sleeved -shirt, in soft cotton, pink or baby blue. Gorgeous!

Cuba! Cuba!
814 Duval Street ☎ 295-9442

This shop is probably as close as you'll get, on this trip anyway, to a shopping excursion in Havana. Stop here for Cuban arts and crafts, cigar label art, a large variety of fine cigars, Cuban foods, books, cookbooks and maps. Great CDs of Cuban and Latin music. Also pillows, towels and flags in Cuba colors.

Peaches
512 Duval St. ☎ 296-0799

Proprieter Susie Rafferty came to town in 1974. She served drinks at the Pier House pool, and was also the Pier House baker. She created the Key lime cheese cake featured for many years on the menu at Louie's Back Yard. Next she put her creative talents to work as a designer of bathing suits and sports clothes under the label "Peaches." Peaches bathing suits, made in luscious colors and fabrics, made every one who put one on look just beautiful! Susie sold them wholesale, right out of her house. Then, out of a shop on Duval Street. In 1991 Susie took a long break from merchandising and travelled the world, visiting every place that had ever interested her. She founded the Earth Dream Alliance, a corporation supported by a small grant and lots of private funding that saves a cloud forest in Equador. It's still there, too. Now, there is a Peaches again, only this time the merchandise isn't bathing suits, since we old-time Key Westers aren't really wearing bathing suits as often as we once did, or could. Peaches merchandise reflects Susie's eclectic tastes and the fruits of her worldliness. She makes regular buying trips to places she loves, and fills her shop with things that catch her fancy. She also promotes local artists, writers, and designers by featuring their creations in her store.

Don't miss Peaches. It's a classic.

Fast Buck Freddie's
500 Duval Street ❧ 294-2007

The windows at Fast Buck Freddie's are not to be missed; each month the windows change, with themed displays featuring merchandise available for sale in the store that month. For example, one Valentine's Day, the display featured Liz Taylor and her eight marriages—but there are only six-and-a-half windows! No problem, because Liz married one husband, Richard Burton, twice. Each of Liz's seven husbands got a window, although Eddie Fisher's was displayed in the window half the size of the others.

Reserve at least an hour to take in this spectacular emporium of glitzy, nutty and beautiful things in the massive space that once housed the Kress Five and Dime. If you're not shopping, explore the place as if it were a museum. In a way, it is because the owners claim it to be Key West's first department store. It certainly is the island's most extravagant superstore. Try on the trendy clothes. Read the glitzy greeting cards. Test the gadgets. Browse slowly through the amazing tabletop accessories. You'll find toys and T-shirts, books, stationery, and fine writing instruments. Zen rock gardens are a big seller. Fast Buck's is open from 11 a.m.–6 p.m. daily. Tony Falcone and Bill Conkle, a couple of former advertising whiz-bangs from New York City, founded Fast Buck's in 1979.

Flamingo Crossing
1107 Duval ✆ 296-6124

The Florida Keys' only agricultural export today is mangrove honey, which tastes best when sampled in combination with walnuts, cream and ice in a cone at Flamingo Crossing, where fresh ice cream is made daily. If this isn't the best ice cream you've ever tasted…well, it is. It just is. And if that weren't enough, it's less expensive than the factory-made stuff at the other places. On the hottest summer nights my neighbor Thea and I sometimes eat double scoops at Flamingo Crossing and call it dinner.

Key West Aloe
540 Greene Street ✆ 294-5592

In 1967 New Yorker Frank Romano came to Key West for a visit and got himself a terrible sunburn. A local friend recommended that, for relief, he try a time-honored local solution: gel of the aloe plant. Romano was amazed at the instant relief; his sunburn healed without blisters and without peeling. As a result, Romano became deeply interested in the magical healing properties of aloe. He researched tropical aloe for two years; then he moved to Key West with master perfumer Joe Liszka, and the two founded Key West Aloe, the first company in America to manufacture its own skin-care and beauty products using aloe gel.

Thirty years later Key West Aloe employs eighty-five people and distributes more than one hundred skin care products all over the world. It also has new owners, and Frank and Joe are retired and having the time of their lives traveling and participating in local philanthropic ventures.

Stop at the shop and lay in a supply of Key West Aloe creams and cosmetics. The best! Hours 9 a.m. until 6 p.m.

Key West Cigar Factory
3 Pirates Alley (at Front Street) ✆ 294-3470

Lately, the cigar industry is enjoying a sudden rebound. Cigars again have become chic, just as they were in the 1800s, before the proliferation of cigarettes helped to wipe out the once-thriving cigar industry. Nowadays it is much more hip to sport a fat, fragrant Cuban cigar than a lowly cigarette. Cigar connoisseurs are buying glitzy magazines with names like

Smoke, The Magazine of Cigars, Pipes and Life's Other Burning Desires, and *Cigar Aficionado*. And they are visiting places like the Key West Cigar Factory, where they can watch cigars being hand made on a cigar rolling table that appears to have been in use since the industry peak in the 1880s. Key West was once a cigar boomtown, producing 100 million cigars annually. Eventually, politics, union strikes, hurricanes, better working conditions in Tampa, and the popularity of cigarettes began the industry's demise. Seventy-five years later only six small factories remained on the island, and by 1963, only one was left; the Key West Cigar Factory is the era's sole survivor.

Now that cigars are again in vogue, the shop's cigar rollers are busy keeping up with the demand. The cigar rollers listen to a Havana radio station and roll tobacco grown in Africa, Brazil, and Colombia. They make cigars called "El Hemingway" and "Cuban Split."

Thirty percent of all cigars smoked in America, a clerk in the shop told me, are smuggled into the country from Cuba. The newest craze for people who have everything—a $30 cigar smuggled from Cuba.

Key West Hand Print Fabric
201 Simonton Street • 294-9535

During Key West's amazing cigar making era, this brick building was constructed as a warehouse for storing tobacco. During the downtown reconstruction in the 1960s, the building was restored and became home to a factory producing hand-print fabrics.

Designers Suzy dePoo and Lily Pulitzer created the famous turquoise, yellow and pink Key West prints that were made into sports jackets, shorts, shirts and dresses. The fabrics were silk-screened, that is, the paint was stenciled directly onto the fabric in full view of charmed visitors. In the '60s and '70s, it was common to see lots of hand print fabric fashions at all the best parties. Miss Pulitzer has passed on, but Suzy dePoo, who is near 90 years old, still designs fabric in a studio in her Key West home.

The Key West hand-print fabric is no longer printed at the shop. The space that once contained the silk-screening operation is now a showroom. It's full of lovely clothes, constructed of Key West hand-print fabrics; particularly sweet are the children's clothes. All are expensive. Shop hours are 9:30 a.m.–5:30 p.m. every day but Sunday, when the shop is open from 10 a.m.–5 p.m.

Kino Sandal Factory
Kino Plaza ✦ 294-5044

Full of fabulous, very affordable, locally made leather sandals, the factory is in Kino Plaza, corner of Greene and Fitzpatrick. But watch out for those heavy glue fumes! The original Kino sandal, $10 for women, $12 for men, is the best value, and made in a simple, sturdy style. You can't always find your size and color, though, and you can't always find a place to sit down and try on your sandals. But persevere. Kino's are a nearly perfect shoe except for one terrible flaw: on wet pavement they're greased lightening, definitely not the shoes to wear on a rainy day. Otherwise, they're really very cool, unique to the island, and extraordinarily long-wearing. This is another item you'll buy for yourself whenever you get to Key West, or take a pair home to a pal—they're cheaper than T-shirts!

From the Ruins
219 Whitehead Street ✦ 293-0897

Amazing assortment of one-of-a-kind garments, handcrafted accessories, and exquisite objects d'art. This is where you'll find the exorbitantly expensive dress that you'll wear for the rest of your life. Over 250 museum-quality garments, designed by artists from around the world, are featured. When you try on these clothes you realize that they've been created by sensual designers who appreciate the womanly form.

The shop's name refers to the timelessness of fashion, and the ancient methods of dying and weaving used in the creation of this collection of wearable art. Kim Harriss, a spectacularly chic woman with a sunny disposition and lust for life, is the proprietress and stylist. Kim will make you beautiful.

There's a mirror propped on a palm tree in the front yard so you can see the clothes in natural light. Kim minds her shop in $2,000 outfits and bare feet. Open 10 a.m.–6 p.m. every day but Sunday.

Peppers of Key West
602 Greene Street ✦ 295-9333

Hotheads, you must not miss this! Proprieters Tom (an amazing and commanding actor, earning a living) and Mike (an impressive Italian chef) promote the ins and outs, the ups and downs, and the fine balance of pain and pleasure, in this emporium devoted to heat. Over 600 fiery food products to choose from with labels like Dave's Insanity. Ring of Fire. Blair's After Death. Goin' Bananas - the Hot Sauce with A Peel. The Extreme Right Wing Sauce - a Jerk Sauce. The tasting table is busy and great fun. Bring your own beer. Join the hot sauce of the month club.

Paradise Tattoo
5160 US 1, Stock Island ✺ 292-9110

People who have been thinking for a long time about getting a tattoo often find their courage at an all-time high right here, while on vacation in Key West. Tattoos have now come into their own as a popular island souvenir. For around $100 or so, you can buy yourself a lifelong reminder of Paradise—a dolphin, a sun, a sunset or a moon. Hearts and flowers are ever in demand, and you'd be surprised how often people ask to have a name tattooed onto themselves. The tattoo artists at Paradise will discourage you from this drastic measure, however.

Body piercing is also big lately. The most frequently pierced body part here in bikini land is the bellybutton.

Paradise Tattoo is open daily from noon till 8 p.m.

The Sea Store
614 Greene Street ✺ 294-3438

It's difficult to say exactly what the hours of operation truly are in this tiny, antiquish, nautical-themed shop, but keep checking. The shop is wonderful and is headquarters for the Florida Keys Chapter of the Audubon Society. The telephone answering machine not only takes messages, it gives a rundown of bird sightings for the week. And the machine is always on.

Sponge Market
Mallory Square ✺ 294-2555

Who better than C.B. McHugh, a fifth generation sponger born in Key West in 1923, to tell you all about sponging in the Florida Keys? C.B.'s been sponge fishing since he was eight years old, and he knows sponges.

At the Sponge Market, C.B. demonstrates, through the miracle of modern videography, the process of gathering sponges and preparing them for market. You'll get a kick out of C.B.'s old-timey and very subjective narration.

"All sponges that grow in the ocean are called saltwater marine sea fossils," explains the Sponge King. "They're not animals. They're not vegetables. And they're not plants. I don't care what they say, they're nothing but common saltwater marine sea fossils. And I'll argue with anybody about that."

Sheepswool sponge is used throughout the world as bath sponges for racehorses, as dandy carwash sponges, and by tile-layers who use it to wipe the grout off tiles. During World War II sheepswool was used as oiled packing for gun barrels. But best of all, the sheepswool sponge is a luxurious addition to a hot, soapy bath. At the Sponge Market you can buy a high-grade sheepswool sponge for $20 to $30, depending on the size, or a less-stellar sponge for considerably less.

The Sponge Market is open daily from 10 a.m. till 9 p.m., except on cruise ship days, when they open at 8:30 a.m.

Fairvilla Megastore
520 Front Street ✦ 292-0448
Intimate fashions, toys for lovers, sensual accessories, exotic movies. And a whole lot more. Big, spacious, bright space where you won't feel creepy shopping for dildoes and vibrators and various magical potions that turn warm and fragrant when rubbed into human flesh.

Leather Master
418 Appelrouth Lane ✦ 292-5051
When shopping for sexy, naughty things , I like to go directly to the traditionalists. This is the place Key Westers have known and trusted formany years when in the market for lubricants, leather condums, and other fun stuff. The leather products are very well made and will last forever. If you don't want to carry your sex toys on the plane with you when you fly down for vacation, send them ahead. Leather Master will hold them for you till you get there, and send them back to you, too.

Second Hand Rows

Consigning Adults
802 Whitehead Street

Dress For Less Consignment Boutique
1021 White Street

Kat's Little Consignment Shop Around the Corner
1102 Truman Ave.

Salvation Army
1924 Flagler Avenue

St. Peter's Episcopalian Church Parish Hall Thrift Shop
800 Center Street

Second Hand Sams
Habana Plaza, Flagler Avenue

The Perfect T

A s you walk down Duval Street, you will notice an overwhelming number of T-shirt shops. Some of them pay people to stand out front and offer you coupons for discounts within. T-shirts has become a big business here in Key West. Yes, we know we have far too many T-shirt shops, but our elected officials can do nothing about that since this is America, when you try to impose restrictions on what merchants can and cannot sell on Duval Street, you invite lawsuits and bigger and more expensive lawyers than this city can afford to fight.

There are several reasons why, from an economic standpoint, the T-shirt business is so successful in this tourist town. First, marketing surveys indicate that the most frequently purchased item that visitors take home from Key West is a T-shirt. Second, unlike many trends and fads, T-shirts don't go out of style And, third, they're cheap to produce. In many shops they're not even imprinted until someone buys them and chooses an image they want from a staggering selection displayed on shop walls. A T-shirt shop's main inventory is inexpensive plain white T-shirts. Thus, you may find T-shirts being sold for $5, or 2 for $20, or any other combination that will bring in the money to pay the rent that day.

There are, however, unscrupulous T-shirt merchants on Duval Street, who advertise T-shirts for one price and then charge considerably more for the finished product after the customer has been invited to choose whatever images he wants imprinted on the shirt. Plenty of people have complained, particularly non-English-speaking tourists. It's a dirty trick, to be sure, and it's been perpetrated often enough that City Hall has imposed laws to protect tourists from these bait-and-switch tactics.

Today, T-shirt shops are required to post a list of prices on all shirts within a shop, but be sure to confirm the total price *before* the purchase. If you're going to order a shirt with many slogans or designs on it, ask for an itemized bill before the printing begins, so that you can decide if the price is in line with what you expected to pay.

If you think you were overcharged, contact the City of Key West Code Enforcement office at 292-8191.

Some favorite T-shirt designs are the **Hog's Breath Saloon, Sloppy Joe's,** which features Ernest Hemingway's face, and the **Half Shell Raw Bar**, sporting a saucy babe in a bikini, inviting one and all to "Eat it Raw" at the Half Shell Raw Bar.

At **Captain Tony's Saloon,** which Captain Tony sold some years back, T-shirts are sold in a shop adjacent to the Greene Street bar. Business is always brisk.

Jimmy Buffett's Margaritaville Gift Shop sells thousands of shirts each week and so does the Wyland gift shop on Front Street. Those local classics will cost you about $20-$30.

Last Flight Out, 503 Greene St., sells a great selection of T-shirts with a sort of getting-away-from-it-all motif. "I'll see you in C.U.B.A." is an old classic available here, as well as the blue plane winging its way into the sky on the last flight out. "We all have a Last Flight Out within us..." I love this place, and these shirts.

Goldman's Bagel and Deli in the Winn Dixie Market Place on North Roosevelt Blvd. sells a terrific shirt—white letters on red. For $10! Sometimes people named "Goldman" come to town and buy them out. The bagels at Goldman's are terrific, by the way.

The **Mel Fisher** "Today's the Day" T-shirts were worn hopefully for years by those who hunted daily for the massive treasure. The day finally arrived for Mel Fisher's Treasure Salvors on July 20, 1985. Shirts featuring the treasure hunting themes are still sold at the Maritime Heritage museum gift shop.

Local character and Key West Fire Chief **Bum Farto** disappeared in 1976, just days before he was to be sentenced for selling cocaine. "Where is Bum Farto?" asked one of the most popular T-shirts of the '70s. Alas, old Bum is still among the missing.

Old Island T-Shirts, at 914 A Kennedy Drive, 296-3329, sells shirts by the pound. If you've got ten friends, or, God help you, ten kids waiting back at home for their Key West souvenirs, this is the place to go. The shirts are inexpensive because they're irregular over-runs from other jobs, possibly flawed in some small, Key West-chic way. Maybe the print is crooked or letters are missing or something like that. Whatever. Most are 100% cotton; buy them for $8.50 a pound. Are T-shirts supposed to be perfect? Nah! You'll find all kinds of interesting designs here, so take your time to hunt through all the bins and piles, and chances are you'll find something for even the most discerning collector. Open from 10 a.m. till 5 p.m.; closed on Sunday. Blank shirts are also available for $8.50 a pound in lots of neat colors.

Another place for interesting T-shirts, many of them designed by local artists, is the **T-Shirt Factory** at 316 Simonton Street. As elegant as T-shirts can be, these are hand-printed in an open-air factory, which you can watch. Prices are around a third less than the same shirts sold in fancy Duval Street shops even though the factory is only a block off Duval. Kids' and adults' sizes all the way up to XXXL. Also sweatshirts. Open daily from 10 a.m. till 6 p.m.

T-shirts are designed also to commemorate just about every local event. Often money raised from shirt sales benefits some group or organization. The Annual Memorial Day Survivor's Party T-shirts, sold at the party and afterwards until they run out, benefit **AIDS Help, Inc.**

Some political campaigns, like **Captain Tony's** when he ran and was elected mayor, sell T-shirts to raise campaign funds. These are found for years after in the chic collections of T-shirt hobbyists everywhere.

An exhibit of Key West T-shirts, which we've never had, certainly would be a fascinating way to tell the story of this island's fascinating history. And imagine the swapping that might go on! Collect wisely and save your Key West T's for this future possibility.

Endless Love

Weddings

IT IS SURPRISINGLY, some might say frighteningly, easy to acquire a license to marry in the Florida Keys. Both members of the couple must appear when the application is applied for and issued, but neither of them needs to produce any kind of identification. The marriage license form will ask for names, ages, birthplaces, and information on just how past marriages, if any, were concluded. They also want to know the date of your divorce, so know that. There is no blood test required. After you finish the paperwork and pay the clerk $93.50, you must wait 3 days. If you are not a Florida resident, you're legally ready for matrimony the minue you get that license. If you're in a big hurry, you can be married by a clerk at the courthouse. The charge is $30, about as cheap as you can get in Monroe County unless you have a friend who is a notary public.

Roughly 200 marriage licenses are issued each month at the Monroe County Court House at 500 Whitehead Street in Key West. Well over half of those are issued to out-of-towners, apparently overwhelmed with the relentlessly rosy romance of an island holiday.

By the way, the cost of and application for dissolution of a marriage (divorce) is $352.50, and you must be a resident of the state of Florida for at least six months to divorce here.

Any legally registered notary public has the power to marry you in Florida. Many of them turn performing weddings into a business. You will see their brochures at the Chamber of Commerce and their ads in the Yellow Pages, as many types of services and ceremonies as there are mar-riage licenses. The more outrageous, it seems, the better.

Last minute nuptials pose no problem for local wedding planners and teams. One phone call will fix you up with everything you need, from location to custom services to photographs, from the very simplest to the most glorious ceremony imaginable. No challenge is too great for local wedding planners.

Many resorts, like the Marriott and Holiday Inn Resort & Marina in Key Largo and the Pier House in Key West, actually employ wedding consultants who are a phone call away. The Butterfly Museum and the Audubon House also advertise themselves as fine wedding venues, because if the weather turns nasty, where will you be then? Plan your wedding inside the Butterfly habitat and you have no worries.

Church weddings for out-of-towners are generally more difficult to arrange in a hurry. Many churches require a counseling session before a clergyman will perform a wedding ceremony. Determination and sincerity may win you the support of a local clergyman willing to tie your knot. Lots of churches are listed in the Yellow Pages. If a church wedding is what you must have, chances are you can find a way to have one. One way is to do the mandatory preparatory groundwork with your hometown clergy and bring certification to present to the local branch of your church here in Key West.

The following is a short, and by no means complete, list of possibilities.

At Your Service Key West Weddings
800-504-5404

Elizabeth Rose, the energy behind this wedding planning business, has charged anywhere from $500 for the very simplest of weddings, to a $9,000 extravaganza. She'll arrange for a wedding on the beach, a reception for you and your friends. Hiring a local planner saves you lots of time and money, she says. It's much cheaper than having a big wedding back home, for most people. Elizabeth says that she won't plan a wedding between August 15 and October 1. That's the hot, sticky, muggy hurricane season zone, and it's also when she takes her annual vacation from her very busy job.

Marrying Sam
296-3640

Marrying Sam advertises discounts to pregnant brides, locals and members of the military, with no charge for renewing vows at any point in the marriage. A longtime local character, Marrying Sam wears a safari hat, and drives a moped. Between vows, she'll snap a couple of photos of the happy pair. This is your basic, no frills deal.

Reverend Debra Benedict
296-7439

If appearances are important to you, and you are hoping for a more dressy and refined sort of affair, you might call on the Reverend Debra, for whom fashion holds a high spot on her long list of avocations. If need be, Reverend Debra will dress the entire wedding party. As an interfaith minister, she performs services of appropriate simplicity or economical grandeur. Like all wedding officials, Debra will perform on the very shortest of notice, and offers assistance in planning of location, transportation, accommodation, entertainment, photography, and video documentation.

Chapel by the Sea
292-5177 ✷ 800-603-2088

A wedding coordinator will handle every detail of your wedding. All you have to do is show up! A ceremony next to the fountain in their tropical garden setting, with champagne and photographs for two, costs just under $200. For around $500, you and your intended and an attending party of four can go on a private sunset cruise, sip beer, wine and champagne, marry at sea next to a bouquet of tropical flowers, and pose for photographs.

Weddings Without Worry
294-6019 ✷ 877-209-6452

Absolutely nothing surprises Key West's wedding brokers. They've heard it all and then some. Sheri Cabanas, a notary public and wedding planner, says the craziest wedding she arranged was a surprise marriage. The groom made all the arrangements, and invited his girlfriend to go with him for sunset at Mallory Pier. Sheri, and the carefully planned wedding, were waiting. All the shocked bride had to say was "I do" and fortunately, she did. People at sunset signed the guest book. Like all the others here, Sheri not only marries you, but can also arrange for flowers, music, location, catering, wedding favors and photos.

Join us on the worldwide web
www.junekeith.com

Weird Science:
The Elena Hoyos Story

COUNT VON COSEL, who wasn't a count at all except in his own mind, was an X-ray technologist at Key West's now-defunct Marine Hospital. In the spring of 1930, a sweet but doomed Latin beauty named Elena Hoyos showed up at the hospital for blood tests and X-rays. Tests revealed that tuberculosis would soon kill the pretty 22-year-old. But von Cosel, a small German man who wore clean white suits, a white Panama hat, and a tiny mustache, was smitten with Elena, whom he claimed to recognize from a dream he'd had forty years earlier. He could not bear to accept the reality of his own diagnosis.

Von Cosel determined to save Elena's life by charging her oxygen electrons with his own invention, a bizarre contraption with electrodes that attached to the girl's wasting body. The treatments were hideously painful for Elena, but von Cosel's weird science was oddly reassuring, too. Elena's poor, heartbroken parents welcomed his devotion and ministrations. He kept their hopes for their daughter's survival alive.

As Elena languished in her tiny bedroom, von Cosel brought her gifts of perfume, scarves, jewelry, and exotic fruits and candies. He bought her an elaborate mahogany bed, that barely fit through the door of the family's humble home. It was in that bed that Elena died on October 25, 1931.

Her family buried Elena in Key West's City Cemetery. According to the memories of those who were there, von Cosel sagged with grief as he watched his beloved being lowered into her shallow grave. (You can't dig a deep grave on an island only a few feet above sea level.) The water! The worms! The flimsy casket! How would Elena's delicate beauty survive the tyranny of the damp earth? After two years of regular visits to Elena's grave, von Cosel could bear the image of her demise no longer. One moonless night he dug up her nearly fleshless bones and took them to his laboratory located in the fuselage of a wingless airplane parked on Rest Beach.

Julia Hoffman, then a young woman dating a newspaper reporter from Ohio, went along when her boyfriend interviewed von Cosel in his Quonset hut on the beach well before Elena's body was discovered. Von

Cosel, Julia recalls, seemed so logical, so convinced of the validity of his bizarre experiments and kooky plans—he was building a plane to fly to Heaven—that she was nearly convinced it could be so.

Von Cosel determined to preserve what remained of Elena's sultry charms with a bizarre series of soaks, washes and regular soapy baths. The mad count replaced Elena's rotting flesh with oiled silk, beeswax and balsam. He replaced her eyes with glass ones. He fought an unending battle with insects, who continually found their ways into Elena's nooks and crannies in spite of his painstaking precautions. Eventually, of course, von Cosel's eerie project was discovered. It's difficult to keep a secret in Key West—especially one as odorous as necrophilia.

Elena's body was removed from the wingless plane and taken to a local funeral parlor where an autopsy was performed. It had been seven years since her death. Doctors noted in written reports that Elena's remains had been the receptacle of physical evidence of von Cosel's love. That's right: intercourse.

Talk about a twisted tale....

Von Cosel was arrested. Elena's body was put on exhibit in the lobby of the funeral parlor, and the townspeople were invited to come by and view the eerie spectacle. Almost 7,000 people came to see Elena. Teachers brought their classes. Reporters came from all over the country. Von Cosel's story caught the fancy of just about everyone in America, in spite of the fact that the bit about the intercourse was considered much too shocking to report in the papers.

More than a few Key Westers suggested that Elena's body be sealed in a glass case and put on permanent display. Wouldn't the tourists love that! There was sympathy for the weird, old man, too. What was his real crime after all? Loving too much?

A local innkeeper named Joe Zorsky, perhaps more tolerant of freaks than most people due to his background in the circus, bailed von Cosel out of jail and let him stay in room 23 of his motel lodge (today the place is Key Lime Village). When the world press arrived to interview von Cosel, they gathered around him, in front of a huge night-blooming cactus.

Eventually the courts discovered that there was no Florida law against not burying a body, and the charges against von Cosel were dropped.

"Can I have Elena back now?" von Cosel reportedly asked the judge, oblivious to the horror of the curious on-lookers who had flocked to the court for his sentencing.

"No! No, you can't!" screamed the outraged judge.

Elena was buried in an unmarked grave. Von Cosel left town in 1940 and spent his remaining years in Zephyrhills, Florida, the place where the natural spring water comes from. He died, alone, in 1952. When morticians came to take von Cosel's body away, they found an eerie sight propped in the corner of the little shack: a life-sized replica of Maria Elena Hoyos.

Songwriter/performer Ben Harrison heard the story of creepy, crawly Count Carl von Cosel, Key West's infamous necrophiliac, and Maria Elena Hoyos, the object of his ghoulish ardor, and immediately felt his songwriting juices begin to gush. Harrison began performing his talk/sing horror story, *The Ballad of Maria Elena Hoyos and Count Carl von Cosel*, at gigs around town. Every time he performed the eerie bit, his audience became enthralled.

"Is that a true story?" people asked him incredulously.

"It is," Ben Harrison told them. "It really is. I promise."

Encouraged by his customers' ghoulish enthusiasm for the tale, Harrison eventually wrote a book about it. *Undying Love* explores every mucky detail of the macabre legend and contains unbelievable quotes from von Cosel's own kooky narrative that appeared in *Scientific American Magazine* in 1940. Next time you've got a few hours to kill (you should pardon the expression), pick up Harrison's book. Halloween Eve might be a perfect evening for this gross and engrossing read. You won't be disappointed.

A Land That's Mostly Water, A Sea That's Mostly Sky

The
Lower Keys

The Lower Keys
...

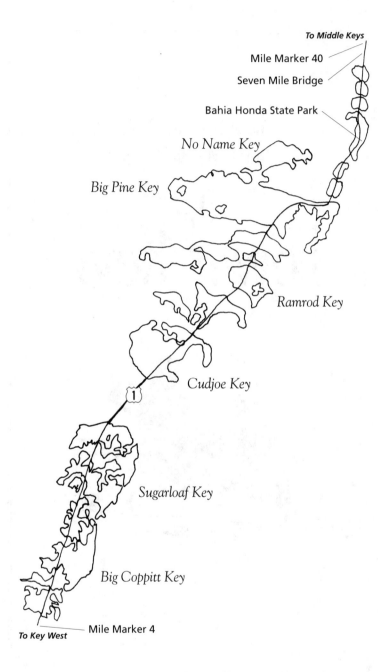

To Middle Keys
Mile Marker 40
Seven Mile Bridge
Bahia Honda State Park
No Name Key
Big Pine Key
Ramrod Key
Cudjoe Key
Sugarloaf Key
Big Coppitt Key
Mile Marker 4
To Key West

A Land That's Mostly Water and A Sea that's Mostly Sky

ANY PEOPLE consider this part of the Overseas Highway, from Boca Chica Naval Air Station at mile marker (MM) 7, to the Seven Mile Bridge at MM 40, to be the most spectacular thirty-three mile stretch in the Keys. The endless expanses are so dazzling that you may find yourself losing the line where the sea ends and the sky begins. It is possible to drive from the urban heart of Key West into some remarkably vast marine flatlands, well within a half hour.

Beyond Key West, development thins out dramatically. With few buildings, no malls, and no fast-food emporiums, but several long, new bridges, many square-miles of mangroves, and lots of water—the Atlantic Ocean on the south side of the highway, the Gulf of Mexico on the north. On this stretch you will find restaurants and accommodations, but not many.

The Boca Chica Naval Air Station, the last major landmark you see as you drive away from Key West, has been here since it was commissioned in 1917. This location was chosen for the air station when Navy research found it to have the most days of perfect flying weather of anywhere in the country. If your car radio is on as you drive past Boca Chica, you will hear a series of little beeps that might make you wonder if your car is being bugged. But no, it's the sky that's being bugged by radar scanning for unwelcome visitors approaching the area by air.

Driving north to Big Coppitt Key, the four-lane highway turns into two lanes. Big Coppitt Key is a predominantly residential community. Many of the residents work at the nearby base; others have moved here to suburbia from Key West to buy affordable homes on the less-glamorous, and certainly less-prestigious, Big Coppitt Key. If you live here, your mailing address is Key West.

The traffic light at MM 17 marks a tiny hub of commerce on the island of Sugarloaf Key. The Bat Tower, a dolphin named Sugar, and a wee airport are all located on Sugarloaf Key.

Cudjoe Key is thought to be named after a guy named Joe who fled the busy city of Key West in the 1880's to homestead on a peaceful island twenty-two miles up the road. Say "Cousin Joe's Key" real fast and you might hear "Cudjoe Key." That's one theory anyway. Another is that Cudjoe Key is named for the joewood tree that grows on the island.

Guarding the sea from a spot high in the air over Cudjoe Key is a 1400-foot-high radar blimp affectionately known as "Fat Albert." The blimp is tethered to a Naval facility on Blimp Road. Fat Albert can be seen from miles away in either direction.

Big Pine Key, eight miles long and roughly two miles wide, is the second-largest in the coral island chain. (Key Largo is largest.) Much of the pineland and hardwood hammocks and mangrove fringe on this island is encompassed in a critical habitat called the Key West Wildlife Refuge for indigenous, threatened and endangered species. The refuge is managed by the U.S. Department of Fish and Wildlife.

Recently the Florida Department of Transportation judged Big Pine Key, the island that begins at MM 29, to be the most congested traffic area in the Keys, triggering an automatic building moratorium. Commercial building is allowed only as long as it does not increase traffic to the island. (How can it not, you might reasonably ask?) The worst time to pass through here is on Saturday mornings between late October and May when the Big Pine Flea Market slows traffic to an inching crawl. All of Big Pine Key, from MM's 29 to 33, is a reduced speed zone— 45 mph by day and 35 mph after dark. Speed limits are strictly enforced.

The beautiful sandy beach that everybody visiting the Keys seems to be looking for is in Bahia Honda State Recreational Area at MM 37, adjacent to Bahia Honda Channel. In this reverently maintained natural preserve are indigenous plants and flowers that, according to park signs, grow almost nowhere else in the world; there's excellent RV and tent camping in the park, too. Many people find the campgrounds in the Lower Keys more relaxed and less restrictive than those to the north.

After the lonely little islands of Ohio, Missouri, and Little Duck Keys, named by Flagler's railroad workers in the early 1900s, comes the majestic and amazing Seven Mile Bridge.

A History Stranger Than Fiction

Sponges and Bats—
Sugarloaf Key's Weird Past

At one point in its history, it looked as if Sugarloaf Key might become the sponge capital of the world. Charles Chase came to Sugarloaf Key in 1910 to establish the Florida Keys Sponge and Fruit Company. Charles and his businessman brother (who lived in Chicago) had studied results of several government-funded experiments in artificial sponge cultivation and determined that they could make a successful business of raising sponges in the large, nearly landlocked, shallow sounds at Sugarloaf Key. The Chase brothers paid $45,000 to buy nearly all of Sugarloaf Key from J. Vining Harris of Key West.

In an astonishingly short time, land was cleared, living quarters were built and occupied by workers and their families, and facilities for processing and planting sponges were established. A disk-manufacturing operation, located in the area of today's Sugarloaf Lodge, constructed

Spongers

thousands of 10-inch round, cement disks upon which sponges would be encouraged to grow. Natural sponges were taken from the ocean floor and cut up into many smaller pieces which were wired onto the disks. The disks and sponge starters were then submerged in shallow water where, presumably, they would mature into uniformly round, sand-free sponges, ready for the already-established, world-wide demand.

When the Overseas Railroad was completed and the first train thundered across Sugarloaf Key in January 1912, the sponge cultivation settlement was a small town with a population of one hundred and a work force of sixty. When the settlement next to the railroad tracks became big enough to require its own post office, it became a town named Chase, after the brothers who'd started it all.

Unfortunately, the earlier experimenters in sponge cultivation had miscalculated on one extremely important point: how many years the sponges would need to grow to commercial size. The Chase brothers had planned on four years; in fact, it was more like six, and so they ran out of money well before their grand scheme yielded a viable harvest.

The brothers solicited money from contacts in their native country of England, and they got it, but before they were able to transfer it back to America, World War I began, and the funds were frozen in English banks.

By the time the Florida Keys Sponge and Fruit Company declared bankruptcy in May 1917, the town of Chase was abandoned. The Chase brothers eventually sold their ghost town and their holdings on Sugarloaf Key to Miamian Richter C. Perky for $200,000.

The Bat Tower

Perky planned to develop the property as a private vacation and fishing retreat. But the future of his planned paradise looked bleak when he realized the severity of the mosquito problem. In an interview years later, a caretaker who worked for Perky recalled that the mosquitoes were so thick that a person could press his hands against a screen and quickly attract so many mosquitoes that, when they pulled away, a clump of hungry mosquitoes in the shape of their hands would remain on the screen.

Perky had heard of an interesting means of mosquito control that had worked successfully in other parts of the country. Following instructions in a book called *Bats, Mosquitoes and Dollars*, Perky built a bat tower on his property. Perky's plan was to rid his island of mosquitoes by filling his tower with mosquito-hungry bats. Then he planned to sell the recycled mosquitoes, in the form of bat poop, as fertilizer; however, the bats never came.

Current tourist literature often makes Perky out to be a crazy man, but scientists say his idea wasn't so outlandish—bats are a natural means of pest control; one bat will eat its weight in insects every night. Obviously, it behooves Floridians to keep their bat populations thriving. Five years ago researchers at the University of Florida in Gainesville built a bat tower similar to Perky's. Today, at least 3,000 bats are living permanently in the gabled stilt house. And recently, more than sixty years after Perky built the 30-foot bat condominium, colonies of bats have been confirmed in the Upper Keys. They are not living in Perky's tower yet, but when they're ready to roost, the bat tower will be ready for them.

Making Charcoal

The Torch Keys were named for torchwood, a small tree that works well in the creation of charcoal because it burns well, even when green. Buttonwood, which grows profusely in the Lower Keys, is another fine wood for charcoal making. Before the use of electricity, and gas or coal stoves, charcoal was the main fuel in Key West. Many settlers in the Lower Keys made their livings creating charcoal, an arduous task. First, trees were chopped down and cut into logs, which were stacked into massive cones and covered with mud or seaweed. Then a fire was started at the center of the tee-pee-shaped construction. The stack of logs was never allowed to burst into flame and burn; instead, the charcoal-maker would keep the interior damp so it would smolder for days. Eventually the wood was reduced to charcoal and transported to Key West, where there was a large and steady demand for the fuel.

Like many Keys and reefs, Ramrod Key got its name from a ship that wrecked near the island in the 1800s. Ramrod, Summerland and Cudjoe Keys were all once centers of charcoal production.

Cudjoe Key

The most famous person ever to live on Cudjoe Key was a trail-blazing woman from Chicago named Lily Lawrence Bow. She came to Cudjoe

Key with her husband and their two sons in 1904. But Mr. Bow didn't enjoy the tropical wilderness of the Florida Keys, and soon he returned to the north, leaving his family alone and without means. The Bows, the only white people on Cudjoe Key, grew vegetables and raised chickens; the boys fished. Eventually Ms. Bow, who'd gone to college, became the only schoolteacher for miles, and Keys, around. Her students' parents paid for her services with food so the Bows were able to stay on Cudjoe Key for two years. Finally they moved to Homestead, Florida, another rough and rugged wilderness. With a homestead grant, Lily Bow built a log cabin and planted a citrus grove there. She became active in civic affairs and helped found the area's women's club. Homestead's public library is called the "Lily Lawrence Bow Library" in her memory.

And in the Keys, Bow Channel, that runs between Upper Sugarloaf and Cudjoe Keys, is named after Lily Bow, and today, just like back in 1904, it still takes an enormous amount of courage to survive near the swift waters of Bow Channel.

The Monkey Keys

They're gone now, but it used to be that on Key Lois and Raccoon Key, islands several miles offshore from Summerland Key, two rhesus-monkey habitats were home to thousands of monkeys, who roamed freely, consumed large quantities of red mangroves, and shrieked wildly while awaiting their turns in the medical research laboratories of Charles Rivers Labs. The monkeys stayed healthy and free from infections, thanks to their isolation, and that made them particularly valuable to the researchers.

Although Charles Rivers Laboratories owns the monkey islands, but were unable to with any accuracy how many test monkeys lived on them. Maybe 1500, they said; maybe 3,000. Environmentalists complained that the monkeys were destroying significant stands of red mangroves that once ringed the islands. They were also concerned about pollution from monkey poop. In addition, Lower Keys residents were concerned that the monkeys might swim to the nearby Keys and invade peaceful neighborhoods. Or there was a fear that hurricane winds might blow the Monkeys into densely populated places like Key West. In a spirit of cooperation, the Charles Rivers Lab agreed in 1992 to pen the monkeys in cages of 300 monkeys each, and to cover the remaining mangrove stands in protective mesh. Environmentalists, as a result, charged that caging the creatures was inhumane.

100-acre Key Lois is on the Atlantic side of the Keys; Raccoon Key, a 200-acre island, is on the Gulf side. You cannot see either island from the Overseas Highway, but local kids on Waverunners enjoy riding very close to the shore of the monkey islands for a closer look. "The monkeys are mean-looking," one kid said. "And dirty. You hear them before you can actually see them." It was illegal, of course, to disembark on Key Lois or Raccoon Key. Hey, who'd want to?

They're gone now. But it was weird thing to see while it was happening.

Earning a Living on Big Pine Key

The original inhabitants of this area were Indian hunter/gatherers who lived on deer, turtles and fish. Later island dwellers found the soil on Big Pine Key to be very productive. Among the 132 people who lived on this part of the Lower Keys in 1870, more than half were farmers; the rest were seamen. The Bahamian farmers grew cash crops of fruits and vegetables which they transported by schooner to Key West. Settlers augmented their diets with white-crowned pigeons, doves, herons and cormorants, as well as green turtle and conch.

A woman who lived on Big Pine Key as a child in the early 1900s recalls that Key limes were so plentiful her family couldn't use them fast enough. Her father made a tool that squeezed a dozen limes at a time. The Key lime juice was called "old sour" and was a popular marinate for seafood, poultry and fish. Key limes sold for a dime a case in Key West.

By 1900, blacks from the Bahama Islands and freed slaves from the American South outnumbered whites in these Lower Keys two to one. They supported themselves, like everyone else, by making charcoal, sponging, farming, or fishing.

Before the completion of the Overseas Highway in 1938, to reach the Lower Keys by car, it was necessary to make two fourteen-mile ferry crossings. Ferries shuttled cars from Lower Matecumbe Key to Grassy Key, and then from Knight's Key to No Name Key. Operation of the ferries created jobs and several small settlements. Today the remains of a cistern and several coral-rock foundations mark the site of the little town that grew up around the ferry landing on No Name Key.

Hammerhead shark

A shark processing plant was the first major enterprise on Big Pine Key. The shark facility was built in 1923 by Hydenoil Products, a company that butchered sharks for their hides and livers. The hides made a strong, soft leather; shark liver oil is rich in vitamins. The products were exported from the Keys via the Overseas Railroad, which operated in the Keys from 1912 until 1935.

The company employed sixty men who caught sharks in nets, where they drowned or clubbed them to death. The Hydenoil Company killed up to one hundred sharks a day. The biggest fish they caught was a 1,752-pound mackerel shark. Among the grisly finds made by shark processors when they cut open the sharks' bellies was a human arm still wearing the remnants of a blue serge suit. The material later proved to be from the

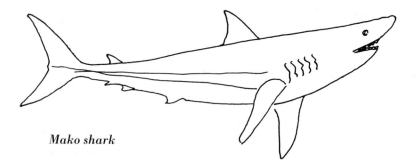

Mako shark

uniform of a Cuban pilot who'd been on a seaplane that had crashed into the ocean days earlier.

In spite of their seemingly successful operation, the Depression spelled hard times for Hydenoil Company, and the Big Pine Key shark plant closed in 1931.

Lower Keys Chamber of Commerce
MM 31, Oceanside ✱ 872-2411 ✱ 800-872-3722

Outside of the Visitors Center a clean, breezy park has benches, picnic tables, public bathrooms and a spreading poinciana tree in spectacular bloom in early summer. Exhibits by the National Marine Sanctuary program post some surprising information, like the fact that the barrier reef ecosystem of the Florida Keys is the third largest in the world.

Inside you can cool off in fine air conditioning while you stock up on brochures promoting every imaginable local feature, as well as lots of things to see and do in Key West, 30 miles away. Yes, 30 miles farther down the road. Many people are surprised that they're not yet at the end of the road by the time they arrive here. Some people even ask "Are we in the Keys yet?" which is enormously amusing for the people who work here.

Videos describing the reefs, Key deer, and the profoundly luxurious offshore resort of Little Palm Island play full-time. If you don't like what's playing, change it. The video of Little Palm Island is as close as most people can afford to get to this exorbitantly expensive bastion of splendor.

"Big Pine Key is all about nature," you will be told. "We have nature." And they do. A kayaking tour of the backcountry, a visit to the Blue Hole, and an encounter with a Key deer are all do-able in a day or two visit. Good restaurants are here, too.

What's everyone's first question when they arrive at the Visitor's Center? Where do we go to see Key deer?

Key Deer

ONE OF THE MOST REMARKABLE CREATURES on the endangered species list, and perhaps the Keys' most cherished, is the endearingly dimunutive Key deer. If you think Bambi was cute, imagine these wee critters. The very largest Key deer weighs 75 pounds and is two-and-a-half feet tall. The very smallest is the two- to four-pound infant, who is born after a 200 day gestation period. At the Museum of Natural History at Crane Point Hammock, MM 50 in Marathon, a life-like exhibit of a mama, papa and baby Key deer is on display.

Key deer are mentioned in some of the earliest written accounts of life in the Keys. At one time Key deer were found all the way from Big Pine Key down to Key West, thirty miles away. They were eaten by local residents as well as by passing sailors who came ashore to hunt. Through the years the Key deer population has been thinned through hunting, poaching, and habitat destruction. And yet, the little guys survive.

By the 1940s, when conservation laws were established to save the Key deer from extinction, there were fewer than 50 of the creatures left alive. Now there are thought to be 300 Key deer living on Big Pine and No Name Keys. The species exists nowhere else in the world.

Although the Key deer has done a remarkable job of adapting to the Keys' limited space and sparse food supply, it is still one of the most threatened species in the country. The biggest threat to Key deer is cars. Each day an average of 30,000 vehicles travel the Overseas Highway during the winter tourist season. Each year the number of deer killed by cars increases, and the statistics look more grim than the year before. In 1995, the number of recorded deer deaths was eighty-nine; sixty-five of those were killed by vehicles. The rest drowned, were killed by dogs, or died of natural or unknown causes. Thirteen of the dead were fawns.

The Overseas Highway now has a reduced speed limit for the length of Big Pine Key, from Mile Markers 29 through 33: 45 mph by day and 35 mph after dark. The limits are strictly enforced.

In spite of state and federal laws prohibiting people from feeding Key deer, many people find it difficult to believe that by providing the deer with food, they are harming them. In fact, deer who are fed may change their behavior, growing overly confident around humans. In addition, unhealthy foods inhibit the deer's ability to reproduce. Laws also prohibit molesting or interfering with the Key deer; violators face $540 state fines and even jail time.

To survive and procreate, Key deer need fresh water and sufficient food sources. They eat red, black and white mangroves, thatch palm berries, and over 150 other species of plants. I have seen Key deer

munching bougainvillea flowers. Accessing their needs becomes more and more difficult.

Roughly one-third of the eleven-square-mile island of Big Pine Key is taken up by the U. S. Fish and Wildlife Key Deer Refuge. Some residents resent the federal government's presence and would like to build an elementary school and other community service buildings on Big Pine Key; progress must go on, they say. Environmentalists argue, however, that overdevelopment of the island has already destroyed wetlands and depleted the fresh water supply. So a bitter environmental controversy rages over the Key deer, which has become a symbol of a community's continuing controversy over land use, and the poster child of the endangered species. Save the Key deer, many believe, and you save the Keys.

And when a hurricane heads our way, how do we protect the Key deer? What will we do with the deer in case of evacuation? It is possible that the entire population of deer could be wiped out by a single powerful hurricane.

Spotting Key Deer

In the novel *Sunburn*, Key West author Larry Shames writes an account of a Key deer-spotting expedition to No Name Key. It's a couple of pages into Chapter 36. No Name Key is described by *Sunburn's* hero as a swampy place with "spiders the size of your fist, leaves that give a rash, alligators that eat Dobermans."

Well, yes, all that's true. But you really do have a good chance of seeing Key deer there. You will be surprised to find how comfortable Key deer seem to be around humans and their vehicles. They don't run away when you show up, but this is not always a good thing. Naturalists say that the more confident a wild animal becomes around humans, the more trouble they are bound to get into.

From around mile marker 31.5 to the beginning of the Spanish Harbor Bridge at mile marker 33, you have a good chance of seeing deer grazing on the gulfside shoulder of the road. Deer seldom travel alone, so if you see one, look around and you will probably see more.

Long Beach Road, which starts at mile marker 33 oceanside, is the eastern border of the Key Deer Refuge. Many times if you simply look down that road from the Overseas Highway, you will spot deer. Drive slowly down Long Beach Road, and you may see good-sized groups of deer.

No Name Key is where the tour buses go with the hope of catching a glimpse of Key deer. To get to No Name Key, you must go over a new cement bridge called the Bogie Channel Bridge. From the bridge you can look over the water and see the Spanish Harbor Bridge out on the Overseas Highway. You can also spot the Bogie Channel Bridge from the Spanish Harbor Bridge.

Before you arrive at the white boulders that mark the end of the road and the ruins of the old ferry town, you will probably see more deer. That's why you must travel very slowly. Follow the road all the way to the end, or simply park on the side and wait. Eventually you are sure to see some deer wandering through the tropical hammock. The creatures blend in very well with the background vegetation, so you've got to keep your eyes peeled. If you get out of the car, beware of poisonwood trees.

It is said that early mornings and late afternoons are the best times to
see Key deer, but we have seen them at all times of the day. They are not
hiding, you will find, and they are very beautiful; yes, very much like
their northern cousins but in miniature.

The Key Deer Protection Alliance
872-0774
Founded in 1989, the goals of the alliance are to help save the Key deer
from extinction by creating and distributing accurate and objective information to the public, and by supporting the preservation of the Key deer
habitat. The Alliance awards scholarships to students pursuing degrees in
biological sciences. They hold regular clean-up days. It is not a place to
visit with Key deer, as some tourists seem to think.

Bahia Honda State Park

The Florida Keys' Biggest and Best Beach

Bahia Honda
MM 37, Oceanside ✒ 872-2353

Here is the most beautiful beach in Florida and possibly the whole country. That's what the travel magazines say anyway. What's most thrilling at Bahia Honda Beach are the brilliant colors. The ocean's magnificent arrangement of blue, green, and azure seems to change from day to day, and even hour to hour. What you see is actually a kaleidoscopic light show as the light reflects up from the bottom of the ocean through clear water. Each type of bottom translates to a different color as light bounces off it and back to the water's surface. Grass meadows reflect dark brown or navy blue; sand reflects yellow and beige; corals reflect various shades of blue. As the winds whip and toss the surface of the water, the hues of each color change. A cloudless day or a heavily clouded day will empower or mute the colors. The time of day and the angle of the sun influence your view, too. Beware: The sea is hypnotic.

The blustery sea air here is filled with graceful sea birds, who seem to be having a fine time gliding on the gentle breezes and gusts of the limitless sky. The sand is fine and the color of cafe au lait. You cannot not be dazzled by this glorious arrangement of sea, shore and sky.

The majority of the people you see have come here for the incomparable beach—and that's it. There's another beach on the other side of the park, on Bahia Honda Channel, and it's dramatically beautiful too, but in a different way. The waters of the Bahia Honda Channel are quite deep, by Keys standards, and the currents are swift not far from the sandy shore. Both beaches are the stuff that tourists' dreams are made of. Where's the beach? It's here, baby.

In addition to the main attraction, the beach, Bahia Honda Park's 524 acres also contain several complex biological communities. You will see more subtropical flowers here, particularly in springtime, than anywhere else in the Keys. Sea birds, white-crowned pigeons, herons, egrets, and gulls, are also in abundance.

Exploring the park is great fun. Deep waters begin close enough to the shore to provide exceptional swimming and snorkeling. Campers catch fish right off the shore and docks in front of their campsites on the channel. Kayaks are available for rent by the hour: $10 for a single, and $20 for a double. There are two boat launches and a parking lot for trailers. Snorkeling trips leave the lagoon twice daily. (There's a fee.)

Hike the perimeter of the park to see a tangled jungle of thatch and silver palms, key tiger lily, key spider lily. Sea lavender and bay cedar give way to a beachfront hammock with trees like satinwood and yellow wood. The plants were brought here from the West Indies via the Caribbean Sea by birds, hurricane winds, and ocean waves.

The Bahia Honda campfire circle, which is really an outdoor theater with a movie screen set against the backdrop of the Atlantic Ocean, is certainly the spiffiest campfire circle you'll ever see. Camping has come a long way since Mom and Dad were scouts....

On a map of the world in the park store, you are invited to push a pin into your home town. The areas of the eastern United States, as well as western Europe, are the most well-represented areas on the map.

Plenty of picnic tables and shelters are scattered throughout the park, many of them deliciously private, as well as three camping areas and a concession, where you can rent a boat or sign on for a snorkel trip to the Looe Key Reef.

The park is open from 8 a.m. until sunset every day of the year. Admission is $2.50 per car with one person. $5 for a car with two, and 50¢ for each additional person. Children five and under go free.

Information: Bahia Honda State Park, Route 1, Box 782, Big Pine Key, FL 33040. Phone: 305-872-3897.

The Waters of the Lower Keys

The Backcountry

You might envision an area located at the end of a long, lonely dirt road when you hear the term backcountry. Down here the term refers to expanses of small, uninhabited mangrove islands, scattered, shallow-water seagrass meadows and tidal channels on the north and west of the main island chain. The islands of the backcountry are accessible only by boat.

Because the backcountry is a haven for a wide variety of wildlife, most of the islands are under the jurisdiction of the Everglades National Park, National Key Deer Refuge, Great White Heron National Wildlife Refuge, and Key West National Wildlife Refuge.

Navigating through the sometimes maze-like backcountry can be difficult for newcomers. Tidal channels are not well-marked, and depth perception is difficult for the inexperienced eye. Running aground is a constant possibility in these very shallow flats, and, unfortunately, it is very easy to damage the backcountry's bottom communities with a boat's propeller. Boats crossing the deeper flats at high speed are almost sure to hit bottom at some of the shallower points on the flats. Propeller digs leave cuts in the seagrass beds and cracks that fill with sand and mud. Although sea grasses can withstand some disruption without suffering serious consequences, environmentalists are now concerned that the cumulative effect of increased boating in the backcountry may have lasting negative impact.

To avoid doing harm, keep your boat in the tidal channels, steer clear of the shallower shortcuts, and proceed with respectful caution. It is much easier to back off a flat that you have glided into gently than it is to back away after you've hit hard aground at a high speed. Lightweight, flat bottom kayaks are becoming the preferred vessel for visiting the backcountry. They're easy to operate, and they work for sightseeing, fishing and snorkeling.

Here's some good news about the backcountry for people prone to seasickness: The waters and lakes of the backcountry are usually quite calm, even when it's blowing hard on the oceanside of the Keys.

Looe Key Sanctuary

In March of 1996, Rodale's *Scuba Diving Magazine* readers chose Looe Key Reef as the best one in the United States. Looe Key gets its name from the HMS *Looe*, a 44-gun British frigate that ran aground on the reef during a winter storm in 1744. The reef is still a threatening one for boat traffic; small boats have scraped and damaged corals. Ironically, a large research vessel from the University of Miami caused massive damage when it grounded at Looe Key in 1994.

The 5.3-square-mile reef became a National Marine Sanctuary in 1981 following the success of the Key Largo Sanctuary, created in 1975. On the Looe Key reef, as well as on Key Largo's reef system, concentrations of fish species are spread throughout. The sanctuary designation means that spearfishing, tropical fish collecting and wire fish-traps are banned in the area of the reef. In the fifteen years since Looe Key became a sanctuary, scientists say, reef populations have become significantly more stable than in other unprotected areas.

Water clarity in the sanctuary is excellent, and sea conditions are generally moderate, permitting the reef's many spectacular inhabitants and features to be observed easily. The reef features over 150 species of fish, with descriptive names like yellowtail, jawfish, parrotfish, surgeonfish, barracuda, lizardfish and peacock flounder, swimming gracefully between the coral heads and sea fans and whips. Fifty species of coral are named for the earthly things they resemble: brain, elkhorn, and staghorn, for example. Looe Key Marine Sanctuary's spur and groove formations are the best developed in the Keys; uncommon pillar corals thrive in the intermediate and deep reefs. The seagrass meadows and sand flats provide fascinating views of sea life.

Stuff to Do On the Water

Dolphin Marina Boat Rentals
MM 28.5, Oceanside ✆ 872-2685

The nice thing about the boats you rent at Dolphin Marina is that they're so well equipped. If you're going diving, everything you need—except the dive gear—is on board: ship-to-shore radios, a Bimini top or transoms to provide shade, and ice chests.

Boat rents start at around $160 for a half-day and $225 for a full day. Boat sizes are 20 to 22 feet. Before you leave the marina, someone will go over charts with you to make sure you're headed in the right direction. You don't have to travel far from shore to find some fun.

If you're interested in fishing, on the flats or in the deep sea, Dolphin Marina will hook you up with a fully licensed and insured fishing guide.

Looe Key Dive Center
MM 27.5 Oceanside ✆ 872-2215

Looe Key is truly the nicest reef to visit in the Keys and the daily reef trip offered here is one of the most affordable. The Kokomo Cat, a 45-foot catamaran, leaves for the reef at 10 a.m. Arrives back at 3 p.m. The trip is open to snorkelers, SCUBA divers, and passengers. They visit 3 locations in the Looe Key Marine Sanctuary, and on Wednesdays and Saturdays they go to the *Adolphus Busch Senior*, a ship sunk to form an artificial reef in December, 1998. The developing reef has attracted lots of big fish, and new growth is coming along well, local divemasters say.

Passengers just going along on the boat for the ride pay $15. You can rent snorkel gear, SCUBA gear, and, if it's all you need, tanks. One of the benefits of diving the Looe Key Sanctuary is that it doesn't take a very

long time to boat out to it. During slow times of the year, Looe Key Dive
Center offers some great specials on reef trips. Call for prices.

Strike Zone Charters
MM 28.5 Gulfside ❧ 872-9863 ❧ 800-654-9560

Larry Threlkeld, owner of Strike Zone Charters, is frequently called to
ultra-posh Little Palm Island to introduce folks like former Vice
President Gore and family, Rod Stewart and his wife of the moment,
David Copperfield, and Ivana Trump to the joys of diving the Looe Key
Reef. Larry says magician David Copperfield did not make Little Palm
Island disappear, in spite of many requests. As for those fashion models
he is hired to ferry out to the tropical retreat of the rich and famous: "We
call them the 'vampire people.' They run from the sun! Their photo
shoots start at 5 a.m. and wrap by 10 a.m."

Of course, you don't have to be a star to sign on for one of Strike
Zone's many excursions. Through Strike Zone you can snorkel in the
Looe Key Marine Sanctuary, tour the backcountry, fish on assorted package tours, or do it all in a popular five-hour excursion designed to
enlighten visitors to the natural history of the living coral reef and the
Florida Keys, as well as the ecology of several Keys marine systems. Your
captain will point out sea birds, marine life, and even help you catch a
fish, which you cook and eat on board.

The five-hour Island Excursion heads out at 1 p.m daily, for a look at
both the Atlantic Ocean and the Florida Bay floors, through a glassbottom boat for small children or other people who are unable, for any
reason, to get into the water. Otherwise you can snorkel. You might see a
manatee. And if you hear music while you're exploring the reef, don't
think you've flipped your lid. Your captain will sometimes lower a big
speaker right into the water for an impromptu underwater rock concert.
Cost is $49 per person, and that covers cost of snorkel and fishing gear.
Kids three to nine years old go for half price; Under 3 under go for free.
This is a great family trip out on the water. Take plenty of sunscreen.

Snorkel and SCUBA dive trips depart for Looe Key at 9:30 a.m. and
1:30 p.m. daily. Snorkelers pay $30; Kids nine and under pay $25. Rent
snorkel gear for $5. SCUBA divers pay $40; gear rental for them is $40.
Strike Zone also offers a deep-sea fishing charter on a 40-foot or 34-foot
sport fisherman. Custom fishing charters are $650 for a full day; $500 for

a half day, and that price includes rods, reels, bait, tackle and your fishing
license.

Jig's Bait and Tackle
MM 30.5, Gulfside ✶ 872-1040

Not only does Jig's sell block ice, custom rods, tackle, snorkel gear, dive
flags, fishing licenses, and just about any other nautical needs you may
have, they'll also hook you up with a captain and charter boat to take
you out into the ocean for deep-sea fishing, or into the backcountry for
flats fishing. Jig's will also find you a kayak tour, if that's what you're looking for. Jig's used to rent kayaks, and by the time you are reading this, if
all goes well, they'll be renting them again. Hours are 6:30 a.m. till 7 p.m.
Monday through Saturday; They close Sundays at 3 p.m.

Bahia Honda State Park Concession
MM 38 Oceanside ✶ 872-3210

Weather permitting, daily snorkel trips to Looe Key depart Bahia Honda
dock at 9:30 a.m. and 1:30. p.m. On the reef trip, snorkelers are assisted
in identifying the wonders of the deep by helpful mates. Adults pay $30;
kids under 18 pay $25. Snorkel set rental is $6 and, if it's really cold, you
can rent a wet suit for $6.

Kayak rentals, single ($10/hour or $30 for a half day) and double
($18/hour or $54 for a half day). Life jackets and paddles are included in
the rent. You'll also find anything you need for the beach at the concession stand, for rent, as in the case of chairs and umbrellas, or for sale, like
sun screen, and snacks.

Big Pine Kayak Adventures, Inc.
At the Bogie Channel Bridge ✶ 872-7474 ✶ 877-595-2925

A full-service kayak tour and rental agency, specializing in Lower Florida
Keys Backcountry adventures, located in the Old Wooden Bridge Fishing
Camp on Big Pine Key. Visits to the Key Deer Refuge and the Great
White Heron National Wildlife Refuge. Find the book *Florida Keys, The
Natural Wonders of an Island Paradise*, for a glimpse of what you'll see,
beautifully photographed by kayak tour guide and nature photographer
Bill Keogh, owner of Big Pine Key Kayak Adventures. Sign on for half or

full day kayaking nature tours or shallow water skiff eco-tours. Or, rent a kayak and head out on your own with an easy to follow laminated chart to show you the way - actually, several ways. For backcountry tours, kayaks and their paddlers are ferried deep into the backcountry aboard a power boat. In the untouched wilderness of the backcountry you'll see sharks, rays, dolphins, turtles and birds. Kayaks are safe and stable and quiet. Paddling, some say, is addictive.

Saltwater rafting

Osprey

Nature Treats

The Blue Hole
Key Deer Boulevard ⚓ MM 30, Big Pine Key

The Blue Hole is an old rock quarry of fresh water that is home to several alligators, many fish, a couple of turtles, and some hawks and herons. It is the largest body of fresh water in the Keys. The alligators swim up to the observation deck to eyeball visitors with their strange, lizardy orbs and seem to think you're going to feed them. Don't do it! When you feed 'gators, you teach them to be unafraid of humans, and brave alligators eat humans, especially small, chubby ones like children. Recently a big 'gator became so tame, so confident about his acceptance by humans, that he begun to snap at tourists. Whoops! He had to be taken away from the Blue Hole.

On Saturdays, you'll sometimes find a volunteer naturalist greeting visitors and telling them about the inhabitants of this strange place. Fresh water is crucial to the survival of Key deer, so you will often see them here, along with fat raccoons.

To get to the Blue Hole: At the Big Pine traffic light at mile marker 30 turn onto Key Deer Boulevard (gulfside). Go through the intersection of Key Deer and Watson boulevards; then continue for one-and-a-quarter miles farther.

Pinewood Nature Trail
Key Deer Boulevard

A two-thirds mile long nature trail is located a quarter-mile past the Blue Hole. The trail winds through an excellent habitat typical of many slash pine and palm hammocks on Little Pine Key. Lots of signs will point the way and tell you what you're seeing.

Key Deer Refuge Headquarters
MM 30, Big Pine Shopping Center ☎ 872-2239

This little office contains a world of information about the unique habitat of Big Pine Key and the wondrous creatures who live here, many of them endangered. You will see a real key deer here. It's stuffed. Before visiting the Blue Hole, the Big Pine Nature Trail, and No Name Key, stop by the refuge headquarters. Hours: 8 a.m. - 4 p.m. Monday - Friday, summertime; Tuesday - Saturday wintertime.

Legal Highs

Fantasy Dan's Airplane Rides
Sugarloaf Airport ✱ 745-2217
Fantasy Dan will fly out to the reef to view Stargazer, a two-hundred-foot-long, seventy-foot-wide 50,000-pound metal sculpture, resting twenty feet below the blue water's surface some five miles northwest of Key West. Stargazer is the world's largest artificial reef. On a very dark night, when phosphorescent sealife light up Stargazer's form, the sight from the air is breathtaking. Dan charges by the flight. In other words, you can be one person or three people on the same trip and it will cost the same. Regular flights: 35-minute sight-seeing flights down along the reef, around Key West and back over the islands of the Keys gulfside, and a 55-minute flight west, out to Boca Grand Key, for a look at several shipwrecks. Dan is a great guide.

Skydive Key West
Sugarloaf Key ✱ 745-4FUN
At MM 17 there is a blinking yellow light. Turn toward the Gulf there (same side as the Sugarloaf Lodge), and you'll come to the trailer that houses Skydive Key West. Inside there are videos of other people's dives to tempt you to sign up yourself. Cost of the tandem dive is $200 if you pay cash, and $220 if you pay with a credit card. Want to take home a video of your skydive? That's $99 more.

Ultralight Rides and Tours
MM 28.5, Barry Ave. ✱ 872-0555
Take an instruction ride, or fly just for the fun of it, aboard an ultralight airplane with Emil Oureick. Emil will let you fly it yourself for a minute or two. Anybody can do it, he says. The tricky parts are taking off and landing, and he'll do those things for you. Open daily, depending, of course, on the weather.

From the Ruins

Bahia Honda Bridge
MM 36, Oceanside

Just after you pass over the new Bahia Honda Bridge, heading for Key West, you will see a rough parking area, oceanside. This wild and wonderful place used to be a ramp for the Overseas Railroad and the Bahia Honda Bridge. Hike to the top of the bluff and compare the old railroad bridge, which was the most difficult of all the bridges to build, to the sleek, new bridge next to it.

The original Bahia Honda Bridge is 5,356 feet long, with twenty feet of clearance above the water and a maximum height of sixty-five feet. The trains for which the bridge were originally built in 1907 traveled through the center of the span, protected on either side by high, steel guardrails. But when the bridge was adapted for auto traffic in 1936, it was found to be too narrow to accommodate two lanes of cars. So the roadway was built over the top of the bridge. Imagine driving across that bridge on that road! You can still see the crumbling road surface.

Across the Bahia Honda Channel you can see Bahia Honda recreation area, where great photo opportunities await in this leg-stretching place. Explore the paths and ancient structures. In springtime a profusion of tropical wild flowers bloom on this ground. The wind is wild, always blustery. The waters in the Bahia Honda Channel are the swiftest currents anywhere in the Keys.

A Freaky Nature Treat
Bahia Honda MM 36

During the full moon in late May or early June, tiny palolo worms hatch from the sponges and rocks in the channel under the Bahia Honda Bridge. Tarpon go into a feeding frenzy, gobbling up the poor little worms. From the bridge you see huge schools of silvery tarpon clouding the surface of the water. Call Bahia Honda and ask a park ranger just how the scene is progressing next time you're in the Lower Keys at the end of May.

The Bat Tower
MM 17, Gulfside

Businessman Richter Perky read, many years ago, that a tower built of cypress and baited with food would attract hundreds of bats, which would, in turn, devour the pesky mosquitoes that discouraged anyone from seriously hanging out on Sugarloaf, where Perky had a fishing and gambling lodge. Perky built the tower, but the bats did not come. Now the tower is a historical monument, visited by hundreds of people annually. You might be disappointed when you see it, but it's only five minutes out of your way. And for Sugarloaf Key, it's a major tourist attraction.

The Bat Tower

The Ferry Ruins
No Name Key ✻ Big Pine Key

No Name Key is connected to Big Pine by the Bogie Channel Bridge, a fairly new concrete span that seems to be used more by fisherman than it is by cars. When you cross the bridge, you're on No Name Key, a place with no electricity and no water, either. The people who live on No Name Key get their power from solar units or generators. The houses are located at the end of long driveways with sinister-looking no-trespassing signs that seem to mean business.

Follow the road all the way out to the end, and you'll come to the ruins of a once-thriving ferry town. Park near the large, white limestone boulders that mark the road's end. Beyond them is the sea. This was once the site of a car ferry landing that carried travelers across a fourteen-mile span to or from Knight's Key next to Marathon. A small village with a school and a post office was established here in 1922. The town was a busy one until the Overseas Highway put the ferry out of business in 1938.

Today the ferry landing at No Name Key is unbelievably quiet. The only sounds you hear are the calls of birds in the trees and the whispering of the soft breezes. There are bold raccoons sometimes in the trees and, often, many Key deer. To the right and just beyond the white boulders is a magnificent and unusual clump of seven Canary Island Date Palm trees, their branches heavy and studded with dates. If you want to taste one, make sure you check for bugs first.

At the Old Wooden Key Fishing Camp you can rent a kayak and paddle from there out here. Or, they'll drop you off in the water here and you paddle back.

Biking

PLENTY OF LONG, SMOOTH, ROADS here are great for biking. On Big
Pine Key, Watson Boulevard and Long Beach Road (MM 33) both
take you past the Key Deer Sanctuary. As you bike past pinelands,
mangroves and tangled jungle, you'll likely spot many deer and ride
through pockets of suburbia-like enclaves that feel absurdly out of place.
A good bicycle tour and lunch break in these parts could take up an
entire afternoon.

On Sugarloaf Key, at mile marker 17, ride Sugarloaf Boulevard all the
way to the end and turn right. You'll ride past three-and-a-half miles of
dense mangroves on your right and, on the left, the entrances to some
elegant estates barely visible from the road. It might cheer you to know
that the Beatles traveled this route in 1964 when they were brought back
here to visit the estate of Florida state representative Bernie Papy.

Big Pine Bicycle Shop
MM 30.9 Gulfside, at County Rd. ✴ 872-0130
At Big Pine Bicycle Shop you can rent adult cruise or mountain bikes as
well as BMX bikes that kids love. Baby seats on some adult bikes. Also,
bike sales, repairs, parts and accessories. Rent for the day or the week.
Lowest prices in town. Open 9 to 5 Monday through Friday; 9 to 3
Saturday, and closed Sundays.

Accommodations

IG PINE KEY really is a bedroom community. Plenty of people,
residents and tourists alike, go to sleep each night and wake up each
morning in Big Pine Key but spend their days and evenings in Key
West. You can do the same thing and save yourself some money.

Several waterfront B & Bs are available on Big Pine, rather spectacular ones actually, and, in the Lower Keys, dozens of great campsites—
many of them right on the water in Bahia Honda State Park or in neat,
old fishing camps. Call ahead and the Lower Keys Chamber of Commerce (800-872-3722) will send a complete list of accommodations. It's
a short list, for sure, but you can discover good values and rare finds along
this serene stretch of blue sea, sky and bridge that joins Marathon Key to
the Lower Keys and the fury and bedlam that lies ahead at the very end
of the road on the island of Key West.

By the way, contrary to what you will probably be told or might reasonably surmise on your own, it takes a lot longer than a half hour to
drive from MM 30 to the end of the rainbow; it often takes twice that
long.

Bahia Honda State Park Campsites and Cabins
MM 37 Oceanside • 872-2353

The beautiful Bahia Honda Park has three excellent camping areas
containing eighty campsites for tents and RVs. Waterfront camping is
available on the Gulf of Mexico, the Atlantic Ocean, and on the Bahia
Honda Channel. The park is excellent for exploring—the beach on the
Atlantic side of the island is often called the best in the Keys, in Florida,
and one of the best in the world.

Bayside camping sites are for tents or pop-up campers only. Camping
units over 6 feet, 8 inches high won't fit through the low underpass you
must take to access the area. There are rest rooms near these seven tent
sites, but bathhouses are not so handy. Tent site #80 is the best one here;
it's surrounded by buttonwoods and features an unobstructed view and
access to the Gulf of Mexico.

Many campsites in the Buttonwood camping area face the Bahia Honda Channel and have great views of both the old and the new Bahia Honda bridge. There are public phones and a bathhouse. The shoreline is sandy and jagged, so you're in a fairly private area.

Three cottages on stilts each contain six units that sleep six people each. You can see the cottages from the highway at mile marker 37; they're on the gulfside of the Overseas Highway. You have to go through the park gate to access the cabins as well as an area of rustic campsites. Furnished cabins are air conditioned, and they have heaters, too. Each unit has two double beds, two bunk beds, and two cots. There's no television, no telephone, no radio, no microwave, and, although the kitchens are supposed to be fully equipped, bowls, pots and pans seem frequently to have been pressed into service as bailing pails and beach buckets.

The artificial lagoon in front of the cabins is not suitable for swimming, due to some polluted thinking in the early '70s. When the ramp for the old Bahia Honda bridge was demolished to make room for construction of the new bridge, a ton of metal rods and planks were dumped into this 35-foot-deep quarry. A park service SCUBA diver explored the lagoon and found a veritable garbage dump beneath the quarry's calm surface. In addition to three junked cars, he found metal barbs and rods standing upright from the bottom. That's why you see signs prohibiting swimming. But fishing off the deck of the cabin is fun. Many folks bring a boat and keep it tied up at their front door. Dining on the deck is popular, too.

Although many people don't realize that they're available for rent, the cabins at Bahia Honda are usually very well booked. To rent a campsite or cabin here or in any Florida Keys state park, you must call Reserve America, at 800-326-3521. Only a very few campsites are left open to rent on a first come, first served basis.

Barnacle Bed and Breakfast
Long Beach Drive ▪ 872-3298 ▪ 800-465-9100
The Barnacle Bed and Breakfast is advertised as "barefoot oceanfront living with panache." That's a good description. As you enter the house, a sign on the door reminds you to remove your shoes. You really do go barefoot here.

The house is built in the shape of a star. The rooms are shaped like points. Someone very creative, and a lover of stained glass and bright colors, has done a brilliant job designing these unique spaces. No two rooms are alike. At the middle of the star is an atrium, the communal space where breakfast is served. There's even a stairway to Heaven— well, to the sun deck on the roof. But if you'd rather, you can take your sun on a natural sandy beach and wait till nightfall to climb up to the roof for some stargazing. The sky is amazing out here.

All rooms have queen-sized beds, private baths, refrigerators, beach towels and ice chests. Two guest rooms are off the atrium where the hot tub is located. One efficiency unit with kitchen, is separate from the main house. If, after checkout time, you'd prefer to lounge on the beach for a few more hours rather than vacate immediately, you are welcome to use an outdoor shower and changing room at no additional charge. It's a nice touch.

No children under 16. No pets. No Smoking. Bikes, paddleboats, hobie cats and BBQ grills are free. Room rates are very reasonable and rise and fall with the seasons, just like they all do.

Big Pine Key Fishing Lodge
MM 33, Oceanside ✹ Long Beach Drive ✹ 872-2351

Beneath the Spanish Harbor Bridge lies a wonderful row of old-timey, oceanside cinder-block cottages, a couple of spanking-new motel units, several rows of RV campsites, and some rustic but very pleasant tent sites. Some RV's spend the warmer months in storage here while their owners summer in the North. Dock your boat on a canal at the back door of your motel for only 20¢ a foot.

The lodge was designed some twenty-five years ago by folks who still live in the area and now operate the Casa Grande B & B on Long Beach Road. From an above-ground pool with a shower and a water fountain, you can gaze out at treetops and enjoy temperate breezes. Downstairs is a lovely clubhouse room with a stage and a bar for private parties.

Prices vary according to type of accommodations—but they're quite reasonable, and that's why guests here are frequently repeaters. Rustic tent sites are directly on the water and look out across the Spanish Harbor to the beautiful Bahia Honda State Park. Take a hike down Long Beach Drive and see Key deer.

Big Pine Motel
MM 30, Gulfside ☎ 872-9090

There has been a slow, but steady upgrading of this motel in recent years. The whole place has been painted a cheery white with yellow trim. The floors in downstairs rooms are now tiled, and there are queen-sized beds. Upstairs, there is new carpet and double beds. Old mattresses have been replaced, and trust me, it was time. The motel rooms are clean, moder-

A view typical of Big Pine Key guesthouses

ately sized, and equipped with televisions, chests of drawers, writing tables, private baths with tubs, air conditioning, and phones, with free local calls.

Rates are posted on a menu board in the front office, which indicates they're subject to frequent changes. They're lowest on weekdays in the off season and highest on weekend nights in the on season. High season rates click in on holidays and special weekends. Motel rooms and several efficiencies. This isn't a ritzy place, but it might be a bargain—depending on the season and what's going on. Europeans return year after year. The owners of the Big Pine Motel live in Texas and hire charming local folks to run it.

Right outside the front office there once stood a very charming Greyhound Bus stop. A tornado, in the winter of 2002, blew it to pieces and so another was built to take its place.

Deer Run Bed and Breakfast
Long Beach Drive ◂ 872-2015

A real-estate saleswoman owns and operates this B & B, which is convenient because if you decide to relocate, Sue Abbott will help you find your own house here in Paradise. The Deer Run got its name from its location at the edge of a wildlife sanctuary. Before she built her home here, Sue says, she came here often to observe the proliferation of Key deer and raccoons in the area. The Key deer that roam here are docile and beautiful and perfectly at ease around this house that has been here for just over a decade.

All guest rooms at Deer Run face the Atlantic Ocean. In upstairs rooms you can open your door and sleep in fresh sea breezes. This is very much a Florida house, designed to blend gracefully with its surroundings. Amenities include a wide wrap-around porch, outdoor hot tub, and a full American breakfast served on the upstairs porch. All units have private baths, air conditioning and even heaters, though they're rarely needed.

The house is in a hardwood hammock and is next to the Atlantic Ocean. The beach is small and sparse, but it's inviting and certainly handy. In addition to the abundant wildlife, Deer Run is home to a couple of obviously spoiled house cats and 21 remarkable birds, including macaws, cockatiels, and a couple of very talky parrots.

Because of its location, you can be sure that you'll find utter serenity at the Deer Run. More than once, Sue says, people have checked into this quiet place and found it to be *too* quiet. But mostly her guests appreciate the tranquility. For restless tourists, bikes and canoes are available, free. And four miles away, the Bahia Honda Beach and Park.

A few house rules: A 50% deposit is required within ten days of making reservations. No credit cards, no children, no spring breakers, no smoking, and if you're coming for Fantasy Fest weekend, book early. Sue's friends and family usually fill the place then.

Little Palm Island
MM 29, Oceanside ☞ 872-2524 ☞ 800-343-8567

The world has been heaping awards and accolades upon the Little Palm Island Resort since it opened more than twenty years ago. *Conde Nast Traveler* magazine's reader polls consistently give Little Palm Island high marks for service, rooms, food, location and atmosphere. Splashy publicity keeps locals regularly informed of its status. Last we heard, it was rated the second best hotel in the world. Which, of course, makes us want to know, who's number one? This we know for sure: Little Palm Island is the only four-star-rated hotel in the Keys. A Noble House Resort.

The Florida Keys' penultimate resort is located on tiny, South Sea flavored Munson Island. You can get there by boat or seaplane only, which is probably a big part of its allure. Nestled amid flaming bougainvillea, oleander, hibiscus and palms are thirty one-bedroom suites designed for privacy and seclusion. Located in 28 stilted, thatched-roof cottages, each suite is equipped with a mini-bar, a coffeemaker, ceiling fans, a private sun deck, an outdoor shower and jacuzzi, a hammock, and a wrap-around balcony with views of the ocean. Robert Wagner and Jill St. John honeymooned in the Mockingbird Cottage.

Munson Island, the five-acre island upon which the Little Palm Island Resort is built, was once a fishing camp visited by Presidents Harry Truman and Richard Nixon, among others. It was owned by John Spottswood, a former Florida state senator and a Monroe County sheriff. Spottswood also once owned the magnificent Casa Marina Hotel in Key West. In 1960, *PT 109*, the story of President John F. Kennedy's World War II experiences, was filmed here. The Great House, which still stands today, was built to house film crews. A number of utilities were piped to the island at that time, including electricity and water, transforming Munson Island into the valuable little paradise that is it today.

Daytrippers are welcome to make reservations and skiff over to the island for a sumptuous lunch or dinner, but reservations are absolutely required. The fifteen-minute ferry ride is free. After dinner, hang around and use the amenities, which include a pool, sauna, windsurfers, sail boats, and canoes. Take the launch at MM 28.5 on Little Torch Key.

Don't be surprised if you have to wait a few days to get a reservation in the Little Palm Island dining room. Everything here is spectacularly delicious, with unbelievable price tags to match. Call for details.

Looe Key Reef Resort and Dive Center
MM 27.5, Oceanside ✺ 872-2215 ✺ 800-942-5397

If you're coming to the Keys to dive—snorkel or SCUBA—you should consider staying here at the Looe Key Resort, where you're always only a half-hour or so away from the Looe Key Reef and on the same premises as a five-star PADI dive center. Looe Key Resort also features a pool, sun deck, tiki bar and restaurant. It's moderately priced and very popular. All twenty motel rooms are located on a canal with a boat ramp and dockage. Motel rooms, all the same, have two double beds, AC, TV and phones.

A 45-foot power catamaran makes one five-hour reef trip daily, from 10 a.m. till 3 p.m. You can snorkel, SCUBA dive or simply be a passenger. The Looe Key Dive Shop will rent you equipment, tanks, and so forth. Walk out of your room and hop in. Motel guests get 10% off the cost of the dive trip.

Old Wooden Bridge Fishing Camp
Bogie Channel Bridge ✺ 872-2241

Twelve little cottages in a row by the bay with palm trees in every yard. Pretty picturesque. Smallest cottages sleep two or three. Larger cottages, four or five. Every cottage has a kitchen. The Bogie Channel bridge, which used to be an old wooden fishing bridge, is a holler away. Fish from the bridge and catch your dinner or make a friend of a fellow fisherman. Is this funky or what? Lots of guests here come just to bridge fish. You can bring your boat and tie up in the bay, or rent one here.

No phones, but new owners, Mark and Julie Shaffer, have upgraded with TVs and they take credit cards. That's new. A pool is under construction as we are going to press. Room rates are the same year-round. Smaller cottages are $150 per day, $950 per week. Cottages for four are $190 per day, $1200 per week. They'll also rent you a single or double kayak or a 19, 22, or 24-foot fishing boat. So besides fishing what is there to do around here? Rest. Take nature walks. Watch the Key deer. Hang out at nearby No Name Pub. That's about it. You'll need a good book and a car.

"We're far away from everything," Mark says.

Sugarloaf Lodge
MM 17, Gulfside ✴ 745-3211

A wonderful, happy place, run by a lovely family. The lodge was built in the '60s and still maintains a '60s feel, physically and spiritually. Surprisingly, there are fifty-five rooms in this motel, some efficiencies. Each is appointed in a sedate, sand-colored decor and overlooks mangrove islands on the Gulf of Mexico, which is a breathtaking vista. The pool area is particularly pleasant, though rarely crowded. Most of the time, folks are taking their sun around the lagoon, which used to be, but is no longer, a sanctuary for Sugar, the dolphin. Her death, of old age, made headlines in local papers.

At the tiki bar, you'll find drinks and good, light meals like burgers and chicken wings. The restaurant inside and bar at the Sugarloaf Lodge are both good and popular.

It is not unheard of for Key West couples to honeymoon at the Sugarloaf Lodge, located seventeen miles from the end of the road. Staying at the Lodge is also a wise choice for the budget-minded. You won't get anything quite this nice in Key West for the same money. The drive "into town," as locals call it, is a pleasant twenty-minute hop. Call well ahead for reservations.

Big Pine Vacation Rentals
MM 29.5, Big Pine Key ✴ 872-9863

Three night minimum stays are required when you lease accommodations from this concern. (The three-night clause is becoming standard practice in the Keys in the past few years, much to the chagrin of tourists.) All homes are on canals with boat dockage and fishing. Rates are deluxe, though still usually less expensive than what you'd pay in Key West for similar luxury.

Some Restaurants

Bobalu's Southern Cafe
MM 10 Bayside ✶ 296-1664

Family-owned and operated. Newest owners, Doug and Debbie, came to the Keys from New Haven, Connecticut and have added pizza and Italian dishes to the menu. The busy little bar and restaurant is decorated with antique tavern paraphernalia. Fourteen tables. It's a small, neat and tidy place with friendly food. Gourmands should definitely go elsewhere. Food is just like home-cooked, and reasonably priced. Jamaican dishes are jerked chicken and chicken with cabbage. Southern cuisine includes fried chicken, liver and onions, baked pork chops, with a daily selection of veggie sides (you get two with your entree) like turnip greens, beans, rice, okra, mashed potatoes and fried green tomatoes. Dinners start around $10. A plate of four veggies side dishes is a deal at $6. And now, submarine sandwiches, chicken parmesan sandwiches, stuffed peppers, or spaghetti and meatballs. Fruit cobblers and a terrific selection of home-made pies. There are menus, but the print is so small it's easier to just make a selection from the blackboard specials menu propped on a chair by your table.

Jimmy Buffett describes Bobalu's in a scene in his novel, *Where is Joe Merchant*. A long row of newspaper vending machines out front features local papers, and if you get panicky for real news—the *New York Times* and the *Wall Street Journal*. Bobalu's is open from 11 a.m. till 10 p.m. every day except Monday, when they close.

Evie's Subs
MM 22.4 Cudjoe, Oceanside ✶ 745-1005

Evie and Joe Venuto have been making their outrageous sandwiches and selling through a busy walk up window for some time now. They're very good at it. Philly cheese steak sandwiches, Cuban mixes and spaghetti dinners. Do yourself a favor and find it. If I can't convince you that eating at Joe's is a treat, the aroma of a Joe Burger, Italian Style, sizzling on the grill, surely will. The bread is imported from Amaroso Bakery in

Philadelphia, and the orange Flavorburst shake will remind you of the Creamsicles you ate as a kid. Chatting with Joe is as much fun as gobbling the greasy, yummy food he sells. Joe is also familiar with the Atkins Diet, and will prepare you a feast fit for Dr. Atkins himself. Breakfast sandwiches, too. Good take-out food, at reasonable prices.

Galley Grill
MM 25, Summerland Key ✷ 745-3446
A homestyle restaurant run by Delores Feinberg and her four daughters. Hubby, Ron, is the repair and maintenance man. Built in the '50s, the grill is a regular stopping place for lots of local folks. The bar (beer and wine only) is busy all day and all evening. Out back there's a canal where boaters, some of whom live on mangrove islands in the area, tie up their vessels while they come inside to eat or drink. Sunday morning and early afternoon are usually packed with dawdly diners who enjoy reading the papers, and drinking gallons of coffee. Open daily for breakfast, lunch and dinner. Traditional local fare: conch chowder, conch salad, catch of the day, shrimp, fish and sandwiches, all cooked to order, nothing frozen or pre-made. People come here for the food, not the bar, though you'll usually find some pretty interesting gatherings at the bar. Nightly dinner specials. Prices are moderate for very good food.

Geiger Key Marina
MM 10.5, Oceanside ✷ 296-3553
Attractions are drinking, live music, and dining on the dock right next to the canal. Don't bother to dress up for this waterfront hideout frequented by locals and a few lucky tourists who find their way to the place. It's been in business since the '60s, but Geiger Key Marina remains relatively unchanged and undiscovered. Happy hour is Monday through Friday, from 4:30 p.m. - 6:30 p.m. Good, live music begins in the afternoon on Fridays, Saturdays and Sundays, and goes on till 9:30 p.m. There's barbeque Saturday and Sunday afternoons; sometimes the main course is ribs; sometimes Jamaican jerk chicken. With fresh fish. You buy a meal voucher from the bartender, then grab a paper plate, and plastic fork and knife, and step up to the barbeque grill where the chef fills your plate. You've heard that food tastes better outdoors? That's true here. Feed the fish, or the gulls, or the pelicans. Pet the wild igunana, Grover.

His favorite food is bread. And when he's had enogh, he slithers into the water and swims back to his home in the mangroves.

Geiger Key Marina is located in a residential area with lots of souped-up trailers surrounded by some very lush foliage. To find it: Turn toward the ocean onto Old Boca Chica Road at mile marker 10.5 (there's a Circle K store there). Geiger Road will appear on your left, after a mile or so. The marina is on the water, on the right side of the road. You'll think, wow! It would be very cool to live in here. But think again. Geiger Key is right under the flight path of the Boca Chica Naval Air Base.

China Gardens
Winn Dixie Shopping Center Oceanside ✽ 872-8861
These same people have been serving or delivering great food to the people of Key West for several decades. Now Big Pine Key residents and visitors can enjoy their quality, classic Chinese cuisine. Call them for a delivery or dine in. They're good, fast and pleasant.

Mangrove Mama's
MM 21, Gulfside ✽ 745-3030
Unless someone recommends this place nearly hidden from view by a luxurious cluster of banana plants, you probably wouldn't go in expecting a great lunch or dinner. It looks funky, and it is, but charmingly so. Locals keep it busy year-round. That's a good sign. There's a main dining room, with a library, and a couple of dogs and cats lying around on the cement floor. On the occasional December or January cool night you might find a fire in the fireplace. A series of smaller dining areas extend from the main room, and you'll probably want to dine in one of those. The bar (try the Key Lime martini) is always busy.

Key Deer Bar and Grill
MM 31, Gulfside ✽ 872-1014
Former NASCAR driver Dan McLaughlin, known around here as "Captain Dan" is the owner and manager of the Key Deer Bar and Grill, a family place with reasonable prices. Items like sandwiches, taco salad, great chili and linguine with marinara, all under $10. Fresh fish and prime rib specials on weekends. Pizza. More pizza. There are a lot of pizza

places on Big Pine Key. Here's another one. Full-service bar. Open daily 11 a.m. - midnight, later if the place is jumping.

Five Brothers II
MM 27 ✒ 872-0702

The people of Ramrod Key are truly blessed to have this authentic Cuban sandwich and coffee shop on their rock. And so am I. It used to be that the Five Brother's Key West location was the only place in the Keys for real bollos, a Cuban treat of ground black eyed peas and garlic deep-fried to greasy perfection. But now you can get them here. I strongly recommend to those who drive the Keys a stop at Five Brother II for cafe con leche and a little brown bag of bollos. Eat them while they're hot, between sips of coffee. Heaven! Try a Cuban-style cheeseburger or Cuban mix or midnight sandwich. Hours: 6 a.m. - 7 p.m. Closed Sundays.

No Name Pub
North Watson Blvd. ✒ 872-9155

Turn onto Watson Boulevard, which is bayside, at the light. Bear to the right onto Wilder Road. Turn right at the stop sign. Bear right. No Name Pub is on the right. This outpost of local color is gaining an ever-larger reputation. Somehow, it's become the place to find when visiting Big Pine Key. You feel you've entered into a time warp here and gone back to the days when bare-footed, beer-drinking expatriate Americans like the ones at this bar, were present at every bar south of Miami. Key West used to be like this twenty years ago. Back then, not owning shoes was a glorious reminder of how far away we were from tradition and adulthood. You'd be surprised to see how tough good soles can become in the right climate.

The beer at the No Name is served in the bottle—no glass. The walls and the ceiling are covered with dollar bills upon which people write their names and the date for posterity. "Do you have any idea how many dollars there are on these walls?" a customer asked a pregnant waitress named Donna. "No, but you're welcome to count 'em," she answers.

Once it was a bar used by married men and their girlfriends, certain that no one would ever find them here. Yet many Keys residents still don't know it's here, since they don't read guidebooks. Lately people from all over the world have been showing up at the No Name Pub to drink in the local color. The pizza, which is renowned, is pretty good. The place is air-conditioned, so it's cool in the summer. Outside, there's a huge beer garden where fundraiser picnics and parties are occasionally held. The entertainment is a jukebox and a pool table. It's out-of-the-way, remote, and believe me, there are no neon signs to help you find it. Open seven days.

Old Road Cafe
MM 22 Gulfside ✔ 745-8888

The heady aroma of growing herbs perfumes the air in an outdoor court-yard at the Old Road Cafe. Words hand-printed on a decorative watering can say "From the earth we are formed. To the earth we return. And in between we garden." People are thrilled to see chef/owner Leslie Artique or her sister Lisa Johnson bustle out of the kitchen and into the garden to snip a handful of lemon basil or dill.

Outdoor dining here is very popular, but indoors is just as interesting. Smoking is forbidden and air conditioning is turned on at the last possible moment; the room is open and balmy—even in summer. A slide show of images of the Keys of yesteryear is projected onto a wall. The pictures are nostalgic, unbelievable, and provocative. Also, there are photographs mounted beneath a sheet of glass on every table. Blue Plate specials are available nightly. A favorite is smoked baked pork chops with sweet potatoes, apple slices and onion. Others are country fried steak. Turkey meatloaf. And the freshest fish.

The menu is short and manageable. Presentation is simple. The Old Road Cafe achieves a soft shimmer of Eastern serenity. Dinner only, from 5 p.m till 9:30. Wednesday through Saturday. Closed April 15 - Dec 1.

Rob's Island Grill
MM 31.2 Gulfside ✔ 872-3022

Rob started out in a tiny stand selling hot dogs down the road from this nice big roadhouse he's in now. He has greatly expanded his repertoire and boasts a full bar and a nightime scene with live music. In addition to great food the place serves up lots of sports, on 15 TVs. Weekend nights are Prime Rib nights, pizza and wings. All sorts of deals for happy hour patrons. Closed Tuesdays.

Key West Fishcutters
MM 25, Gulfside on Summerland Key ✒ 744-3335
New to the area, and receiving a hearty welcome. There is always a crowd at Key West Fishcutters., which serves up very fresh shrimp, conch and locally caught fish like hogfish, grouper and snapper, fried or grilled. The menu is short and to the point, that point being simple, nicely prepared fish. Buy it to go, or order off the menu. Several excellent alternatives for people who don't eat fish. Catch of the Day sandwich with chips is a deal at $5.95. But try the mango coleslaw. Open from 11 a.m. till 9 p.m. with the same manu.

Parrotdise
MM 28.5, Gulfside on Barry Ave. ✒ 872-9989
You can drive a car or or a boat to the Parrotdise waterfront bar and grill. It's right on Big Pine Channel so while you sip a beer at the bar you get a stunning view of traffic ambling over the channel bridge. After a while the view begins to feel surreal. From time to time you hear the shatter of breaking glass. It's the sound of beer bottles smashing into the recycling bin at the foot of a two story chute into which the barmaid cheerfully tosses dead soldiers. The frequent shattering gives the place a sort of bawdy atmosphere. There are real characters sitting at this bar, like a guy with a parrot on his shoulder and a bandana wrapped around his head like a modern day pirate. The food is good, sometimes great, and you get real silverware, not plastic, and I like that. The service is good and the barmaids and waitresses are friendly. From your table, or bar stool, you can see fishing charters coming in from a day of fishing. Walk to the end of the pier and see the days catch. If you bring your own catch, cleaned, they'll cook it for you and frame it with soup or salad.

Raimondo's
MM 21 457 Drost Dr., Cudjoe Gardens, ✒ 744-9800
Turn onto Drost Drive at MM 21. Raimondo's is less than a mile in, on the left, located in a residential neighborhood, next to the little Cudjoe Gardens Marina. There is a nice, long bar, and a dining room where they keep the lights very dim, because it's more romantic that way, my waitress told me. Eat in the dining room outside on the patio. Subdued atmosphere. The food is very, very good. Prices are moderate. The hog fish puttenesca is grand and so is the shrimp fra diavolo. You'll see people dining on pizza, too, and they seem quite happy with it. There are several

traditional Greek dishes like dolmas, saganaki, souvlaki and gyro. Italian dishes mostly, and that includes hot subs and sandwiches. Dine in, take it out, or order a delivery. Open noon till 10 p.m. every day except Tuesdays.

Big Pine House of Music
MM 28.5 Gulfside ✱ 872-9000

Members of the Angus Bangus band, Angus, Kathleen and Mark, are owners, managers, as well as the core of the house band at the Big Pine House of Music, which opened in 2004. In addition to being talented rock musicians, the trio is well versed in marketing and business management. They seem determined to establish a rock 'n fun locus right here in little Big Pine Key, bringing big name bands to our islands with affordable ticket prices. There's something going on every night, like kareoke on Tuesdays and open mic night Wednesdays and taco night Thursdays, accompanied by Smokin' Blues Band. Even the Sunday brunch buffet is accompanied by music. Dine, dance, or dally till you find your groove.

Shops

Artists in Paradise Gallery
MM 30, Big Pine Shopping Center, Bayside ✻ 872-1828
This is a co-op gallery, which means the artists and painters of the Lower
Keys are well-represented in person as well as visually. Every day there is
at least one artist, or a close relative of one, on duty to answer your questions about their work, or about work by any of the other 25 artists
represented here. The gallery features mostly tropical art, expressed in
watercolors, oils, prints and etchings, embossings, stained glass, sculpture,
pottery, weavings and metal wall hangings.

Occasional public receptions showcasing new works by one of the co-
op's artists are well advertised, but not regularly scheduled. If you're
interested in collecting regional art, or just in collecting regional conversation with Keys artists, you should drop in or phone the gallery for a
schedule of currently scheduled events. Artists In Paradise Gallery is
open from 10 a.m. till 6 p.m. daily.

Baby's Coffee
MM 15, Oceanside ✻ 744-9866
Don't forget your Baby's Coffee! Baby's Coffee Roasters started out on
Duval Street, in Key West, in 1991. The business soon perked its way
right out of those original digs and moved into its current location on
Sugarloaf Key. Stop in for a cup of rocket fuel coffee, and browse through
Baby's interesting collection of Baby's branded shirts and hats. Also
locally authored books, snacks and gifts. Fresh baked rolls and coffee cake
are excellent accompaniments to Baby's coffee to go. Choose from a
number of tantalizing blends. Baby's does a huge mail order business, and
the fist step to becoming a Baby's regular is this initial visit to the shop
and your first cup of Baby's delicious coffee. You will be ruined for anything but Baby's! Warning: One pound of Baby's coffee in your trunk will
infuse your car with the unimaginably rich aroma of freshly roasted coffee
beans in a matter of minutes. Don't buy it unless you love it!

Out of the Blue Gallery and Gifts
MM 29.7, Oceanside ✺ 872-8864

The Blue Moon Trader offers all the things I love in a store—great shop-keepers to chat with, two rooms full of very cool recycled and consignments clothes and miscellaneous items, a children's corner of books, toys and related items, new age books and CDs, gifty items like scarves, boxes, jewelry and wind chimes, and all of it with a new age theme. Upstairs, you'll find message therapy and the Floating Island, a separate shop featuring what the shopkeeper describes as "kitchen pretties", linens, ceramics, and beautiful one-of-a-kind pots and plates. Also fine chocolates. It will take you quite a while to to get through the Blue Moon Trader. Sometimes, in the area beneath this stilted building, there are psychic fairs. If you hear of one, go and have your horoscope or your tarot cards or your palm read. Hours are 10 - 6; 10 - 4 Sundays.

Caribbean Cobbler
MM 25, Oceanside ✺ 745-9966

A full service shoe, boot and leather repair shop located in a rather unlikely location, featuring a very interesting and opinionated lady cobbler who knows feet and shoes and the myriad problems of their coming together. Do your feet get bigger as you get older? Oh yes. They spread, too. That's why your favorite leather boots seem to get tighter year after year. Why not switch to forgiving Minnetonka moccasins, or Nyot sandals? Available for sale here. Or a big, rough and tough-looking pair of leather engineer boots. Also, beautiful leather bags, belts and vests. You can pick up some amazing bargains on marked down leather goods. Also, adorable little shoes and sandals for toddlers and little kids. A cool place.

The Good Food Conspiracy
MM 30.2 Oceanside ✺ 872-3945

Marney's health food store is an important landmark in this community. In addition to the usual vitamins, food supplements, extracts and herbs, there's an excellent juice bar, with the Keys best, and certainly most nutritious, smoothies and sandwiches. Fresh island fruits and vegetables, like papayas, key limes, starfruit, arugula, mustard greens and sprouts, are delivered daily—all of it grown right here in the Lower Keys. The barefoot dentist next door often orders smoothies for his patients undergoing long procedures. Every-day specials, created of whole foods, are fairly priced and wonderfully delicious. Dine at the juice counter or in a courtyard out back. In front of the store, an excellent free box overflowing with clothes and shoes and all manner of second hand stuff, lots of it really nice. The Good Food Conspiracy is open every day from 9:30 a.m. till 7 p.m. Stop in and get better.

The Nut House
MM 10 Bayside • 292-8688

A nut and dried fruit emporium on Big Coppitt Key. Big sellers are Keys Crunch, a bark-like brittle of nuts, seeds and honey, Duval Crawl, spicy Chinese crackers, and hot stuff like Scorned Woman Hot Sauce and Bloody Mary Mix. Also wonderful and unique gifts and decorative items. Shop owner Ann Labriola is usually in view, wrapping gift trays of gourmet goodies for shipment to Bloomingdales, Saks, and a slew of other fancy food boutiques. As she works, Labriola chats easily, laughs often, and answers many questions. All the while, her hands, ever graceful and sure, are moving.

There is an art to all of this, and in fact, she is an artist. Labriola is a renowned and well-respected sculptor whose monumental works have brought her fame, but not fortune. Making a living in the pricey paradise of the Florida Keys is an ever-constant challenge. She never planned on making money on her sculpture, Labriola says, and she never has. In the twenty years since she arrived in the Keys with a MA degree from the San Francisco Art Institute, she has cleaned houses, maintained yards, waited tables, and developed photographs in a home lab to pay the bills.

She has also created several colossal sculptures, all designed to promote her artistic vision: the union of art, nature and archaeology. Her most notable work, *Stargazer*, is 200 feet long, 70 feet wide, 10 feet high, and wrought of 50,000 pounds of steel. Holes on *Stargazer*'s surface form patterns of star constellations. Resting on a sandy bottom, in 22 feet of clear, blue water, *Stargazer* is five miles from Key West, and points due southwest toward the Sand Key Lighthouse. The project took three years and $125,000 to complete, Labriola raising most of the money herself. Once she wore knee pads and knelt before one art patron to beg for money. He wrote her a check for $500.

"I'm used to people looking at me as if I'm crazy," Labriola, a native of Armonk, NY, says, shrugging. "But it takes a lot to give something lasting to the world."

True Art Bakery and Bookstore
Quail Roost Trail (at MM 30) ✹ 872-0200

Just a bit off the beaten path, but you really should find it. Turn at the light on Big Pine Key, onto Chapman, then right onto Quail Roost Trail, and you'll see the little shop that's been enchanting visitors since it opened in 2004. Art and photographs by local artists. Funny, crazy 'fridge magnets, ceramics, and jewelry. Also black caviar from Iceland, olive oil and whole wheat pasta from Italy, and cookies and candy made by Trudy, the industrious founder of the shop. Soup mixes, teas and dips, and not a speck of preservatives. If you like, buy something packed into whimsical and one-of-a-kind boxes Trudy imports from a mother/daughter team in California. Cole's Peace artisan bread arrives daily from Key West, a great idea because there's nothing like it and having it available in Big Pine Key means locals can get it handily. Books by the ounce are over-runs, purchased from esoteric publishers. Some recycles. All of them quite interesting, and you won't every spend more than $10 for a book. Check it out. You'll dig it.

Second Hand, Fleas and Junk

Big Pine Flea Market
MM 30.5 Ocean ✹ 872-4103

8 a.m.–2 p.m. Saturday and Sunday — a good time to avoid driving through Big Pine Key, if you can. The traffic jam is absurd.

Big Pine Methodist Church Flea Market
Key Deer Boulevard ✹ 872-2470

Saturdays only, same hours as the Big Pine Key Flea Market.

Salvation Army Thrift Shop
MM 25, Oceanside ✹ 745-3327

Join us on the worldwide web
www.junekeith.com

Marathon
and the
Middle Keys

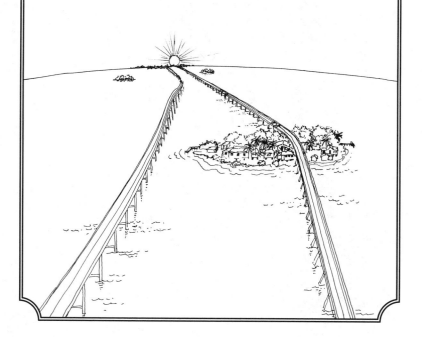

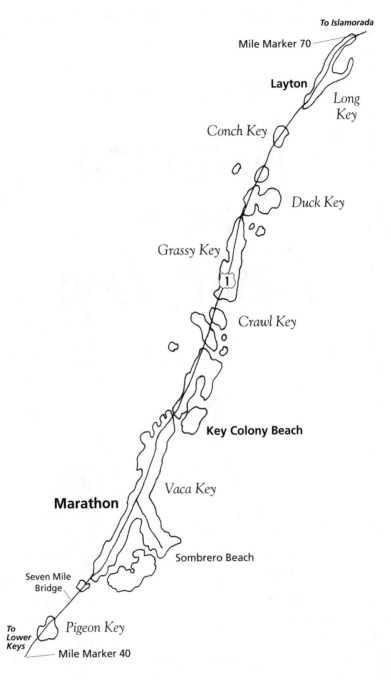

To Islamorada

Mile Marker 70

Layton

Long
Key

Conch Key

Duck Key

Grassy Key

1

Crawl Key

Key Colony Beach

Vaca Key

Marathon

Sombrero Beach

Seven Mile
Bridge

To
Lower
Keys

Pigeon Key

Mile Marker 40

Marathon & The Middle Keys: Nothing Succeeds Like True Grit

WHILE KEY WEST is ever-polishing and refinishing its surfaces, fast erasing the last traces of the rough and salty exterior that brought tourists there in the first place, Marathon is proud and satisfied to be a last holdout of that indescribable, but-you-know-it-when-you-find-it, Keys island charm.

The citizens of Marathon are proud of the way they've managed to preserve the magic of the Florida Keys and the coral islands' intrinsic seaside languor. "Why hurry? Why gripe?" Marathon's attitude seems to say. "Here it is. Here's what we've got. This is the way we do things." There's the faintest trace of haughtiness in residents' patient responses to your questions as you sample their food, their shops, their resorts. You can't blame them; you're only visiting. These people live here, not just for two weeks, but for every day of their lives, in this hazy paradise of endless summer.

In Marathon, a man wears a shirt that says, "This is as dressed up as I get." Believe it.

Marathon is said to have the largest year-round, live-aboard population at anchor of any place on the east coast: an estimated 100 boats year-round, and up to 300 in the winter when it's too cold for boat-living in the rest of America. The shore is lined with funky marinas that give way to tiny streets of jumbled trailer parks.

Marathon's attractions are limited, and that's part of its allure. It is truly laid-back, a characteristic often described, but seldom actually found anymore in the ever-more-busy Keys. Marathon's charms are subtle; you have to root them out. Make friends with the locals you meet who are tending bar or running the boat rental shops. From the woman who runs a shell and gift shop, I learned that every morning, around 8 a.m., a group of stingrays assembles in the water at the Pigeon Key end of the Old Seven Mile Bridge and seems to greet the folks walking and biking above them. Walking clubs have formed around this phenomenon.

The area of the Middle Keys is a historian's bonanza, much of its magic lying in its remarkable past. The Seven Mile Bridge, built in 1909, remains one of the world's greatest engineering feats. Pigeon Key, the tiny island beneath it, is a shrine to the unlikely heroes who built the bridge and the miracle that was the Overseas Railroad. From Knight's Key, huge steamships once departed for Havana, Cuba, heavy with passengers delivered to Marathon by train from places like Montreal and Boston and New York City.

The Long Key viaduct at mile marker 65.5, no longer used, runs alongside the modern Long Key Bridge. The two-mile bridge is said to have been Henry Flagler's favorite. Since it was built in 1909, it has been one of the most photographed places in the Keys. Long Key, now an attractive State recreational area, was once the location of a posh fishing camp, whose membership list included presidents, writers, and other business and cultural icons of the first part of the 20th century.

The Marathon area has a private 18-hole championship golf course, a public 9-hole golf course, a children's museum, several dolphin facilities, and a couple of good biking and hiking trails. Also, oceanside camping.

Bargains in the Middle Keys include accommodations and food. It's also a terrific central location. For vacationers interested in exploring the Keys, this is the place to be. The brochures all claim that when you're in Marathon, you're only an hour from Key West or Key Largo, but in fact, it's more like an hour-and-a-half. Marathon has a fine, modern airport, but unfortunately, major airlines have not it profitable to service the little airport. Right now, charter flights servicing the area are very expensive, but they are available. Several major rental car company's are headquartered in the building.

The area of the Middle Keys begins around mile marker 70 and ends at the southern end of the Seven Mile Bridge, at mile marker 40. Middle Keys, in my book, are comprised of Long Key, Conch Key, Duck Key, Grassy Key, Key Colony Beach, Knight's Key and the City of Marathon, which is located on Key Vaca.

Marathon (Key) and The Name Game

A bunch of Marathon business people recently came up with a plan to change the name of the Middle Keys community known as Marathon to Marathon Key, with the hope that the new name would let people know that Marathon is a bona fide part of the Florida Keys, and hence inspire them to book their vacations here. The Monroe County Commission agreed and gave the plan their blessing. But when word of the planned change got around, there was an outcry from citizens opposed to the addition of "Key" to Marathon. After all, they reasoned, Marathon isn't an island or a key at all; it isn't a town or a city—it's a community, on a key, and that key's name is Vaca. But Vaca Key is hardly a romantic name for a tropical island. Marathon Key isn't a lot better…but it beats Vaca, which in Spanish means "cow." And everybody already knows Marathon.

For a while the editorial pages of the local papers were filled with letters on the subject, arguments both pro and con. Finally, just before the matter was to be turned over to the U.S. Board on Geographic Names for a decision, the Marathon Economic Development Council withdrew its name-change petition and the identity crisis was over.

"I've never seen the town come together in such a way to fight a group of big money guys. It's wonderful," said Gail Swanson, a Keys historian and Marathon resident.

History

EY VACA is found on a map of the Keys drawn by Spaniards in the 1500s. Historians believe it was named for the manatees, or sea cows, that thrived in the area's waters. For Keys Indians, manatees were a delicacy reserved for only the most important people in the tribe.

A young Spanish sailor, shipwrecked near Key Vaca in 1575, was captured by prehistoric Indians and lived with them for eighteen years. He was freed by a crew from a passing ship. Back in Spain, Escalante Fontanada wrote an account of his life with the Indians, but historians believe he recorded his memoir nearly thirty years after his captivity. His is the only written account we have of those times. Unfortunately, many of the references are puzzling and do little to broaden our knowledge of the Florida Keys.

In the early 1800s, Key Vaca was settled by Bahamians as well as several fishing families from Mystic, Connecticut. During the 1820s, Key Vaca was a port for a small fleet of wreckers and one of the first three settlements in the Keys; the others were Key West and Indian Key. Bahamian farmers raised limes, guavas, avocados, sugar apples, sapodillas, and sea isle cotton. Eventually these settlers abandoned the area, frightened away by the Indian Key Massacre in 1840. The seafarers from Connecticut moved to Key West, and the Bahamians fled to other islands. In the 1845 election, only nine citizens from Key Vaca were registered to vote. By 1860 only twenty-six people lived on Key Vaca and, of those, twenty-four were of one family. After the Civil War, only two farmers were known to be living in Key Vaca.

When the Overseas Railroad reached Key Vaca, the area became construction headquarters. By 1910 the population was 600; a small town had sprung up. Key Vaca was renamed Marathon by the railroad workers who lived in wooden dormitory buildings on Marathon and adjacent Pigeon Key. From 1909 to 1912, Flagler's railroad operated between Miami and Marathon, which had, by then, become a major depot and administrative center for the railroad. Marathon had wooden sidewalks and a two-story hotel, built in 1908 near the site that is today Marathon Yacht Club.

Knight's Key was the terminus of the Overseas Railroad while the Seven Mile Bridge was under construction. Passengers heading for Key West, Cuba, or the Caribbean got off the train at a wharf on Knight's Key and boarded ferryboats to complete their journeys. In 1912, the train tracks were finished all the way down to Key West.

By 1920 only a few families remained in Marathon, although it was still an important fishing town. The Miami Ice & Fish Company operated hundreds of boats on the waters surrounding Marathon. Fish was iced, loaded onto the trains, and shipped to Miami.

In 1935 the Overseas Railroad which, in its twenty-three years of operation had never turned a profit, was destroyed by the Labor Day Hurricane. In 1938 the Overseas Highway, built atop the remains of the railroad, was completed, linking the Lower Keys to the rest of the country. Marathon became a tourist resort and sport-fishing area.

Hurricane Donna demolished much of Marathon in September 1960. Many people still living in Marathon remember Donna well. Sometimes on the anniversary of the storm, at community get-togethers, survivors describe their memories of the event. Very scary....

A History of Long Key

Long Key was first named Rattlesnake Key by those ever-inventive Spanish explorers. The name refers to the island's shape, historians say, not to rattlesnakes who live there. Yes, the Keys *do* have rattlesnakes.

The Spanish government deeded the unsettled 965-acre island of Long Key to Don Francisco Ferreira, a St. Augustine man in 1814 as a reward for service to the crown. Ferreira sold Long Key to Charles Howe of Indian Key for $1500 in 1827. Around 1838 Howe, then the postmaster at Indian Key, and botanist Dr. Henry Perrine started up a partnership called the Tropical Fruit Company. They began clearing the land for a mulberry tree grove with the hope of starting a silk industry. Unfortunately, Dr. Perrine died in the Indian massacre at Indian Key in 1840, before the plans yielded fruit or profit.

In 1880, a couple of guys bought Long Key and planted it with coconuts. 17,000 coconut palms were growing on Long Key when it was purchased in 1884 by two brothers from New York City. The brothers frequently visited their coconut plantation on their yacht. The entire population of Long Key by 1900 was ten people; twelve when the New Yorkers were in town.

In 1906, Henry Flagler's Overseas Railroad reached Long Key. Flagler thought the coconut grove so beautiful he bought it and created a super deluxe fishing camp, in keeping with his tradition of marking the route of his railroad with spectacular inns and hotels.

Flagler's fishing camp had a clubhouse, a lodge, a post office, and four-teen cottages connected by a boardwalk. Among the Long Key Fishing Club members was Zane Grey, a dentist from Zanesville, Ohio, who was also a novelist. Grey, whose most famous novel is *Riders of the Purple Sage*, is known as the "father of the American Western." Grey served as president of the club from 1917–1920. Presidents Herbert Hoover and Franklin Roosevelt were among the fishing enthusiasts who stayed there.

In September 1935, the Long Key Fishing Club, that magnificent coconut grove, and much of the Overseas Railway were destroyed in the Labor Day Hurricane. The Long Key Fishing Club was reactivated near the camp's original location in 1968. Baseball player Ted Williams was a charter member, as were Jackie Gleason, Arthur Godfrey, Mike Douglas, and President Jimmy Carter, who was not yet president. The club disbanded for the last time when Long Key was turned into a state park.

Long Key State Recreation Area was created by the State Parks Department and opened to the public in 1969. The original Long Key Fishing Club is remembered with a historical marker located around mile marker 66 and with Zane Grey Creek Road, named after the author.

Flagler's Railroad: The Eighth Wonder of the World

When Henry Flagler was 37 years old, he formed a very fortuitous part-nership with John D. Rockefeller. That business was the Standard Oil Company, and, in short order, both men were millionaires. There were no income taxes in the United States back then, so Flagler and Rockefeller literally made money faster than they could spend it.

In 1886 Flagler formed the Florida East Coast Railroad, which ran from Jacksonville to Miami by 1896. The train was convenient for folks who traveled to South Florida's tropical paradise with its balmy weather and remarkable environment. Flagler built several fabulous hotels along the Florida coast so that his clients would find not only the country's most marvelous weather but comfortable accommodations as well. Through his hotels, his railroad, and his oil company, Flagler just kept getting richer.

But Flagler's successes only whetted his appetite for more acquisitions and a bigger role in America's economic future. During the Spanish-American War, Flagler noted that the Army shipped supplies to its troops in Cuba via railroad to Tampa, and then by sea, out of Tampa's deep-water harbor. Although Miami is closer to Cuba, its harbor was too shallow for trade. Key West, however, had a magnificent deep-water harbor. Flagler knew Key West's excellent harbor could easily become a valuable gateway to Cuba, the Caribbean, and the Panama Canal.

Building a railroad to Key West, Flagler believed, would open up trade with far-flung ports of the world like China, Japan, and the Far East. He was propelled by visions of cargo moving by rail from America's great northern cities all the way down his Florida East Coast Railroad route, and then on down the East Coast Extension and into Key West.

Key West was the very last in a chain of coral rock islands, overgrown by subtropical jungle, mostly untouched by civilization, and separated by varying spans of ten to thirty-feet-deep ocean water. More than half of the planned railroad would have to traverse water. To most people the idea of building a train over the ocean and through jungle was sheer madness.

When Flagler was asked how he could possibly build a railroad down the Keys, he replied, "It is perfectly simple. All you have to do is to build one concrete arch, and then another, and pretty soon you will find yourself in Key West."

One associate's reply to this was, "Flagler, you need a guardian."

In 1905, in spite of the general consensus among his peers that he was off his rocker, Flagler hired the best engineers his bottomless pit of money could buy and work began. The world called the project "Flagler's Folly."

As the first team of workers, 300 blacks from Florida and the Bahamas, slashed their way through the first thirty miles of jungle between Homestead on the mainland and the thirty-mile-long island of Key Largo, they were bedeviled by merciless heat, mosquitoes, sand flies, alligators and rattlesnakes. Halfway through Key Largo, workers discovered a mile wide inland lake that had been overlooked by surveyors. Appropriately, they named it Lake Surprise.

As construction of the railroad moved down the Keys, a sizable fleet of ocean-going vessels was employed to transport the enormous amounts of gasoline, concrete, dynamite, crushed rock and coal, as well as water, food, medical supplies and goods for a work force that was at times 3,000 to 5,000 men.

Workers lived aboard huge floating houseboats, or quarterboats. When a disastrous hurricane hit the Keys in 1909, one of the quarterboats with 160 men aboard broke from its moorings and was carried out to sea by winds of over 100 miles per hour. Some men, terrified of drowning or of being eaten by sharks, swallowed deadly doses of laudanum from first-aid kits and lay down to die. After the barge broke apart, a few survivors clung to planks and were picked up out of the sea and taken by freighters as far away as Liverpool, England.

In addition to the loss of nearly 130 lives, the hurricane wreaked terrible damage on the railroad and the fleet of boats that carried the equipment and materials. Construction that had been started on the Long Key Viaduct was badly damaged.

Many workers died in dynamite explosions, in hurricanes, in fights and disputes often fueled by alcohol. Keeping workers was an enormous problem for the railroad. The job was simply too challenging for most men. Workers from the Cayman Islands, out in the Caribbean where the weather is similar to the weather in the Keys, did far better than most. Men from places like Norway or Canada might show up from time to time but usually lasted only long enough to collect their first paycheck before heading back to civilization.

Speculation grew that skid-row bums and winos from the streets of New York and Philadelphia had been enlisted to work on the railroad by nefarious methods. But a governmental investigation into Flagler's hiring practices later cleared him of these charges.

Laborers hired from New York were promised $1.25 a day, free room and board, and free hospitalization to work on the railroad. In those days, a man could live well on $2.50 a week, so railroad pay was substantial.

Flagler strictly forbade alcohol in any of the workcamps, which opened opportunities for bootleggers from Key West who arrived with clandestine boatloads of hootch. To counter the damage done by "booze boats," Key West churches sent boatloads of "preacher boats" to camps to hold services.

In spite of the horrific hardships, the Long Key Viaduct was finally completed in 1907, which meant the railroad to Key West was roughly half done. The bridge was built on 186 35-foot reinforced concrete arches, extended over 2.15 miles of water. It required 286,000 barrels of cement, 177,000 cubic yards of crushed rock, 106,000 cubic yards of sand, 612,000 feet of piling, 5,700 tons of reinforcing rods, and 2,600,000 feet of dressed lumber. Imagine the maneuvering required to transport all those materials to their destination.

By 1908 the railroad reached Key Vaca, one of the first two settlements in the Keys. A bustling station on nearby Knight's Key became the train's terminus for the next four years. In Key Vaca, one railroad worker exclaimed, "Building this railroad has become a regular marathon." The name stuck and later became the name of the town that is known today as Marathon.

A busy city grew up on Key Vaca, populated by various employees of the railroad. Regular passenger service began in February 1908. Steamships of the Peninsular & Occidental Steamship Company, also owned by Flagler, met the trains on Knight's Key. The number of passengers and the amount of freight between Florida and Cuba quickly increased.

In January 1909, the first through passenger train between New York City and Knight's Key began regular service every day but Sunday. The train left New York at 2:10 p.m., and arrived at Knight's Key dock at 7:30 a.m. two days later. Passengers slept in Pullman berths, dined in dining cars, and unfortunately missed the most breathtaking scenery, the islands of the Florida Keys, as the train passed over them in the dark. The ferry to Havana then took six hours.

The hurricane in September 1909 severely damaged preliminary work on the Seven Mile Bridge. It took two years to repair the damage. Finally, the Seven Mile Bridge was completed, and the railroad construction continued on, advancing slowly past Little Duck Key, Ohio and Missouri Keys (named by homesick railway workers). Finally, it reached the Bahia Honda channel. Named by Spaniards, the name means "deep bay." The job of bridging the Bahia Honda channel was fraught with terrible difficulties. The deeper the water, the higher the wave; therefore, Bahia Honda's bridge had to be very high. The finished bridge required thirteen

A steam train on the Seven Mile Bridge

spans 128 feet long, thirteen spans 186 feet long, and nine arches of con-crete, each one 80 feet long. Just when that bridge was completed, a second mighty hurricane struck in September 1910 and displaced a center span.

When one superintendent was caught in the hurricane, he tied him-self to a tree with his belt to avoid being blown or washed out to sea. Only after it was too late and the storm was at the height of its fury, did he realize with horror that he had tied himself to a manchineel, the most poisonous tree in the Keys. As he watched helplessly, the white toxic sap of the tree ran into the wounds torn into his skin by the flying debris. He did not die, but he spent many months in the hospital recovering from the poisoning.

Although the train was scheduled for completion by 1913, the sched-ule was pushed ahead when it appeared that Flagler, now an old man in failing health, might not live long enough to see his Florida East Coast Extension reach Key West. Workers had luck on their side for the remainder of the construction, and on January 22, 1912, an engine pulling five passenger cars filled with dignitaries and notables, including Flagler himself aboard his private car, arrived in Key West.

On the day that the Overseas Railroad reached Key West, Flagler announced that, in his opinion, "Key West will have a population of over fifty thousand people within ten years from this date."

The governor of Florida, a number of congressmen, and even foreign ambassadors were in Key West to celebrate the arrival of the steam-powered train. The citizens of Key West, always ready for a party, turned out in full force. The mayor spoke and the schools closed; a three-day party celebrated the "Eighth Wonder of the World." Flagler was weak and nearly blind, so he was led from the train, uttering his famous and much quoted statement: "Now I can die in peace."

At that time trains were restricted from crossing any bridge faster than 15 miles per hour and trains did not chance crossing the longer bridges when the wind was blowing faster than 70 miles per hour as measured by wind gauges on bridges. Under the best of circumstances the train's maximum speed was 35 to 45 miles per hour. According to schedules, the train time between Key West and Miami was four-and-a-half hours, but that was seldom the case. It was more like six or seven hours. Trains were often late, sometimes up to twenty-four hours behind schedule.

Flagler's Overseas Railroad made very little money; it never even began to earn the cost of its construction and it didn't even cover the cost of its upkeep.

And yet it was one of the most remarkable and memorable experiences many people had ever had. There are folks still living in the Keys who remember riding through the islands on the train, stopping at tiny stations to drop off mail and ice, and thrilling to the magical sensation of riding suspended over the water. Children were put to bed as the train passed northward through groves of Florida palm trees and awakened the following morning to find themselves rolling past tall oaks and pines.

From the last timetable printed, we know that a roundtrip ticket from Miami to Key West was $4.75; and only $2.50 on Sundays. A round trip from Miami to Havana, via Key West, was $24.

During Prohibition, booze came into the country from Havana, smuggled past customs in trunks and sometimes caskets, taken off ferries and shipped by train to New York. Cuban pineapples were another main cargo. Pineapple harvesting in Cuba was very profitable because of cheap labor available there. Ironically, Flagler's train provided the Cubans with a viable and profitable trade route for their cheaply produced pineapples, and it delivered the final knock-out punch to the staggering pineapple farming business of the Upper Keys.

By the time it was twenty years old, the railroad that had cost Flagler twenty-five million dollars and five hundred railroad workers their lives, and 25,000 more untold suffering, was bankrupt. The railroad was in receivership when the 1935 Labor Day Hurricane destroyed over forty miles of the roadbed. Rather then spending the $1.5 million to rebuild the tracks, which was the estimated cost of the repairs, the receivers decided to sell it. All of the property, the railroad bed and bridges, were sold to the state government for $640,000, which was less than the cost of one of its still-standing bridges. The Overseas Highway was superimposed on the railroad's right-of-ways, across the amazing Long Key Viaduct, the Seven Mile Bridge, and the lofty Bahia Honda Bridge. When the highway was completed in 1938, it became possible to drive a car all the way to Key West, the very end of the coral chain. The link to the mainland would change life in the Keys forever.

Henry Flagler's Doomed Wives

Henry Flagler became a widower for the first time in 1881, when he was only 51 years old. By then he was very, very rich. Unfortunately, his first wife Mary was a sickly woman, usually an invalid never really well enough to share or enjoy her husband's fine fortune.

Henry's second wife, the woman who'd been nurse to his first one, was named Ida Alice Shrouds. Shortly after the marriage, Alice began communicating with a Ouija board and became convinced that she was destined to marry the Czar of Russia. Eventually a doctor friend of Henry's diagnosed Alice as being mentally unstable. She was committed to a sanitarium and eventually judged to be legally incurably insane by the New York Supreme Court.

Meanwhile, Henry had met singer and pianist Mary Lily Kenan. Mary was 24 years old; by then, Henry was 70. Henry and Mary hoped to wed, but what to do about Alice the lunatic? Henry changed his residence to Florida and campaigned friends in the Florida Legislature to draft a law recognizing insanity as grounds for divorce. In 1900, Henry Flagler, with his huge fortune and great visions for Florida, was a powerful and well respected man in the sparsely developed state. In spite of the brewing scandal, the law passed and Henry was finally free to divorce his mentally incompetent wife. He and Mary Lily were wed in 1901.

As a wedding gift, Flagler built the sumptuous Whitehall estate on Palm Beach for Mary Lily. Today, Whitehall is a fantastic museum offering many daily guided tours to a clamoring public. A visit to Whitehall is an amazing glimpse of American wealth at the turn of the century, as well as an intimate portrayal of a winter/spring marriage. In the regal Whitehall ballroom, a secret stairway leads to Henry's bedroom. This stairway enabled Henry, who was never much of a party animal, to exit the festivities when he became tired and leave his young wife in charge.

Flagler died May 20, 1913, in Palm Beach when he was 83 years old. Shortly before his death, he made arrangements for him and Mary to be buried in the resplendent St. Augustine's Memorial Presbyterian Church. Flagler had built the church in memory of his daughter Jennie, who had died in 1889. Henry and Mary Flagler are buried there still.

According to Henry's will, Mary Lily Flagler inherited $108 million when he died. A few years later Mary Lily wed Robert Bingham, a Kentucky politician. Only eight months after the wedding, she died. Bingham had signed a prenuptial agreement foregoing any financial gains he might make in the event of Mary Lily's death. But one month before she died, a codicil had been added to Mary Lily's will stating that Bingham would inherit five million dollars.

Mary Lily's outraged family suspected foul play. They arranged to have her body exhumed and autopsied at New York's Bellevue Hospital. They promised that the results of the autopsy would be made public. But the results were not publicized and the question of exactly what killed Mary Lily was never answered, which gave rise to speculation that she had been a user of laudanum (a form of opium) and had accidentally overdosed. There was also a rumor that Bingham was so furious at Mary Lily's family for interfering in the matter that he threatened to release a story that she had died of syphilis if the family didn't back off.

Bingham's fortune then financed his purchase of the *Louisville Courier* newspaper.

In his will Henry also left his divorced wife Alice with two million dollars for her care. She lived comfortably until 1930, when she died at the age of 82. But for the remainder of her life, it is said, Alice told anyone who would listen about her planned nuptials with the Russian Czar.

The Old Seven Mile Bridge
and Pigeon Key

The Queen mother of Florida Keys historic bridges is the Old Seven Mile Bridge, which runs parallel to its replacement, the sleekly modern, and all new Seven Mile Bridge. The new bridge, completed in 1982, was built in three years. It took four years to build the original bridge 75 years earlier.

Once the new bridge, with its wide lanes, sturdy guard walls, and pale gray cement was in place, there was talk of taking down the Old Seven Mile Bridge. But engineers surveyed the structure and deemed it nearly indestructible. The cost of tearing it down, they said, would be prohibitive.

Besides, the citizens of the Florida Keys had grown attached to the old girl. She has survived devastating hurricanes and several million cars. She has starred in a number of feature films, and dozens of television commercials. The black charred areas you see on the bridge are left over

Pigeon Key and the new Seven Mile Bridge

from explosions staged by the makers of *True Lies*, an Arnold Schwarzenegger film.

Every Christmas season someone manages to get to a lone shrub, growing through a crack in the concrete midway across the ancient span, and lace it with strings of white, battery-powered lights. Every night, year-round, the fishing areas at the near and far end of the old bridge are crowded with fishermen. And every day, all day long, you'll see walkers, joggers, bikers and skaters enjoying the sun, the magnificent air, and the spectacular view from the Old Seven Mile Bridge.

She is a marvel, a miracle and a monument to visionary Henry Flagler. The Overseas Railroad, once dubbed the Eighth Wonder of the World, chugged across the bridge thrice daily for 23 years. The Labor Day Hurricane of 1935 that delivered a killing blow to the railroad, spared the Seven Mile Bridge.

Today, the first two miles of the Old Seven Mile Bridge is a recreational site and connects the mainland to Pigeon Key, an historic, 3.2-acre island nestled beneath the bridge. Beginning around 1908, Pigeon Key was a camp for the work crews who built Flagler's railroad. In 1912, once the railroad was complete and underway, Pigeon Key became home to the workers and families of maintenance crews and bridge tenders involved in the operation of the railroad.

Among the permanent work force was a full-time paint crew. The crew worked on the Seven Mile Bridge and the Bahia Honda Bridge. The tracks, plates, girders and even the spikes were painted to preserve them from the salt air. As soon as both bridges were completely painted, it would be time to begin the massive job all over again.

For 25 years Pigeon Key was a small, tidy village with a store, post office, school, and dock. The little island is only four feet above sea level, situated on a shallow reef. From the island's dock it is possible to wade for some distance into the shoal waters abounding with marine life. The children who lived there had a playhouse under the bridge, and a swing hung from a trestle. Imagine what a wonderful place it was to grow up!

A woman who spent her childhood days on Pigeon Key, recalls a huge poinciana tree in the yard by the railroad tracks. When the tree was in bloom, she says, the train would stop so the passengers could take pictures. Pigeon Key is still said to be one of the most photographed places in all of the Florida Keys.

The village of Pigeon Key was abandoned after the train shut down in 1935. For many years it was empty. Later it was leased as a research center to the University of Miami for $1 per year. Environmental researchers and students from around the world ate and slept in the aging white clapboard cottages.

Today, the Pigeon Key Foundation, a non-profit organization dedicated to the restoration the island's historical buildings, operates the island as a park and and educational center for kids, who come with

A poinciana tree

school-organized trips to learn history and marine science in this glorious dot of land. (The foundation does not sponsor or organize educational retreats.)

All seven structures surviving from the days of the settlement of Pigeon Key have been restored, one by one, financed by private funding. Also brand new are modern rest rooms, a children's interactive marine exhibit, and a gift shop. Preservationists promise that Pigeon Key Village looks pretty much as it did at the height of its glory in the 1920s, and they've worked hard to get it this way.

Visitors are invited to tour the island and admire the simple, sturdy construction of the buildings. The Bridge Foreman's House is a favorite subject of painters. The Negro Quarters is a stop on Florida's Black

Heritage Trail. The Section Gang's Quarters, the largest structure, was the first to be restored.

A long dock juts into a flat, shallow bay where snorkeling is likely to turn up artifacts from Pigeon Key's rich past—buttons, bottles, bits of china—as well as a wonderful show of marine life. Pigeon Key's grassy lawns are perfect picnic sites.

For a few weeks in the fall, it is possible to watch the sun sink at the juncture of the old and the new bridges where they meet at the horizon. It is a popular phenomenon, bringing scores of thrill-seekers and photographers to the island every year.

Admission to the park is $8.50. That includes a round trip ticket on the Pigeon Key Express, a replica train-tram, operating between Pigeon Key and a visitors center on Knight's Key every day from 10 a.m. till 5 p.m. Bring lunch and snorkeling gear and make a day of it.

Want to know more? Call them at 305-289-0025.

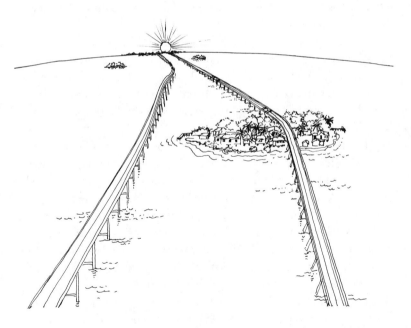

Sunset between the two Seven Mile Bridges

Nuts and Bolts

Marathon Chamber of Commerce
MM 53.5 Gulfside ❧ 743-5417 ❧ 800-262-7284

Anytime you walk into the Chamber of Commerce Visitors Center you are urgently requested to sign the guest book. It seems an important point to the people who work here. But once that detail is out of the way, these folks will chat you up and down again.

When you sign the guest book, check it out. You'll be amazed at the variety of countries represented by this list of visitors. Most are Americans, but Canada and Germany and the United Kingdom send lots of travelers, too. Over half of all those who sign the book name Key West as their ultimate destination. But many others list Marathon and the Middle Keys as their primary destination.

The Chamber's carefully tended charts and tables point out that Marathon and the Middle Keys' popularity as a vacation destination is growing. That's understandable—you'll find good bargains in accommodations in the Middle Keys as well as something even rarer than that: several surviving pockets of old-time island styles and attitudes that once prevailed in all of the Keys.

The most often asked question at this chamber, as in all others in the Keys, is "Where's the beach?" These chamber people have good answers: The Middle Keys have beaches; Sombrero Beach is free, rarely crowded, lovely, and nearby; Bahia Honda, called by travel writers one of America's most beautiful beaches, is a twenty-minute drive away.

In some flowery promotional literature, Marathon is described as a sleepy little fishing village. Well...not that sleepy. The local radio station DJs call it "beautiful, downtown Marathon." And though they're probably poking fun, to some people it really is beautiful in a seedy, crumbling kind of small-town way. Every day another weather-beaten layer of local color is scraped away by progress; what's not yet gone is Marathon's honest-to-God character.

George Dolezal Library
MM 48.7, Oceanside ✎ 743-5156

The local library is on a crest between the Sheriff's Station and the Fisherman's Hospital. Slow down or you'll zoom right past the hidden driveway. The library is spacious and user-friendly. The children's room is wonderful and the staff is warm and helpful. You could pass many hours in this cozy, air-conditioned library.

Friends of the Marathon Library sponsor some pretty good coffee-and-discussion hours and presentations Wednesday afternoons during winter months in the library's lovely assembly room. This past winter for the reading of works by Dorothy Parker, the place was packed. The reader, a former Broadway actress now retired in Marathon, was terrific, and she didn't seem to mind, or maybe she didn't notice, when several of the older gentlemen in the crowd began to doze. The coffee and cookies were tasty and plentiful; the crowd was mostly friendly, retired citizens.

A chess club, a computer club and an amateur ham radio club also meet at the library. Their meetings and activities are open to the public, too. Call the library, or stop by for a schedule of meetings and special events. The hours are 10 a.m. till 6 p.m. Monday through Saturday. Late nights—open till 8 p.m.—are Monday and Wednesday.

Marathon Airport
MM 52 ✎ 289-6060

Many people don't even know it's here; even travel agents don't know. The formerly funky airport terminal building was fabulously upgraded into a multimillion-dollar terminal, and has won a slew of design awards. With its earthy Spanish tile, fancy rest rooms, high ceilings, and works by local artists, the terminal is eminently cool and relaxing. It's a beauty!

Several small airlines provide limited service between Marathon and Key West, Tampa and Ft. Lauderdale airports. You'll also find several rental car agencies. Town movers and shakers are working hard to get some bigger airlines to stop here and provide more routes to the mainland, and hopefully, by the time you're coming, they will have done it.

The Marathon Airport is a full-service facility for private aircraft.

Paradise Air
Marathon Airport ✽ 305-743-4222

Twin engine jet prop planes fly between Marathon and Ft. Lauderdale. The plane is plush and offers much more comfort than you would expect on a commercial airline. Seats are individual captains' chairs, wide and soft leather. No more than 9 passengers per flight. Visit them at the airport, or call for schedules and rates. They'll even arrange to have your rental car waiting for you when you arrive.

Conch Air
Marathon Airport ✽ 305-395-1117

Fly on a Waco bi-plane, promises pilot/owner Paul Goodwin, and you'll understand why dogs love hanging their heads out of moving car windows. Take a half-hour aerobatic ride aboard Paul's 1988 model Waco, Sweetie Pie 2, (his dog is Sweetie Pie 1) or a basic, sight-seeing roller coaster flight. Swoop into sunset. Take an aerial photo of the Seven Mile Bridge. Goodwin promises you'll fall in love with the grace of bi-plane flying.

SeaCoast Airlines
866-302-6278

Offers charter flights to Marathon from Zephryhills Municipal Airport outside Tampa and St.Petersburg-Clearwater International Airport on Florida's west coast

Florida Coastal Airlines
888-435-9322

Connection flights from Ft. Lauderdale to Marathon Airport.

Museums

The Museums of Crane Point Hammock
MM 50 Gulfside ✽ 743-9100

The museum is on Crane Point Hammock, a 63-acre environmental and archaeological preserve. Displays of several small, natural communities feature a family of endangered Key deer and a mangrove community of Keys birds.

There's a photo exhibit of the Florida Keys, shot from space, which illustrates clearly the ancient coral reef that emerged to form the delicate and isolated Florida Keys. An exhibit of photographs of the construction of the Overseas Railroad is a monument to Henry Flagler's vision and amazing role in history.

A self-directed nature trail leads you along a winding path through the unusual and exotic vegetation of the Crane Hammock. Ten endangered plant and animal species live here, as well as 160 native, and fifty exotic plant varieties. Carefully placed plaques tell the story of this rare palm and hardwood hammock. The quarter-mile trail passes a sinkhole or pit, where the top layer of earth has been worn away by a millennium's rainfall, exposing ancient ocean fossils that were once beneath the water's surface. You'll see these same brain corals beneath the water on the living reef.

Another trail leads to the Adderly House, built in 1906 by George Adderly, a black Bahamian immigrant who was a sponger, boatman, and charcoal maker. The house is very simple: one story with a hip roof, in the masonry vernacular, similar to residences built by blacks in the Bahamas during the 19th century. The floors are made of Dade County pine, a wood so resilient that nails can hardly be driven into it. Its walls are two feet thick and were considered to be Indian-and hurricane-proof. Adderly, a lay Episcopal minister, lived until 1950 in this house which is listed as a stop on Florida's Black Heritage Trail.

The Crane Point Hammock and its natural history museum are open 9 a.m. to 5 p.m. Monday through Saturday; noon to 5 p.m. on Sundays. Admission to the museum is $7.50 for adults, $6 for senior citizens, $4 for students. Free for children six and under.

The Turtle Hospital
MM 48.5 Gulfside ✴ 743-2552
The turtle hospital is the only state-certified veterinary hospital in the world for turtles. Since being established in 1986 to repair injured sea turtles and return them to the wild, to conduct research in conjunction with state universities, to work for environmental legislation to make the waters safe and clean for turtles, and to educate the public through

outreach programs, the hospital has treated and released over 500 turtles! The five species of sea turtles found in the Florida Keys are Loggerhead, Green, Hawksbill, Leatherback, and Kemps Ridley. The hospital treats turtle troubles like flipper amputations caused by fishing line and trap rope entanglements, shell damage caused by boat collisions, and intestinal impactions caused by ingestion of foreign material such as plastic bags, balloons, and fishing lines. The most common surgery is the removal of viral tumors called fibropapilloma,which grow on the soft body tissue and leave a turtle unable to feed or avoid predators. The green turtle is most vulnerable to these tumors.

A one-and-a-half hour tour of the Turtle Hospital is now offered by hospital volunteers at 10 a.m., 1 p.m. and 4 p.m., providing there are no turtle emergencies going on at the time. The program is limited to 20 people at a time and is on a first-come, first-served basis. So make your reservations ahead of time. Part of the program is out of doors and requires minimal walking. Cost is around $15 for adults, kids 4-12, $7.50 and free for kids 3 and under.

Theater

Marathon Community Cinema
MM 51, Behind Marathon Liquors & Deli ✱ 743-0288
Formerly known as the West Side Cinema, it was purchased by Marathon Community Theater and is operated by them to support live theater next door. Generally one major motion picture at a time, showing at 7 p.m. and 9:30 p.m., with weekend matinees at 2.

Marathon Community Theatre
MM 51, Next door to Cinema ✱ 743-0994
Live community theatre. Season runs October through April. Comedies, musicals, dramas staged with all the verve and enthusiasm of community players everywhere. Exciting and fun. Summertime readings. Very reasonable ticket prices. The performances get better every season, and the playhouse does, too, as the group grows and community responds to theatre. Productions sell out quickly. If you're thinking of going to the theatre, buy your tickets right now!

Beaches

Coco Plum Beach
Coco Plum Drive, Oceanside ☙ MM 54
Coco Plum is a very funky patch of beach, but, since beaches are at such a premium in the Keys and held in such high esteem by travelers, it's been included here. Down at the water's edge you'll find a ribbon of shells—the most shells you'll ever see on a Keys beach. A patient beachcomber will find plenty to look at here, including coral, interesting bits of flotsam and jetsam, and weird evidence of sea life, like the snow-white cartilages of man-of-war jellyfish washed ashore. Mangy tangles of silver driftwood are poetic, somehow. This is public property, but there are no facilities here. The beach has not been improved or cleaned or touched in any way. The beach is in its natural state. If you're looking for privacy, you can find a comfortable place to sunbathe or meditate or watch the ocean from a shaded place beneath the Australian pines. Dogs are welcome and their are clean up bags at the beach for them.

To find it, turn onto Coco Plum Road at MM 54. About a mile down the road, on the right, you'll see a sign for the beach.

Sombrero Beach
MM 50, Oceanside (Turn onto Sombrero Boulevard)
Follow signs for about a mile to arrive at the Sombrero Beach. The signs that point the way to this family beach are small, so you've got to look for them. The 12.6 acre beach has a grassy park and a crescent of rough sand next to the ocean, with picnic tables, grills, rest rooms, a volleyball net, a softball diamond and a terrific, kid-pleasing playground. Often you'll see a group of students being instructed in scuba diving technique at the far end of the beach. For the rest of the beach, a wide and deep swimming area is surrounded by a protective net. Explorers will find lots of crabs and even tinier creatures endlessly washing up on shore in the gentle, barely-there waves of the Keys waters. Pick up a handful of seaweed and shake it. You'll be amazed at what lives in there!

You'll find plenty of free parking here and clean rest rooms, sometimes utilized by tour vans. The annual Fourth of July celebration and fireworks show brings the whole town to this beach.

On one windy January day we bought an Italian sub and took it to Sombrero Beach. We sat at a picnic table in the sun to eat and watch the action. It was a slow, beautiful day. A grandmother walked her two little grandkids to a water spigot right near our table. She turned the water on and rinsed the sand from the little children's feet. First the girl. Then her squirming little brother. All at once the little girl stopped jumping, stood perfectly still, looked into the sky full of gulls, seemed to shimmy from head to toe, and smiled broadly into the day. It was a shudder of pleasure, a moment of sheer joy, expressed with pure exuberance. A few minutes later, a pair of dolphins way beyond the shore began leaping out of the water, thrilling the people on the beach. The show went on for about ten minutes. Surely those dolphins knew what they were doing.

Long Key State Recreation Area
MM 67.5 ❦ 664-4815

Campsites in this park are popular because of their proximity to the water's edge, a place vacationers in the Florida Keys desperately want to be. To reserve a camping site, in this or any other Florida State Park, you must call Reserve America, at 800-326-3521.

The beach is a half mile of natural shoreline from which you can walk way, way out; the water is very shallow and the bottom is sandy. It's a good, fun place for kids and for snorkeling. With roughly one hundred of the park's nine hundred sixty-five acres submerged, you can enjoy many wading bird species and abundant marine life in the shallow waters of Long Key. When you drive into the park, you choose one way which leads to the boardwalk and the nature walk, or the other, which leads to picnic areas and campsites.

The boardwalk is popular with folks stopping in for a nature hit. The rest area adjacent to the parking lot has clean bathrooms and a couple of showers. A sign at the entrance to the nature walk promises you will see egrets, herons and other shore birds. The boardwalk takes you over extremely dense mangroves and over a tidal lagoon. If you climb the tower with two sets of stairs to take you to the top, you will see a prime exhibit of red and black mangroves. (Red are the ones that curve around and burrow back into the mud below them. Black are the ones that sprout up out of the muck.)

This is not a long walk by any means. If you take your time and read and carefully consider the information plaques along the way, you can stretch the walk out to fifteen minutes. If you walk fast, it will take you only five. Neat campsites along the way make you long for your own cozy, little tent in the mangroves. In addition to the abundant marine and bird life, plenty of mammals live here too. Raccoons are very bold and will help themselves to campers' food if it isn't sealed well, but, in spite of their seeming lack of concern about your presence, it is wise to keep your distance from raccoons. Park rules forbid you to feed or touch any wild animals here.

A few feet from the beginning of the boardwalk you'll find the Golden Orb Weaver Nature Trail named after the spiders that live here. Huge and amazing webs are spun by the red and gold female of the species. These are harmless spiders…still, they look pretty scary. And to help you tell the trees apart, labels identify gumbo limbo, poisonwood, mahogany, and Jamaican dogwood trees in this tropical hammock.

The quiet around you is deafening—spooky if you're used to lots of modern-day noise. All you hear is the rustling of leaves as the wind passes through the canopy above. You'll want to go slow in this serene place.

Choose the other direction at the fork in the road just after the park entrance and find a row of shoreline picnic sites—tables and grills under shelters, right on the water. Get to the park early, though, if you want to set up your party here because these areas are in big demand, and at no extra charge. Farther down the same road, you'll come to a gate that marks the beginning of the beachside camping sites. Since Hurricane George took down so many trees, it is actually possible to see the strip of beach campers from the Overseas Highway. But the trees and foliage are growing back, slowly but surely.

Canoe rentals with a marked, one-and-a-quarter-mile winding canoe trail are popular because you go at your leisure, paying for the canoe by the hour. Bike rentals work the same way and several very pleasant bike paths run within and immediately outside of the park.

From January through April, on Wednesdays, at 9 a.m., rangers lead nature tours; Thursdays at 9 a.m., birding expeditions; Fridays at 8 p.m., campfire chats.

The park is open from 8 a.m. till sundown, year-round. Admission is $3.25 per car, plus fifty cents per person.

Veteran's Memorial Park and Beach
MM 40, Oceanside at the Seven Mile Bridge

Located at the western end of the Seven Mile Bridge, this is just the place to stop for a picnic on your way to, or from, Key West. This sweet little beach used to be mostly empty. Now, it seems it has been discovered and at the height of most afternoons, you'll find it nearly full of daytrippers, who arrive in campers and SUVs, to spread out for a day at the shore. Shallow waters and sandy ocean floor make it fun, and safe, for people of all ages. No concession stands. Bathrooms. Just a beach, a boat ramp, and 5 old-fashioned picnic shelters. Open from 7:30 a.m. till dusk, daily. No overnight parking. Free!

Nature Hikes

Layton Nature Trail
MM 68 Bayside

This is sort of tricky to find. Look for the green historical marker for the Long Key Fishing Camp. A tiny sign, close to the ground, marks the beginning of the trail, part of the Long Key Recreational Area which is headquartered on the other side of the street at mile marker 67.5.

This is such a short trail, you could hardly call it a hike. Still, it is an opportunity to guide yourself, at your own pace, through a thick but narrow hammock and out into the clearing that is the Florida Bay, with water very clear and calm. Dried sea grass forms a soft, brown cushion over the rocks. Some trees are labeled: poisonwood, wild coffee, Jamaican dogwood, gumbo limbo, seven year apple, buttonwood, wild dilly and wild lime. If you've hiked anywhere around here, by now you are beginning to recognize some of these indigenous plants. On this trail you'll also see some new ones and a surprise: Spanish moss—the first we've seen in the Keys. From the ancient diary of a Spanish shipwreck victim who lived among the Keys Indians for eighteen years in the 1500s, we know that the native American women of this region fashioned loin clothes, their only garments, of this feathery light material.

Old Seven Mile Bridge
MM 40-47

Walking or riding a bike or roller-blading over the magnificent span that once carried the Overseas Railroad across a seven mile stretch of ocean, is an almost religious experience, particularly around sunrise. Or sunset. The wind whips your hair. The birds swoop and dive into the cobalt-blue water below. The air is clean. The sky stretches endlessly. Your mind expands too, and anything seems possible. The round trip is almost four miles, but there's a nice layover at Pigeon Key. In the early morning it is possible to see tarpon, sharks, and stingrays in the water beneath the bridge. The big treat is to see an angler, on a boat in the water below the bridge, fighting a tarpon.

As you walk check out the side rails. They're constructed of the old rail ties from the railroad. Imagine. They've been baking in the Keys sun since 1912, when the bridge was completed.

The parking lot is at Marathon end of the bridge.

Crane Point Hammock Nature Trail
Museum of Natural History ✺ MM 50 Gulfside

Crane Point Hammock, a 63.5 acre land tract of rare palm hammock, is one of the most important historical and archaeological sites in the Keys. The area contains evidence of pre-Colombian artifacts, and once was the site of an entire Indian village. You'll have to pay admission to the museum to get to the trail, but it's worth it. The museum is quite fascinating.

Curry Hammock State Park
MM 55, Oceanside ✺ 664-4815

The state park people, who view this as a sister park to Long Key State Park just up the road, hope to turn Curry Hammock into another oceanside camping area, but so far, that hasn't happened. This quiet, peaceful, natural area is a nice place for a hike and a picnic. These 600 acres form the largest uninhabited terrestrial tract between Key Largo and Big Pine Key - see it now. It's a last chance to see how the Middle Keys used to be.

Big Fun

Bike Paths

The safe and scenic paths in Marathon provide great opportunities for bicycle rides. Here are some favorites:

Coco Plum Drive
Mile Marker 54

Look for a sign for Coco Plum Drive. Perhaps the loveliest bike route in the area, it's our favorite. You'll bike past a number of stately condominiums, flowering trees, and flat tracks of open land until you arrive at the very end, a natural beach. Sit on the point and watch the boats for a while. It's a wild, windy beach. Chances are good that you won't encounter another vehicle or person on this road.

Key Colony Beach
MM 53.5 Oceanside

The wonderful biking and walking path on this island will take you past lovely homes, stretches of seascapes, and on to a terrific oceanside restaurant and bar called the Tavern-by-the-Sea.

Marathon Bike Path

Starts at MM 47 (the Marathon end of the Seven Mile Bridge) and runs parallel to the Overseas Highway to MM 54. Lots of local folks regularly use this path as their main means of transportation up and down the island. When the path runs past the Marathon Airport, you can watch the bellies of little planes and jets as they come and go. Just past the airport, on the gulfside of the island, you'll see occasional picnic shelters.

Sombrero Beach Loop

Turn off the bicycle trail at MM 48 and follow the bike path toward the ocean. You'll go to Sombrero Beach and loop around the golf course. It's a nice ride. Sombrero Beach has picnic tables and shelters, showers and clean rest rooms.

Bicycle Rentals

Bike Marathon Bike Rentals
 ☎ 743-3204
Call and they deliver your rental bikes to wherever you're staying in Marathon or Key Colony Beach. Bikes sized for adults and kids. Kiddie carts for toddlers. $10 for a day, 3 day minimum. $45 for a week. $99 for a month. Cash or personal check only. No credit cards.

The Equipment Locker
MM 53, Gulfside ☎ 289-1670
Bikes rent for $10 for 24 hours/$50 for a week. Adult and children's bikes. Baby seats for rent. You need a credit card or a cash deposit to rent a bike - or anything else around here.

Golf

Key Colony Beach Golf Course
MM 53.5 (turn at light) ☎ 289-1533
A nine-hole par three course in the truly beautiful island city of Key Colony Beach. Hours on the public course are 7:30 a.m. till dusk, daily. Clubs and pullcarts are available for very affordable rental rates. Year-round rates are $9 per person for nine holes.

Sombrero Country Club
Sombrero Boulevard ☎ 743-2551
A full length golf course on 135 acres. The club is strictly private. Reportedly the club plans to bring a halt to the reciprocal agreement that allowed members in good standing of other country clubs to play here while Sombrero members were allowed to play there. Seems that more folks wanted to play here than folks here wanted to play there and the deal got a little lopsided. Guests at Hawk's Cay Resort (page 379) are invited to play on Sombrero Country Club greens. Those arrangements are made through the resort, and this is the only resort with this arrangement.

Gyms

Keys Fitness Center
MM 49.7 Oceanside (next to Marathon Liquor) ✆743-6350
A very affordable fitness center for both men and women, featuring modern work-out equipment, shower and sauna facilities, personal trainers (for additional fees) and a friendly and enthusiastic staff. Special annual rates for locals. Visitors to the area are welcome to sign up for a day, a week, a month. Open weekdays from 6: a.m. till 9 p.m. Saturday - Sunday, 8 a.m. - 8 p.m.

Curves
MM 50, Publix Shopping Plaza ✆ 289-3211
Curves gals know being away from home is no excuse for missing a work-out. Bring your travel pass from your home Curves and do just what you do there, here. Call for hours.

Tennis

City of Key Colony Beach
MM 53.5 Oceanside, at 8th Street ✆ 289-1533
Key Colony Beach Tennis courts are open to the public. Play is $4 per hour for singles, $6 for doubles. Two lighted courts available daily from 7:30 a.m. till 10 p.m. daily. Phone ahead and reserve your time and court.

Skate

Marathon City Park Skate Park
39th St. & US 1, Bayside ✆ 743-3323
An area of the city park is dedicated to skate boards and in-line skating. New this year, BMX bike trails, too. Marathon Skate Club runs events and skill clinics. Full gear required. They'll rent gear to you if you don't have your own. Also available: Play station. TV. Pool table. Supervision at all times. Admission is free to all. Closed Mondays. Otherwise open 3 p.m. till 9 p.m. Tuesday - Saturday. Noon - 6 p.m. Sundays. But look for these times to change with the seasons.

Fishing

IN THE GULF STREAM OFF MARATHON lies an underwater platform rising from depths of 1,000 feet or more, to a peak of 480 feet below sea level, known as the "Marathon Key West Hump." This hump creates a popular feeding ground for gamefish like blue and white marlin, mako shark, blackfin tuna, and amberjack. This area is a favorite stop for private fishing charters, and it's the reason that fishing off Marathon is considered by most serious anglers to be some of the best in the world. Marathon is different from its neighbors to the east (Key Largo and Islamorada), in that the gulfside in the Middle Keys is deeper and more open in this area, giving an extra dimension to local fishing. On a day when it's too rough to fish offshore or on the reef, the Gulf is an excellent alternative, as it's usually calm even in a stiff breeze.

Since 1991, six world record catches have been made by anglers fishing with Marathon guides.

Flats fishing

A True Fish Tale

On June 23, 1912 sport fisherman Charlie Thompson of Marathon, caught a 30,000-pound whale shark (15 tons, 45 feet long) just off the Seven Mile Bridge. It took 36 hours to land the monster, using five harpoons and 151 bullets. The fish was towed to Miami, where it was embalmed and then taken on a railroad tour through America. I am not making this up.

Marathon Guides Association
PO Box 500065 ⚓ Marathon, FL 33050-0065
For a complete list of the Middle Keys fishing captains, their specialties, and an informative brochure on fishing off Marathon, write to the Marathon Guides Association (MGA). In the brochure you'll also learn about what fish you can expect to catch at what time of the year, and where you can expect your captain to take you to find them.

Party Boats

Marathon Lady
MM 53, at Vaca Cut Bridge ⚓ 743-5580
This great party boat has been taking people out fishing for more than 40 years. They specialize in families with kids and feature nighttime fishing trips during the unbelievably hot and humid times between Memorial and Labor Days. Nighttime trips leave the dock at 6:30 and return around midnight and cost adults around $40. Two days trips leave at 8:30 a.m. and again at 1:30 p.m. Half day trips are $33. All day (which means you go out and in and back out and back in again all in the same day) is $48. Rod and reel rental is $3. Special rates for kids aged 12 and under. Fish cleaning service available.

Bridge Fishing

It seems that you see more bridge fishing in the Middle Keys than anywhere else in the Keys. Fishing from a bridge is a simple alternative to expensive charterboats. Lots of people say it's the only way to fish because it's such a great way to mix with locals, and what is fishing about after all, if not camaraderie? Excellent fishing can be had from the Long Key Bridge, both the bridges at Toms Harbor, and the east and west ends of the Old Seven Mile Bridge. At night, when you drive over the Seven

Mile Bridge, you will see the twinkling lights of fishermen on the old bridge.

Non-Florida residents need a fishing license to fish from the bridges. Numerous bait and tackle shops in the area's marinas have everything you need to get started—including the license.

Some Marinas

Captain Hook's Marina and Dive Center
MM 53 at Vaca Cut ✺ 743-2444 ✺ 800-278-4665

Vaca Cut is the waterway that connects the Gulf of Mexico with the Atlantic Ocean. Captain Hook's, tucked against the shore just under the Vaca Cut Bridge, isn't a huge marina, but it's a busy one. Rent or charter a boat, buy bait, or hook up with a fishing guide. Sign up for scuba diving lessons. A 30-foot Reef Hopper heads out to the reef with 14 scuba divers, or 22 snorkelers, every day at 8 a.m. and 12:30 p.m. Walk around the corner and find the *Marathon Lady* charter fishing boat as well as a number of fishing boats for hire.

Captain Hook's marina store is full of useful stuff. Soda, beer, ice, bait. Stuff for the water. I found featherweight Polaroid sunglasses for $12. Once you've worn featherweights, you won't go back to Foster Grants.

At Captain Hook's Marina, there's a small, clear lagoon alive with moray eels, stingrays, sharks, and parrotfish. Each day at 4 p.m. the fish are hand-fed in what has become a major attraction. Kids love it. And it's free!

Key Colony Beach Marina
MM 53.5, on the Causeway ✺ 289-1310

Here at one of the area's more upscale marinas, park in the convenient lot and stroll the dock for a look at some fine vessels or to find a charter to your liking. The Landing Restaurant and Bar at the end of the docks overlooks the harbor.

Diving

YOU CAN EXPLORE fifty dive spot destinations in Marathon waters, according to promotional materials distributed by the Chamber of Commerce. In addition to its beautiful coral reefs, Marathon has numerous artificial reefs in depths ranging from 25–200 feet. Even the shallow waters just offshore offer plenty of marine life habitats to explore. Hard bottom areas support sponges, golf-ball corals, soft corals, lobsters and tropical fish. Sandy bottom areas and grass beds are home to shrimp, crabs, small fish and anemone. The grass beds are also an excellent place to find conch, but remember: it is against the law to disturb conch or coral!

Some Famous Marathon Dives

Sombrero Reef Marine Sanctuary and Lighthouse
About four miles offshore, the Sombrero Light Tower marks a stunning spur and groove reef system. At 142 feet, the Sombrero is the tallest light tower in the Keys. It was built in 1858. You can see the Sombrero Light from shore, and it will take you about thirty minutes to motorboat out there. This is the first reef in the Middle Keys to have mooring buoys, which provide boats with a place to tie up so they don't have to drop their anchors on delicate corals and risk damaging them. The Sombrero Reef is very easy to find and fascinating to dive.

On Sombrero Reef, two fingers of coral meet to create an eight-foot natural coral bridge under which divers enjoy swimming. In the same area, giant brain corals, and mountain star and elkhorn corals, as well as barracuda, French grunts, trumpetfish and yellowtails all make their homes here.

Coffins Patch
The remains of an old lighthouse can be seen scattered along the shallow reef in this area at the east end of Marathon. Snorkelers particularly

enjoy this dive because in many places the water is only seven or eight feet deep.

Yellow Rocks

Three-and-a-half miles off Key Colony Beach lies a set of ledges running east and west for more than 200 yards, rising nearly twelve feet from the bottom. Maximum depths are twenty-eight feet, making this a good area for lobsters and plenty of marine life.

Thunderbolt

One of the most famous and most often requested scuba destinations in the Middle Keys is this one-time Navy research vessel sunk in 1986. The *Thunderbolt* sits upright 120 feet below the surface. Stripped of doors, hatches and windows, the interior now features a teeming community of sea life. You are free to enter the vessel to explore the dark hold and swim five floors up into the pilot house. A thrilling dive—for scuba people only.

The Barge

Dive masters adore this 100×30-foot wreck, lying on the ocean floor twenty-two feet below the surface. This is a terrific first-wreck dive, fascinating enough to keep a scuba diver entertained for an hour or so but not terribly skill-challenging. The area is particularly photographable.

Some Dive Charters

Abyss Dive Center
MM 54 ⚑ Holiday Inn Marina ⚑ 743-2126 ⚑ 800-457-0134

Volumes could be written describing the wonderful, enthusiastic dive charter people you will meet in Marathon, as well as in all of the Keys. They're so darned nice, I think, because they're blissed out all the time. Whether they're talking about the reef, riding on a boat to the reef, or actually diving the reef, they're deliriously happy. Why not? What's not to be happy about, arranging for people to have one of the finest experiences available on the planet?

Heidi and Bill Ferrell run the Abyss Dive Center, including a full-service dive shop, at the marina of the Holiday Inn. Their operation features a 34-foot boat; reef trips are limited to six divers at a time. A dive trip visits two locations, chosen according to the skill and requests of the people aboard. You get lots of personalized attention from the captain/instructor on Abyss Charters.

A dive package—one night in the Holiday Inn, including breakfast and two dives—is around $90, per person. A dive trip to the reef is $53 per person, which is the going rate for reef trips in this area. They'll rent you snorkel or SCUBA equipment, too.

Spirit Snorkel Trips
MM 47.5 Gulfside • 289-0614
Snorkeling trips (no SCUBA, ever) to the the 30-acre coral reef surrounding the historic Sombrero Lighthouse. Spirit's 34-foot catamaran can handle 40 people. Specializes in families and first time snorkelers. Daily reef trips are at 9 a.m. and 1 p.m., year-round. Cost is $24, and that includes equipment. There are $2 off coupons around town. Even if you don't have a coupon, just say you do for the $2 off deal.

To the Sea

Marathon Kayaks at Sombrero Resort Marina
MM 50 Oceanside, 19 Sombrero Blvd. ☏ 743-0561
Rent a kayak and get up close and real personal with the marine nature of the Keys, some of the most fascinating you'll find in America. It's all so simple. Owner David Kaplan and staff will teach you everything you need to know about kayaking before sending you out to perfect your paddling technique. You get a map, too, with plenty of sites to visit during the 4- hour rental time. Or, rent for the day.

If you're not so much the adventurous type, sign on for guided cruises, like the 4-hour Red Mangrove Ecosystem Tour, an exploration of the channels and lagoons of Boot Key, an area only accessible to paddlers. The tour takes you through serene mangrove forests, the nesting places for many of the sea's most fabulous, and delicious, fishes! Also, the Seven Mile Bridge Tour, a day long exploration of the little islands and waters beneath the amazing bridge. Lunch is included in the cost of the tour. There's a sunset tour, too. Take it on a full-moon night and paddle back to shore by the light of the silvery moon. You might think paddling a kayak is hard work, but it's really not so bad. Tourists of all ages have successfully paddled on Marathon Kayaks. Rent a double kayak for two for around $40 for a half day, $60 for a whole day. Half day tours are $40 per person; $80 for a full day tour. And that includes lunch. And there are many packages and prices in between.

Marathon Jeff's Boat Rentals
MM 54 ☏ 743-9992 or 888-352-5397
Rent a jet ski, or a bunch of them, one for every member of your party, from Jeff. And if you need a boat, Jeff says forget about trailering your boat to the Keys. Just rent one from him. He may have a good point. Have you tried managing a boat and trailer in Keys traffic? Why not let Jeff manage the headaches? He'll deliver your boat to your hotel, too.

The entire fleet of Jeff's boats is replaced annually, like rental cars, so every boat is in great shape. Jeff will rent you rods, if you need them.

Middle Keys Accommodations

EW B & Bs, but a couple of very nice oceanfront resorts, and a bunch of really neat, inexpensive motels. (I mean inexpensive by Keys standards.) Waterfront is standard here; in the rest of the Keys you pay big for it. The Middle Keys location is terrific if you have a car and a restless spirit. You can save substantially on a Keys vacation with the kids by checking into one of the condo-like units equipped with kitchens, and located on the beach. Find the right place, and you won't have to get into your car for the length of your visit. Key West is a good hour and a half drive away, but it's a spectacular drive, featuring some of the most incredible scenery in America.

In the past I've quoted room rates on motels and inns, but prices change so frequently that I don't like doing that any more. I've tried to update with ballpark figures, and when prices are really low, I've quoted them. Remember that every price on every room, item or menu is subject to change. When shopping for a hotel, don't forget to check for cost of extra people, kids or pets (when allowed) in your room. Also, there's an inescapable 11.5% tax on all accommodations. When booking, ask lots of questions and get what you want. Marathon people are some of the friendliest in the Keys. It comes with the rough hewn territory.

The Chamber of Commerce (800-262-7284) will send you lists of local marinas, fishing guides, restaurants, RV and commercial camp sites, or whatever other information you ask them for. Be specific.

The following list of accommodations is a sampling of some of the interesting places I've uncovered in the Middle Keys. It is by no means complete, but it does list accommodations from the most basic to the most extravagant.

Long Key State Recreation Area Campsite
MM 67.5 Ocean ✆ 664-4815

Campsites right on the Atlantic Ocean in a row of sixty narrow sites in a grove of Australian pines. Usually there are more RVs than tents. To reserve a campsite here you must phone Reserve America, 800-326-3521, which is the number to call to reserve campsites in all Florida state parks. Otherwise, you can try your luck at finding a place available without a reservation. The park keeps 10% of its sites open for drop-ins. Each site has a picnic table and grill. Beyond a small bluff and a wide ribbon of brown seaweed, you come to a strip of natural sandy beach on clear, blue ocean water. It's a fun place to snorkel. And plenty of bathhouse rest rooms are available. The area, behind a combination-lock gate (only campers know the combination), is pleasant and breezy from the nearby surf, cool and shaded from the pines. At the far end of the camping area is a clearing with benches around a pit for a campfire circle. A large white screen, like a mini drive-in movie screen, is for visual presentations.

On the boardwalk six campsites are reserved for the Boy Scouts. If there are no scouts camping when you're there, you can have a tent spot on the boardwalk real cheap. No electricity or water hook-ups, of course, but the rest rooms with cold water outdoor showers are nearby. The drawback is that during daylight hours, when the park is open, you'll be observed by a small army of tourists cruising the boardwalk. Once I was on the boardwalk and heard a happy camper from within a boardwalk tent snoring very loudly. At 3 p.m.! That's how close you are to them. Campsite #6 on the boardwalk, the last one, is the best one. It's right where the boardwalk ends. You actually have a sliver of waterfront right behind your tent.

Banana Bay Resort
MM 45.9 Gulfside ✺ 743-3500 ✺ 800-BANANA-1
The lushly tropical Banana Bay Resort is on ten secluded acres directly on the Gulf of Mexico. Amenities include one of the Keys largest freshwater pools, an outdoor Jacuzzi, two tennis courts, snorkel area (practice for the reef). In the recreation area there is bocce ball and and beach chess, which people love posing for photographs with. BBQs and picnic tables. Conference rooms with full catering facilities, a poolside restaurant and lounge, sunset tiki bar, and a fifty-slip marina. Come in your boat if you like, but make reservations with the dockmaster before you arrive. Cost is $1.50 per foot and there's a 20-foot minimum.

If you don't have a boat of your own, rent one here and cruise to the areas many seaside bars and restaurants. Vacationers appreciate the on-site charterboats for fishing, sailing and diving.

All guest rooms feature king or two double beds, refrigerators, Bahama fans, TVs, hair dryers, and clock radios, irons/boards (if you're still ironing your clothes you have not yet achieved true relaxation). Decor is Caribbean plantation style, and truly, once you enter this lovely inn you'll feel that you're someplace very tropical, and far, far away.

A daily poolside breakfast of seasonal fruit, muffins, bagels, juices and coffee is substantial. Room rates range between $185—$225 during the season; $85 and $185 in the off season, depending on type and view. Always ask about packages when you call to book a stay. Many people take advantage of the Banana Bay wedding package and marry here. For a price almost as cheap as eloping you get a seaside ceremony, flowers, photography, and champagne. Combine that with the Romantic Escape Package and you're definitely starting things right. It's a family place, too, so bring your kids.

There's a second Banana Bay Resort in Key West and it's just as nice as this one. However, it's an adults only facility. Ask about splitting up your Keys vacation with a few days here and a few days there. Now that's paradise!

Bayview Inn Marina
MM 63, on Conch Key ● 289-1525 ● 800-289-2055
Built originally as a fishing camp, this is the only guest lodging on Conch Key, a sixteen-acre island of lobster traps and lobster fishermen's houses. During the summer season (April—July is the off-season for lobstering), you'll see the traps stacked everywhere. The Bayview Inn's units—5 efficiencies and 4 bedrooms—are clean and inexpensive. Efficiencies have tiny kitchens and all rooms have refrigerators. The Bayview offers boat rentals (14, 17, or 22-foot Boston Whalers) and a dock and boat ramp. Dock your own boat for $1 a foot, or make a "boatel" deal. You dock your boat outside and rent an efficiency, in which case the dockage is free, providing you book a stay for at least 3 days. A little bit of everything sort of store stocks groceries, bait and tackle and dive supplies.

Proprietors Robert and Carolyn Lyne will hook you up with the area's best fishing captains for flat or deep sea fishing.

Many customers have been coming for years. They know what to expect in this no-frills, family oriented, family-run place. Pets by arrangement only. Tiki bar and sundeck, but no pool. Call for rates, which vary according to the time of year and type of room.

Bonefish Bay Motel
MM 53.5 Oceanside ✺ 289-0565 ✺ 800-336-0565

Besides the good deals on room rates, the Bonefish Bay offers free use of their bicycles, and in Marathon you can bike in some terrific places. (Otherwise, bikes rent in this area for about $10 a day.) Bonefish Bay is centrally located, and full of lazy charm. The clean and tidy units in the sixteen-unit motel are located in white stucco cottages with bright, yellow doors and window frames, with a sort of Jamaican feeling. At a private beach a mile away at the Cabana Club, Bonefish Motel guests are welcome for $3 per person. The beach is fantastic, one of the nicest in the entire Keys, so don't feel ripped-off about the $3. Otherwise, hang out at the cute pool at the Bonefish; you'll feel part of a little neighborhood here. Often a card game or a barbeque is going on in the yard. At the boat ramp, there's no additional charge to dock your boat. Rooms and apartments have the usual amenities, with the addition of a couple of extra movie stations on the TV. Unit #12 is right on the water; backyard fishing is popular here. Rates are all over the place, but they're a bargain. You can bring a small pet, but it'll cost you an extra $10 a night.

Faro Blanco Marine Resort
MM 48, Gulfside ✺ 743-9018 ✺ 800-759-3276

At Faro Blanco you can sleep in a lighthouse or on a houseboat. The lighthouse apartment is a two-bedroom unit carved into the second level of the gulfside white lighthouse that is the marine resort's logo. Air conditioning blows through ornate vent grates that look like old-fashioned heat vents up north. There's a little gabled room with a single bed, cushioned window seat, and child-sized bathroom, perfect for a romantic little girl, but definitely not for a boy. The adult-sized bedroom also features a window seat, English cottage feel, and windows on the world. In the

living room, the couch pulls out to a queen-sized bed. In the fully
equipped kitchen, a communal dining table is a wide wooden plank with
a bunch of bar-height stools. Easy to imagine a gang of adventurers putting away a few pounds of steamed shrimp and a couple gallons of beer
right here. All the ceilings are low; walls are old-fashioned wainscot
paneling; the floors are dark and wooden. The living room furniture is
modern, and actually, so is the place. But they've done a good job of
making it feel old and funky. Two couples or a good-sized family could
make use of the additional cots in the walk-in closet and have themselves a fine vacation. It's a unique retreat. Dock the family yacht right
out in the harbor, mere seconds away from your door. "You'll either love
it or hate it," a woman at the resort's front desk told us, handing us the
key. We loved it. Faro Blanco's houseboats are located less than a mile
away in a funky marina at the end of 15th Street. It tells the story of
Marathon's past, present, and future, all in one weird mesh of old, new
and newer. The houseboats are the newest. For people who get only two
weeks of salt air a year, this is a wonderful place to breathe in their
money's worth.

The Faro Blanco houseboats are tied so firmly to the dock that though
they rise and lower with the tide, they barely rock; the water is quite
serene. If you're hoping to be lulled to sleep by the action of the sea,
you'll find it's not quite as dramatic here as you might have expected. As
we hunted for our houseboat in the labyrinth of uniformly gray and white
houseboats, young and clear-headed on a bright sunny day, we wondered
how it would be to hunt for our lodgings if it was nighttime, and we
weren't so clear-headed. So consider this possibility for yourselves if you
plan to sleep here.

Word around town is that the Faro Blanco has been purchased by the
Spottswood Company of Key West. They plan to turn the resort into a
condominium complex. That may take a while, but it will happen.

Flamingo Inn
MM 59.5 ✎ **289-1478**
Here's a roadside mom-and-pop motel that looks good enough to eat,
like a dainty *petit four*. It's got AAA's two-diamond rating, and it even
landed a small—but important—role in a television series. A few years

ago the Fox Television Network came to the Keys to film an ill-fated series called *Key West*. The show, which aired six times before it was banished forever, used a number of Keysy, colorful locations like this one to tell their weak story. So how did the Flamingo fit in?

"It was a Norman Bates kind of scene," says proprietor George Richter.

"How much does it cost to rent a room?" one of the characters asks a weird-looking guy who is supposed to be the innkeeper.

"By the hour? By the day? Or by the week?" the weird innkeeper asks.

"And, of course, he gives these outlandish prices," laughs George.

Besides appearing in *Key West* the Flamingo's adorable facade, painted in pink, white and lime green, also appears in a number of guidebooks, George says. And, by the way, it only rents by the day. Or the week.

Very clean rooms with a '50s-kitsch decor: TV, AC, phones in every room, but if you use them, you pay 50¢ a call. Efficiencies with kitchenettes available. Also a three-room apartment. A freshwater pool encircled by a red brick walkway. No pets, please. There's a boat ramp a hundred yards down the street. Prices on a par with everybody else in the area . Winter rates and minimum-stay rules may apply during holidays and special events.

Hawk's Cay Resort
MM 61, on Duck Key ✶ 743-7000 ✶ 800-432-2242

Big families and major corporations frequently choose Hawk's Cay as a retreat destination because of its something-for-everyone atmosphere, and its 25,000 square feet of conference center and banquet facilities. A new 5500 square foot ballroom can be divided into three.

Built in 1959 by a local contractor, the Hawk's Cay Resort is a self-contained community sitting in the middle of Duck Key, a private, sixty-acre island located between the Atlantic and the Gulf of Mexico. The resort, originally called the Indies Inn, has changed hands several times through the years. Current owners purchased the property in 1983; they refurbished and renamed it. In spite of its many incarnations, or perhaps because of them, the property glows with a lovely patina. There's a vaseline-on-the-lens softness to it. On a busy weekend it feels kind of like an aging Catskills resort in the summertime. Kids are everywhere, and maids wear authentic maid costumes. Uniformed doormen, too.

Two children's program provide seven-hour days of supervised activities for kids. Island Adventures is for kids ages 6–12. Little Pirates for kids 3–5. Kiddie pool is one of the best in the whole country. Honest. It's a hoot and little kids love it. Ask about the Dolphin Connection's programs for little ones, too.

There's a quiet, very dignified library, with a remarkable photo display of some people of renown who have stayed here. Arnold Schwarzenegger, his wife Maria Kennedy Schriver, and Jamie Lee Curtis, were all here for the making of the film *True Lies*, partially filmed on the Old Seven Mile Bridge. The movie stars look so small in these pictures! There's a mounted 158-pound tarpon caught by Don Johnson. According to a plaque on a bridge that leads to Duck Key's plush residential area, even President Harry Truman once vacationed here—in March, 1964. The library features a fascinating aquarium. Though the room is lavishly appointed, there's nothing stuffy about it. It's comfortable.

There's a beach and 5 freshwater pools. Jacuzzis. And golfing at nearby Sombrero Country Club. Eight well-tended tennis courts and a fitness center. Green grass lawns. Water activities available at Hawk's Cay Marina—for a fee, of course—include snorkeling, scuba diving, deep sea and backcountry fishing, sunset cruises, sailing, and glassbottom boat trips.

Breakfast is served daily in the Palm Terrace, a bright rotunda suffused with sunshine filtered through several large skylights. An extravagant breakfast buffet features baked goods and pastries, tropical fruits, made-to-order omelettes. Tables are draped with dusty-rose tablecloths, set with casual elegance.

There are 160 guest rooms and 16 suites in the Hawk's Cay. New are 250 villas, which means that at the height of season the place really bustles.

Key Colony Beach Motel
MM 53.5, Take the causeway to East Ocean Drive ✶ 289-0411

If you build a moderately priced motel on the Middle Keys' nicest beach front, the tourists will come. Here it is—a moderately priced motel that backs up to the Atlantic Ocean. The rooms are like motel rooms everywhere: two beds, TV, AC. Clean, though a bit shabby, with tiled showers, and carpeting that has been cleaned and fumigated too many times. All rooms have fridges. But who cares what the rooms look like as long as they're comfortable? Four rooms are oceanfront, overlooking the pool (call to reserve them). There's also a good-sized freshwater pool. Key Colony Beach is a very good place to headquarter. Biking, walking, tennis and golf are available nearby. And that white sand beach. Rooms on the beach rent for around $90 in season and $80 in the off. Rooms not on the beach are a little less. Prices are "subject to change," this motel's advertising notes. As in the majority of Keys motels, all holidays use winter rates.

Kingsail Resort Motel
MM 50.5 ✶ 743-5246 ✶ 800-423-7474

There must have been a big resort-building boom in Marathon during the 1950s because here comes another resort with charmingly out-dated decor to make you nostalgic for the simpler days of white brick, blond wood paneling, and wrought iron furniture.

What's great about the Kingsail Motel is the staff's dedication to upholding the Keys' balmy reputation. Forget about the rest of the world, put away your city clothes, and head out to the pool. Every day begins with complimentary coffee on the docks.

During the summer many guests arrive by boat. Or arrive with a boat on a trailer. There's a boat launch, and a place to park the boat trailer. Dock at the Kingsail for $10 a night. It's located on an inlet, on the Gulf of Mexico. There's a little laundromat on promises. A charter fishing

boat is available at the dock, and when enough people sign up, they'll go
out for a day of fishing. He takes a summer break, back for season.

All forty-four units have phones, TV, and air conditioning.
Efficiencies have full kitchens; motel rooms have refrigerators only. Rates
on efficiencies are $80 - 130. Motel room rates range from $65–$95.
Rates are hiked a bit for special events and holidays, no matter what time
of year they occur, but there is no minimum stay requirement.

Lime Tree Bay Resort
MM 68.5, Layton ✽ 664-4740 ✽ 800-723-4519

AAA approved and an award winner, the Lime Tree Resort's location is
its finest feature: The bay beyond the motel is breathtaking. Many units
have tiny decks and chairs for taking in the view. The pool is built on a
platform that overlooks the bay; sit in the jacuzzi and marvel at the glory
of it all. There are inviting groupings of chairs in the lawn on the bay,
and a couple of hammocks as well. It's quite charming. If you stay here,
plan to set aside some time for bay watching.

Layton, a two-mile-long city with its own mayor, commissioners, and
police force, is the smallest city in the state. It's a clean, neat place,
founded by a guy who loved fishing and was dedicated to the pursuit of
happiness. At mile marker 68 you're in a good position to find it. You're
close to some of the Keys most interesting sights, restaurants and
beaches. And yet, you can get the feeling of a true retreat here. If your
sole purpose is relaxation, you're in the right place. This is definitely *not* a
party place. It's slow and quiet.

There are 31 units, several types: waterfront motel rooms and efficiencies, one-bedroom cottages, and two-bedroom apartments with names
like the Hemingway Cottage and the Zane Grey Suite. Non-smoking
rooms are available. Call for a well-prepared list of unit descriptions and
prices. Discounts available for extended stays. No pets.

A watersports concession on the grounds rents boats, Waverunners,
kayaks, sunfish sailboats, snorkeling gear and fishing rods. Fish right off
the dock. You can also tie up your boat here at the Key Lime Bay dock.

Ocean Beach Club Hotel & Resort
MM 53.5 Oceanside, Key Colony Beach
289-0525 ☞ 800-321-7213

Key Colony Beach is located a few minutes from Marathon's fine, recently updated airport, and yet it feels quite detached from the rest of Marathon. Key Colony Beach is a tiny city, all on a man-made island, with only about a thousand citizens. The island is spacious and wind-swept, connected to the mainland by a causeway. Many retirees winter here and rent their condos out to tourists when they're not here. You'll find a wonderful and well-utilized walking and biking path, and several very good restaurants.

If you've got to have a beach available twenty-four hours a day right outside your room, this is the place for you. Out back you'll find one of the very nicest beaches anywhere. Two hundred feet of lush, natural sand.

The Ocean Beach Club was built on the ocean in the late '50s. Its thirty-eight units are modest, spotless and roomy. Not luxurious. Thanks to Hurricane Georges (9/ 98), the older '50s-era furniture has been replaced. There are lovely king-sized beds in all suites and pretty comfy pull-out couches in the living rooms. Dark wood paneling, also ruined by Georges, has been torn out and replaced with white painted walls - an improvement actually. Next door there is the fabulous Tavern-By-The - Sea, a quite fabulous bar and seaside restaurant featuring excellent food at reasonable prices.

Rent a room with an ocean view for around $200 in season; Suites with kitchen, around $260. A room on the other side of the building—non-ocean view, sorry—is $165. Amenities include complimentary morning coffee and sweet rolls in the lobby, a big, ocean-side pool and jacuzzi, a lighted fishing pier, and that terrific restaurant next door. Also, one of the nicest desk and management crews in the islands. When you call for information, ask about specials. They can be very creative with specials.

Rainbow Bend Resort
MM 58. Oceanside, on Grassy Key ☞ 289-1505 ☞ 800-929-1505

The big draw here has always been the free use of a Boston Whaler motorboat. Or you can use the sailboat, canoes and kayaks. Full breakfast

is free every morning, too. There are twenty-three seaside units, pretty
simple, with that good old '50s feel so prevalent in Middle Keys rooms for
let. There's a not very sandy beach and a pool and jacuzzi. Rooms, efficiencies, one and two-bedroom suites. Rates are all over the place,
depending upon the size of your unit. Figure on paying anywhere from
$165 to $270. When you consider the complimentary breakfast and boat
time, it's a deal. And the on-site restaruant is a winner. You won't have
to leave the place for anything if you don't want to.

Seascape Ocean Resort
76th Street Oceanside (turn at MM 50) ✒ **743-6455** ✒ **800-332-7327**
The Seascape is at the oceanside end of a sedate residential street in
Marathon. Sometimes miscalled "the sea escape" by hopeful guests, the
property is a quiet and breezy compound of nine units, well off the beaten
path, and yet, conveniently close to it. Spectacular views of the Atlantic
from sunrise to sunset are endlessly fascinating. Hypnotic. From a cement
jetty on the deep-water marina, the light tower on Sombrero Reef is
faintly visible some five miles off shore. Guests are welcome to arrive by
boat and dock at the Seascape at no additional charge. (That no additional charge is a deal—usually you pay to dock.)

Monroe County's one-time commissioner of tolls built this lovely seaside villa in the early '50s. In a spacious wing facing the sunrise, he built three apartments for his three adult daughters and their families. New owners eventually chopped the estate into apartments. Finally the Seascape's intrinsic value as a resort was recognized. The apartments were divided into two, creating six units where there originally had been three. Seascape became an inn—but not the snug, blond on white ocean-side retreat you see today. It took the artistry and dedication of artist Sara Stites and her photographer husband Bill to bring the Seascape to its current state of bright charm.

Five beautifully landscaped acres feature a freshwater pool on a terraced jut of land with more breathtaking views of sky and sea. A walled garden is one of several serene retreats on the property. Also, two hammocks strung between trees, so close to the water's edge that at high tide you have to wade through water to get to them. Use of several kayaks and a tiny row boat is free to guests.

A breakfast of fresh-baked muffins, fresh fruits, and gourmet coffee is served in a pleasant, whitewashed community room. A tiny library features books by local authors, including a couple of Bill's sumptuous photography books. Around sunset, complimentary wine and hors d'oeuvres appear. All nine units are airy and light, some with complete kitchens. No phones. Sara has painted the designs on headboards and the mirror frames. The mattresses, Bill says, are the best that money can buy. And so are the New Age air conditioners...quieter than a whisper.

Rates start around $165 and go up to $245, depending on the type of unit—efficiency or room—and time of year. This is a good place to disappear, or . . . to escape.

Siesta Motel
MM 51 Oceanside ☙ 743-5671
Seven small, neat units so clean that phrases like "neat as a pin" and "clean as a whistle" come to mind. Ancient terrazzo floors feel wonderful on hot, tired, *tourista* feet. Several units are efficiencies. Others are simple rooms for two. New mattresses dressed in old, white cotton sheets, worn to dreamy perfection, are hypnotically restful. Newest owners, Frank Catchpole and Chris Kessler, have worked hard to keep things just as they've always been, with some minor, and much-appreciated moderniz-

ing. They've added coffee pots and television remote control units in all the rooms. They accept Mastercard and Visa. It's officially gay friendly, too.

Ginger Tolle opened the Siesta Motel with her husband in September, 1960—the same month Hurricane Donna slashed a swath of destruction right through Marathon. The furniture for the new motel arrived late, which turned out to be a blessing. Had it arrived on time, Ginger says, Donna would have torn it apart. Some of the furniture from that 1960s shipment is still in use in some of the rooms! And some of the guests, or the children of the guests from those days, are still coming, too. There's lots of repeat business, enough to keep the place quite full. If you're one of those repeat customers, Frank and Chris will give you the place at the rates you're used to. The current rates, $65 - $95 in season, are still good.

No pool. No phones. No beach. No frills. Just clean, comfortable rooms in the heart of the Keys. Two very nice inn-keepers. Siesta is a good name for the place.

Valhalla Beach Resort Motel
MM 56.5, Oceanside ☎ 289-0616

The sheets on your bed in this little motel were dried in sunshine and tropical breezes. That's the way it's done here. There are no clothes dryers. Everything is done as simply and no-fuss as possible. Even the office is stark. The price list is written and hung on a bulletin board on the door. Up until recently you clanged a bell to summon someone when you were ready to check in or out. But now there's somebody in the office pretty much all the time. That's progress for you.

This is where Key Westers go to vacation. It's an hour from home, and a world away, all at the same time. Owner Bruce Shofield inherited the Valhalla from his parents, who built the place as a fishing camp in 1951. It's been running continuously since then. Located about a half-mile-lane away from the Overseas Highway, the Valhalla feels quite remote and removed from the rest of the world. Until you see the sign, you might think you're about to become lost in the weeds. The complex includes ten units located on a tidal lagoon, with water on three sides. There's a very nice, not very sandy beach, with shade if you want it, and great wooden lounging chairs. Hammocks. Picnic tables. Flowers. Palm trees. Birds from the surrounding mangroves fly around and squawk happily.

Canoes are free to guests, and the area is perfect for exploration. Parents with children will find this a comfortable retreat. In the summertime, boaters often arrive pulling their boats. There's a launch on the property and no charge to dock here while you're a guest. You can fish off the pier, too.

All efficiencies and rooms have AC and TV. Also refrigerators. No phones. Efficiencies start at $110. Motel rooms at $95, based on double occupancy. Extra people in a unit are $10. Kids are $7. Rates are the same year-round. Two night minimum, although there's flexibility on that if you happen to show up when there's an opening. If you want to stay here, make your reservations early. The Valhalla does not advertise but is featured in many guidebooks because it is rustic and real.

Yellowtail Inn
MM 58.5 Oceanside, Grassy Key ✺ 743-8400
Hurricane Georges ripped this place apart pretty badly in 1998, which inspired (and required) a massive overhaul and redecorating. Now it's a lot spiffier than it used to be, and the landscaping is much more lush. It's still got wonderful sea front on the Atlantic Ocean and the sultry, salty sea breezes everywhere. Grassy Key is one of the most mellow and still natural areas in the Keys. A private, natural beachfront with imported sand runs the length of the property offering sun worshipers and beachcombers many hours of pleasure. Rent a boat and head out in search of new horizons. The grounds are scattered with plenty of BBQ grills and lounge chairs, and they get lots of action. BBQ is very popular with Grassy Key Beach guests.

Rooms are infinitely comfortable, and someone who worked there for a while told me that he was happily surprised that there were absolutely no complaints about the rooms for the length of his employ. He's worked in other Keys resorts, and complaints are more common than you might imagine. (Eg,: People don't like finding expired lizards under their $200-a-night pillows.) Many units are half trailer/half cottage. Sounds a little weird but the blend has been gracefully executed. The whole place is painted purple. You'll find refrigerators, coffeemakers, TV, AC, and private baths in all units; two big oceanfront units (one house, one apartment) have full kitchens. No two units are the same; they're all different, with different evolutionary stories. Grassy Key is popular with Europeans, particularly in the fall. Prices are very fair.

Dining

Barracuda Grill
MM 49.5 Gulfside ✒ 743-3314

This is one of the places innkeepers in Marathon invariably recommend to their guests. It's also a favorite eatery for locals. Dress is casual, but that doesn't mean the scene isn't top shelf. The food is divine; the wine list is sophisticated and well thought out. The service is meticulous. The servers are well-versed on what they're serving and answer every question you might have about the menu with authority. Eat inside or out under the stars. The short menu features the dishes that have proven most popular through the years. Sweet scallops from Argentina with creamed fresh spinach will make you moan with delight. Fran's Voodoo stew, featuring Andouille sausage with spicey shellfish is bewitching. The lobster bisque will bring tears to your eyes and make you feel sorry for the rest. Nightly specials are truly special. The stucco walls are adorned with elegant photographs, including some touching images of the owners' children. The whole scene is sleek and precise and soothing. The husband and wife team of Jan and Lance Hill are the chefs, in a kitchen so spotless I heard one food delivery man say you could eat off the floors. The prices are steep, but certainly approprite to the menu and the presentation. Don't drag the whole family along to this particular restaurant. There are lots of fish houses in Marathon perfect for a raucous family supper. Save this for a time when you can really relax, and take in all the pleasures dining at the Barracuda Grill has to offer.

Annette's Lobster & Steakhouse
MM 49 Bayside ✶ 743-5516

The first thing I can think to say about Annette's is that she serves the very best mashed potatoes this hungry writer has ever had the pleasure of not being able to finish. Honest. Alone, on a cold January night, I found myself enjoying the evening special of potato pancakes, lobster, shrimp and scallops, in Newburg sauce. The sauce was sublime. The pancakes were made of mashed potatoes, dusted in slivered almonds and sauteed in butter. (The waiter told me how it was done.) The seafood was cooked just right. I could not eat it all.

A few days later, I had occasion to lunch in Marathon with friends. I suggested Annette's and, as per my suggestion, my friends ordered sides of mashed potatoes to go with their Reuben sandwich, beef tips in wine sauce, and club sandwich. They agreed that the mashed potatoes were the best they'd ever had - of course it's not like anyone could tell me they weren't . . . Our sandwiches were terrific, too. Annette's has a lovely, simple soup and salad bar, featuring fresh, colorful salad fixings. Soup, on the evening I was there, was tomato basil. Excellent. Dessert was out of the question, on both visits to Annette's, but since Annette is a former pastry chef, I'm sure you can count on the same high quality. I've also heard that if you're craving something that's not on the menu, Annette will try to make it for you.

Prices are medium at lunch, and somewhat high for dinner. My seafood and potato pancake extravaganza was $25. But remember, everything is fresh, and prepared with care and respect. I like Annette's a lot.

Island Tiki Bar and Restaurant
MM 54 Gulfside ✶ 743-4191

A one shop stop for food, drinks and watersports. You hang out at the funky tiki bar, or in the air-conditioned comfort of the dining room, while the more ambitious in your party hit the watersports concession. Watch them soar past, high in the sky via Aloha Parasail (289-9412), which operates oh the same property. Menu is what you'd expect to eat on the waterfront. Shrimp every which way imaginable, conch ceviche, salads, clams, crabcakes and BBQ. Burgers, chicken wings and chowders. Be here for a great view of the famous Florida Keys sunset. Fantastic!

Burdines Waterfront
15th Street & Ocean Ave ❧ 743-5317

The turn for 15th Street off US 1 is fortunately located in a 35 MPH zone, so you're going slow enough to find it. Drive through a neighborhood of trailers and keep going, past the dry-docked boat that marks the right-hand turn-off to the Castaway Restaurant. You'll pass a row of very nice big boats. Admire the yachts, and find a parking place. By now you should see the sign for Burdines, which is a weather-beaten building on the left. Don't get upset if you don't find it right away. Look again. You can't get lost! And there are stops on 15th Street definitely worth finding.

Burdines is no relation to the Florida department store. It's an upstairs bar perched over a lagoon, with a great breeze and a spectacular view of the sunset. The atmosphere is divine — salty, rough, and reminiscent of the way Keys bars used to be when everybody knew everybody else and there were more locals than tourists. The waitresses at Burdines will remind you of your mom, if your mom had chucked it all and run away to the Florida Keys right after you left her nest empty. Now if all this isn't enough to make Burdines one of the best spots in Marathon to sip a beer or wine, the food is terrific! If you're weary of fried fish, try a grilled fish sandwich, or yellowfin tuna chunks, skewered and grilled with onions and peppers. Garden salads, with or without chicken or fish. Quesadillas, black beans and rice. The fresh-cut fries and homemade coleslaw really are fresh and homemade. Old fashioned, fresh squeezed lemonade is shaken, not stirred. Live entertainment on weekends. Simple, good, basic food and drinks with prices to match. Beer and wine only. Visa and Mastercard.

Castaway Restaurant
MM 47.8, 15th Street Oceanside ❧ 743-6247

John and Arlen Mirabella sailed into Marathon and bought the Castaway Restaurant in the winter of 2000. Their sailboat, the *Darcena*, is parked right outside and they live aboard her still. The California natives have done an admirable job of recognizing and maintaining the funky character of the Castaway, which is cherished by long-time fans for its out of the way location in a nook of harbor just seconds off U.S. 1. (See directions to Burdines, above.)

This official historical landmark, established here in 1951, is a bit tricky to find, and parking is somewhat difficult. There's a small parking lot for the whole place, so it fills quickly. Don't take a chance in a tow-away zone, either. In this marina of shrimp and lobster houses, houseboats and residential trailers, the Castaway fits quite nicely. The dining room is a screened-in porch, with ceiling fans turning at top speed to keep the warm air moving. There's a newly opened, very tiny air-conditioned dining room, which fills up first in warmer weather. The floor is cement. The chairs don't match, and you might find a shrimp shell, left over from an earlier patron's dinner, under your table (we did). The rough-hewn ambiance reminded one guy in our party of his '50s era summer camp back in South Carolina. It's fun to sit at a table with a window on the canal, when the lights of the low-rent neighborhood glitter off the after-dark water.

The food at the Castaway is great. It had better be, right? As always, a basket of luscious honey buns appears on every table as soon as you sit down. It's a tradition at the Castaway, no matter who's running the show. Chef John, formerly a nuclear engineer, prepares nightly specials like blackened yellowfin tuna with teriyaki sauce. In the short time he's been here, his fine food has already earned several awards. "We're just overwhelmed with happiness," John says, as he rushes between kitchen, dining room and front door to welcome newcomers. Menu selections include fried or sauteed fishes, shrimp and lobster. A woman at the table next to ours, who always visits the Castaway during her family's annual Marathon vacation, raved about the experience of dining at this long-time establishment. "We eat here once a year, and we always get lost trying to find it," she laughed. "It's all part of the tradition with us."

Prices are moderate. Beer and wine only. Major credit cards. Lunch Monday - Friday only. Dinners nightly from 5 p.m.– 10.m.

Cracked Conch Cafe
MM 49.9 Oceanside ▪ 743-2233
Gee whiz. Absolutely nothing went right on the day we visited the Cracked Conch Cafe. But everything looked perfect at their indoor

dining area, bar, and outdoor dining room, enclosed by white-washed cement blocks. Lots of boughs of tropical green creep and poke around the room among little tables for two or four, and one table for up to six people. The waitresses are sturdy-looking gals with some good stories to tell—you just know it when you see them. This place was featured on *TV Diners*, a program that goes on location to feature curious culinary sites all over the country. Since you don't often see cracked conch on a menu, it is easy to imagine how the chewy mollusk that figures big on this menu, as well as in the name of the joint, caught the attention of the *TV Diners* scouts.

So we were expecting to eat one fine lunch. It was 1 p.m. and the place wasn't crowded. We had 2 'o clock plans. Surely enough time to have a quick sandwich, right? *Wrong.* Twenty minutes after we had ordered, our waitress came to the table to confess that she'd forgotten to put our order in to the kitchen. She brought us a couple of cups of nothing-to-write-home-about chowder to make up for the delay. "Men like red and women like creamy," the waitress said.

Finally, our sandwiches arrived. The deep-fried conch sandwich was chewy, but good. My poor friend's fish sandwich wasn't cooked all the way through. In fact, he realized after a couple of bites, the damned thing was very close to raw. Time was ticking away. The waitress took the raw fish sandwich off our bill. She would have taken it back to the kitchen and had it cooked through, she said, but we were running late for our 2 'o clock plans and didn't have any more time to spend at the Cracked Conch Cafe.

Since this crazy day a few years back, we've dined at the Cracked Conch and enjoyed it a lot. Which goes to show you that every restaurant has it's ups and downs. Don't cross it, or any place that you find inviting, off your list of possibilities.

Fish Tales
MM 53 Oceanside ✆ 743–9196
If you were a fan of the Grassy Key Dairy Bar, which wasn't a dairy bar at all but a seafood restuarant on beautiful Grassy Key, you'll recognize the people who own and run this bustling little seafood market/eatery. The owners, George, Jackie and Johnny Eigner, have moved to town and are on the premises of their new endeavor, making sure that every dish and

product they sell is as fresh and well prepared as it can possibly be. Every fish or shellfish here is harvested from local waters. You can count on that. They've given the old place a great overhaul, too. It was pretty funky and junky a few years ago, which it perhaps had a right to be since it's supposedly the oldest fish market in Marathon.

Dine in on the usual seafood dinners, fried fish baskets, sandwiches, or burgers, or one of the house specialties like the German Snapper sandwich, served on grilled swirled rye with cole slaw, fries & muenster cheese. Try the smoked fish spread, or order it to go. You can also buy a Key lime pie to go, or even homemade sausages or hand-cut aged steaks . Prices are very reasonable. Have a glass of wine or beer while you wait for your to-go order.

Herbie's
MM 50.5 Bayside ✹ 743-6373

A Key West friend says he always stops in at Herbie's on his way to or from Miami. So we figured we should try it, although there's nothing about the way it looks from the outside to entice you to go inside. Unless you're encouraged by long lines... But it's a fun bar, and the fried fish sandwiches are yummy. Gee whiz, what else do you want? Around 8 p.m. on Friday and Saturday nights, people stand in line to get into Herbie's to eat, which might give you the idea that the food is extra fantastic. Why else would they wait when there are so many other places? The waitresses are super fast, but the prices are like fried fish prices everywhere else. It's one of those been-here-forever joints. An institution. No credit cards. Closed Sunday and Monday.

taking orders for the day's special: ribs and French fries with coleslaw. Food is not fussy, but it's great; we enjoyed every greasy bite.

On the menu we noted that the severity of the heat in the spicy-hot Hurricane Wings is rated by force, just like a hurricane. Get it? "Force 1" is mild. "Force 2" is not so mild, and so on. The menu states that, to order "Force 6," you must be over eighteen and willing to sign a release form. Other menu selections are fried fish baskets and Philly cheese steaks. The full bar features lots of beers. The waitresses are cool; the laid-back atmosphere is big with local, funky Keys characters.

Key Colony Inn
MM 53.5 Key Colony Beach ✒ 743-0100

Off the beaten path, but not too far off. The food here isn't ultra fantastic; it's just very good, very satisfying, kind of like Mom's home cooking. Prices are somewhat less than at comparable restaurants on the main highway. At this no-nonsense restaurant you can count on finding a good selection of nicely prepared, beautifully presented dishes based on American and Italian cuisine. Service is excellent and personable. Lots of variations on local seafood. Salad is served family style, in a big bowl with more than you can possibly eat. This place feels like a country club dining room up north; a little old-fashioned, but nicely so. And everybody knows everybody else. Order the Grand Fisherman's Platter, sauteed or fried, or simple ravioli with tomato sauce and mushrooms. The well-designed children's menu has very good prices, too. Lunch and dinner only; full bar.

Weekends feature lots of weddings, so you'll see people in wilted wedding clothes wandering through the dusk, looking dazed and sort of beat, the way you feel at the end of a long wedding day. The Inn opens around 11 a.m. every day.

Keys Fisheries Market and Marina
MM 49, take 35th St. to the bay ✒ 743-4353

A Marathon motel owner told me that the same people who own Joe's Crab House in Miami also own this simple eatery, which is used as a recipe test kitchen. I don't know if that's true, but it makes for a good story. People love this place, I think, because the walk-up order window harkens to an easier, softer time in our past when such places dotted the highways of America. A seafood market, too. And, it's right on the water. Great sunset view at dinnertime. Menu is on a big board next to the window where you order from polite and efficient staff members. While you wait for your food, pick out a table, arm yourself with plastic silverware and napkins, condiments and drinks. If you want beer or wine, bring it. Wander the marina. Check out the fish market.

Fried fish with potato pancakes was the all-you-can-eat special one night. And at the height of the season, an all-you-can-eat special on stone crab claws for around $25. That's a deal. Fish sandwiches served in baskets with fries. Crab cakes. Cole slaw. Conch salad. Chowders and seafood bisques. Dinnertime steamed broccoli with garlic butter is divine! Fried, whole belly clams are a rare treat, though frozen and imported. Prices moderate. Credit cards. Open daily from 11:30 a.m. till 9 p.m. Fun, easy and informal. You'll be back!

The Hideaway Restaurant
MM 58 Oceanside at Rainbow Bend Resort ✻ 289-1554

Dining at the Hideaway will cost you plenty, but your dinner will be memorable. The enclosed dining room faces the ocean. Dinner is served from 4:30 till 10 p.m. nightly. The Hideaway describes itself, in its ads, as as "casual gourmet" and that's accurate. You don't have to get dressed up to eat here, but the food is definitely dressed up. House specials are the 2-pound stuffed Florida lobster, Beef Wellington or Seafood Wellington, lobster and seafood crepes, roasted whole duck, NY Strip, lamb, Caesar salads with every entree, and appetizers. Skip the desserts. You'll be too full and besides, they're not quite as magnificent as the main courses. Entrees are $20 - $35, but there is plenty on every plate. Every bite of every dish is truly delicious. Great wine selection. Service is personable and terrific. If it's possible, the chef will come out of the kitchen and greet you. Make reservations. Save this place for a special occasion. You won't be disappointed.

Little Italy
MM 68.5 ✻ 664-4472

The name of "Little Italy" is a bit of a misnomer because the place serves much more than just standard Italian dishes: fried conch and fish; Lunchtime Reuben and chicken parmesan sandwiches are robust and affordable. Salads are substantial and fresh. They aim to appeal to locals, and they do. Regular customers are staff members from the nearby Dolphin Research Center. Area motels send more business, and regular Keys travelers know they'll find consistently good food and reasonable prices here. The Little Italy opens every day at 6:30 a.m., serving break-fast dishes like battered and fried dolphin with eggs and home fries, blueberry pancakes and yummy stick-to-your-ribs standards. Lunch is served till 2:30 p.m. Dinner hours are 5 p.m.–10 p.m. The dinner chef makes a mean shrimp scampi. Dolphin - the fish, not the mammal - is prepared many different ways. This place closes only for Thanksgiving and Christmas because it's a family sort of place. The parking lot is always full. The place is always jumping.

Porky's BBQ
MM 47.5 Bayside ✹ 289-2065

Perched between the Overseas Highway and a very tranquil saltwater lagoon, Porky's indoor/outdoor shack dining room is painted with fishes, moons and slogans like "swining and dining." Porky's may not look like an important restaurant, but it is. The atmosphere and the attitude here represent all that is sweet and goofy about the Keys. While you wait for your ribs or BBQ sandwich or beer, you may find yourself chatting with folks at the next table. They might be locals; they might be visitors. They might be Miami tourists who stop by every couple of weekends on their way into or out of the Keys. If you're looking to rent a boat, have a look at Captain Pip's selection on the right side of the marina. Ring a ship's bell and Captain Pip will appear to handle the arrangements. The reef, Captain Pip will explain, is about about five miles out.

Lunch or dinner for two—there's only one menu—is around $25. The food isn't as good as the atmosphere, although it's definitely good. Our gripe was that the ribs were reheated. Same for the barbecued beef and pork sandwich. We've heard that some of the area's winter residents rush straight to Porky's as soon as they arrive back in town each season for some of Porky's southern-style barbeque. Porky's caters some of the best area parties, too. We'd like to go to a party catered by these folks. Beer and wine only. Porky's is open every day. They close only for bad weather.

Seven Mile Grill
MM 47 Bayside ✹ 743-4481

Buy a T-shirt. See live Marathon characters like a very hungover guy picking up a to-go order in a shirt that says *If I'd known you were gonna care about me this long I woulda taken better care of myself.* The food complements the area's borderline shabbiness.

The foot-long hot dog with all the trimmings used to be special and terrific because of the old-fashioned grilled roll. Lately they've stopped grilling the roll, which seems like a sign of the times. Is nothing sacred?

"The bakery doesn't send us those rolls anymore," a waitress, who I think owns the place, explained. The waitresses who work here have been around forever. Fried fish, stuffed crabs, burgers and a yummy shrimp bisque are all specialties. (Long ago a Seven Mile Grill employee told me the bisque is made of evaporated milk, Campbell's cream of asparagus and cream of mushroom soups and tiny canned shrimp. You figure out the proportions, she said.)

The Grill features traditional roadside, deep-fried food served at a long, old-fashioned lunch counter. Decor is old diner—walls full of license plates, wooden plaques with dumb fishing cartoons, and signs that say stuff like "No Snowmobiling." Pitcher of draft beer is around $8; also canned and bottled beer, and wine.

We always stop at the grill for something or other; usually we eat. You can dine in the air-conditioned dining room, but then you're missing the point. Not so long ago, there were few other choices, and that's when my family and I got hooked forever on the Seven Mile Grill. New owners have promised to keep the joint open every day of the year. That' s new, and welcomed!

Tavern By the Sea
401 East Ocean Drive, Key Colony Beach • 289-3131
Sit beneath a sheltering umbrella, outside, on the large seaside terrace and dig the heady joy of the magnificent view of the Atlantic Ocean. You get the full effect of dining on the ocean here, which is something you don't get to do very often, even in the Florida Keys. Or, belly up to the horseshoe bar and feel the wild wind in your hair and the brine of the sea in your nose as you sip a cocktail. The view is just as good from the indoor tables, thanks to walls of windows and the cool comfort of air conditioning.

You might think that with all this fabulous atmosphere going on the people who run the Tavern might not feel the need to worry much about the food. Wrong! The food is excellent, and the menu so varied and full of delicious sounding salads, sandwiches and entrees your biggest problem will be what to order. So take your time. Ask lots of questions. Our servers have always been warm and friendly and interested in making us happy. Prices are medium for high quality food. There's a kids' menu, and on Sundays, a very affordable brunch buffet.

The Tavern by the Sea seats up to 350 people, and is popular for weddings. Live entertainment on weekends. Walk to the end of the fishing pier and look for dolphins. Can you tell I love this place?

Village Cafe
MM 50 Gulfside Village Shopping Center ☎ 743-9090

Enjoy a terrific Sunday breakfast buffet from 8:30 a.m. to 2 p.m., with all the usual breakfast goodies, for $6.95. The Sunday dinner buffet, served from 5 p.m. to 9 p.m. for $12.95, is attractive, and the atmosphere is perfect for Sunday evening, when everybody is a little tired but feeling warm and fuzzy. The regular menu is very nice, and the food really well-prepared at this family operation. The waitrons here seem to be going crazy at lunchtime, but, in spite of the hubbub, they keep on smiling. They shouldn't be surprised it's so packed because this is one of the best places for pasta meals, and most reasonably-priced, in the Keys. The fresh pastas have terrific sauces, and the clam sauce is heavenly. The fresh tomato and basil is good, too, and reminded me of New York Italian cuisine. Good salads, good service, and a very nice presentation. Considering all that, particularly as it stacks up against what else is available in the area, it's one of Marathon's best deals. Breakfast, lunch and dinner every day except Christmas and New Year's.

Wooden Spoon
MM 50.5 Oceanside ☎ 743-7469

The grill's on at 5 a.m. Heavy-duty fishermen's breakfasts attract many hungry locals, fisherman, and hung-over tourists. Crowded from the crack of dawn on. Buy a box lunch and take it on your fishing boat. The waitresses in here call you "Hon" and are so good at anticipating your needs, it seems as if they are reading your mind.

The Wreck & Galley Grill
MM 59, Grassy Key ☎ 743-8282

Right next door to the Dolphin Research Center. Don't be put off by the sports bar sign. It's very much a family place for lunch and dinner. The children's menu is unlikely, but much appreciated. A wonderful stop for tourists and locals alike. There are TVs everywhere, but they're not terribly intrusive. Go out on the deck if you don't want to know the score. There's even a grassy side yard where your kids can work off excess energy.

This place used to be Crockagators until a family from Michigan arrived to take over, totally repaint the building, inside and out, and set about serving solidly delicious and affordable fresh local seafood as well as the sideline stuff you like to nosh while watching the game. They claim to have the largest Buffalo wings in the Keys, and you can order them as hot, or tame, as you like. Calamari rings, jalapeno poppers, stuffed potato skins, are all great. Chowders are very good, particularly the New England clam chowder, thick with clams and potato chunks. Fish sandwich is perfect every time you order it. Hamburger is as pedestrian as the fish was outstanding. So order fish. If you're a frog leg lover, you won't want to miss All You Can Eat Frog Legs Night.

Friday night is Big Ass Prime Rib night, and on the Friday night we were there, the place was packed with carnivores. Also, excellent service. Our server came from Michigan, and so did most of the staff. Prices commensurate with sports bar prices everywhere.

Nightlife

The Brass Monkey Lounge
MM 50 ✺ 743-4028
Rock 'n' roll rules! Tonight and every night in this longtime-popular local bar. The Brass Monkey boasts live entertainment nightly (except Mondays) and no cover charge. Happy hour daily, 4 till 8, and on Friday, what has become a tradition: the Friday Happy Hour Buffet. House star is Freddie Bye. His band plays anything you request. Open till 4 a.m. every day.

Sombrero Marina and Dockside Lounge
MM 50, Oceanside; on Sombrero Boulevard ✺ 743-0000
This dockside lounge with a full bar and live music, overlooks scenic Boot Key Harbor. The party-hardy atmosphere blends Caribbean music and limbo contests with Hawaiian luau food and hula dances. Patrons are encouraged to dress accordingly. The goal of the Sombrero Dockside Lounge is to make you feel at home no matter what side of the continental divide you're from—and to rent you a Waverunner or a sailboat the following day.

Shops

Bougainvillea House
MM 53.5 ✎ **743-0808**

Within this ancient, sun-silver wooden building, beneath an explosion of brilliant pink bougainvillea, you'll find a fabulous collection of paintings, photography, pottery, ceramics, hand-blown glass, handwoven baskets and jewelry, all created by local artists. A very nice, not-to-be-missed browse. Open daily from 10 till 6 in season. Hours and days vary during summer months.

Blond Giraffe
MM 50, Oceanside ✎ **743-4423**

Everybody down here claims to make the very best Key lime pie in the islands. I make that claim. Because honestly, it is not difficult to make a lovely and amazing Key lime pie. The nice Brazilian couple who founded Blond Giraffe have made a major project out of baking big batches of Key lime pie and selling them to people who would rather pay $25 a pie than take a few minutes to make their own. They also sell frozen Key lime pie on a stick, and single servings of pie. And they're doing very, very well. Now rum cake is another deal altogether. As far as I know, you have no choice but to go to Blond Giraffe to get that buttery treat. Indulge in all things Key lime at this sparklingly clean shop. Send a pie home to the people who have never heard of Key lime pie. If you really love them, send a Key lime rum cake. Open daily, 9 a.m. - 8 p.m.

BP Cargo
MM 49.5 Oceanside ✎ 743-0555

The first question every customer asks upon entering this shop is this: "Do you always play Jimmy Buffett music in here?" The answer is "Yes. For 9 hours every day."

"Actually, fortunately, I like Jimmy Buffet's music very much," says manager Sandy Spear. "I can't imagine doing this if, say, Wayne Newton had an apparel line."

Merchandise here is every Jimmy Buffett CD, tape, and book, trinkets and doodads, and anything else related to Jimmy Buffett worship. Don't just sing along to the Jimmy Buffett songs. Wear one! In a shirt inspired by Buffett songs and lyrics. Caribbean Soul is Jimmy Buffet's apparel line, and there are shirts here to fit tall and big parrot heads up to size 4X! Take home some Margarita mix. The store opens, and the Jimmy Buffett music starts playing, every day at 9 a.m.

Marathon Discount Books
MM 48.5 Oceanside ✎ 289-2066

Stop in for a talking book to keep you company on the Overseas Highway, a spicy tell-all biography for the beach, or a stack of picture books to occupy the kiddies. How about a collection of June Keith's *Postcards From Paradise*? A book on sharks or one on pirates? They've got all that and more at Discount Books. And the prices on many selections are reduced! Some quite drastically. The clerks behind the counter are always good for tourist information. They know about the newest dining hot spot, shop, or attraction in the Middle Keys. And they've read a lot of the books they're selling. Ask them for their reviews. A book store lover's dream book store.

Food For Thought
Gulfside Village ✎ 743-3297

OK. So I love book stores. And here's another great one. For a long time this was the only book store in Marathon. They've done an admirable job of assembling a fine selection of reading into fairly small quarters. The bargain table always has something sensational like a giant book of photographs and trivia about the king of rock 'n roll: *Graceland: The Living Legacy of Elvis Presley*, which sold originally for $50. I got it for $9. Amazing, huh? Also bestsellers and books by Keys writers, postcards and nice boxed notecardy things. Check out the community announcement center posted in the window, with its great array of posters and ads for all sorts of events and services. It's a fun browse, and you'll probably find something crazy or interesting to do or see.

On the other side of the shop, you'll find a health food store with whole foods, organic beauty products, and vitamins. Food for thought...get it?

Quay Village Shops
MM 51 Bayside

The various proprietorships of these little sun and wind-worn storefronts seem to change frequently. Merchants come and go, so you never know what sort of merchandise, and what atmosphere or attitude you'll find in each individual shop from season to season. No matter who shows up, or who departs, this has always been a wonderful place to while away a morning or afternoon in Marathon. At a place called Small World you'll find the cutest imaginable tropical-flaired clothes for kids. A grandparents' bonanza. Next door to that one a shop sells Jimmy Buffett CD's and Caribbean Soul, Jimmy's line of island-inspired clothing. At the far end, the last shop in the chain is Shipwrecked by Design, my favorite. The guy who owns this shop is a cigar aficionado, with a penchant for heat — as in Velvet Elvis Hot Sauce, his very own brand. No matter who's running this show, it remains quite fascinating. Mosey around this collection of Keys kitsch and schlock, gifts and souvenirs, and then, treat yourself to a hamburger and a beer at the tiki hut behind the Quay Restaurant. The hamburger here is one of the island's best. (Don't go to the Quay Restaurant! It's the tiki hut, out back, on the water where you'll get good food.)

This is a good place for mixed-interest parties. Send the non-shoppers out to the tiki hut. They'll have a ball, and so will you—shopping.

Islamorada

Village of Islands

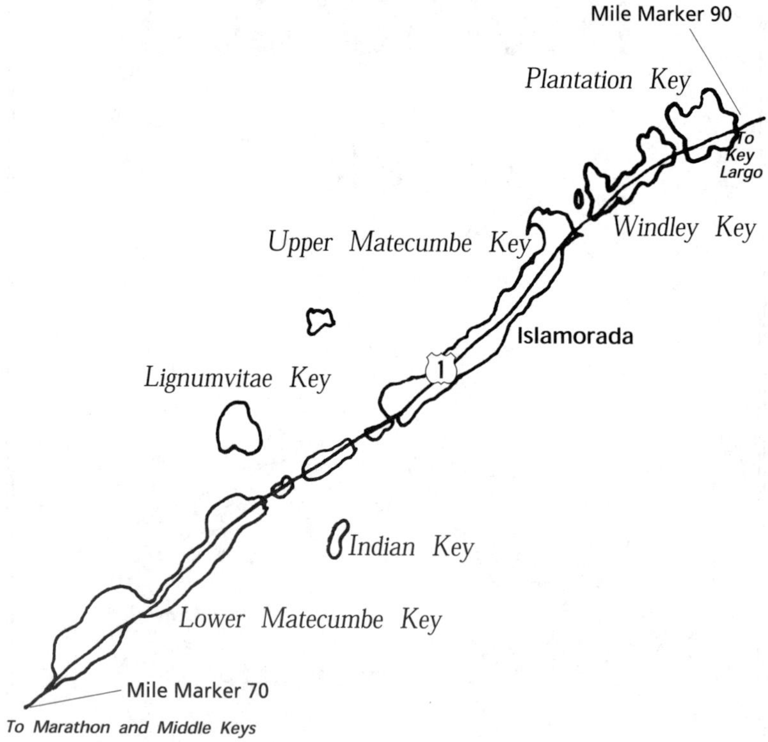

Mile Marker 90

Plantation Key

To Key Largo

Upper Matecumbe Key

Windley Key

Islamorada

Lignumvitae Key

1

Indian Key

Lower Matecumbe Key

Mile Marker 70

To Marathon and Middle Keys

*...Marlin fishermen suffer from a rare psychological
disorder that I call the Ahab Complex—
an obsession to pursue and conquer a monster
of the depths regardless of the consequences to
one's bank account, career and family life.*

– Phil Caputo, Pulitzer Prize winner

The Purple Isles
and Their Number One Passion

"The Purple Isles." That's what the early Spanish explorers called this little group of islands. But no historian is quite certain what purple inspiration those sailors saw. Flowers? Shrubs? Tree snails? Seashells? Like many of the descriptive names given these islands by Spaniards long ago, this is another without a clear-cut origin. All we know is they saw purple and, since Islamorada is such a pretty name, we're glad they did.

The area we know today as Islamorada is comprised of six islands also known as "the Matecumbes." The meaning of the word "Matecumbe" is also unclear. In some places you will read that Matecumbe is the mispronunciation of the word "Guarugumbe," which was the name of one of the islands. Another theory is that Matecumbe is a contraction of two Spanish words: matar, "to kill" and hombre, "man." Obviously, controversies over the meanings and origins of Keys names are quite common.

When Islamorada incorporated in 1997, they changed their name to "Islamorada, Village of Islands." The islands they're talking about are Plantation Key, Windley Key, Upper Matecumbe, Lower Matecumbe, and the offshore islands of Lignumvitae Key, and Indian Key.

The fundamental differences between the Upper Keys areas of Key Largo and Islamorada spring from their respective primary tourist industries: diving and fishing. Consider the differences between people who dive and people who fish, the differences between communing with nature and, well, *challenging* it. Key Largo is a diving town, and Islamorada is a fishing town—the "Fishing Capital of the World."

Fishing can be an extraordinarily expensive passion. The guides, the gas, the gear, the vessels and the licenses all carry big price tags to be passed on to the tourist. But for devotees, the fat price tags are part of what makes it such a noble sport.

Hardcore anglers will find their heaven on earth in the fish-rich waters of Islamorada. The people of Islamorada understand the allure of angling—perhaps better than any other community you will find in the world. So the place feels kind of country-clubish, and the theme everywhere, always, is fishing.

On T-shirts and coffee mugs, posters and menus you'll see this whimsical sentiment: "Islamorada, a quaint little drinking town with a fishing problem."

If endless vistas of sea and sky tinged with the scent of diesel fuel and fish bait bring you no joy whatsoever, do not despair. There is much else to do on Islamorada's shores. Some of the Keys' most remarkable history happened right here. You can stay in some truly unique resorts, motels, and inns, visit great places to shop, eat and drink. Or just sit and read in the unbridled breezes of the mighty Atlantic, or on the sultry side of the islands that face the Florida Bay.

The area of Islamorada, the Village of Islands, covers the miles from Anne's Beach at mile marker 73, all the way up to mile marker 90, near where the big island of Key Largo begins.

Islamorada Chamber of Commerce
MM 83.2 Bayside ☛ 664-4503 ☛ 800-322-5397
Of the Florida Keys chambers of commerce, this one is probably the friendliest, and most fun. The place is run by a handful of industrious women, who call themselves Chamber Maids. These bright specialists are in charge of telling the world about Islamorada and keeping records on who wants to know what. (That's why they always ask you where you're from. They like to keep track of who's coming here from where.) They

handle over one hundred telephone calls a day and answer thousands of in-person tourists' questions. They work very hard, for less money than you might think. Every last one of them is crazy about Islamorada, and it shows. If you're looking for a place to eat, sleep, drink, party or shop, these women, of varying ages, backgrounds and tastes, will come up with all the answers to your questions. Just don't expect them to know all about Key West, or Big Pine Key. They know about Islamorada!

One of their more appreciated attributes is their honesty. They won't pretend to know about something if they don't. And when they do know about something, they will share the news with open hearts and minds.

Also in the Visitors Center you'll find a dizzying selection of brochures and pamphlets. Islamorada is particularly good at brochures. The Caboose is set back a bit from the road, so keep your eyes peeled for it. There are often traffic jams in the tiny parking lot, but do be patient, find a good spot and come on in for a good time.

If you're not here yet, call ahead and they'll send you a list of charter-boat captains, a list of accommodations and restaurants. But you've got to ask for each specific item.

A Bloody History

W E KNOW FROM SPANISH sea charts, dating from as far back as the 1500s, that the freshwater wells on Lower Matecumbe Key have long been of great importance to passing ships as well as to Indians who originally inhabited these islands. Archeological evidence points to several Indian communities having been here. Easily accessible from the Atlantic Ocean, the Matecumbes were visited frequently by seafarers who came ashore for fresh water.

It is believed that Indians began communicating and interacting with Cuban fishermen as early as the 1500s. Native Americans incorporated Spanish words, as well as Spanish names, into their cultures. The Keys Indians were proficient divers and were the first salvagers of ships wrecked on the dangerous reefs that run parallel to the island chain. The items they found on wrecked ships were often useless to them and their society. However, items like fanciful clothing were much appreciated, and, always, Indians were delighted to find barrels of rum. Sometimes the victims of the frequent shipwrecks were enslaved by the Indians, and sometimes they were killed. It is said that Keys Indians were tolerant of Spanish-speaking people, but suspicious and extremely hostile to others.

Just after the Civil War, Bahamian settlers arrived in the area and survived by raising cash crops of melons, limes and vegetables, which they transported by trade schooners to Key West or northern Florida. According to the census taken that year, in 1870 the population of the entire Keys outside of Key West was three hundred.

Early settlers of the Upper Keys faced unimaginable hardships: bugs and mosquitoes, poverty, isolation. Many settlers came to the Keys, settled on the open land, tried for a few years, and then went away again beaten by the harsh conditions.

In the 1820s and 1830s, however, a little community was founded, and it flourished quite remarkably on Indian Key. But the town was burned in 1840 by warring Indians during the Second Seminole Indian War.

The arrival of the Overseas Railroad in the early 1900s brought little change to the area. But the Overseas Highway, completed here in 1928, changed life in Islamorada forever, just as it would do everywhere in the Keys. Still, those changes came very slowly; the population figures from the mid 1800s through early 1900s are unbelievably small.

When the Matecumbe islands, where the ocean is always just a few feet away from anywhere on shore, became accessible by car, tourism slowly began as a trickle and then grew steadily. Besides the terrific climate, deep-sea fishing was the draw. Then in 1935, the United States' most devastating hurricane nearly wiped the Lower Matecumbe islands off the map, and so the area had to start up fresh from scratch once again.

Tourism was established as the Keys' most important industry by the time electricity was installed here in 1942; fresh water, via an extravagant pipeline stretching from the mainland all the way to Key West, came in September of the same year. Mosquito control began in 1952. Today, area jobs and businesses are nearly all tourist-related.

The Indian Key Massacre

There is scant record of anything going on in the Keys before the early 1800s. When the U.S. government began a settlement at Key West Harbor in 1822, the Keys were wild and ungoverned and filled with a handful of people who liked it that way. One of the few places outside of Key West to attract any settlement was Indian Key. The eleven-acre island was situated close to the treacherous reefs that brought increasing numbers of ships aground. It was also less than a mile from Lower Matecumbe Key and its important source of fresh water for seafarers. The island was a busy rendezvous for pirates, smugglers, privateers, and all sorts of rugged seamen on often nefarious journeys.

The first store in the Keys, outside of Key West, was founded on Indian Key around 1824 by a Spaniard. The tiny general-supply store was doing a brisk trade when an aggressive wrecker and scofflaw named Jacob Housman showed up on the island. Recognizing its many natural assets and its potential for development, Housman settled here with plans to take over.

The Infamous John Jacob Housman

Born in 1799 to a Staten Island, New York, sea captain, John Jacob
Housman grew up around the sea. His father was in the shipping business. When he was twenty-two years old, Housman was piloting one of
his father's schooners when he became struck with wanderlust. Without a
backward glance, he commandeered his father's boat and set sail for the
West Indies. But before he got to his destination, he went aground in the
Florida Keys.

Hanging out in Key West while he waited for his ship to be repaired,
Housman became intrigued with the lucrative business of wrecking, which,
in one way or another, employed every able-bodied man on the island.

Wrecking, at that time Key West's number one business, was the
exciting and extremely profitable business of salvaging goods from vessels
that had run aground, or wrecked, on the dangerous reefs off the Keys'
shores. Once ashore, owners of the wrecked ships would negotiate with
wreckers, in a wrecking court, for a share of the recovered cargo.
Wreckers were often awarded half or more of the salvaged goods, which
might not seem like such a good deal. But to a shipper, losing half his
cargo was better than losing all of it.

Jacob Housman ditched his plans to go to the West Indies and went
into the wrecking business. But the Key West wreckers didn't take kindly
to outsiders, and Housman felt the wrecking courts were unfairly bal-
anced in favor of the locals. He may well have been right. Even the
judges owned wrecking businesses!

After five or six frustrating years in Key West, Housman sailed to
Indian Key, 75 miles away from Key West's wrecking court, and 75 miles
closer to the most dangerous reefs in all of the Keys. There he prospered
with a wrecking business of his own. With the proceeds of his growing
business, on his 30th birthday Housman bought himself a very big gift:
the island of Indian Key.

During the years between 1831, when he purchased Indian Key, and
1840, when Indians destroyed the community, Housman turned the place
into a busy wrecking center. He owned four wrecking vessels, wharves,
warehouses, workshops and thirty cottages—most of it built by his twelve
Negro slaves. Eventually there was even an Indian Key post office. The
planned city was a tiny, breezy paradise, featuring paved streets, a neat
town square, and even a conventional inn, the Tropical Hotel, often busy
with guests.

One notable guest at the Tropical Hotel was bird artist John James Audubon, who visited the island twice in the spring of 1832. Indian Key is depicted in the background of Audubon's painting of the brown booby. In his journal, Audubon glowingly describes the island's many natural charms, as well as an evening at the hotel:

> *The bouncing of brave lads and fair lasses shook the premises to the foundation. One with a slip came down heavily on the floor and the burst of laughter that followed echoed over the isle. Diluted claret was handed around to cool the ladies, while a beverage of more potent energies warmed their partners.*

In spite of outwardly charming appearances, life on Indian Key was not so pleasant under the iron rule of power-hungry Jacob Housman. The citizens who lived here, mostly turtlers and wreckers, were dependent upon Housman's good will and, often, his charity. It was common practice for Housman to forgive debts at the general store in exchange for favors—many of them slightly illegal, or at least unethical.

In 1836, Housman came up with a scheme to give his settlement independence from Key West. He convinced a friend who was a representative in the territorial legislature to push through a bill that made Indian Key the county seat of a new county named Dade. Dade County, at that time, was vast, unsettled and very scarcely populated. To be the county seat of a barely existent county doesn't sound like much today, but to Housman, it was the first step in making Indian Key a port of entry, complete with its own courts, over which Housman imagined himself having domain.

For a while things went well for Housman and his tiny kingdom. Not only was his wrecking business reaping huge rewards; he also earned big bucks from his shoreside enterprises like rents on docks and warehouses. The general store, where ships routinely stopped for supplies, earned him over $30,000 annually.

In 1838 Housman, described at the time as "a man of unprincipled disposition," was finally busted, doing what many people believed he'd been doing all along. It was proven that he had embezzled goods and money from a vessel he'd salvaged. His wrecking license was revoked. Without the enormous income his salvaging business had provided and the decrease of commerce in his village due to the Seminole War begun in 1836, Housman's fortunes began to dwindle.

In 1839 Housman came up with yet another of his self-serving, money-making schemes for which he had grown famous. He proposed a deal with the government whereby he would "catch or kill all the Indians of South Florida for two hundred dollars each." The congress, however, did not go for Housman's proposal.

Perhaps the Indians learned of Housman's plan, or perhaps they were simply after Indian Key's store of gun powder. In any event, they attacked. On August 7, 1840, just after midnight, a band of warriors arrived on Indian Key in seventeen canoes. Their plan was to wait until dawn to begin the assault, but someone with insomnia spotted them well before daylight. Gunshots were exchanged and the raid was on, in the dark.

Jacob Housman and his wife escaped through their back door and into the water at the end of their dock, just as the Indians burst through the front door of their house. Their terrified dogs followed them into the water, barking and clamoring. When he could not calm them, Housman was forced to drown both dogs with his bare hands.

The next morning as the sun came up, the Housmans and a group of Indian Key survivors watched from a Navy schooner as Indians set fire to every building and wharf on the island.

Housman and his wife moved to Key West, where he auctioned off the remainder of his possessions: several boats and his Negro slaves. He went to work as a seaman on a wrecker and was killed in a freak accident at sea less than a year later, when he was only forty-two years old. Mrs. Housman took his body back to Indian Key and marked his grave with an elegant stone. Eventually the marker on his grave was smashed by vandals and even his remains were stolen.

Dr. Perrine

Botanist and physician Dr. Henry Perrine arrived on Indian Key with his family at Christmas, 1838. Like Jacob Housman, Henry Perrine was born on Staten Island, only two years earlier than the wrecking king, in 1797. Perrine had big plans to begin a settlement dedicated to agricultural experimentation on a six-mile square land grant in southeast Florida. However, until the Second Seminole War was over, he was reluctant to take his family into the Indian-infested wilderness. So they came to pretty little Indian Key to wait out the war.

Several of Perrine's children kept journals of life on Indian Key, and it is from these writings that we are able to piece together a picture of their lives when Indian Key was at the height of its brief glory.

The Perrines did not socialize with anyone on the island but the Charles Howe family. Mr. Howe was the postmaster; he had a wife, three children, and seven slaves. Dr. Perrine and Mr. Howe were business partners in a joint agricultural venture on nearby Long Key.

The Housmans were considered socially beneath the Perrine family—not because of Mr. Housman's famous loose morals, but because of Mrs. Housman's bad reputation, presumably brought all the way from her hometown of Charleston, South Carolina.

Modern-day descendants of the tropical seeds Perrine planted in the 1830s still thrive on Indian Key, Lignumvitae Key, Long Key, and even Cape Sable, where he reportedly risked confrontations with warring Indians to go ashore and scatter his exotic seeds.

On the night the Seminoles attacked Indian Key, Dr. Perrine hid his wife, two daughters and one son in an enclosed area beneath their dock where turtles were penned. Then he climbed into a cupola at the top of the house to hide himself. But the warriors soon found him and as his horrified family shivered in their hiding place, they listened to his screams as the Indians murdered Dr. Perrine.

Most of the inhabitants of Indian Key managed to live through the attack by hiding out in various spots around the island. Some died in their hiding places. One boy hid in a cistern under a warehouse and was presumably boiled alive before the burning building finally collapsed. An infant was torn from his mother's arms and thrown into the sea. His horrified parents were then scalped, their bodies left to burn.

One of the first things the Indians did when they invaded the village was to help themselves to the hotel's liquor supply. Consequently, the warriors grew progressively drunker, and progressively easier to duck, too as the night wore on.

After the massacre, in which eighteen people died, the island was briefly occupied by the Navy. Several barracks, warehouses and a hospital were erected. During an outbreak of malaria, fifty sailors died in the hospital on Indian Key.

At the time of the Labor Day Hurricane of 1935, Indian Key was operated as a fishing camp by two brothers. One brother left the island to seek shelter on the mainland before the storm struck. The other brother secured himself in a large cistern built nearly a century earlier by Jacob Housman. His body was discovered two days after the storm.

Later, Indian Key became a shipbuilding yard and, after that, a strange sort of tourist attraction. Tourists paid to be delivered to the abandoned island and given a shovel with which to dig for buried treasure that they imagined had been forgotten by pirates and/or the infamous Jacob Housman. But all their digging, and eventually, even dynamiting, failed to turn up treasure...or so history has it.

In 1972, the State of Florida purchased the abandoned island. Today it is part of the state park system, and it's open to the public.

The Killer Hurricane of 1935

No one knows for sure how many people actually died in the catastrophic Labor Day Hurricane that battered the Matecumbe Keys with 200 mile-per-hour winds and swamped the land with a tidal surge of over eighteen feet. The coroner's report said that 423 bodies were found after the storm, but there is no doubt that many, maybe even hundreds, of victims were washed out to sea.

The hurricane was a category five, so rare that only one or two occur in a century. Hurricane Andrew, the storm that hit the Miami area in August, 1992, was a category four hurricane. Andrew's winds were clocked at around 160 mph; the tidal wave was twelve feet. Damage from Andrew was estimated at $20 billion. But only 35 people died from storm-related deaths.

In the days after the Labor Day Hurricane, Red Cross workers and volunteers suffered through the heart-breaking job of sorting through the dead. Identifying the victims' bodies was often impossible. Most of the dead were so mutilated they barely resembled humans at all. Some were without faces, their flesh having been sand-blasted into raw pulp. Many of the dead were World War I veterans. President Franklin Roosevelt's New Deal had given 650 veterans both homes and temporary work. They were building the highway that would eventually link Miami with Key West. Their homes were makeshift work camps in Islamorada.

On the first day of September in 1935, few signs warned of the hurricane's approach or of its power. Storm-tracking was a very imprecise science then; forecasting the route a hurricane might take was pretty much hit-and-miss. Citizens of the Keys were given two days' notice that a hurricane was heading in their direction. Key West was prepared for the storm, but was spared the devastation that would savage the Matecumbes a day later. Only the outer bands of the storm, strong winds and heavy rains, passed through Key West on the night of September 1.

Then, as hurricanes often do, this one wandered a bit before resting for a day over the Atlantic Ocean. There it gathered power, expanding into a storm of enormous strength. The barometer dropped to 26.35 on the afternoon of September 2, indicating to natives that they were in for a horrific storm—a normal barometer reading is 30.00.

Murphy's Law

Overseas Railroad officials sent a train from Miami into the Keys to transport local families and the veterans to higher ground. But through a series of mishaps, bungled communications, and manpower shortages due to the Labor Day holiday, the train was tragically delayed. As the doomed train finally headed down the tracks toward Islamorada, people climbed on at stops along the way. Local legend has it that the clocks of Matecumbe stopped at 8:30 that evening. That's just about when the rescue train arrived in Lower Matecumbe, where it collided with the storm. Part of the train was tossed off the tracks and laid on its side by the 200-mile-per-hour winds. The engine remained upright, and it is there that several men survived the tempest. A monstrous tidal wave surged over the island, and then scraped nearly everything in its path into the water, leaving the ground clean, right down to its raw, white coral base.

Aside from the many vets who lived in workcamps, the Upper Keys were scarcely populated in 1935. Twelve members of the Parker family miraculously survived the storm in a small, sturdy cottage. They huddled under a mattress on an iron bed. The survivors were those who found shelter in houses that floated. After the storm, they found themselves, and their cottage, atop the bare, battered branches of a lime tree grove. Fifty members of the pioneering Russell family perished in the storm. Many of their bodies were never recovered.

Victims also died by being swept into the Florida Bay, or sucked into the Atlantic by the undertow after the wave passed. Others were struck by flying debris. Of the 423 bodies accounted for, most were thought to be the veterans. It was suggested that the dead vets should be transported for burial at Arlington National Cemetery, but the idea was wildly impractical. The Upper Keys did not yet have electricity, or refrigeration, or even a train for transporting bodies. The Overseas Railroad had been destroyed by the storm, most of its tracks impassable. Finally, there was no choice but to burn the bodies in four massive fires.

The Hemingway Spin

Ernest Hemingway was living in Key West with his wife Pauline and two young sons at the time of the hurricane. In 1935 he was at the height of his famous literary career. He arrived in Islamorada by sea on the day after the storm. In an article for a socially conscious magazine called *The New Masses*, he described the sight of trees completely stripped of their foliage; once-developed land, raw and resembling a river bed; massive railroad cars toppled onto their sides. He wrote graphically of dead seabirds tangled in the mangroves; two girls who ran a sandwich shop and filling station hanging lifelessly in the trees, their bodies rotting in the sun; a man whose fingers had been eaten by land crabs; another man, out of his mind, walking through the devastation.

Later in the article, which was entitled "Who Murdered the Vets?" Hemingway lambasted the U.S. government for sending the bridge workers to their doom. He also made the following point about the Keys' natives who died in the storm:

"It is not necessary to go into the deaths of the civilians and their families since they were on the Keys of their own free will: they made their living there, had property and knew the hazards involved. But the veterans had been sent there; they had no opportunity to leave, nor any protection against the hurricanes; and they never had a chance for their lives."

There is a legend that in 1965 a car with 1935 tags and five skeletons inside was dredged up out of a coral rock quarry. For many years skeletons were found on mangrove islands in the backcountry. No doubt, more remain.

The Hurricane Monument

Historic Landmarks

The Hurricane Monument
MM 82, in the Median

A memorial to the hundreds of people who lost their lives in the Labor Day Hurricane of 1935, this monument was created in 1937 by artists and craftsmen as a Works Projects Administration art project. The art deco slab marks a community grave that holds the ashes of more than four hundred people.

When the Hurricane Monument was dedicated two years after the Florida Keys' worst disaster, 5,000 people showed up to observe the sad occasion. In March 1995, the memorial was added to the National Register of Historic Sites.

Whale Harbor Tower
MM 83 Oceanside ✶ 664-4959

The stone tower at the entrance of the Whale Harbor dining room still has the high-water mark established during Hurricane Donna on September 9, 1960. Go inside and explore the gallery of mounted fish and historical photographs. A sign in the tower says: "This tower served as a shelter for six people during Hurricane Donna's 200-mile-per-hour winds and seven foot tides."

The Pioneer Cemetery
Cheeca Lodge Grounds ✶ MM 82, Oceanside

In 1992, the Cheeca Lodge restored a tiny cemetery on its property and brought in Miami historian Josephine Johnson to research its history. Names on the grave markers—Pinder, Russell, and Parker—are from the area's pioneering families who arrived in the rough wilderness in the late 1800s. Some of the descendants of these families still live in the Keys today. In fact, many of them are employed by the Cheeca Lodge.

Tourists are welcome to visit this site and see the cemetery's most famous marker, the angel with the broken wing. In the 1935 Labor Day

Hurricane she was picked up and thrown over 1,000 feet to land on the Old Highway which runs parallel to the Overseas Highway. But she was soon returned to her rightful position as guardian to the grave of Etta Pinder, who died in 1914.

The angel with a broken wing at Pioneer Cemetery

The Pioneer Cemetery was recently dedicated by the Historical Association of Southern Florida. It is an easy walk or short drive from the Hurricane Monument. Go to the Cheeca Lodge—the entrance is just north of the monument—and head around to the back of the main lodge. The Pioneer Cemetery is on the beach, about fifty yards south of the pier.

Windley Key Fossil Reef State Geologic Site
MM 85.3, Bayside ✷ 664-5574   4815
During the Depression, Windley Key was the site of a work camp for WW I veterans employed by the Civilian Conservation Corps (CCC) to construct the Overseas Highway. Coral rock quarried from this site was sliced very thin, polished, and used as an attractive and cheap facade in construction. Keystone, as it came to be called, was used as a decorative face for many historic buildings in South Florida and beyond. The Viscaya estate in Miami uses lots of keystone. Cut and highly polished slabs of keystone were used in the creation of Islamorada's commemorative Hurricane Monument. You can see it in Key West on the Federal Building on Simonton Street, which was completed in 1934. Today expensive and chic keystone furniture is seen in many fine homes in the tropics.

Rock cutters left behind an amazing display of fossils formed by corals millions of years ago, making this the only place in the world where it is possible to walk inside an ancient coral reef and see how it is constructed. And you won't get wet. In fact, it's hot and dry in the quarry. The site was bought by developers in the 1980s. They planned to build a complex of condominiums here, and fill in the coral quarries with water. Local environmentalists battled to save the quarry from development. Ultimately the environmentalists prevailed, and in 1985 the quarry was named a state park. When you visit this strange place, you can still see some of the rusted remains of the equipment used to slice the slabs of keystone out of the sides of the quarry.

This 32-acre park is open from 8 a.m. till 5 p.m. Thursday through Monday. Well informed and enthusiastic park rangers lead tours and answer your questions in the brand new, air-conditioned environmental education center. There's an interesting collection of books and specimens for sale. We bought a tiny square of coral rock. Fascinating.

Outside, it's fun to capture particularly fanciful fossil images with pencil and paper rubbings.

Nature News

Florida Bay Research Radio broadcasts news of wildlife happenings and scientific research. Bulletins accompany National Oceanic and Atmospheric Administration weather reports every two minutes, around the clock. Tune in to 1610 AM (a program of Everglades National Park).

Helen Wadley Library and Hurricane Shelter
MM 81.5 Bayside ☎ 664-4645

Built as a hurricane shelter in 1936, the building that today houses the Helen Wadley Branch of the Monroe County Library has been a school, a church and a Coast Guard station. The structure was built to withstand winds of 150 mph, and did duty as a hurricane shelter in 1960 when Hurricane Donna passed directly over Islamorada. Both the building and many local residents who sought shelter in it came through the storm unharmed. During a recent face-lift and expansion, a 1,000 square foot meeting room and disabled-accessible bathrooms were added to the library.

Offshore Islands

Indian Key
MM 78.5

In 1972, the State of Florida purchased the abandoned island. Today it is part of the State Park system. Each October, Islamorada celebrates Indian Key's turbulent past with a weekend-long celebration. Boats ferry people from the mainland to the island for tours and history lessons led by guides dressed in period costumes of the 1830s, Indian Key's golden decade. During the weekend of the celebration, visitors can send postcards, hand-cancelled with the Indian Key postmark.

Indian Key State Park is open Thursdays–Mondays from 8 a.m. till sunset. Visitors pay $1 to tour the area. The island has no rest rooms and no shops of any kind. Park ranger-guided tours leave the dock at 9 a.m and 1 p.m.

What remains on Indian Key are parts of the foundation of Jacob Housman's house and a replica of his original gravestone. Some unidentifiable rubble is thought possibly to be part of the Tropical Hotel or ruins of the Naval installation. Visitors to the island may be surprised at how little there is to see, considering its remarkable past. An imaginative and well-informed guide will make the place come alive. Otherwise, it can be a bit of a disappointment, particularly for kids, who expect so much....

How to Get There

Access to Indian Key and Lignumvitae Key is by water only. Robbie's Marina (664-9814) at mile marker 78 runs a state-sanctioned shuttle boat service to both Keys. Roundtrip boat service to either Indian Key or Lignumvitae Key is $15 per person; $10 for children 6 and under. To see both Keys, you'll pay $30; $15 for kids. Boats arrive at the Keys in time for daily tours. For further information on Indian Key contact the Florida Park Service at 664-4815.

Lignumvitae Key State Botanical Site
MM 78.5, Offshore, Gulfside ☛ 664-4815

Some say the best time to visit Lignumvitae Key is in the spring. Others say the worst time to visit Lignumvitae is in the spring. The 130 species of trees on the island bloom and blossom magnificently in the springtime; 130 million mosquitoes, also on the island, regenerate quite gloriously in the spring.

Because of its location on the Gulf of Mexico, and its thick, leafy canopy, Lignumvitae is ten degrees cooler than the mainland. Keep that in mind as you don your long-sleeved shirt and ankle-length pants. And don't forget the insect repellent. Any area of exposed flesh is fair game for these sub-tropical devils.

A wealthy Miami chemist named William Matheson bought the 280-acre island in 1919 for use as a family vacation retreat. Matheson had the house built of coral rock gathered on the island. Its power was generated by a huge windmill, still there, although today power is provided by a generator. The island's water comes from a 12,000-gallon cistern filled by rain falling off the roof. The cistern has run dry only twice since the State of Florida has been in charge of the place, beginning in 1970. Behind the house there is a small building where the estate's caretaking family lived, and behind that building a smaller one. It is not known what the small mystery hut was used for. The hurricane shelter beneath the house, our guide described as "scary and dark."

The house was damaged in the deadly 1935 Labor Day hurricane but not annihilated, like most buildings of the Matecumbes. The house is built at the island's highest point, sixteen feet above sea level, which is also one of the highest points within the entire length of the Keys. The winds of the 1935 storm tore the roof off the Matheson's house. It was reinstalled with steel rods—you can see them—that hopefully will hold the roof tight in future blows.

The Matheson house contains collections of shells, stones, colored glass, seafans, a turtle skull, and driftwood. In addition, a megaphone the family used to call to each other across the island.

At the beginning of the tour, visitors pass a small slice of lignumvitae wood from one to the next to experience its surprising weight and its remarkable gloss. You rub it briefly with your thumb to bring out its built-in sheen. Wood of the lignumvitae—Latin for "tree of life"—is denser and more resilient than iron, so it does not wear out, and it does not dry out or easily rot.

Lignumvitae wood has been used to make bowling balls and even false teeth. The wood of lignumvitae was used in making hinges for locks on the Erie Canal; these hinges remained functional for one hundred years. It is said that Columbus was so impressed with the amazing proper- ties of the lignumvitae tree that he carried logs of it back to Spain after his second voyage to the New World. Indians believed that the gum resin of the lignumvitae was good medicine. One species of tree snail, liguus,

Lignumvitae
leaf and flower

prefers the lignumvitae tree over all others in the virgin forests of Lignumvitae Key.

Some of the plants and trees on this botanical preserve have been growing here for a thousand years. The settlers and pioneers saw some of these very same ones when they arrived in the Florida Keys so very long ago.

Visitors walk on the trails originally cleared for the horses, pigs, goats and chickens that were once raised here. Sisal, planted in the Keys by botanist Henry Perrine during his brief stay in the 1830s, is prevalent. Your guide will cut a piece from the plant and show you exactly why Perrine was so enthusiastic about sisal's potential as a cash crop for South Florida. Its leaves are laced with a strong, twine-like core. Until the 1940s and the invention of nylon, sisal was the main component of rope.

Park rangers are always anxious to point out the scary poisonwood tree, to spare anyone the misfortune of wandering too close to its treacherous leaves and bark. They compare its properties to those of poison ivy. Plenty of poisonwoods are scattered throughout the hammocks of the Keys, they say.

"So why don't they cut them all down?" asked an attentive seven-year-old.

"Because poisonwood berries are the white crown pigeon's favorite food," the ranger replied, launching a talk on the graceful symmetry of a successful ecosystem.

Other interestingly named trees you will encounter are gumbo limbo, mahogany, Jamaican dogwood, mastic, pigeon plum, stopper, wild coffee and strangler fig. Scattered throughout the trees are delicate tree snails, other-worldly in their design, and butterflies, swirling gracefully in the peaceful woods. All are protected from removal, even the pretty shell you believe to be uninhabited. That must stay, too.

Sisal

As the tour loops down by the shore, the types of trees change. You see buttonwood, which grows next to the shore up and down the Keys, wherever concrete has not taken over. You'll be introduced to red, black and white mangroves as the ranger explains the mangrove's unique filtering system.

Nearly a 3,000-foot coral-rock wall runs from the center of the island all the way down to the water, which is somewhat of a mystery to historians. Who built it? Why? The wall is not on the general tour, but a ranger is happy to take you to it if you ask. It resembles a stone wall you might see in the forests of New England.

Beaches

Anne's Beach
MM 73, Oceanside

Once known as Islamorada Public Beach and located on Lower Matecumbe Key south of Caloosa Cove Resort, it is dedicated to local environmentalist Anne Eaton. Anne began her life as Anne Kinder Jones. She was a schoolteacher until she met and married wealthy industrialist and banker Cyrus Stephen Eaton in 1957. Although polio left her wheelchair-bound when she was only twenty-four years old, Anne and her husband traveled the world, meeting politicians and international leaders in science and industry. After her husband's death, Anne heard about the Florida Keys, the only frost-free place in the continental United States, and knew she had found her heaven on earth. Of all the places the wealthy seeker of world peace had been, she is said to have loved Monroe County best. Anne Eaton lived in the Keys until she died in 1992. Her home in Lower Matecumbe, near the beach dedicated to her, is called the Last Resort.

A small parking area is located at each end of Anne's Beach; the two are connected by a marvelous boardwalk. At low tide the beach is alive with crabs and other crawly creatures. At high tide, you might wade out far enough for a swim. The public bathrooms recently received a much needed restoration and are currently in pretty good shape.

Islamorada County Park
MM 81.5 Bayside

Locals call this the Library Beach because of its close proximity to the Islamorada library. Located on a natural creek that runs from the Florida Bay, the tiny park is on one side of the creek; a line of mangroves is on the other. You need to swim across some fast currents to get to the mangrove's edge, but once you're there, the snorkeling is great. Many wonderful fish babies hatch and grow to maturity here. There is nowhere quite like the busy and complex worlds that exist in and around the roots of the islands' anchoring mangroves. Meanwhile, back on shore there's a terrific playground for the kids, plus a few picnic tables.

The current makes this not an ideal place for kids to swim. There's a little sandy beach good for wading, or water and sand play. For a change of pace, there's a nice children's reading room inside the library.

Islamorada Founders Park
MM 87 Bayside 853-1685

This lovely property used to be a privately owned yacht harbor and inn. Before that it was a pineapple plantation. A few years ago Islamorada, Village of Islands, incorporated and its nearly 7,000 residents voted to buy this grand piece of mahogany treed and bayfront property and turn it into a community park. They installed a progressive skate park (full gear required), lighted tennis courts, and an olympic-sized, heated swimming pool. Because this is the warmest place in the continental United States, the Founders Park pool often hosts college athlete swimmers during Christmas breaks, and was a training center for Olympian swimmers the winter before the 2004 Summer Olympics in Athens.

The gulfside park boasts a wonderful sandy beach, a nice, new playground, and kayak, hobie cat and paddle boat rentals. There's a little dog park, too, where you can unleash your dog and let him run with the locals.

Guests of Islamorada hotels(with proof of registration) as well as local residents enter for free. Visitors pay a small fee to enter the parik. Everyone pays a daily fee to use the skate park and the pool. Beach is free, once you're inside. Fees are reasonable.

The Sandbar
Oceanside, off MM 84.5

On perfect Saturday and Sunday afternoons, you'll see dozens of boats crowded around a wide sandbar just offshore, right around mile marker 84–85. Locals call it "the Islamorada Beach." There's only one way to get to it—by boat. Rent one from a concession at Pelican Resort or at Holiday Isle Resort. Rent will run you around $100 for a very simple, motor-driven skiff—but you and four other friends will meet and play with Islamorada's most devoted partyers.

Fishing

SLAMORADA IS PROUD of the many high-profile celebrities who travel regularly to this island cluster to partake in the world's best sports fishing. But you don't have to be a big shot to fish in the same ocean as President George Bush, Sr. and friends. Everybody is welcome in the Fishing Capital of the World. Earlier visitors to this area were President Herbert Hoover, British Prime Minister Winston Churchill, and *Riders of the Purple Sage* author Zane Grey.

The area's wonderful proximity to the Gulf Stream has spurred the development of a number of fine enterprises—tackle shops, concessions and marinas—and the largest concentration of fishing boats in the Florida Keys. Some of the sports fishing related businesses here have been passed down through several generations of islanders. These people know their stuff.

First time visitors are sometimes surprised to learn just how much it costs to drop hooks in the Gulf Stream. Chartering a boat, captain and crew who will devote themselves exclusively to your comfort and happiness will cost $800 or more a day, depending upon the type of boat. A much less expensive way to get out on the water is to buy aboard a party boat (around $30 for a half day), in which the heavy charter fees are divided among a crowd of anglers. Good for families.

People catch plenty of fish off bridges, too. All you need is a fishing rod, a license, and lots of patience. Buy a license in any bait and tackle shop. There is no thrill comparable to catching your own fresh seafood dinner. Many area restaurants understand this and will happily cook your catch for a small preparation fee.

A Big Deal of a Tourney

President George Bush, the most famous angler at Cheeca Lodge, hosts an annual bonefish tourney every August. It's a high stakes, all release fundraiser. Entry fee is $1,000 per angler. As part of the tourney, participants—who are some very, very high rollers—rub elbows with the former

Marlin fishing

President during the kick-off dinner and several other events. The whole of Islamorada looks forward to this very important, and always spectacular, fish party.

Proceeds go to the Everglades Trust, a non-profit organization formed to restore the Florida Bay and the Everglades. Info: 664-4651.

Florida Keys Fishing Tournaments, Inc.
P.O. Box 420358, Summerland Key, FL 33042 ⚓ 872-2233
"Tourneys Are Us." Christina Sharpe, a member of one of the Florida Keys' most important fishing families, runs this very busy year-round organization. If competitive fishing is your bag, this is an important resource for you. Christina and her staff will direct you to all the fun. It is a rare weekend when something isn't going on in the area, or at least somewhere in the Keys. For an extensive list of local and Keys fishing tournaments and events, write for a free brochure. If you can't wait, phone them during business hours.

How To Find a Fishing Captain or Guide
Go for a walk through a marina—they're easy to spot—and get a first-hand feel for the place. Nobody is friendlier or more helpful than a captain or a guide trying to put together a party for a day of fishing. Can you think of a better way to make a living?

The Islamorada Chamber of Commerce (800-322-5397) has a list of fishing charterboat captains and backcountry fishing guides. Call or write ahead, and they'll send the list; then you can do the research before you get here.

Florida Keys Fly Fishing School
P.O. Box 603, Islamorada, FL 33036 ✻ 664-5423
Learn casting, fly selection, fly tying, and knots and leaders from a staff of instructors that reads like the Who's Who guide to the world's most famous saltwater fly fishermen. If you're a fly fishing enthusiast, you'll recognize the names of these champs: Chico Fernandez, Flip Pallot, Sandy Moret, Jose Wejebe, and Rick Ruoff. At the Florida Keys Fly Fishing School, these stars are your teachers.

The structured fly fishing course is on six times a year. Included in the cost of the course is a Friday-night reception at the glittery Cheeca Lodge, breakfasts and lunches, as well as the nuts and bolts of fly fishing, rods and reels. In the 14 years since it was founded, the Florida Keys Fly Fishing School has graduated around 1300 fly fisherpeople. This course is the fastest way to learn this sport of cunning and finesse.

Cost of the course is around $895. Call or write for a spiffy brochure that tells you all about it.

Some Marinas

Bud 'n' Mary's Fishing Marina
MM 80 Oceanside ✻ 800-742-7945 ✻ 664-2461
You'll probably notice the huge, fiberglass replica of a 417-pound shark, hung by his tail and glistening in the sun, just at the door to Bud 'n' Mary's tackle shop. Caught in the late 1980s off the coast of Australia, this great white shark once held the record for being the largest fish ever caught with a rod and reel. Alas, the record was broken mere weeks later! If you don't stick your head into the shark's mouth and have your picture taken, you're no fun.

The Gulf Lady, a 65-foot, air-conditioned party boat is docked in the marina. Day trips are $55, rods, reels, bait and tackle included. Boat leaves the dock at 9:30 a.m.; return and dock at 4:30 p.m. You bring your own food and drink. Summertime night fishing trips are $45; from 7:30 p.m.–12:30 a.m. On a party boat like this, the captain and mates will bait your hook and help you reel in the big fish. *The Gulf Lady* is also available for sunset cruises and private charters. Group rates are available, too.

Also, fourteen off-shore charter boats available for deep-sea fishing; thirty back-country boats with guides. Don't be surprised to see a political or media or sports star here. This is the place where they can feel comfortable because here everybody is treated exactly the same. "Famous people really like that," one guy behind the counter told me, referring to the swarm of secret service men who had just left the dock after depositing their famous politico boss on a boat bound for the Gulf Stream for a day of sport fishing.

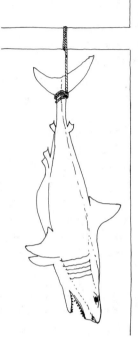

***Bud 'n' Mary's
replica of a
417-pound shark***

Catch and release is popular these days, but if you do want to eat your catch, they'll clean it when you get to shore. Then you take it to a local restaurant to have it cooked. If you want to have a spectacular catch replicated in fiberglass, they'll know where to send you for that, too. (Fish are no longer stuffed and mounted in the old-fashioned way. Nowadays your prize fish is replicated.)

Rent an unsinkable fiberglass boat 16 or 18 feet and take it out to Indian Key or Lignumvitae Key. Call 664-0091 for boat rentals for half or a whole day, beginning at $100 and up to $250. Weekly rates available, too. Bud 'n' Mary's rents rooms, too.

Bud 'n' Mary's Fishing Marina, in business since 1944, is open seven days; 7 a.m. till dark.

Holiday Isle Marina
MM 84 Oceanside ✦ 664-2321 ✦ 800-327-7070

You may have to park your car in the lots across the street because this place is always very crowded. A fleet of sixteen off-shore fishing charter-boats, and fourteen backcountry fishing boats and guides are lined up at this busy marina. Also, party boats, which are the least expensive. Best time to go shopping for a charter is before 8 a.m. or after 4 p.m. because most boats leave the dock for the day between those hours. Many visitors find that a good way to chose a captain and boat is to observe anglers arriving back at the dock after a day of fishing. Do they look happy? Disappointed? Friendly toward their captain? Holiday Isle is a very friendly, very informal place. The offshore charters at Holiday Isle Marina charge between $750 and $1000 for a full day of fishing. They'll supply the fishing gear; you bring food and drinks. Each boat sets its own prices. They are all privately owned and operated, renting space at the marina.

Papa Joe's Marina
MM 80 Bayside ✦ 664-5005

Directly across the street from Bud 'n' Mary's Marina, it's the place to go to find a guide for backcountry fishing. Twelve skiffs are available for private charter-flats fishing daily, and a family fun boat to transport you to Indian Key, Lignumvitae Key, Horseshoe Key or take you on a sunset cruise. Sturdy Papa Joe's T and sweat shirts and bill hats are available in the tackle shop, as well as fishing licenses. There's a nice bar atop Papa's Marina, from where you can gaze upon the ocean and the bay.

Robbie's Marina
MM 77.8 Bayside ✦ 664-9814

Robbie's is located beneath the Lignumvitae Bridge, home of the hungry tarpon dock where you feed the fish, and the Hungry Tarpon Restaurant, where you feed yourself. Rent a boat for a ride into the backcountry, or take yourself to Indian Key or Lignumvitae Key. (Lignumvitae Key is closed to the public on Tuesdays and Wednesdays.) Boats from 14 to 25 feet rent from $80 to $195 for a full day.

Or take a shuttleboat to Indian Key and Lignumvitae Botanical Site State Parks for $15, adults; $10, kids.

Whale Harbor Marina
MM 83.5 Oceanside ✆ 664-4511

You'll find up to sixteen offshore sport-fishing boats at the Whale Harbor docks. The boats come with a captain and a mate, and will cost you, depending on the size of the boat, anywhere from $750 - $1,000 for a full-day trip. Best time for a visit is early mornings or later in the afternoon when the fleet returns with the day's catch.

The 65-foot party fishing boat *Tradewinds* (664-8341) costs adults around $30 and kids around $25 for a half day of deep sea fishing. Trips leave 9:30 a.m. and 1;45 p.m. daily. Weekends there are night trips that leave the docks at 7:30 p.m. and cost a few dollars more.

On most fishing excursions you take along your own food and drinks for the day. Buy it at the ship's store or at the Harbor Bar & Raw Bar, a neat dockside bistro with a great view of the marina and the ocean. They'll sell you a box lunch and/or breakfast from 6 a.m. Raw bar menu served from noon til midnight. Live entertainment every evening, except on Sundays. The Whale Harbor Inn was once a hotel made popular by radio personality Arthur Godfrey, who vacationed here often in the '50s. Remember him?

Diving

Some Famous Islamorada Dives

Alligator Reef Light

In 1823, the USS *Alligator*, part of an anti-pirate squadron commanded by Commodore David Porter, battled with pirates near Indian Key. The battle was won by the anti-pirate forces, but Naval Commander W.H. Allen was killed in the fray. In honor of his dead comrade, Porter went back to his home port of Key West and renamed the settlement "Allentown." A year later the USS *Alligator* went aground on the reef where the Alligator Light now stands. Porter's attempt to rename Key West failed, too.

Pickles Reef

Pickle barrels containing a mortar-like construction material ended up on this reef in the 19th century. The wood of the barrels rotted away in the saltwater, but the barrel-shaped blocks of solid mortar are still visible on this 10–25 foot deep reef.

The Eagle

One of the first big artificial reefs created in the Keys, the *Eagle* was sunk in 1985. Since then, the *Eagle* has become gloriously encrusted with numerous corals. It is a popular hangout for many large fish, and a terrific and very popular dive for scuba divers.

Hens and Chickens Reef

Tourists from everywhere in the world ask to visit and dive the Hens and Chickens Reef. This reef is excellent for snorkelers because it is shallow, and it contains enormous coral heads full of caves and holes; it's also veined with narrow valleys of sand.

Horseshoe Reef
Another Jesus guards this reef. Several born-again Christian divers stuck this little Jesus into a car tire full of concrete.

Davis Reef Ridge
A small, fat Buddha smiles benevolently at the south end of this ledge that rises six to eight feet from the flat sandy floor. Schools of sergeant majors here can be so dense they block your view. Underwater photographers say this reef is the most picturesque in the Keys.

Cheeca Rocks
About 600 yards straight out from the Cheeca Lodge, a comfortable dive for snorkelers.

San Pedro Underwater Archaeological Preserve
Located 1.3 nautical miles south of Indian Key, the *San Pedro* was part of the Spanish fleet that sailed from Havana Harbor in 1733. A few days after it took to sea, it was driven into the reefs by a powerful hurricane. Today the remains of the *San Pedro* anchor a shipwreck park dedicated in 1989. A popular underwater nature trail features varied populations of fish, crustaceans, mollusks, and corals, as well as bricks and pieces, much picked over by now, from the doomed *San Pedro*.

Some Dive Charters

Holiday Isle Dive Center
MM 84.5 Oceanside ✺ 664-4145 ✺ 800-327-7070
Whoever books the trip first gets to choose the reefs visited on that trip. Holiday Isle's 35-foot powerboat carrying scuba divers or snorkel divers, or both, departs at 9 a.m. and 1 p.m. to visit two reefs. If you are hoping to visit specific reefs, tell the dive center and they'll book you on the appropriate trip. A minimum of two must sign on for the trip to go out. The maximum is twenty-two people.

A snorkel trip with gear rental is around $40. A two-tank scuba trip is $50; to rent additional scuba gear, you'll pay around $20 more. No discounts for kids. The trip is roughly three-and-a-half hours long. Two trips a day are scheduled, but enough people are interested, they'll take you out for a night dive.

Key Dives
MM 79.8 Bud N' Mary's Marina ✺ 664-2211 ✺ 800-344-7352
They'll carry your scuba gear to the boat and set it up, break down your gear, rinse and store it for the next day of diving. All you have to do is breathe and kick! Just follow your diver guide around and they'll make sure you see all the cool stuff you should see when diving in the Keys. Unguided dives, too. Competitive prices. Dive boat is the lovely Coral Sea, fully stocked with fresh fruit and ice water. A cooler is available for those who prefer their own beverages and snacks. The trip is roughly three-and-a-half hours long. Two trips daily. Rental gear available.

Big Fun

Fish Bowl
MM 83.5 Bayside ☙ 664-9357

Bowling in Paradise? Sure. You'd be surprised how popular these air-conditioned lanes are on steamy summer evenings, where relief from the heat is worth more than gold. Fish Bowl, which has been serving bowling enthusiasts for over two decades, is the only public bowling available in the Keys. Open bowling on weekdays is from 6 p.m. till midnight; Saturdays 3 p.m. till midnight, and Sunday, 1 p.m. till 10 p.m. Snack bar, pool tables, and video games. Shoe rentals, and discounts for kids. Twelve lanes with bumpers. Hours seem to change frequently here so call ahead and see what's going on.

Islamorada Tennis Club
MM 77 Bayside ☙ 305-664-5340

Everything you could want or imagine in a tennis club is here—where you'd least expect to find it—in the fishing capital of the world. Owners are USPTA Professionals, T.J. Cardwell and Kris FitzPatrick. If you are wandering around solo, itchy for a game, call the tennis club, and they'll hook you up with one. Play is on one of six lighted courts, two hard, four clay. Figure to pay around $16 for a day pass. Open clinics are $25 for non-members. Ball machine rentals are around $25 per hour for non-members. The enormous pro shop is full of the latest state-of-the-art goodies. Private, semi-private and group lessons available. Open from 8 a.m. till 8 p.m. daily.

Feed the Tarpons/Robbie's Marina
MM 77.5 Bayside ☙ 664-9814

As long as the sun is bright, and the tarpons are hungry—and the tarpons *always* seem to be hungry—there's something wild to do at Robbie's Marina. Between 8 a.m. and 5 pm. daily you can buy a bucket of fish for $2 and pay $1 per person to walk out to the end of the dock. Feed the bucket of little fish to the big fish. Once the tarpons figure out it's feeding

time again—it goes on all day—you'll have dozens of the huge, glittering
fish swarming frantically beneath the dock. Some of these guys are up to
six feet long. Pelicans are a bit of a nuisance, though. They're so used to
humans that they'll take a tiny fish right out of a little kid's hand. Don't
worry, pelicans don't have teeth. Usually the marina dog chases pelicans
away. If you're lucky, whoever's in charge of taking the money will let
some of the smaller kids go for free. Lots of fun. For tots, it just doesn't
get any better than this.

Pelican Cove Boat and Waverunner Rentals
MM 84.5 Oceanside ✺ 664-4435

Keith and his beautiful assistant watch their customers very carefully to
be sure that Waverunners are operated safely and respectfully. Basic fee
for a half-hour of wet and wild thrills is $45 for one rider, and $55 for
two. You must be 18 years or older with a Boater's Safety Card, or 21 and
able to prove it.

Rent a 16-foot, flat-bottom skiff from Keith for $125 for half a day,
which is 4 hours. Again, Keith will have to convince himself that you
know what you're doing before he'll let you go. He'll show you where to
find the channel, and how to avoid hurting turtle grass. Only five people
at a time on the boat.

Theater of the Sea
MM 84.5 ✺ 664-2431

When the Overseas Highway was completed in 1938, and traffic picked
up real well in these parts, it seemed a good plan to create a tourist
attraction based on the natural resources at hand—the sea and its
remarkable inhabitants. And so this marine park was created on the site
of several abandoned quarries dug at the turn of the century during the
construction of the Overseas Railroad. The family that established this
14-acre park in 1946 owns and operates it still. Over 100,000 visit the
park annually.

Marking the entrance to the bustling theme park are the masts of a
pair of tall ships. On a wide, grassy plot in front of the park are shrubs
sculpted into mermaids and leaping dolphins. A treasure ship will titillate
your imagination, and inside, all sorts of wonderful creatures of the deep
will charm and delight children as well as their grateful parents.

Inside the park's three acres is a saltwater lagoon, home to dolphins, sea lions, sea turtles, tropical and gamefish, sharks, and stingrays. The lagoon is also a refuge for several endangered species who, due to injuries, would not survive in their natural habitats. You can also observe a blind American crocodile, who lost his sight as a result of shotgun wounds, and several sea turtles, most of them missing flippers from disastrous entanglements with monofilament fishing lines. The aim of the park is to educate as well as to entertain with these rare creatures.

Since 1987, the Theater of the Sea has been offering several human/dolphin swim programs for various groups. The most popular swim-with-the-dolphin experience costs $150. Participants who are not yet 18 years old must have a completed parental consent form. Kids 7 and under must always be accompanied by an adult to swim, or wade with the sea lions or dolphins. The thirty-minute swim is preceded by a thirty-minute educational orientation. Two very special groups, Make-a-Wish and Children of Dreams Foundations, whose patients are undergoing critical care or who are terminally ill, work in cooperation with the park to help their clients realize life-long dreams of swimming with dolphins. In addition, an intern program for college students is designed to award college credits after completion of an intensive course in marine animal care.

Tours of the park and shows begin at 9:30 a.m.; the last tour starts at 4 p.m.; the park closes at 5 p.m. Plan on spending two to three hours at the park to take it all in. Admission is around $24 for adults; $16 for kids ages 3–12. Kids two and under go free. Parking is free, too.

Write to the Theater of the Sea (P.O. Box 407, Islamorada, FL 33036) for specific information on any of their programs or for an enormous amount of information on the park. Also, get good fact sheets on dolphins, sea lions and sting rays. Handy for those "what I did on my vacation reports".

Tours by Land, Sea and Air

Robbie's Rent-A-Boat to Indian Key or Lignumvitae Key
Robbie's Marina ♦ MM 77.5 Bayside ♦ 664-9814

To visit Indian or Lignumvitae Keys, it's easiest to take a shuttle run by Robbie's Rent-A-Boat. Shuttle service to Indian Key at 8:30 a.m. and 12:30 p.m. and Lignumvitae Key at 9:30 and 1:30. Round trip cruise to the island of your choice is $15 per person. Once on the islands, which are actually state parks, park rangers lead tours. Cost of the tour is included in boat shuttle ticket fee. Tours are around $3 per person if you get yourself out there in your own boat. Parks are closed Tuesdays and Wednesdays.

Tour of Indian Key, setting of the Indian Key massacre of 1840, is quite fascinating for history buffs. Imagine this lonely little island as a bustling island city, and the county seat for Dade County, with a fine hotel, excellent homes, and a bustling economy. Modern kids thrill to images of Indians in warpaint, gruesome murders, and children boiled alive in cisterns when Indians burned the town down.

Meanwhile, on the Florida Bay side of the narrow Overseas Highway, Lignumvitae Key has its own interesting, though certainly softer, charms: flowering plants, trees, and mangroves. And a coral-rock house built in 1919. Unfortunately, excitement-wise, it doesn't hold a candle to Indian Key's grisly past. So don't take the kids on this trip. They'll probably be bored silly.

SCUBA Dive & Snorkel Tours
Bud 'n' Mary's Marina MM 80 Oceanside ♦ 664-2211

Both the Coral Sea, a 40' Burpee, and the Delphine, a 29' Island Hopper, are pressed into daily service. Snorkel trips to two locations—snorkelers swim for around 45 minutes in each—leave Bud 'n Mary's Marina at 1:30 p.m. daily. Scuba dive tours depart at 9 a.m. and 1:30 p.m. daily, and anchor at two spots for dives of around 50 minutes each. Dive sites are chosen on each trip, according to weather, and desires of snorkelers or divers. Snorkel trips are $30 excluding gear, $35 if you need to rent the gear. Scuba trips are $75 including tanks and weights, guided by a dive-master or instructor.

Adventure Snorkel Cruise
Theater of the Sea, MM 84.5 Oceanside ✴ 664-2431
This four-hour tour visits sites of environmental and historic interest in the waters of the Atlantic Ocean and the Florida Bay. Tour destinations are sometimes altered to accommodate weather conditions but generally take you to historic Indian Key, the Alligator Light Tower, and Cheeca Rocks Reef. A naturalist on board describes the ecosystems of ocean, backcountry, and the plants and creatures that thrive therein. Dolphins hopefully will appear somewhere along the way in their natural habitat, which is a treat and a bit of a revelation: these creatures are natural born showoffs! You'll cover thirteen miles of coast, snorkel for thirty minutes at a nearby reef. $65 for adults and $40 for kids 2 - 12. Rent snorkel equipment on board. The boat leaves at 8:30 a.m. and 1 p.m. daily from the Theater of the Sea.

Nautilimo Tours
Matecumbe Marina ✴ MM 80.5 ✴ 517-9501
You've got to see this. Captain Joe Fox, designer of the Nautilimo is also the chauffeur and/or tour guide in this 1987 white Cadillac, mounted on a barge and motored by a 100-horsepower Yamaha engine. The Nautilimo seats four and is very popular for weddings. Nobody will beat these wedding photos! Take the Nautilimo out for a sunset cruise, and or a tour of Islamorada. Ask Captain Joe to take you past his houseboat, once a prop in the 1960s TV show "Surfside 6." Is Captain Joe a fun guy or what?

Sunset Waverunner Tour
Pelican Cove Resort ✴ 664-8892
An hour-and-a-half guided tour on Waverunners for up to eight people— 2 or even 3 to a Waverunner. (Larger groups can be accommodated.) Guides are master storytellers, well-versed in island lore and legend, as well as current events. The cruise winds out of Pelican Cove, under the Snake Creek drawbridge, and into the flat waters of the Florida Bay. Points of interest are inlets once prowled by pirates, Indians, and modern

day smugglers. You sort the fact from the fiction. Also, nature treats like osprey nests, and the tale of an osprey who swooped right out of the sky to steal a big old snapper right out of a fisherman's hands. Just after sunset, the tour ends up back at the Pelican Cove dock. Cost is $150 per Waverunner. Call for reservations. The tour won't go until passengers man at least two Waverunners per trip.

Accommodations

OTELS, MOTELS, INNS AND GUESTHOUSES around here follow some mighty complicated guidelines when it comes to figuring their rates. Generally you can't stay for only one night of a weekend. On holiday weekends they'll often only sell three-day packages. Off-season rates do not apply on holiday or big Keys events weekends. At those times, expect to pay full high-season fare. (Check the Annual Events chapter in this book. We celebrate holidays down here that you haven't even heard of!)

Remember, the sales tax and the bed tax, all together, add 11.5% to your bill.

Unfortunately, a shortage of B & B-style accommodations exists in the Upper Keys. Possibly, by the time you get around to visiting, more options will be available. If you're a B & B person, phone the Islamorada Chamber of Commerce at 1-800-FAB-KEYS and ask for information on area B & B's. Call around before you make reservations. Decide what you're looking for, and ask for it. Will you be spending lots of time at your inn, or using it simply as a bedroom? If you're interested in doing all the fishing and diving you can during your time in the Keys, choose a place that features a marina and dive shop. You won't even have to get into your car. Got pets? Kids? Handicaps? Do you want sand on your beach, or will a fabulous pool with a spectacular sunset view do? Sunset is bayside; sunrise is oceanside. There are some sandy beaches here in Islamorada…but the sand is imported. It comes. It goes.

Bed & Breakfast of Islamorada
81175 Old Highway, MM 81 Bayside ✺ 664-9321
Dottie Saunders is a high-energy woman whose dedication to aerobics keeps her trim, enthusiastic, and tough enough to trek the world armed with nothing but a backpack, camera and endless curiosity. One of her sons is a pilot, and that's how Dottie gets all those plane tickets to the far corners of the world. She says she doesn't mind roughing it, and neither should you if you choose to stay at her laid-back bed-and-breakfast. Dottie smokes, so you can, too. If you don't like smoke, don't stay at

Dottie's. Each of the three rooms has a TV and a clean, very modest bathroom. That's it, amenity-wise. It's not on the water, and there's no pool, but it's inexpensive, $50–$65 (less if you pay with cash, Dottie says), and lots of information about the area is conveniently collected in several looseleaf notebooks in the living room, including menus, brochures and numbers to call (Dottie charges 25 cents per call). Dottie has fished, snorkeled and partied in the area for many years and names the Lorelei as her favorite watering hole.

Ask to see Dottie's collection of news clips, too. One travel writer from the *Washington Post* wrote that Dottie reminded him of "Ava Gardner in her role as innkeeper in *Night of the Iguana*," which, frankly, isn't at all far-fetched when you consider that Tennessee Williams also roamed these Keys for many years…he had to get his inspiration for those characters from somewhere.

The Bed & Breakfast of Islamorada is located behind Sid and Roxie's Green Turtle Inn at mile marker 81. After dark, when the lights go on and the green neon turtle begins his nocturnal laps above the doorway to the restaurant, it's real easy to find the turnoff to Dottie's.

Caloosa Cove Resort
MM 73.8 Lower Matecumbe Key ⚓ 664-8811

Nearly seventy years ago, this area was ground zero when the worst hurricane ever to hit the United States tore through Lower Matecumbe Key and wiped it clean of vegetation, buildings—and people. Centuries before that, several Caloosa Indian settlements thrived here. These grounds are steeped in history. Oh, if these coral rocks could talk!

Today, the Caloosa Cove is a particularly lovely arrangement of thirty oceanfront condominiums, built with care and lots of closet space. Every unit has a spectacular view of the ocean, and the resort is far enough away from the busier sections of the Overseas Highway that you don't have to see or hear anything other than the soothing sights and sounds of Paradise.

If you don't want to buy a luxury condo in Islamorada, you can rent one of these—when they're not booked by time sharers—for a day or a week or longer. Efficiencies start at $175 nightly and $750 weekly; they are comparatively spacious units, certainly as big as a deluxe New York City efficiency. The bedroom suites with dens have couches that pull out, and kitchens, modern, very clean, and well-equipped. Rates are $250 nightly and $1,500 weekly.

The Safari Lounge pays homage to the owner's trip to Africa. On display are photos of a white hunter posing between two dead lions, and a proud Masai warrior. Also antelope antlers, and carved wood, evocative of the dark continent. Lazy paddle fans and a great view of the ocean make it everything a tropical Keys bar should be. Cool, dark, spacious, kind of mysterious.

Back out in the sunshine, explore the long, good-for-a-walk beach; enjoy the BBQ pit and picnic tables, or a game of volleyball, tennis or ping-pong. Or swim in a very big, heated pool. Very inviting.

The Caloosa Cove Marina, a place that looks quite a bit spiffier than most marinas in the area, is fun to explore. *Poverty Sucks*, a 53-foot Hatteras Sportfisherman offshore charter fishing boat, is popular with tourists. They like standing next to it and having their pictures taken. Phone 664-9256 to schedule a trip.

Casa Morada
MM 82.2 Bayside ✺ 136 Madeira Rd. ✺ 664-3030 ✺ 888-881-3030
An Italian furniture designer, weary of running his Miami retail business, and deeply enamored with the sultry charms of the Florida Keys, recently turned this little 1950s era bayside hotel into a very chic European-flavored retreat so many turns off the beaten path that some guests complain they have trouble finding their way back to their suite after dark. And surely, that's the worst thing anyone has ever said about this place.

Sixteen suites (no rooms, just suites) feature cable TV, phones with modem ports, refrigerators, electric water kettles, electronic safes, and hair dryers. Owners will arrange for anything all this luxury whets your appetite for, like a message or a pedicure, or a bottle of good wine delivered to your suite. They'll also hook you up with fishing or dive charters, tours, and dining recommendations. Garden suites all feature private terrace overlooking the private gardens. Bay suites overlook the Florida Bay. A bayside pool is stunning, simple and elegant. You really will feel like you're in Europe.

But this isn't just a hotel. It's a living catalog of designer furniture. Every piece of furniture here is for sale! The mahogany desks and shelves, tile-topped tables, curved wrought iron beds, pigskin chairs and ottomans, or double chaise lounge. Just put in your order at the front desk. It will be made especially for you, and shipped to your door.

Naturally this kind of luxury is pretty pricey, but there are some interesting packages that make it a deal. Recently, for example, when you stayed at the Casa Morada Sunday through Wednesday, you got Thursday for free! Ask about similar promotions and discounts when you call for reservations.

Casa Thorn Bed & Breakfast
MM 87, Bayside ☞ 114 Palm Ln. ☞ 852-3996

If you remember the Chiquita Banana girl with the castanets who danced in the television ads in the mid-50's, you will recognize proprietress Thorn Trainer, actress, model, singer, romantic, entrepreneur, personality, and hostess extraodinaire whose eclectic tastes and spirit of adventure are brilliantly visible in this fantastic collection of wrought iron and wooden furniture, coral rock walls, cheetah and zebra rugs, animal print pillows, books and beautiful things big and small. Nothing is coordinated. Each piece of furniture, each work of art, each curtain, shutter or drape, is an object d'art unto itself. Everywhere you look, there's something fabulous to see. It's stuff that Thorn loves and that's the whole story.

"I acquired all these things one piece at a time," Thorn says. "I love anything at all remotely related to the tropics, everything except fish. You won't find a fish in the place."

You don't know who you might meet at Thorn's breakfast table. There are attorneys from New York City who look way too young to be attorneys, gay policemen from New Jersey, a beautiful gentlewoman from London traveling with her handsome son, wealthy retirees from Key West overnighting on their way to Miami for a shopping spree, and local friends of Thorn's. She's been in South Florida for nearly 40 years and she knows a lot. On a baby grand piano in the living room check out the photos of Thorn hob-nobbing with Frank Sinatra, Eddie Fisher (with whom she once did a show), and Morton Downey, Sr.

Thorn's place became a guest house by accident. She once worked at a nearby restaurant and from time to time rented out her extra room. Taking advantage of a good thing, Thorn added another room to her home, and then another. Today there are 5 guest rooms, each of them dramatic, unique and entirely different from the others. Two of them, the

Tiki hut and Room #4, share a bath. Others have private baths. Further, Thorn delights in frequently rearranging the rooms and the gardens. Rooms are stocked with VCRs, films, CDs, books and magazines, elegant white terry cloth robes. Pond in front and waterfall in back are new.

There's a pool, and comfy community areas. Do find a time to chat with Thorn. She's a trip, and she knows where to eat and where to shop and what to do. Casa Thorn is located in a residential area. You'll recognize the place by the life-sized camel in the front yard with the sign "Casa Thorn" hanging around its neck.

Cheeca Lodge
MM 82, Oceanside ▪ 664-4651 ▪ 800-327-2888
Simply the best; older—in the best sense of the word—and better than all the rest. News here lately is the ultra-chic, 5,000 square foot Avanyu Spa. Big-name stars are sometimes spotted here, being mud wrapped or practicing yoga poses in this posh retreat. Now you know how they stay so beautiful. At the spa, you can feel beautiful, too.

The original hotel on this location was the Olney Inn, comprised of 22 bungalows, built in 1946 by a hotelier from Washington, D.C. The inn's very first guest, Cheeca history has it, was President Harry S Truman. In 1960, after Hurricane Donna nearly demolished the place, it was sold to Carl and Cynthia Twitchell. A&P heiress Cynthia's nickname was "Chee," and from that, the Cheeca Lodge got its name. The Twitchells built the four-story lodge that stands today, and operated the inn with 86 rooms. In 1987 a Chicago concern bought it and invested a reported $33 million into a massive up-date and expansion of the property.

Today the Cheeca features both fresh and saltwater pools, six tennis courts, a three-hole golf course, several restaurants, watersports, 203 units, and there's even a heliport!

If you can't afford to stay in a room or villa at the Cheeca Lodge, you can still visit the place, have a cocktail in the Light Tackle Lounge, and dine in the palatial Atlantic Edge dining room, where my husband and I enjoyed the very finest dinner we've ever had in 25 years of living in the Keys. Have lunch at the indoor/outdoor Ocean Terrace Grill, or come for the spectacular Sunday brunch. In the lounge, notice the room-rate card from 1962, way before the Cheeca became so intensely posh. Room rates then were $25–$40 a night. Also on display: snapshots of the rich and famous who have come to the Cheeca Lodge to fish and be photographed with members of the Twitchell clan.

Members of the Islamorada Chamber of Commerce staff will tell you that President George Bush Sr. stays in the Cheeca's $1,000 plus presidential suite. Each year Bush comes into town to head up a very high-stakes fishing tourney, the proceeds of which go toward preserving the endangered Everglades. The Bush connection is one of the Cheeca Lodge's many claims to fame, and Cheeca employees say that the former prez is a dream to work with, "a real nice guy."

The Cheeca Lodge sprawls on 25 acres of oceanfront property that once was one of the Upper Keys' earliest settlements. You'll find substantial beachfront and a long, narrow, sun and wind-worn wharf jutting into the Atlantic that is quite irresistible—you *have* to walk to the end of it. A neat, sandy beach on a small, safe lagoon is perfect for families. During the winter season, as well as most weekends, kids can take part in an in-house children's program that is something like a day camp at a country club. The theme of the program is marine environmental awareness and responsibility. Kids are taught by four counselors with some pretty spiffy credentials and degrees.

All this luxury costs plenty, but the Cheeca really does have just about everything you could ask for in a resort. Cheeca employees are known for their friendliness. Many of them are descended from those founding families represented in the Pioneer Cemetery out on the beach of the property. Guests at the Cheeca Lodge are treated very, very well indeed.

Holiday Isle Resorts & Marina
MM 84, Oceanside ✶ 664-2321 ✶ 800-327-7070

The penultimate spring breakers' resort, this massive complex of bars, restaurants, shops, concessions and motel rooms has it all, and more. It jumps! It swings! It stops traffic! The size of the traffic jam on the Overseas Highway outside the Holiday Isle complex indicates how busy the resort is that day. Weekends it is always packed; sometimes it's packed to capacity, and people are turned away.

A young crowd features people who look stunning in bikinis. If you don't look so good, you'll be happier elsewhere. Even the Monroe

County Sheriff's deputies eat lunch here. Oceanside barbeque hamburgers and hot dogs are the same here as anywhere, but, oh, the view!

This complex has extensive facilities for watersports, including wreck diving and windsurfing, five restaurants and nine bars, including a tiki bar, shaded by palm fronds. Bimini Walk is an array of shops featuring art and posters, and swimwear and T-shirts, the clothes you need to fit in at this very hot beach. For information and reservations call 800-327-7070 and ask for a brochure. There's so much here! The Horizon Restaurant is on the sixth floor; just take the glass-sided elevator. Guests are curious women and their patient husbands. The college kids can't afford to eat up here—they're doing hot dogs and hamburgers on the beach. Who cares how the food is? It's a novel place to dine.

Holiday Isle goes all out for the spring break crowd in March and April, with lots of parties, specials, and bikini contests with big cash prizes. An information person on duty on the beach can help you, just in case you're looking for something to do.

The Islander Motel
MM 82.1 Oceanside ✹ 664-2031 ✹ 800-753-6002
The Polynesian arch over the driveway harkens back to the '60s, and it might discourage travelers looking for more modern digs. In fact, there has been some local controversy over whether or not the arch represents the sort of image that the Village of Islands wishes to create. Most of the old timers love it. The Islander has undergone a fantastic renovation. The cottages appear just as they always have, but the interiors are much more modern. It's sleek and funky, but oh-so-charmingly so. The Islander Motel maintains a style of old-time Keys oceanside resort that is becoming more and more difficult to find. The place is very attractive, that is—it attracts you, and the ocean breeze beckons. Broad expanses of white coral rock, stark beneath the hot, tropical sun, make you feel like pinning a hibiscus in your hair and wandering around in a flowing cotton gown on the very pretty beach. Many tons of sand have been imported and spread on the 1,100-foot beach. Lots of slouchy beach chairs rest at the edge of the seawall. The twenty-five-acre grounds are absolutely opulent by local standards. You could almost get lost.

In all 114 units of the Islander, you'll get good beds, refrigerators, telephones and televisions; some have fully equipped kitchens. Villas with screened-in porches are popular with families who rent them for weeks at a time at very reasonable rates. In fact, this is surely one of the best deals in the Keys. Help yourself to simple, complimentary breakfast every morning in the lobby. The freshwater pool and the saltwater pool are heated. Snorkeling or fishing right off the 200-foot lighted pier is good fun, not to mention shuffleboard. (Does anybody actually play shuffleboard anymore?), basketball, and volleyball, all near the BBQ patio.

When you stay in this family-oriented vacation resort, you're close to all the local sights, but you may not want to go to all the trouble of seeing them. A true sense of being well away from it all may be enough for you. Venture to the front office, however, it's worth a visit: several shelves of books, a bunch of board games, and oodles of brochures promoting area highlights—maybe these will inspire you.

Islamorada Motel/Inn
MM 87.8 Bayside ✺ 852-9376

This small, clean mom-and-pop joint on the highway—no ocean, no bay—was operated up until recently by a real mom and a real pop. Then the pop split for higher ground. But Mom and some of the kids are still running the place. All thirteen units, rooms and efficiencies, are on a deep, pleasant property. The furniture, including the beds, is perfectly preserved, '60s-era cane, wicker and rattan, all in good shape. A good-sized saltwater pool, a BBQ pit, and a diving gear clean-up station with a hose are all out back. Also, a nifty, thatched-roof tiki hut out front, sheltering a round wooden table and a bunch of chairs, looked like a very fine place for six or eight people to have a lot of fun. The circulating pump was on the fritz on the day we visited, so the pool was leafy—but not gross. All in all, the grounds of the Islamorada Motel were not as pristine as the interior but certainly comfortable enough. A long clothesline in the sun looked like a very good idea.

Mom says that as long as you don't expect a fancy resort you'll be happy here. The rooms are equipped with televisions and air conditioning and dial-out phones. Complimentary coffee and sweet rolls are served in the office every morning. The maid proudly told us that all linens are changed every day! Prices go from $70 up to $110, depending on the unit and the time of the year.

Key Lantern Motel and Blue Fin Inn
MM 82, Bayside ✿ 664-4572

Truly dedicated tourist/explorers may choose to spend their time and money in pursuit of adventure, not luxury. If all you need at night is a clean, safe place to bathe, catch up on broadcast news, and grab a few hours of cozy sleep, this set of motels (same owner/same management) is what you're looking for. Rooms rent for around $60, throughout the year, and each is equipped with TV, AC, and a bath. There's no catch. It's a nice place, clean and affordable. And very busy. If you want to book these cheap and pleasant accommodations, call in advance to reserve your room.

Sunset Inn
MM 82.2, Bayside ✿ 664-3454

Recently purchased by the same folks who run the Key Lantern and the Blue Fin. They are slowly bringing the very funky place up to snuff, with new air conditioners, new beds (very comfortable, I can personally attest) and more. The pool is small, but better than no pool at all. Location is excellent, too. If you're bargain shopping, try any one of these three for a clean and affordable place to stay in the area.

Pelican Cove Resort
MM 84.5 Oceanside ✿ 664-4435 ✿ 800-445-4690

Found: one sandy beach, the sandiest beach we saw anywhere in the area. Maybe they just brought it in; they do buy sand here and spread it on the beaches. Anyway, if you're longing for the kind of sand you sink in up to your ankles, this is the place for you.

Every room in the Pelican Cove has an ocean view, including hotel rooms, efficiencies and suites. The beach, the oceanside pool and the jacuzzi behind the hotel are all meticulously tended. Also a boat ramp and dock, tennis, a poolside cabana, a bar and cafe. The watersports concession on the beach is run by some truly lovely young people who are as nice as they look.

If your parents suggest a family week in the Keys, tell them you want to stay at the Pelican Cove Resort. They'll love it and so will you. Here's the deal: You check in, get the folks settled. Then you put on your best swimsuit and head over to the Holiday Isle—it's right next door!—where you immerse yourself in the thick of the Keys' wildest party scene. It rocks around the clock. Then, when it's time to check in with the folks, come back over to the beautiful, genteel Pelican Cove Resort. Boy, are you smart! Your parents will love their balcony overlooking the ocean. Every room has one. Sweet jazz or show tunes from the Pelican Cove's beachside cabana float up to the balconies. The ocean glitters in the distance. Room rates are on the expensive side here, but guests lulled to sleep by palm fronds rustling in Caribbean breezes believe it's worth it. It's fair to call this place luxurious—and expensive.

Ragged Edge Resort
MM 86.5 Oceanside ☙ 243 Treasure Harbor Road ☙ 852-5389

Jackie Barnes, of Barnes-storming fame, a cheery guy in a straw hat, may be the first person you meet when you arrive at the Ragged Edge Resort. Jackie is proud as punch of the place and will patiently show you around until you find the accommodation you really want. All ten units are built with guests' comfort and safety in mind. For instance, the tiles on the floors of one newly remodeled room have non-skid surfaces; one little apartment is wheelchair accessible and right on the water. All the screened-in porches are perfect perches for taking in sea breezes.The kitchens are conducive to serious food prep. They're certainly not the barely equipped kitchens you often encounter in other Keys apartments and efficiencies. "We even supply the filters for the coffeemaker," says Jackie, opening the cupboard to show us. Also on the premises are a washer, a dryer, and a clothesline. The phones are for out-going calls only, so don't stay here if you're waiting for a phone call because you'll miss it. Outdoors, by the dock, lucky anglers will appreciate the fish cleaning area.

"Don't even think about cleaning your fish in our kitchens," Jackie says, "Your mama won't let you clean fish in her kitchen, and you can't do it here, either."

Jackie then shows us a little marina, sheltered and calm, and a boat launch, a few yards down the street. A freshwater pool overlooks the Atlantic, and a lookout tower is a popular setting for weddings performed at the very crack of dawn. From the dock you can look out into the distance and see the light slash of turquoise against the horizon that marks Crocker Reef, some four miles out.

Jimmy Lee has owned the Ragged Edge for twenty-two years. He likes sitting at a picnic table in the yard and talking about the people who have stayed at the seaside lodge through the years. The Ragged Edge got a whole chapter in a travel book by a London writer who recorded his adventures in a book called *Hunting Mr. Heartbreak*. Ask Jimmy to show it to you.

Both Jackie and Jimmy know what's going on in the area. Jackie knows the kitchen crews in area restaurants and can often call ahead to the bistro of your choice to find out the specials of the evening. Knowing Jackie is like having a best friend in Islamorada.

During season, a nifty studio or efficiency goes for $109 a day. Off season it's 30% less. Weekly and monthly rates are 10% off that. Rates here are among the best in the area.

"We haven't caught up with the rest of the world," Jimmy Lee explains, "and we don't want to."

Dining

Bentley's
MM 82, Oceanside ✵ 664-9094

People who work here seem to be having a good time serving the fish and pasta platters. People who run the hotels in the area often recommend this place. The bar here is full of beer posters and neon slogans, kind of like a frat rumpus room. Prime ribs, a house specialty, are so huge they barely fit on the plate. An appetizer called "drunken sweet potato," with brown sugar and dark rum, butter, cinnamon, and nutmeg, is so wonderful you'll try to recreate it when you get home. Dinner samplers feature shrimp or fish served in several different sauces on the same plate. Kind of weird, but they seem to please Bentley's customers. The place is packed every night, and has been since the day its doors opened. Most major credit cards are now accepted.

City Hall Cafe
MM 88.5, Bayside ✵ 852-3354

What I love about the City Hall Cafe is the menu. Any one who has ever worked in city government anywhere will appreciate the clever plays on words associated with government. Appetizers, for example, are on a list called The Planning Department. Growth Management names the salad section. Get it? Subdivisions are sandwiches. Wrap Sessions are sandwich wraps. The Mayor's Vote is a daily special, an authentic Reuben sandwich, or a roast beef wrap with horseradish sauce. Prices here are somewhat below the swankier places, and more customers are local than tourist. Being located right between county and village office complexes means the City Hall Cafe serves its fair share of beaurocrats. Only ten tables, so service is intimate and personable, ambiance basic and honest.

Prices go up at dinnertime, but are still very fair. Beer and wine only. Children's menu. Wheelchair accessible. Credit cards.

Green Turtle Cay
MM 81.5 Ocean
The Green Turtle Inn, which has been a landmark at this location since even before the infamous hurricane of 1935, is gone. New owners are restoring the building as we go to press. The good news is that master chef Dawn Seiber, formerly of the Cheeca Lodge, and currently of the sublime Kaiyo Restaurant at MM 82, has been brought on board to create a new eatery to be named Green Turtle Cay. It will feature fresh fish, in keeping with the theme of the area, and you know it's going to be fantastic because Seiber is in charge. There will also be a high-end liquor and wine store, an art gallery, and a new location for the Florida Keys Outfitters (664-5423).

Athens Cafe & Grill
MM 82.2 Oceanside ✆ 664-0848
You may think you know how pita bread tastes, but until you have it in a real Greek restaurant, hot off the grill, you don't really know pita at all. Eat pita and a whole lot more in this tiny and scrupulously clean restaurant, the outdoor table for two facing the sunset is nice, or order the food to go. They'll even deliver to your hotel if it's located between MM 74 and 90. Locals are mad for this place and refer visitors to it frequently. Food is absolutely fresh and scrumptuous. Try hummus with pita, traditional Greek salad, brimming with glistening tomato and cucumber slices and served with a perfect oil and vinegar dressing, or the popular Greek gyros, pork, chicken, beef, lamb, or vegetarian, or combos. Prices are very reasonable.

Mangrove Mike's Cafe
MM 82.2 Bayside ✆ 664-8022
Like every other breakfast place in the Keys Mike's is packed every morning and the food is just fine. Breakfast specials are such hopeful dishes as Craig's Hangover Helper and the Super Special, which seems to be a Keys rendition of the grand slam breakfast. Lunch, too, but no dinner. Old-fashioned dishes like hot turkey or roast beef with gravy platters. The watiresses are fast. Fastest of all is the one the locals call Gramma. Gramma wears her hair in a long ponytail and does her work with pride,

efficiency and true grit. After you eat, head over to Roxie's Fluff and Brew and the Girl E. Girl Boutique. While the women fluff, that is check out Melody's excellent display of tropical chic clothes (including large lady sizes) and high-heeled flip flops, the men chill out at Roxie's horse-shoe bar next door, where she'll pour you a coffee, or a beer while you wait for the ladies.

Island Grill
MM 85.5 Oceanside ☎ 664-8400

Sometimes there are live bands and sand-dancing beneath the moon in the backyard beach at the Island Grill. It's right on the water, just before Snake Creek Bridge if you're heading north, just after the bridge when you're heading south. It's a little tricky the first time you find it, but find it. Menu is very creative. Nightly specials are comfort-based dishes. Full bar. A wholesome, clean joint on the water. Take your family. The place is mobbed with tourists as well as locals at dinnertime.

Hog Heaven
MM 85.3 Oceanside ☎ 664-9669

How did they get that airplane in the side of the building? The people who worked that out are gone now, and so is the bar mascot, B.L. Dinner, the pot-bellied pig. B.L., who loved showing off her painted toenails, has moved on to a petting zoo in Miami, where she reportedly lives very happily entertaining a much less raucous crowd than her friends in the Keys.

This is a sports bar, with 19 televisions tuned to nothing but sports in a funky marina with great food and a laid-back atmosphere. You can dine, or drink, outside or in. Great lunch and dinner specials, from 11 a.m. till 4 a.m. Jukebox, weekend DJs, two pool tables, video games, and what brings many people here, the NTN Trivia. Sit at the bar, ask for a play box, and test your skill. Your score goes up against all the others in the nationwide NTN scoreboard. And it's free. Best selling dish here is the fried chicken wings, with blue cheese dressing made on the premises. More free fun: How long can you balance on the pink barrel? Kind of like log rolling, only it's a barrel, in the ocean, with ropes to guide you.

At happy hour, Monday through Friday, from 4 p.m. till 8 p.m., draft beer and well drinks are half price.

The Horizon Room at Holiday Isle Resort
MM 84, Oceanside ✆ 664-2321

In the Holiday Isle complex, it is possible to do some serious bar-hopping without ever leaving the premises. Remember the song "Kokomo" by the Beach Boys? Originally, it was a fantasy place, nonexistent, but when people began arriving in the Keys, asking directions to the mysterious and wonderful-sounding place called Kokomo, the folks at Holiday Isle quickly rushed in to answer their dreams, and a bar named Kokomo was born. So there you are—in Kokomo till the wee hours. There's live island music—reggae, Caribbean, rock—at Kokomo, and more of the same at the nearby Tiki Bar.

Rum Runners, a triple-decker thatched-palm tower featuring bars and cocktails on breezy alcoves and terraces, is the very hottest watering spot in the Keys, a must-visit, according to one of my more dedicated fun-chasing friends. Tuesdays, 6 - 7 p.m., catch Girl's Night Out, a live radio show hosted by Arthur Godfrey's cousin, Pam Godfrey. Catch it on EZ 96.9 FM.

The Hungry Tarpon
MM 77.5 Bayside, at Robbie's Marina ✆ 664-0535

You've heard of grunts and grits, the staple dish of the Florida Keys Depression-era diet, but have you ever tried it? Folks who frequent the Hungry Tarpon Cafe will tell you that eating grunts and grits is no hardship. In fact, many return again and again to this Bahamian-style fish house, built nearly a century ago of saltwater concrete, for this legendary treat. Other eye-opening specials are huevos rancheros, breakfast burritos, and hash browns topped with sausage gravy and cheese. At lunchtime feast on terrific chowders, a truly fine version of black beans and rice, fresh salads, fried fish baskets and sandwiches. Because it's a really tiny place, a few tables and stools at the counter, you can watch your food being prepared, and it will never take long to get it. Prices are fair on the Hungry Tarpon's creative menu. Come hungry! Portions are huge and satisfying. It's tricky to find because it's under a bridge on the bayside of the island, but if you like local and funky, you must find it!

Islamorada Fish Company
MM 81.5 Bayside ✱ 664-9271 ✱ 800-258-2559 (to order fish)
At the Islamorada Fish Company you can eat your lunch or dinner on the water, on a bayside sun deck, or, on windy days, on a deck out front. Everything is served on plastic or paper. Prices are what you'll find in most places for fried or grilled fish sandwiches. The Fish Company offers some terrific, fresh shrimp and tuna salads as great alternatives to the fried fare. For twin lobster tail dinner with fries and coleslaw runs you'll pay market price. Chicken dishes and burgers, too. The Fish Company serves lunch and dinner only, and is open daily at 11 a.m. till around 10 p.m. Full bar, in fact, two bars. One with food, and next door, a plain old waterfront bar.

If you're feeling guilty about all the fun you're having in Paradise sampling the wonderful bounty of indigenous seafood, why not ship a slab of fish, a couple of Florida lobsters or a pound or two of ground conch to the folks back home? The Islamorada Fish Company Retail Store will pack and ship fish anywhere in the continental United States. The packing room is always busy. At Christmas time it's a madhouse, so order early.

Kaiyo
MM82, Old Highway ✱ 664-5556
Chef-owner Dawn Sieber, former longtime head chef at the elegant Cheeca Lodge, blends the very best and most beautiful of East-meets-West cuisine in this tea house-like restaurant. Tempura-fried striped bass and strip-fried shrimp with soba noodles, bok choy, and miso butter broth are winners. Stunning sushi bar, exotic teas and sakis, excellent wine list, and certainly the most beautiful restaurant for many miles around. Wind chimes welcome you through the front door. A floor-to-ceiling collage of chunks of tile and glass, with many hues of greens and blues promotes serenity. Staff members are radiant and seem to take pride in their gentle surroundings and in what they have to offer. A special place.

Lazy Days Oceanfront Bar & Grille
MM 79.9 Oceanside ✺ 664-5256

We tried the Lazy Days Restaurant for the first time on a Saturday afternoon in March. "Sorry–No Vacancy" signs were posted on every hotel, motel, and inn in the area. The restaurants were packed, too, and traffic was bumper to bumper. We'd had a busy day and felt we owed it to ourselves to seek out the best fish sandwich the area had to offer. And guess what? We found it. The crunchy yellowtail sandwich at Lazy Days Bar and Grille was spectacular. Several area restaurants are now adding crunchy yellowtail sandwiches to their menus, too. This one is the original. We ordered fried conch, too, but we wouldn't order it again for two reasons: first, because of the many other truly tasty choices on the menu, and second, because it was so tough that all the chewing in the world wouldn't tenderize it. (Everybody knows the trick to succulent conch is to thoroughly tenderize it and then to cook it very briefly.) Considering the business of the day, the cook may have forgotten it on the fire for a few minutes too long. Or something. The French fries at Lazy Days are terrific. They're worth the visit, hand-cut, not frozen, amazing. You won't ever want to go back to the other yucky kind.

Lazy Days has been featured on a Food Network show about great waterfront eateries and has been named one of 22 Great Spots for Seafood in the USA by Coastal Living Magazine. While you're waiting for your food to arrive, check out the view. To the right you'll see a point of land with a heliport and a row of magnificent palms. No, it's not a public facility; it's the multimillion-dollar retreat of a Chicago businessman. To the left is Bud 'n' Mary's Marina.

Lazy Days offers what every hungry tourist is hoping to find: oceanfront dining and good, fresh seafood. Of course, you pay a bit more to get things so exactly right. Because the entire restaurant is about a story-and-a-half up from the ground, there's a soft breeze that you can probably count on finding year-round. Otherwise, eat indoors. There's a long, busy bar (2 for 1 Happy Hour 4 - 7 p.m.) and great servers. Lazy Days is open 11:30 a.m. to 10 p.m.

Lorelei Restaurant and Cabana Bar
MM82 Bayside ☛ 852-4656

Lorelei was the legendary German mermaid who haunted the Rhine River. Lorelei's plaintive songs lured sailors and fishermen into destruction on the rocks that lined the river. Nice gal, huh? And who knew rivers had mermaids? Eventually Lorelei was carried away by the currents, but her sad singing is still heard late at night along the banks of the Rhine, some believe....

Lorelei, the place on the Florida Bay, evokes a much happier mood than its namesake. Lorelei herself is recreated outside in a glittery splash of all-weather sequins.

On a walkway leading into the complex a plexiglass photo gallery contains pictures of President Bush arriving for dinner; and a barefoot couple getting married: she in a white swimsuit and veil; he in a black bathing suit and bow tie.

Dining in the Lorelei Restaurant is dockside, or indoors in a rather elegant dining room. The restaurant opens for dinner only, from 5 p.m. till 10 p.m., 10:30 p.m. on weekend nights. Early bird specials from 5 p.m. Food is pricey; quality is rather inconsistent, but you don't go to the Lorelei for the food. You go for the ambiance. You go to celebrate sunset on another day in Paradise with people who make their living on the water.

At the Cabana Bar, breakfast and lunch are served daily. Fishing guides, sailboat captains and dive masters come to the Cabana Bar to unwind in the late afternoons. Live music plays about always. And on Sunday afternoons, local celebrity Big Dick plays.

Once locally owned and operated, the Lorelei is now part of a New York-based corporation that owns thirty-five properties around the world. Here's one you might have heard of: The Tavern On The Green in New York City's Central Park.

Marker 88
Guess where? Bayside ☛ 852-9315

Dinner only; 5 p.m.–11 p.m. Boy, does this place get mixed reviews! Some say the food is strictly gourmet, extensive list of fine wines, complete bar, creative menu. Others say the tables are too close together, it's too noisy when it's full, it's way over-rated, and take plenty of money.

Entrees expensive, and mostly a la carte. Food critics praise the Key lime baked Alaska dessert. Closed Mondays, reservations strongly suggested on weekends.

Papa Joe's Landmark Restaurant
MM 79.7 Bayside ✱ 664-8109

Recently named a Historic and Cultural Landmark by the Monroe County Board of Commissioners, this seafood restaurant and bar sits pretty as a postcard on the dock o' the bay. Interior has low ceilings and lots of cedar beams, and a nautical theme with no apologies. The outdoor bar is really the nicest place to eat, if the weather permits. Yet another great view of the sunset. A good place where a party traveling together can split up for a spell to pursue separate endeavors. Maybe all you want to do is sit at the bar and watch the sun glitter off the waters of the Florida Bay. Your more ambitious companions are cruising out to Indian Key or Lignumvitae Key for a local history lesson. Papa Joe's is just the place from which to launch this perfect afternoon in Paradise.

Food is not gourmet or trendy, just simple fare, well-prepared and nicely served, and a great children's menu with terrific prices. If you've got kids, ask for a table near the aquarium. Lunch is from 11 a.m. till 3:30 p.m. Daily specials, like country-fried steak with mashed potatoes and gravy. Early-bird dinner specials from 4:30 p.m.–6 p.m. Prices on lobster, shrimp, or prime rib dinners are very reasonable. There's always a crowd at Papa Joe's because the food's good, and the prices are right. Plus—it's on the water!

Closed Tuesdays. All major credit cards accepted.

Whale Harbor Inn
MM 83.5 Oceanside ✱ 664-4959

Attention hungry whales! The world famous seafood buffet, featuring troughs overflowing with shellfish, roasted beef and hams, and seventy-five accompanying hot and cold dishes, caters to the early-bird crowd from 4 p.m. till 5:30 weekdays, and 11 a.m. till 4 p.m. Sundays. Buffet prices: $21.95 for early birds; $24.95 otherwise. Teens are $17.95. Kids are $9.95. Children under 5 years of age eat for free.

It is interesting to imagine what the Haitian workers who dish out the endless servings of food—shrimp, oysters, clams and roast beef—must be thinking as they watch the excess and the waste. The food looks quite a bit better than it actually tastes; even the shrimp, which you peel for yourself, loses its appeal a lot faster than you might think. When you get tired of eating, go for a walk. The gift shop is a terrific place to wander through, and the prices are affordable on stuff you might need, like a bigger sweatshirt.

Tour buses stop here, so don't be surprised to see one, but do consider going elsewhere and returning at a less riotous time. Certain bus loads, one waitress told me, are comprised of particularly demanding and pushy tourists. If you are a part of a bus load, make reservations and ask about discounts for parties of twenty or more.

Woody's Saloon and Restaurant
Mile Marker 82 ✿ 664-4335

And now, for something completely different! Advertised as Islamorada's hottest night spot. At 9 p.m., the house band, Big Dick and the Extenders, goes on. At 10 p.m., lead man Big Dick, a Don Rickles-type comedian, does his famous hour-long harangue, one of the area's most notorious attractions billed as "adult entertainment." You are warned not to sit in the front row unless you want to swap witticisms with Big Dick. One Islamorada resident told me that Big Dick is "really dirty." Another says, "Big Dick is obnoxious, but you gotta see him once."

Big Dick and his Southern rock and blues band never turn down requests to appear, generally for no pay, at local fundraisers, and in the Keys, there are plenty of those. With a heart that big, how bad can Big Dick be?

Woody's also has sensational, award-winning Chicago-style pizza and very good Italian dishes.

Lately, there's something brand new at Woody's. They're called the Sassy But Classy dancers and the controversy over just how much flesh these girls are allowed to flash here in the Village of Islands is a raging and on-going debate. See the girls Tuesday through Saturday nights. Big Dick and the band play Wednesday through Saturday. The joint is open from 6 p.m. till 4 a.m. every night.

Zane Grey Lounge
Mile Marker 82 ✍ 664-4335

Because I am a huge fan of Zane Grey, this is one of my favorite stops on the long drive to and from the mainland. Zane Grey was born in Ohio, practiced dentistry in New York City, and had a passion for big game fishing. He was also a prolific writer. His novels, which were serialized in magazines and made into many films, made him America's first author millionaire. Grey came to the Keys for the first time in 1911. He was around 40 years old, and was to spend the next 15 winters at the Long Key Fishing Lodge, located a few miles south of this namesake lounge. In his rustic and cozy cottage he wrote for a few hours early in the morning, and then headed out for long days of deep sea fishing. Unfortunately, he never wrote any books about fishing, or about the Florida Keys. In 1935, the Long Key Fishing Lodge was destroyed by the Labor Day Hurricane.

The Zane Grey Long Key Lounge is designed to pay homage to Grey and his passion for Keys fishing. The walls are paneled in dark wood, and there is a sumptuous fireplace and thick, soft carpet. There are photos of Zane Grey and a shadow box containing rods, gaffs, and books actually used by him. There is a full bar and beyond it a cigar humidor. It's a smokey bar, but you can go outside onto a wide, bayside veranda and enjoy your cocktail or meal there, if you like. Food is very rich, to match the dense atmosphere of the room. Chowders are thick and tasty; sandwiches are served just so. Salads are crisp and fresh and brightly colored. On weekends they bring in a live blues band. It's a fancier place, I think, than Zane Grey preferred. But surely he'd approve of our modern day reverence.

Shops

Caribbean Village Shops
MM 82 Oceanside

Here is an interesting row of shops. At the Sandal Factory, you'll find a great selection of offerings, with names like Birkenstock, Mephisto, and Bass, at good prices. Resort wear and T-shirts, too, but the sales force is very, aggressive, which actually discourages me from spending much time here. Angelika Clothing Company features lovely, unique, expensive, clothing. Wish it had been here when I was looking for an island romantic wedding dress, because they've got them. Divine gowns. Chic, pricey sportswear, too.

Earth Naturals
MM 82.6 Oceanside ✹ 664-4252

Family and friends of the late Helga Andrews, founder of this bead shop, carry on her work with great classes in basic beading, macrame, peyote stitch and wire wrapping. A wonderful selection of breathtakingly beautiful beads. Also beading and jewelry-making materials. Come in and spend an hour or two at the bead table creating your own souvenir. It's a good way to take a private break from the hustle and bustle of your Keys vacation. To get into the mood for beading, lunch at Kaiyo. You'll be inspired.

Hooked On Books
MM 82.6 Oceanside ✹ 517-2602

A good of selection books, on local as well as worldly topics, and terrific greeting cards, too, in a bright and comfortable shop. You're on vacation, relax and have a good look! If you're looking for something in particular ask Penny. She's happy to advise and to help.

MS.Cellaneous
MM 82.7 Oceanside ☎ 517-9990
The best of both worlds: old and new merchandise. Gifts, clothing
(women's clothing in sizes 0 - 3X), art, curiosities. Check out the
decoupage floor created by the very creative proprietor, Ms. Rae
Cavanaugh. She is a lifelong explorer of fleas, consignments and thrifts,
and a collector of interesting stuff. Who better to open this fascinating
shop? I bought some beautiful sheets here once, and they're still serving
us well. Amazing. You won't leave empty-handed.

Treasure Village
MM 86.5 Oceanside ☎ 852-0511
It all started with a replica of a Spanish fort built in 1949 by treasure
hunter Art McKee, who is known around the world as the father of
modern treasure diving. McKee's guests were invited to view McKee's
collection of recovered loot and then to climb the winding stairway to
a lookout at the top of the fort. All went well, local legend has it, until
someone fell from the top of the fort and broke his neck. A long litiga-
tion followed, the details and results of which have been lost in time.
Eventually, however, all was apparently settled and the fort changed
hands to open in its next incarnation as an anchor store for a spiffy, new,
leafy shopping complex filled with island goodies.

As you encounter the 37-foot spiny lobster replica at the entrance to
the Treasure Island Village Shops, imagine how the lobster feels when
the tables are turned and he is facing a hungry human diver on the ocean
floor. Surely this is the biggest spiny lobster replica in the world. As you
gaze upon the Spanish tower, imagine how fine it must have looked to
tourists in the 1950s. Also remember: the bathrooms are located in the
tower.

The shops of Treasure Village are arranged on a boardwalk that encir-
cles a shady courtyard, with picnic tables and open space for antsy kids.
The courtyard provides a lovely time-out zone for those in need of a
break or some quiet time. Half your party can shop while the other can
sit in the courtyard digging on the reggae music that never seems to quit.

The Rain Barrel Artisans Village
MM 86.7 Bayside ✒ 852-3084

The mood here is serene, soft and green, and very friendly. If you're the sort of person who likes to schmooz a bit with the artist before you buy the art, here's your chance. Shops and boutiques feature artistic expression in pottery, clay, glass, custom frames, airbrushed T-shirts, paintings, stained glass, jewelry, with more merchandise being created all the time. Works are displayed in a main gallery as well as in a series of smaller shops that radiate from the center. Creations are on the expensive side but look and feel as if they will last a long time.

The Garden Cafe serves simple, wholesome food (no fried fish sandwiches or French fries here) in a lovely courtyard. Usually in the late winter or early spring the Rain Barrel artists stage an arts festival. In addition to resident craftspeople, there are live demonstrations by visiting artisans; live music and food. Admission is free.

Why is this gathering place of artisans called "The Rain Barrel?" Owner Carol Cutshall says the arts and crafts center is named after the 5,000-gallon rain barrel in the center of the garden. "Because rain is water and water is needed for the existence of life," she says. Open daily.

The World Wide Sportsman
MM 86.7 Bayside ✒ 852-3084

Don't miss this huge, fun, fascinating emporium of everything to do with fishing and the outdoor living. Fishing poles, tackle, lanterns, ice chests, and diving flippers that really fit your feet! Deck shoes and sandals, and upstairs great women's clothes. Also, the Zane Grey Lounge.

Most wonderful of all, a life-size replica of the *Pilar*, Papa Hemingway's beloved 38-foot, diesel-powered fishing boat, for which he paid Wheeler Shipyard in Brooklyn, NY, $7500, a lot of money in 1934! At the time he was at the height of his career, and living in Key West. Hemingway spent some of his happiest days aboard the *Pilar* and once wrote about her: "She is a really sturdy boat, sweet in any kind of sea."

Key Largo

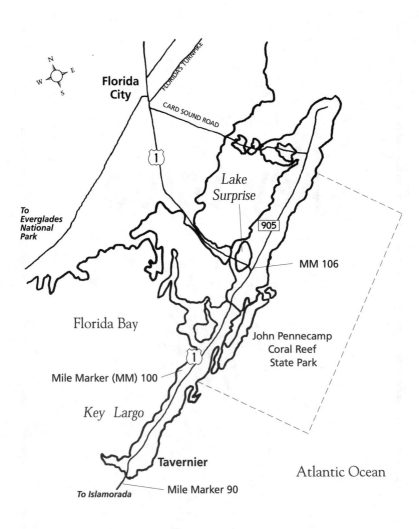

George was right.
The Keys are different from anything
I've ever seen—and hotter.

– HUMPHREY BOGART'S FIRST LINE
IN THE FILM *Key Largo*.

Sooner or Later, Everyone Comes to Key Largo

KEY LARGO is a sun-baked and weather-beaten island, built on bleached coral rocks and populated by people often as sun-baked and weather-beaten as their surroundings. Key Largo feels dry and flat and windswept. It is the first island you come to when you drive into the Keys, and the last one you see when you drive back out.

Key Largo is the longest, largest, and easternmost island of the Keys chain. It is bordered by the Florida Straits and the Atlantic Ocean on the south and the Florida Bay and the Gulf of Mexico on the north.

Since no natural fine-grain sand beaches exist here, local folks working in the tourist industry spend a lot of time and energy explaining to disappointed visitors that Florida's sandy beaches do not extend all the way down to the craggy shoreline of Key Largo. The rest of Florida's coast has beaches, while the Florida Keys have the living reef, the only one in the continental United States. The community of Key Largo seems a support system for that reef, and that's not a bad thing; it gives the place a purpose it would not otherwise have.

Much of the upper part of Key Largo is federally protected land and unsettled wilderness, encompassing the Crocodile Lake National Wildlife Refuge. The refuge is a 6800-acre hardwood hammock and lake that has become the primary breeding ground for the endangered American crocodile. Other endangered species in the refuge are the indigo snake, wood rat, Key Largo cotton mouse, and Schauss' swallowtail butterfly. Because crocodiles are timid, particularly around matters of reproduction, this area is closed to the public.

Visitors, however, are invited to roam the Key Largo Botanical Site on upper Key Largo and, on lower Key Largo, the Wild Bird Sanctuary for an up-close and personal visit with some remarkable species of Keys birds.

Aside from these sanctioned areas, the island of Key Largo is quite heavily populated. Its main street, which is the Overseas Highway, is lined with motels, shops and restaurants. Several shopping centers attract residents from several Upper Keys communities. In spite of four lanes, the highway here is curvy, and traffic is often thick and slow.

Key Largo's biggest attraction is John Pennekamp Coral Reef Park, the first underwater park in the United States, and Florida's most popular state park. It's the largest diving destination in the world, receiving over two million visitors each year.

Diving is very big business in Key Largo. Everywhere you look you see dive shops offering to sell or rent just about anything you need for a day, or a week, of reef or wreck diving. One shop advertises, "We supply everything but your bathing suit." Endless combinations of dive packages are available, too, and every motel and resort in Key Largo is ready for divers, pretty much assuming that's why they've come.

Like everywhere else in the Keys, fishing guides and charter captains are easily available in Key Largo to take you to the quiet, shallow waters of the backcountry, where cagey anglers, such as former President George Bush, go to outsmart snook and bonefish, or out into the deepest, scariest part of the ocean—the Gulf Stream—where burly sportsmen do battle with leaping marlin and sailfish.

Hollywood director John Huston, back in 1948, filmed several brief scenes for the movie *Key Largo* in the Caribbean Club in Rock Harbor, a small settlement on the island of Key Largo. When the film *Key Largo* was released in 1952, area businessmen saw an opportunity to cash in on their island's sudden glamour, spread far and wide via the silver screen by Humphrey Bogart and Lauren Bacall. Promoters decided to drop the name Rock Harbor and call the place Key Largo. Some folks didn't like the idea of the name change, but business interests prevailed, and Key

Largo has been promoting itself in relation to the film classic of the same
name ever since.

For purposes of this guide, the area of Key Largo begins roughly
around MM 90 and ends at MM 106, where the Overseas Highway splits
into two roads, U.S. 1 and Card Sound Road. Either one will take you,
in under a half hour, to the beginning of the Florida Turnpike or the
Everglades National Park. Take Card Sound Road; the other way is much
too hectic and, statistically, much more treacherous.

The Key Largo Chamber of Commerce
MM 106 Bayside ☛ 451-1414 ☛ 800-822-1088
If you're home, and your trip to the Keys is still in the planning stages,
call ahead and tell a Chamber staff member what you're most interested
in doing in Key Largo. Someone will answer your questions and send a
comprehensive list of the area's features.

This center is often the first stop for folks arriving for the first time in
the Keys. One chamber woman told me that many people come to Key
Largo to see the living reef but are confused about how to find it. At least
once a day, she says, she must explain that the reef is located miles offshore and beneath the water. "You can't see it from the road," she
explains. "You can't drive your car to it. It is only accessible by boat."

You Are Here
On a blustery Saturday afternoon in January, business is brisk at the Key
Largo Chamber's Visitors Center. Planted among the milling crowds are a
half dozen telephone stations from which travelers may phone ahead to
reserve rooms for the night. Each station is equipped with a pencil and a
tiny pad of paper. Couples are busily conferring, and it appears that nail-
ing down a room reservation is a man's job, for it is usually the men who
are doing the negotiating with the motels. The men repeat what they are
hearing to the women: "He says we're still two-and-a-half hours away," a
man says. "They say the room is definitely on the water," another assures
his wife, "but it's $30 more."

Yes, Key West is only a hundred miles away, but those are hard miles.
Late afternoon is not the best time to head into the Lower Keys; it would
be better to settle in for the night at one of Key Largo's funky motels or
sleek resorts. At the very least, stop for an hour and enjoy the setting sun

from some cozy vantage point on the bay. It's no fun at all driving straight into the blinding sunset, and that's exactly what you'll do if you head out for Key West around 6 p.m. on a January evening.

History

KEY LARGO (in Spanish, Long Island) was named by Spanish sailors in the early 1500s. It is one of the oldest named places in Florida. However, for centuries, having a name did not lead to having a population. The isolation, lack of fresh water, mosquitoes, sand fleas, and heat prevented much of anything at all from happening until several pineapple plantations got the civilization ball rolling in the later half of the 1800s.

Archaeologists have uncovered evidence of an Indian village site in North Key Largo that dates back almost 3,800 years. Thought to be a ceremonial altar, it is a high mound made entirely of coral rocks, each measuring from eight to twelve inches in diameter. The site has been plundered by curiosity seekers as well as campers from a nearby campground, who use the rocks for encircling camp fires. In the 1950s, before the rocks were pilfered, the mound was 15 feet high, 100 feet long, and 15 feet wide, with a flat top and several wide ramps leading to it.

In the mid-1800s, several families received land grants to settle in the Key Largo area, but not one of them survived the harsh environment, and the area remained unsettled.

Then in 1866 a successful Key West wrecker named Ben Baker, perhaps growing weary of the seafaring life, planted 6,000 pineapple plants on a large piece of property he owned in then-desolate Key Largo. Baker reaped a very profitable harvest from that first crop, which encouraged other farmers also to begin growing pineapples. For the next forty years, pineapple farmers slashed and burned huge areas of tropical hardwood trees to make way for the pineapple plantations that provided jobs and livelihoods for the area's sparse citizenry. Pineapple workers were often native Bahamians who were accustomed to the harsh environment, and were unable to find work on their own islands.

One acre of land yielded nearly 7,000 pineapples in eighteen months. But making a harvest pay was not always easy. Ripe pineapples were transported to Key West on small schooners and then loaded onto larger ships bound for northern cities. Transporting perishable cargo in the days before refrigeration was an often frustrating business. Getting the fruit to market before it began to rot depended mainly upon favorable weather conditions.

In 1906, the Overseas Railroad linked the Upper Keys communities to the mainland. Plantation owners had hoped that the railroad would help overcome their shipping problems, but in that same year a hurricane destroyed enormous tracts of pineapple plants, then came a devastating blight. Those events marked the end of pineapple farming in the Keys.

The Overseas Railroad linked the Upper Keys communities with the mainland, but having a train station didn't promote a population boom in Key Largo. Even after the turn of the century, panthers, crocodiles, alligators, bobcats and huge populations of mosquitoes and sand flies continued to proliferate. Without jobs or fresh water or electricity or telephone service, the Upper Keys were understandably unappealing to settlers.

But all of that began to change when, in 1942, fresh water flowed into the Keys via a pipeline from Florida's mainland. The pipeline, built by the U.S. Navy, ran 130 miles all the way to Key West. Electricity also became available in Key Largo through a private enterprise around the same time. With those amenities in place, and property selling for as little as $110 an acre, Key Largo began to attract developers.

Meanwhile, far away in the south of France, Jacques Cousteau and Emile Gagnan were testing the world's first self-contained underwater breathing apparatus or, SCUBA. The invention was to revolutionize the sport of underwater diving. Before 1950, skin and scuba diving were known to very few people because of the expense and scarcity of equipment. As the development of sport diving equipment evolved, making the reef more available to the general public, so did Key Largo's fame as one of the world's most important diving centers.

In 1952, mosquito control arrived in the Keys, wiping out the most profound of the Upper Keys detriments to development. Homes, schools and churches were built; businesses, particularly those serving the tourist trade, were established to respond to the burgeoning trend of middle class folks seeking out vacation getaways. From the late 1950s onward, Key Largo's population and business community boomed.

Key Largo, The Movie

Humphrey Bogart plays a good guy. Edward G. Robinson plays a bad guy. Lauren Bacall is a beautiful young war widow. Lionel Barrymore is a lovable old gent, father of Bogie's army buddy who died in the war. Bogart has come to Key Largo to meet his dead army buddy's dad and wife, who run a hotel. Guests at the hotel are a gang of bootleggers, who take the other people in the hotel hostage when a hurricane threatens and their plans are blown off course. After the storm, the bad guys kidnap Bogart and force him to pilot the boat full of rum. But Bogart is too smart for them, see. He quickly knocks off the bootleggers and turns the boat around for Key Largo.

In the last scene of the film, Bacall gets word that Bogie is on his way back. She joyfully rushes to the windows, pushes aside the curtains, and lustily slams open the shutters. Bright sunlight pours into the Key Largo Hotel. The storm is over. The sun is shining. Happy days are here again!

All this, and neither Bogie nor Bacall ever set foot in the Florida Keys. Most of the movie *Key Largo* was shot on a sound stage in California. But that's beside the point to the people of Key Largo. Never have you seen a town so thoroughly milk an opportunity.

Key Largo, The Song

In 1980, songwriter Bertie Higgins's girlfriend Beverly told him she wanted to end their romance. "I figured the only way I could get her attention was to get a song on the radio," Higgins says. So he wrote the song "Key Largo," based on the couple's many romantic times here. In 1982, the song was a smash hit. Beverly married Bertie and they had two kids.

Higgins grew up in Tarpon Springs, Florida, and has been coming to the Keys since he was a little kid. Other Bertie Higgins songs are "Just Another Day in Paradise" and "Casa Blanca." What he needs now is another song on the radio... Beverly's gone again.

Historic Sites

The African Queen & The Thayer
Holiday Harbour Marina, MM 100 Oceanside ✶ 451-4655

You've got to admire the people at the Key Largo Holiday Inn for taking a couple of boats with illustrious pasts—the *African Queen* and the *Thayer IV*—and blending them into a theme that is used again and again throughout the resort. The gift shop carries black-and-white poster-sized photos of Humphrey Bogart and Katherine Hepburn. You can buy hats and shirts like the ones they wore in the film *The African Queen*. And after you look through the gift shop, you can have a sandwich at Bogie's Cafe.

If you remember watching the the *African Queen* floating through the jungle in the film, you probably remember the boat as being a bigger vessel than it actually is. When you see it in real life, it's quite small and

The African Queen

plain. Sometimes the *African Queen* goes on the road to make guest appearances in other places. Sometimes her aging engine is out of order, but other times when everything is working just fine, she will take you for a ride. An older friend of mine went for a ride on the *African Queen* and thought it was one of the high points of his life! Others will find the trip quite tame, no matter how illustrious the stars who once occupied it may have been.

Charter groups of up to fifteen can rent the 1912, thirty-foot English steam-powered *African Queen* for a party or wedding or whatever they like. Call for details.

The battered-looking Chris Craft baking in the sun in the white pea-rock yard by the Holiday Inn pool is supposed to be the *Thayer IV,* which appeared in the Oscar-winning film *On Golden Pond.* But recently one of the ladies at the counter in the Bogie, Bacall and Katherine Hepburn-themed Holiday Inn gift shop, told me that the real *Thayer* is in storage because the tropical sun was frying it into oblivion. The one in the yard is the real *Thayer's* movie double.

The Community Center Building
MM 91.7 Oceanside ❧ 451-9401

Originally, this neat little building was a Methodist church, located somewhere on the other side of the street. Later, when it was a masonic lodge, the masons moved the building to the oceanside of the Overseas Highway where it still stands today. It was built of debris following the infamous 1935 hurricane, and indeed the beams are old and battered but also substantial looking. Now, it houses a real estate company.

The Albury House
MM 91.7 Oceanside

When a Key Largo postmaster named Albury built his island home in 1913, he used huge beams at the foundation so that, in the event of hurricanes, the house would float. And that's exactly what it did when the 1935 Labor Day Hurricane hit the Upper Keys. Albury's house knocked the Key Largo train station over on its side, and then, when the waters receded, ended up sitting squarely on top of it. They don't build 'em like that anymore.

Caribbean Club
MM 104 Bayside ✷ 451-9970

Locals call it "the Crib". Supposedly one or two exterior scenes for the movie *Key Largo* were filmed here, although the majority of the film was shot on a Hollywood sound stage. Still, a big sign out front says: "Where the famous movie *Key Largo* was filmed." A serious drinker's bar, this place opens daily at 7 a.m. and stays open until 4 a.m. If you show up for a Bloody Mary first thing in the morning, no one will look twice. Why not enjoy your eye-opener at a picnic table out back with everybody else? Live music some nights is enjoyed by a mixed clientele of locals, tourists, and curiosity seekers. You're as likely to spot a bona fide Keys character here as anywhere else. At the Waverunner rental place next door to the Caribbean Club, we spotted a topless girl sunbathing as the traffic on the Overseas Highway sped past. Also, bikers! Happy hour is a busy time at the Caribbean, so prices must be very good, because not one person came outside to ogle the topless girl in the yard next door. Filming for the edgy movie *Blood & Wine*, starring Jack Nicholson, Michael Caine, and Jennifer Lopez, closed the Caribbean Club down for a week in January 1996. And this time, the stars themselves showed up, unlike Bogie and Bacall.

Join us on the worldwide web
www.junekeith.com

John Pennekamp
Coral Reef State Park

John Pennekamp Coral Reef State Park
MM 102.5 Oceanside ✸ 451-1202 or 451-1621

The gates to this hugely popular state park open daily at 8 a.m., often to a line of waiting cars. On particularly busy days, the park has been known to reach capacity crowds and shut its gates as early as 9:30 a.m. At first glance the park might seem small, but actually it is quite large, encompassing 53,660 acres of submerged land and 2,350 acres of uplands. You can see just about the entire above-ground areas of the park from the observation tower. Well over a million people visit the park annually.

This is America's first and only underwater state park. We can thank *Miami Herald* newspaper editor John Pennekamp for alerting his readers and government leaders to the importance of preserving America's only living coral reef. Before the 1960s when Pennekamp began writing his fiery editorials urging Washington to take a stand on maintaining South Florida's unique natural assets, tourists and divers were well on their way to destroying the reef's population of queen conch, live coral, and tropical fish. Aggressive visitors carved, tore or even dynamited chunks of living coral for souvenirs, perhaps believing that what they were taking away would be replaced by nature. Or perhaps not thinking at all.

In 1963 a gift of several million dollars was anonymously donated to the Florida Park Service for use in acquiring the location of the park's headquarters.

The Coral Reef Theater

A very comfortable visitor center features a giant reconstruction of a living patch reef in a floor-to-ceiling circular aquarium. It is the first opportunity most people have to observe the bright, little inhabitants of the underwater world—swimming, eating and resting, just as they do at the reef. Visitors can then check out several topnotch natural history exhibits, too.

Perhaps later your kids will have questions about sharks, eels, and other scary creatures of the deep. Find the park marine biologist in the theater, who will be happy to answer them.

In the Reef Theater a terrific slide show provides an enormous amount of education and much that you need to know to negotiate the reef. You learn how delicate the living reef is and how you can do your part to preserve it for future generations: simple stuff like not touching the coral and using diving buoys instead of anchoring; these make a big difference. After you visit the Reef Theater, you'll understand why reef etiquette is so vitally important.

Warning: nothing will whet your appetite for a visit to the reef like a visit to the Reef Theater first.

The coral reef

Pennekamp Diving

The living reefs are spectacular aquatic gardens of hard and soft corals. The reef is home to 600 species of tropical fish—more fish by far than in any other reef in the world, thanks to its proximity to the grasslands and mangroves of the Florida Bay, spawning grounds to hundreds of species.

These reefs provide 75% of the sport fish and 90% of the commercially-harvested sealife in South Florida.

Along with the 600 varieties of tropical fish there are more than fifty species of hard and soft corals live there too, with fanciful names like stag, elkhorn, brain, and tree. Soft corals are the fans and whips that undulate in the soft currents. Diving trips to the reef, both snorkel and SCUBA, are managed by the Coral Reef Park Company. Snorkeling tours depart three times a day and cost around $26 per person. SCUBA trips leave twice a day and cost a few dollars more. Combined snorkeling and sailing on a half-day combo tour aboard a 38-foot catamaran are around $39 per person. Diving instruction and equipment are available for an extra charge.

Michelle Lane manages the dive shop inside John Pennekamp State Park. Like many of the people who live and work in Key Largo, Michelle has enormous enthusiasm for diving America's only living reef and truly loves getting people out onto the ocean and into the water. Michelle is proud that her facility has been awarded the 5 Star Gold Palm designation from PADI.

"Diving never gets old," she says. "It's always different, every time you go."

The last time I talked to the dive people at the park, they told me that the term "diving" refers to SCUBA diving only. Otherwise, it's snorkeling. If you call to book a boat, or get information, make sure you say which you mean.

Pennekamp Beach

For the non-diver there are beaches, albeit man-made, and not at all wild or rugged, or terribly tropical. Still, they're nice enough for a couple of hours. Look for a sunken Spanish galleon off one beach where beginning snorkelers can practice and even go home with true stories of wreck diving. You can enjoy swimming, picnicking, and fishing, and boat ramp access on the beach, too. If all you want to do is lie in the sun while the rest of the gang heads out for the reef, fine. You'll be happy here—and close to shelter, food and water.

Pennekamp Camping 800-326-3521

The way you go about booking a camping site at Pennekamp Park, as well as all of Florida's state parks, has changed. "Reserve America", a private agency, now makes all reservations for camping. Call them at 800-326-3521. In every park, only ten percent of the sites are left open and available daily on a first-come, first-served basis. During the summer months your chances of finding a site are good, but during the season, from around mid-December through April, procuring a camping site in the state park without a reservation is a hit-or-miss affair. Ninety percent of the campsites are booked through Reserve America. And you can reserve a campsite up to 11 months in advance. If you can, do.

The maximum stay in a state park campground is two weeks. Yes, some campers stay for two weeks, drive out of the park, and then drive in again to get around the regulation. But such maneuvers don't work very easily in wintertime.

At the Pennekamp Park, you'll have a dump site but no individual sewer hookups. Forty-seven campsites for tents or RVs each cost around $26 per night. Electricity is an additional $2 per day. Scouts or school groups can stay in the youth camping area, which is quite inexpensive at $2 per youth, and $3 per adult, for up to twenty-four people, providing most of them are kids. This is for tent camping only, and this is a no-frill camping area. There's no water or electricity. And you have to walk in. No cars allowed.

Camp bathhouses are pristine, and the campsite areas are also clean and well maintained. The majority of the campers are in long, sophisticated RV campers; a few are in tents. During summer months tents are hot; bugs are hellish. In summertime, those big, mobile campers make the most sense. Pennekamp campers have 24-hour access to the beaches and the areas throughout the park that are often mobbed by day. (Not the buildings, of course.) Imagine a full moon rising over the sandy-edged lagoon....

All can enjoy the interpretive programs, nature walks and talks at Pennekamp. An ever-popular presentation is the Wednesday night "Delicate Balance of Nature" series. Audiences of up to one hundred nature lovers turn out for these free lectures. Friday evenings, January, February, and March, join community campfires. For a list of Wednesday night talks scheduled during your visit, phone the ranger station during daylight hours.

If you are planning to tent camp, camp managers advise you to bring air mattresses for more comfortable sleeping. Remember, the Keys are actually the gnarly spine of an ancient coral reef. In the summertime, stay in a spot where you can sign on for an electricity hook-up, and bring a fan. If you're lucky, the fan will blow off some of the bugs.

To Know More

The brochures and charts created for John Pennekamp Park are translated into German, French, and Spanish. Write John Pennekamp Coral Reef Park, P.O. Box 487, Key Largo, FL 33037, or phone the Coral Park Company at 305-451-1621, for information on diving and scuba tours and boat rentals. For camping information and reservations, in this park or any other Florida state park, phone Reserve America at 800-326-3521.

Diving

Getting Your Divers License

The Professional Association of Diving Instructors, or PADI, has designed a Discover SCUBA Diving course for tourists. Local instructors call it the "resort course" and in it you'll learn enough to know whether or not you like SCUBA diving enough to get further certification, which you really will need to take up the sport. The resort course is offered just about anywhere you find PADI divers. Or, ask about it your hotel. The class begins early in the morning, breaks for lunch and then boats out to the reef for two instructor-accompanied dives. The course costs around $175 per person. Sometimes you'll get a deal if you have a group.

If, after the resort course, you decide to go for the three-day (usually 3, sometimes 4) PADI certification course, you may get a break on the price if you take the course at the same place you took the resort course. Generally it will cost you around $500. You'll need some books and supplies, too.

PADI certification is recognized all over the world. Some people will take the preliminary instruction for certification in their hometowns and then complete the final diving segments of the course here in the Keys. Remember, hours spent on the resort course do not count toward a full certification course, the driver's license of diving. The resort course is a one-shot deal—instant gratification for people in a hurry. If you are unsure whether or not you are interested in diving as a lifelong avocation and have only a day or two in the Keys, the resort course is probably for you. If you're certain that you're going to SCUBA frequently, skip the resort course and plan your visit to the Keys around the certification course, or take it in your hometown, if possible, before you get here.

For information about the dive courses described here, and a few others, like the Advanced Course, Rescue Diver Course, and Divemaster Course, ask at any dive shop.

Some Famous Dives

Key Largo Dry Rocks and The Christ of the Abyss Statue

"This is as close as most of you will ever get to Jesus," the dive master says as you prepare to enter the water for a look at the submerged Christ of the Abyss statue. The 4,000-pound, nine-foot sculpture stands in twenty-five feet of water; it's a replica of a statue of the same name located in the water off Genoa, Italy. This underwater sculpture, located six miles east-northeast of Key Largo's South Cut, is said to be the most photographed underwater sculpture in the world. The famous statue was donated to the Underwater Society of America by an Italian diving group in 1961, but it wasn't until 1965 that it was placed in the park. Christ's hands are raised toward the surface, gesturing a welcome to hundreds of daily visitors. It's the area's most requested snorkel dive, and it really is dramatic. Several diving lovers have been married here.

Molasses Reef

It's the most popular dive destination in the world! Five miles straight out from Key Largo, the Molasses Reef features a classic spur-and-groove pattern. (Spurs are the high towers of coral; grooves are the areas of sand that run between them.) This spectacular and radiantly healthy reef covers around seventeen acres, and contains several variant types of topography. The Molasses Reef begins near the water's surface and slopes away from the light to a depth of fifty-five feet. Schools of spadefish, permit, goatfish, and horse-eye jacks share the reef with turtles and manta rays. Molasses Reef is the sole destination of area glass bottomed boat tours as well as many smaller dive boats. Visibility is usually good here, thanks to a regular flushing from the north-flowing Gulf Stream current.

French Reef

North of Molasses, about four-and-a-half miles southeast of Key Largo's South Cut, the reef sits below forty-five feet of water and is marked by a black piling. Scuba divers swim through cave-like passages filled with small fish; a favorite is Christmas Tree Cave.

The Elbow

Where the reef makes a sharp turn back toward the shore, this part takes on a crook-like, elbow formation. The water is clear here, thanks to its proximity to the Gulf Stream, so you can see a couple of moray eels as well as angelfish, filefish and barracuda. The *City of Washington* wreck is located in this area, too, about twenty-five feet below the water's surface. Also, Mike's Wreck—which is not actually the true name of the sunken ship. It's unknown, so a diver named Mike decided to name it after himself. A third wreck nearby is the subject of much controversy. Nobody knows its true name either, and no one has come along to name it in the meantime.

Grecian Rocks/White Banks

About three-fourths of a mile south/southwest of the Christ of the Abyss area, this dive is popular with snorkelers because the water is shallow, twenty-five feet at deepest. In fact, in some areas the corals nearly touch the surface, so watch your belly. Don't touch the corals; just look!

The Carysfort Light

Because this area is so far north—nearly five-and-a-half miles from Key Largo Harbor—few dive boats travel here. It just takes too long to get to it. Divers, after all, would rather be in the water doing what they came to do rather than cruising over the water on their way to some far-flung area of the reef.

The Carysfort Lighthouse marks a reef that is treacherous for boats but divine for divers. The shallow waters around the 112-foot lighthouse are rich with hard corals and schools of grunts, angelfish, parrotfish, butterflyfish and pufferfish. It's also rich with great history.

In the early 1800s, the Carysfort Reef, which got its name from the wreck of the HMS *Carysfort* that went aground here in 1770, was considered the most dangerous to shipping of all the reefs in the Keys. In 1826, the U.S. government anchored a lightboat here to warn vessels away from the treacherous shoals. The seven men who lived aboard the lightboat one day rowed to the shore, and then to an unsettled wilderness, to plant a garden of vegetables and fruit. That garden is believed to have been in the area that is today the headquarters of Pennekamp State Park.

In June 1837 during the Second Seminole Indian War, another group of men from the lightboat rowed ashore for some fresh supplies from their garden and were ambushed by a band of Seminole warriors. Two men were killed that day; one was Captain John Whalton, whose descendants live in the Keys today.

In 1852 the lightboat finally was replaced by the Carysfort Reef Lighthouse, the first of the six iron screw-pile structures that light the Florida Keys reefs today.

The Duane and Bibb

Two Coast Guard cutters were sunk intentionally to form an artificial reef a mile south of Molasses Reef. The twin 327-foot boats were laid to rest on a white sand bottom in 1987. The *Duane* landed upright with its crow's nest just sixty feet below the surface; the *Bibb* lies one hundred feet deep. Visibility is good, but the current is sometimes strong enough to make diving inadvisable. This is a dive for expert scuba divers, not because of the depth—although it is deep—but because of that powerful current.

Aquarius Underwater Habitat

For scuba divers only, this underwater habitat rests in sixty feet of water and, for up to nine days at a time, is home to researchers working for the marine sanctuary. A support barge on the surface marks the location of the *Aquarius*.

City of Washington Wreck

Just offshore of the Elbow reef lies the remains of the ship *City of Washington*. The wreck, in twenty to thirty-five feet of water, is known for its abundant and friendly fish population. Besides the wildlife, the scattered wreckage provides an excellent backdrop for underwater photography.

The Benwood Wreck

The Benwood was a 285-foot-long freighter, accidentally rammed while running without lights during WWII, and then torpedoed by a German submarine as it attempted to ground itself for later salvage. Its hull now lies in around fifty feet of water and is home to several huge groupers.

Spiegel Grove

The largest vessel ever intentionally sunk as an artificial reef. The vessel is 510 feet in length, 84 feet wide. This is a deep dive, and conditions and currents can get rough. Dive charters will take only the most qualified divers to the site.

Key Largo Undersea Park's Emerald Lagoon
MM 103.5,Oceanside Transylvania Ave. ✆ 451-2353

On windy days, the Emerald Lagoon is the busiest dive site around because it's protected from strong winds so the water doesn't get choppy or stirred up. That's why people say, "There's no such thing as a bad day in the Emerald Lagoon." But that's not the only reason to visit the lagoon; because the habitat is so different here from that of the reef, you will see different sealife as well as a shipwreck and several archaeological sites. Sometimes a manatee finds its way into the lagoon, to the great joy of staff and visitors alike.

Dive Shops & Charters

Amoray Dive Resort
MM 104.5 Bayside ✆ 800-4-AMORAY

Amy Slate has been performing underwater weddings for over two decades. She'll supply tuxedo T-shirts, veils, pearls, and conch shell bouquets to couples taking the big plunge. Receptions are often held on the *Amoray Diver*, a 45-foot catamaran. If you want to do it beneath the surface, call the Amoray Resorts wedding coordinator, and they will hook you up with dive photographers and videographers, entertainers and caterers. Then you can spend your diving honeymoon at the Amoray Resort. This is a very popular way to marry. Amy Slate performs around three weddings a week during the winter season. By the way, you'll also find lots of other stay/dive packages at the Amoray Dive Resort.

It's a Dive
MM 102.5 Bayside, Marriott's Key Largo Bay Beach Resort
453-9881 • 800-809-9881

What a name, huh? But it was recognized as the number-one day-boat operator in a readers' poll of *Scuba Diving Magazine*. "It's a Dive" also ranked number three for best operation in the United States. We spent an hour talking to a wonderfully kind and helpful young woman at It's A Dive and came away thinking she was the nicest person we'd ever met. Then we wandered through many more dive shops and discovered that dive people are simply a wonderful bunch! It's A Dive has added a second location at the Hampton Inn in Islamorada. For that shop call **866-664-0095**. The two locations share the same great guides, captains, and instructors.

John Pennekamp Coral Reef State Park
MM 102.5 Oceanside • 451-1202 • 451-1621

Here's a great dive concession with terrific employees, and these state park prices seem a tad lower than private businesses. See the John Pennekamp Park Diving section for more on this shop.

Sea Dwellers
MM 100 Bayside • 451-3640 • 800-451-3640

This is a PADI 5-Star facility, which means they offer all levels of dive instruction, from basic certification to Divemaster or Master SCUBA Diver. Rob Haff and Jeff Cleary, the guys who own and operate the Sea Dwellers Dive Center, have been living in Key Largo and introducing visitors to the wonders of the deep for over 25 years! And they do it with such enthusiasm and excitement you'd never dream they're old hands at this stuff. In their brochure they promise to make every dive trip an extraordinary adventure, and by golly, that's just what they do.

Sea Dwellers offers SCUBA and snorkel trips daily, leaving from the Holiday Inn Marina, to diving sites in the Pennekamp Park (America's first and only underwater state park) and the Florida Keys National Marine Sanctuary. They operate two custom-built dive boats, crewed by friendly, helpful young folks who know the reef as well as you know your bathtub. Never snorkeled before? No problem. With a little help you'll get the hang of it in no time.

Lots of people like booking the Sea Dwellers Dive Adventure packages. You stay at the Holiday Inn, get a daily continental breakfast, and a couple of dives each day, plus dive equipment, for snorkelers as well as SCUBA divers. There are several packages, so if you're interested call Sea Dwellers and ask for information.

Sharky's Dive Center
MM 106.2 Bayside 451-5533 • 800-935-3483

This is Sharkey's central shop in the Keys, where you come to buy or rent anything to snorkel or SCUBA diving, and to book dice trips on one of Sharkey's amazing vessels.What a name, huh? But it was recognized as the number-one day-boat. The most famous is Sharkey's Machine, a double-decker dive boat that is still the only one of its kind in the islands, and the Extreme Machine. Divers on sharkey's boats appreciate the fresh water showers, and cold free water on every trip. Bring your own refreshments and chill them on Sharkey's ice.

Sharkey's prices are competitive with other dive tours in the area, and Sharkey's offers some great rates on family packages, like a terrific deal on a snorkel trip for two adults and two kids, and a two-day snorkel package for adults. If you don't have equipment, they'll rent it to you.

Why choose Sharkey's? "We have the fastest and newest toys," one happy Sharkey's employee says.

Dolphins In Paradise

OLPHINS ARE WONDERFUL, mysterious and very much at home in the waters of the Florida Keys. For many people, there is no greater thrill than to see dolphins up close and enjoy their remarkably sweet vibes. Many tourists list their interest in dolphins as a prime motivation for visiting the Florida Keys, where dolphins are as much an icon as palm trees.

For centuries man has been intrigued with the sea's most popular denizen. Dolphins are playful, sociable and smart, and they appear to enjoy humans as much as humans enjoy them. Do dolphins have a natural affinity for man? No, says one trainer, but, he adds, dolphins in captivity do come to associate humans with fun, toys and food.

Caring for dolphins is a much-coveted job in the Keys. Dolphin trainers who often have degrees in psychology or zoology, are dedicated and passionate about their charges, and very patient.

"You don't get a five-hundred-pound animal to do anything it doesn't want to do," says one.

Dolphins, who are very trainable, have excellent long-term memory which enables them to use past experiences to form new judgments. They have highly developed sonar or ultrasound-like mechanisms they use to find objects as small as coins tossed into their areas, and they even have the ability, many trainers believe, to detect tumors in humans.

Dolphins are sexy creatures, too. Males denied sex by the objects of their affection become frustrated and irritable. Dolphins in captivity are taught that sexual excitement, as evidenced by erections that grow to an average length of eighteen inches, is not appropriate when swimming with humans.

Play between dolphins can be surprisingly rough, but they are gentle and cautious with humans, particularly so with those who are physically or mentally challenged. Therapists working with autistic children find that dolphins are inexhaustible when coaxing disturbed children to respond to them. Long after humans have run out of endurance and

patience in dealing with this strange disorder, dolphins will continue
activities to stimulate a child.

This hypersensitivity is one of the dolphin's most remarkable and
endearing charms. Nonetheless, pregnant women are generally not
allowed to swim with dolphins for two reasons. First, a dolphin detecting
two heartbeats in one human may become intrigued and curious and,
sometimes, wholly fascinated with a pregnant woman, ignoring everyone
else for the duration the swim. Second, a startled dolphin can propel
itself at speeds of up to twenty-five miles per hour; this torpedoing dol-

phin could, conceivably, do great harm to a pregnant woman. Though chances of this happening are slim, no one wants to risk it.

Here in the Keys we have Atlantic bottlenose dolphins, which are found along the east coast from New Jersey to the Gulf of Mexico.

Female dolphins tend to stay together, while bachelor males also form their own groups, as do adult males. A lone dolphin in the wild will often seek out human companionship.

When dolphins give birth, they are assisted by companion females, who often stick around to help raise the calf. Dolphins nurse their young up to three years. A mother dolphin is very protective of her first calf, less so with her second, even less with her third, and so on. An adult male dolphin can weigh up to 600 pounds and grow to nine feet long. Females are slightly smaller. Dolphins live for around thirty to forty years.

Dolphins do not drink sea water; they absorb water from the fish they eat. They do not sleep because they do not breathe involuntarily. Instead, they put themselves into a resting state and shut down half of their brains while the other half remains conscious to attend to matters of survival.

The brains of dolphins and humans are about the same size. The odd sounds dolphins make, a series of clicks and whistles, may or may not be a form of dolphin communication. Scientists are not sure, although they do know that each dolphin makes its own distinct sounds, just as humans do.

Because dolphins are such an important part of what makes the Keys wonderful and unique, many opportunities exist here for visitors to observe dolphins, learn about them, and experience a truly rare encounter—a swim with the dolphins.

Since this is one of the most popular activities in the Florida Keys, reservations for classes or swims with dolphins at marine and dolphin centers should be made six to eight weeks in advance at the three facilities listed below. These are the only places in the Keys, at this time, offering the opportunity to swim with dolphins.

A final opportunity, and the one purists like best, is to encounter dolphins in their own territory, the open sea. You might see an impromptu dolphin show performed by dolphins in the wild. We saw one in January at Marathon's Sombrero Beach. Some charter boat captains specialize in knowing where to go to encounter dolphins. Dolphins in the wild socialize when the whim strikes and then disappear in a split second if they catch an odd or threatening vibe.

Dolphin Swims

Dolphins Plus Research Center
MM 100.5, Key Largo ✆ 451-1993

Not a theme park or a show, Dolphins Plus is a research and educational center. How dolphins relate to humans and the dolphin's role in zoo-therapy with disabled children is studied here. The center claims that their dolphins are not captive, since several times each month, they are given the opportunity to swim out of the canal and into the ocean. They *choose* to live at the center.

Two types of dolphin swims are offered at Dolphins Plus, and to participate in either one, you should be a good swimmer, and comfortable in water over your head. You must be experienced with snorkeling equipment for the Natural Swim. First, you'll receive an hour of instruction about dolphins, and learn the names of the dolphins you'll be swimming with. Then you'll swim and dive along side the dolphins for at least 30 minutes. They'll look at you, and you'll look at them, and you may be surprised at the depth of character and personality you'll see in their eyes as they observe you, their guests. You don't make physical contact with them. You're not even allowed to reach out to them. Just swim with them. Children 8 - 12 must be accompanied, in the water, by an adult. Kids 13 to 17 must have an observing parent or guardian present.

You can now swim with sea lions, too. It's new and it's being done here and at a few other places in the Keys.

In the Structured Swim you'll wear a floatation device, and interact hands-on with the dolphins under the direction of a trainer. There is no free swimming and no snorkeling equipment. Kids ages 7 - 12 must be accompanied by an adult. If you don't want to swim with dolphins but are curious about them anyway, it costs only around $10 to take the pre-swim part of the program and stick around to watch your classmates swim with the dolphins. To take the class and the structured swim that follows (you *must* take the class to swim) costs $160 per swimmer. Or buy the Combo Program, both types of swim. Reservations are definitely a must, but during the off season you have a chance of reserving a space on short notice. You'll be asked for a deposit to secure your reservation.

Dolphin Cove
MM 102, Bayside ✺ 451-4060 or 877-365-2683
Sister facility to Dolphins Plus, Dolphin Cove offers one daily Natural Swim ($100) at 9:45 a.m. Three Structured Swims ($150 per swimmer) go on daily, too. Read about these programs in the section about Dolphins Plus on page 495. There is no Combo Package offered here. You will also find several great snorkel trips and environmental tours leaving out of Dolphin Cove daily. Call for information.

Dolphin Care
MM 100 at Ocean. 31 Corrine Place off U.S. Highway 1 ✺ 451-5884
Island Dolphin Care in Key Largo, features recreational, motivational and educational dolphin-assisted therapy programs. Recently they've opened the Fonzietorium, named for Fonzie, the original IDC dolphin. Display tanks with correlating touch-screen interactive activities let children play games while they learn about the marine environment. In addition, visitors can get up-close and personal with Pacific and Atlantic reef creatures, marine predators and seahorses. Families can explore the underwater world together at a handicapped-accessible touch-tank. New displays explain echo location, the dolphins navigation system, and introduce visitors to marine mammals.

Dolphin Research Center
MM 59, Grassy Key ✺ 289-0002
This is the oldest dolphin facility in the Keys, founded in 1946 as "Santini's Porpoise School", a marine educational facility. Swimming with dolphins started here around 35 years ago. The giant statue of a bottlenose dolphin out front is a replica of Mitzi, who starred in the feature-length movie *Flipper*, the forerunner of the television series. Mitzi died here in 1972, but her daughter and grandson are still at the center.

Dolphin swims go on in a natural lagoon of the Gulf of Mexico. The trained dolphins are retained by plastic mesh fencing. Here, as in all dolphin facilities, before you swim with dolphins you must learn about them. You'll be briefed on how to conduct yourself and what to expect of them during your twenty-minute swim. The rule of thumb is always this: swim as though there were no dolphins in the water at all. Play innocent. You will also be advised to use your arms as little as possible to avoid alarming the dolphins. No other creature swims like a human, instructors warn.

Although there are long waits to swim with the dolphins most of the time, there are times when people don't show up and it is possible to walk right in and take a swim with a dolphin. Call before you write it off completely. Children under 12 must be accompanied by an adult. You should plan on spending three-and-a-half hours on this, since the training is considerably longer at this facility than at the others.

Theater of the Sea
MM 84.5 Oceanside, Islamorada • 664-2431

You must speak and understand English, not be pregnant, or under the influence of drugs and alcohol to swim with the dolphins here. You are also required to be at least five years old. Kids aged 5, 6, or 7 must be accompanied by a parent or guardian. Thirty-minute structured dolphin swim is preceded by a half-hour of instruction. Swimming is in a natural ocean water lagoon with trained dolphins and includes fun interaction like the dolphin foot push, dorsal tow, and kisses. You may get to snorkel free form for a while, too. Price of the swim includes admission to the park's fine marine shows and a ride on the bottomless boat.

An alternative to the dolphin swim is a three-hour dolphin/sea lion trainer-for-a-day program. For this, you don't even need to get wet, but you might get splashed a little when you feed the dolphins and the sea lions their lunch. You'll learn to prepare fish for dolphins to eat, and discover why and how dolphins do the quirky things they do. You'll learn how these remarkable creatures are trained to perform so nicely for humans. But remember, you won't get to swim with them in this program. There is no guarantee that you will not beg to sign up for a swim with the dolphins or sea lions after you spend a few hours learning about them.

So many people contact the Theater of the Sea about jobs as dolphin trainers that they have a pre-printed sheet of information. Write for it or any other information about the dolphin programs.

Dolphin Encounters

Dolphin Watch
Key West ☎ 294-6306

Captains Alma Armendariz, John Baltzell and Ron Canning take turns piloting their boat out into the wild to look for dolphins, and they know where to find them. They've been visiting one particular pod of dolphins for over a decade. The captains decide where to look for the dolphins based on a number of varying factors each day: the weather, the phase of the moon, the tides, and the number of children in the party. Dolphins love human children and they also love dogs. Captain Alma says that observing dolphins leaping and chasing fish in their natural habitat is an amazing experience, and the captains have the utmost respect for their freedom and privacy, too. Up to six people can go aboard the 31-foot catamaran "Patty C" for a four-hour cruise. The charge is $85 a person, and there is a four-person minimum. It is important to call ahead for reservations; call also for a brochure or for more information.

Dolphin Connection at Hawk's Cay Resort & Marina
MM 61, Duck Key ☎ 289-9975 ☎ 888-814-9154

Dolphins live in a fenced-in, saltwater lagoon along the coast of Hawk's Cay. You do not swim with the dolphins here, but you can get into waist-deep water and touch, feed and play with them. The cost is around $130, less if you're a guest of Hawk's Cay Resort. Also Dockside Dolphin is a great adventure for children and families. Participants do not get into the water with the dolphins, but play a few games with them from the dock. Trainer for a Day is another 3 hour training course. Two to a class, students get to see the in side of the captured dolphin world, the part about handling the frozen fish they eat and cleaning up after a day of interacting with humans. The course is not cheap, around $285. But if your child is talking about a career in marine biology -- so many kids are these days- - this might be an ideal introduction. Call the toll-free number above for a description of all three programs. You need to make reservations way in advance.

Natural Wonders

Harry Harris Park
MM 92.5, Oceanside

Follow the signs to the park and, on the way, as you pass through a residential area, you'll see where the waitresses, fishing guides and shopkeepers of Key Largo actually live. (This is a good destination for bicyclists—a chance to get away from the noisy, beaten path.)

Harry Harris Park is the site of one of the Upper Keys earliest settlements, the town of Planter. In the late 1800s, Planter had seven farms, a chapel, a post office, a general store and several piers. Pineapples were the main crop. But in 1906, and again in 1909, Planter was hit by devastating hurricanes. When the pineapple business began to fail due not

Pineapple

only to these hurricanes but poor agricultural procedures, and blights, people began leaving for higher ground and easier lives elsewhere. By the end of 1942, nothing was left of Planter but memories.

This same site is now Harry Harris Park, which is a pretty super little park containing a man-made lagoon with clear ocean water, a well-maintained beach, a kid-pleasing playground, and rest rooms, picnic tables and BBQ grills so clean you'll want to run out and buy charcoal and hamburgers. The park, rarely crowded, opens at sunrise and closes at sunset. On weekdays it's free and open to the public; on weekends and holidays, visitors from outside of Monroe County—your license plate gives you away—must pay $5 per person to enter and $10 to use the recently upgraded boat ramp. All kids under 12 always enter for free, no matter where they're from.

The county employee who sits in the booth at the park's entrance will kindly entertain your questions about the beach, the birds and the islands you spot from the shoreline. Maybe he doesn't know all the answers, but he's friendly and helpful, and he's happy for the diversion.

Dolphins Plus Research Center
MM 100.5 Oceanside (Call ahead for directions) ✆ 451-1993
"Experience the thrill of swimming with the dolphins" says the brochure. Understand that this is not an amusement park or a dolphin show. For $10 you can learn a lot about the dolphins who live here. You get to know their personality traits, their names, and then, you can watch them interact with humans. Take photos or buy a dolphin themed souvenir in the gift shop. Maybe you'll decide you want to get into the water with them. Sometimes you can get lucky and find yourself in the swim by that afternoon. But not usually. They're booked way in advance. (See page 495 to learn about swimming with the dolphins.)

Everglades National Park
242-7700
Florida's river of grass is a 1.5-million acre ecosystem and the only one of its kind in the world. The park runs west from the bay side of Key Largo, around the southwest corner of the Florida mainland and then north all the way to Everglades City. Much of the Florida Bay is within its nearly

10,700 square miles. Within the park live 300 species of birds, plus alligators, crocodiles, deer and bobcats. Mosquitoes can be horrific, especially in the spring and summer. You'll definitely need bug repellent if you venture into these amazing marine wilds. Eco-tours and fishing expeditions easily access the park via the Florida Bay. While it is possible to rent a skiff and head into the Everglades National Park on your own, it is not advisable. Hire a guide and leave the driving to the experts. The park is a huge labyrinth of creeks, lakes, rivers and shallow plains of seagrass.

State Road 9336 is the main road into and out of Everglades National Park. To get to the closest entrance to SR 9336, you must go to Homestead, approximately twenty-two miles north of Key Largo.

For a list of available guided tours as well as canoeing, fishing, camping and hiking information and accommodations inside the park, call 242-7700. Or write: Park Headquarters, 40001 State Road 9336, Homestead, FL 33034.

Geology Lesson at MM 103

For a look at the geological makeup of the Upper Keys' fossilized coral rock, stop at the bridge that crosses over the Marvin D. Adams waterway. The banks of the man-made cut, a neat cross-slice through the island, provide a look into the make-up of the coral rock foundation of the Upper Keys: staghorn coral, coral heads, and other formations are petrified in the walls. It's really difficult to slow down enough to see anything close up, so stop the car, get out, and walk—carefully, with an eye out for traffic.

Wild Bird Rehabilitation Center
Mile Marker 93.6 Bayside ✷ 852-4486

Although the primary purpose of the center is to provide emergency and recuperative care to injured birds, the bird center has evolved into a popular nature information center. Several daily tours through the area and on a boardwalk along the Florida Bay feature plants, mangroves, and berry trees that are food to birds, but poison to man! The 5.5 acre sanctuary is kept as close to the sea birds' natural habitat as possible.

Injured birds are brought to the center for rehabilitation. Pelicans, which are quite comfortable around people, are the center's biggest cus-

Pelican

tomers. Director and founder Laura Quinn says that birds who hang around humans get into lots of trouble. Most of their injuries are from baited hooks and fishing line carelessly tossed aside by fishermen. You'll recognize the birds' broken wings by the bright blue "casts" they wear on the injured appendage. The center is also a convalescent center for cormorants, egrets, herons, and the rarely seen roseate spoonbills. You will see treatment areas and the laboratory. If you are lucky enough to see a roseate spoonbill, you'll understand why the fantastic pink feathers of the bird were so attractive to hat designers in the years before the world understood that the supply of birds was finite. They were nearly done in for their fine plumes! There are exhibits designed to educate the public on ways of ensuring the safety of these fascinating creatures.

This is a non-profit organization and there is no admission fee, but you will have the opportunity to contribute money toward the upkeep of

Great white heron

the natural hammock and the medicines, medical supplies and food the birds consume in great quantities. Being around at lunchtime is great fun. You can't imagine how clumsy hungry pelicans are on dry land! The center is not government-funded and not likely to be in the near future. It is solely supported by private donations. Quinn started the bird sanctuary in 1991. Since then, she says, the Keys environment has become

more and more perilous for birds, and the center is constantly full of
needy birds. Some of the birds you'll see are permanently disabled and
live at the center full-time. However, Laura's goal is to rehabilitate the
injured birds and send them back out into the wild.

Laura's cats share the grounds with birds here, and all seems to go
well. You can see Laura's artwork, wooden bird carvings, in the gift shop.
Laura Quinn is a special woman, and so are the volunteers who work
with her.

Key Largo Hammocks State Botanical Site
Route 905, Upper Key Largo
451-1202 (Pennekamp Park Ranger Station)

This fascinating hammock is also called "Port Bougainvillea" and is
located less than half a mile before or after U.S. Route 1 and SR 905
converge in Key Largo, depending upon which way you're headed. One
thousand acres of tropical hardwood forest were partially developed
before the State of Florida began acquiring the property for the formation
of the present Key Largo Hammock in 1982. Port Bougainvillea was
planned to be a massive community of pink stucco condos smack in the
heart of a natural habitat to nearly all of the Keys twenty-two endangered species. Environmentalists fought wildly to keep the place holy.
And what a glorious battle it was! You can still see the entrance gate and
the proliferation of bougainvillea planted there by hopeful developers.
Today, it looks a little like the faded entrance to an abandoned southern
plantation.

If you take a good look at the fountain just past the beginning of the
trail, you'll get some idea of just how grand a place Port Bougainvillea
was to have been. Now, that fountain is a gigantic birdbath serving several species of birds. The turkey buzzards seem not to mind a human or
two walking by, but the great blue herons mind very much and lift off
into the sky with a noisy and dramatic shudder of their wings the minute
you approach.

At 10 a.m. on Thursdays and Sundays Pennekamp park rangers lead
nature walks through the botanical site. Otherwise, brochures at the
entrance will lead you on a self-guided tour. Plants and animals that live
in the area include poisonwood, lignumvitae, dollar orchid, prickly apple
cactus, golden leatherfern, American crocodile, and Key Largo cotton

mouse. For information about the area and the guided tours, call the Pennekamp Park Ranger Station.

A Very Cool Library

Key Largo Library
MM 101.5, in Tradewinds Plaza ✸ 451-2396
As libraries go, this one's quite large and plush, with soft-carpeted floors and comfortable reading tables. Good surplus books are on sale for 50¢; surplus magazines and softcover books are free. On exhibit are a huge shell collection and a tiny raft made of canvas and rope and inner tubes that carried four Cubans to Florida. It seems unbelievable that the flimsy raft did the job.

Don't miss the racks with pamphlets and brochures on local attractions and natural wonders. A family could easily spend a hot afternoon cooling off in the air-conditioned environs of the Key Largo Library and, as part of the deal, come away a bit wiser. The library is open every day except Sunday from 10 a.m. till 6 p.m. and until 8 p.m. on Monday and Wednesday. Call ahead for information on Saturday morning children's programs.

Big Fun

Biking

A bicycle and walking path begins at MM 106 and runs beside the Overseas Highway all the way down to MM 91. Eventually it will run smoothly, all the way to MM 0 in Key West. Right now it's sometimes there and sometimes not there. The completed segments of the trail are nicely paved and make for good traveling in northern Key Largo, a little rougher as you move south. It becomes treacherous in places where cars are pulling on or off the road, in and out of shops and restaurants, driving across the bicycle path in a big hurry. So be careful! When you rent a bike, ask the shopkeeper to refer you to various side trips off the busy Overseas Highway.

Tavernier Bicycle and Hobby
MM 92 Bayside ✴ 852-2859

Rent a sturdy coast and brake bike or a sleeker style with gears. Bikes come with locks and helmets. Baby seats are available at an additional cost. You must wear your helmet as you peddle out of the area, though you can take it off later. It's not legally required to wear a bike helmet in Florida. But the guy who owns this place has a special respect for helmets. On a bicycle trail in Vermont his daughter fell from her bike. She wasn't injured but when he retrieved her helmet, which had fallen off, her dad noticed that it had been gouged dramatically. From then on, helmets for everyone. "That could have been her head!" he says. Ask for a bike path map. Particularly popular is the one that winds around to Harry Harris Park. This place repairs bikes and is also a well-stocked hobby shop featuring remote control cars, planes and boats, models, balsam wood, and all that stuff model builders love and need.

Tavernier Towne Cinema
MM 91.5 Bayside ☞ 853-7003
Only movie theater in the Upper Keys. At least 5, and sometimes 6, newly released feature films go on here daily. Matinees, too. Schedule varies according to length of movies. Call ahead for details. Recently renovated, cool and comfortable retreat from your hot and hectic vacation.

Watersports

Caribbean Watersports
MM 97 Bayside, Sheraton Key Largo ☞ 852-4707
Why take a lonely parasail when you can pair-a-sail? That's right. Now two people can share a parachute and take to the air for 15 minutes of thrills and views together—providing their combined weight is less than 300 pounds, and the wind is blowing in the right direction. This would not be a good time to fudge on the truth about your weight . . .

Also at Caribbean: sailing lessons, Waverunners and wind-surfers. Two daily reef trips for divers, snorkeling only, and they'll hook you up with SCUBA dives, too. Just ask.

What is SNUBA?

Surface Nexus Underwater Breathing Apparatus, or SNUBA, is an alternative to SCUBA. It's simpler, though, because you don't have to carry that tank of air on your back. You breathe through a tube connected to SCUBA tanks of compressed air that float on a raft on the surface of the water. You can learn SNUBA in the morning in a pool, and go out to the reef and SNUBA dive to depths of 20 feet or more that afternoon! Snuba was conceived in 1988 in California. Founders sold franchises to entrepreneurs in regions featuring shallow, visually exciting diving, like the Florida Keys. Jeff Tamlyn was the first to bring SNUBA to the Keys. Right now, it is unavailable in the Upper Keys. Too bad. Stay tuned. It's likely to be back. People loved it and Jeff Tamlyn, a native of New Brunswick, Canada, trained thousands of people to experience the amazing experience of swimming with the sharks. Now you gotta go to Key West to Snuba.

Fishing

A T THE HOLIDAY INN MARINA at mile marker 100, you can find out just about anything you want to know about Key Largo fishing: Deep sea, backcountry, party boats, private charters. Follow the canal-side harbor walk, which continues around to the Marina Del Mar boat basin, and you'll find dozens of boats for hire. Charter people never mind telling you about their services. And if you hang around and watch for a while— boats generally come back to shore around 4 p.m.—you'll soon get the hang of how things work around here.

Otherwise, check with the Key Largo Chamber of Commerce for a comprehensive list of fishing boats and guides.

Party Boats

Sailor's Choice II
Holiday Inn Marina, MM 100, Oceanside,
☎ 451-0041 or 451-1802
Enjoy a half day of fishing aboard this all aluminum, 65-foot party boat. Trips are from 9 a.m. till 1 p.m., and from 1:30 p.m. till 5:30, daily. Families and children are welcome. No fishing experience required. Catch a snapper or grouper and take it to your favorite restaurant to be prepared for you. Or, just catch and release. Rod, reel and bait all included. Party boat crews are very nice people. You'll have a ball! And all for around $35 per person.

Tours by Land and Sea

Captain Ray Cramer's Airboat Tours
852-5339

Ray Cramer will take you on an Everglades airboat ride and nature tour. Ray will point out birds, plants, blooms and alligators. But what many folks like best are his Indian stories about the Tequesta and Caloosa warriors who once ruled the 'Glades. Call Ray for times and rates, which vary according to the number of people in your party, and the time of the year.

Everglades Ecology, Nature and Safari Tours
MM 102, Dolphin Cove Marina, bayside ✺ 853-5161 ✺ 888-224-6044

Captain Sterling Kennedy has been taking folks on nature tours of the Everglades National Park for well over 20 years. His vessels are a trio of 25-foot deck boats, and a custom built 48-foot pontoon, all docked at the Dolphin Cove Marina. The boats are designed for the one-to-two-feet-deep shallows of the Everglades and the backcountry.

Kennedy offers several ecology and nature tours in the liquid fringes of the Florida Keys. The most popular is the Everglades Ecology Tour, for a maximum of six people or a minimum of two. The tour takes you into the shallow, clear waters of the Everglades where you may see manatees and dolphins, and a rare crocodile. Crocodiles are endangered, and tours are not allowed to enter areas where they are most prevalent. You'll be in the saltwater portion of the Everglades, so you won't see alligators at all. They're only in fresh water. The tour visits two bird rookery islands, where pink roseate spoonbills, herons, pelicans, cormorants and dozens of species of migratory birds are plentiful. There are 18 tours available daily. Cost is around $45 for adults, $30 for kids. The tour is about one-and-a-half hours. A daily sunset cruise departs at 5 p.m. in the winter, and 7 p.m. in the summer. The champagne sunset cruise is out for about an hour or so and is $49 for adults, $19 for kids. The size of your boat will depend upon the number of people looking to cruise the sunset that day.

Captain Kennedy will perform your wedding. Several wedding packages range from $299 - $499. Marrry on the boat or at a super little private beach Captain Sterling knows about. Or, have it your way. Just tell the captain what you want. You'll even get a video of the ceremony. Private charters are also available.

Florida Bay Outfitters Kayak Tours
MM 104, Bayside ✒ 451-3018
What Frank Woll started out as a one-man operation out of a local bike shop not so long ago is now one of the largest and most popular paddling specialty shops in Florida! Florida Bay Outfitters is all about the sport of paddling, in kayaks and canoes. Frank and his wife Monica even married in a kayak wedding. Half or full-day kayak or canoe rentals are available here, as well as excellent guided tours of the Florida Bay. Frank Woll and his staff know what tours people like best; what tours go untaken. A popular trip is a 7-hour tour of Indian Key and Lignumvitae Key. There are a number of overnight paddle/camp trips to various spots in the area. There is an overnight trip to North Nest Key and a 7-day paddle and camp tour of the Keys! You get the guide, all the camping gear, food and supplies. For a camping trip on the far-flung Dry Tortugas, you and the kayaks travel out to sea on a big boat. Want to be alone? Take a self-guided tour. They'll give you a map and rent you the camping gear. Call or stop by. They'll FAX you information, too.

Witt's End Sailing Charters
MM 100 ✒ 451-3354 ✒ 745-1476
An utterly romantic getaway for fairy-tale types. Sail from mile marker 100 in Key Largo at sunset. Cruise to an uninhabited island and anchor for the night. If you like, you can get married; just bring the license and the Witts will take care of everything else. Later enjoy a sumptuous wed-

ding dinner and sleep in your own private stateroom. The next morning, enjoy a gourmet breakfast on deck. The overnight wedding package runs around $500. But you don't have to marry, you can just cruise and enjoy. There are all sorts of packages and prices for them. Witt's End, by the way, is renowned for its fine food.

Glass Bottomed Boats

This is one of the most popular attractions in the Keys. The beauty of glass bottom boat tours is that you get to see some of what divers who actually get into the water see—but not all of it. The boats don't really have all-glass bottoms, of course, it's more like they have plexiglass windows that slant from the floor outward, giving you a series of windows into the sea and the reef beneath. For younger or non-swimming children, older folks, or anyone interested in not getting wet, glass bottom boat tours allow for a pretty remarkable glimpse at the other world below the surface of the deceptively calm-looking sea.

It's a good show, especially since, unlike a snorkler, you'll have a skillful and enthusiastic guide to point out the highlights and to tell you what you're seeing. Often, a trip to the reef will convince you to don snorkeling gear yourself and go for a longer look. All of the glass bottom boat tours in the Key Largo area go to Molasses Reef, which is marked by a 50-foot tower, so you'll know when you're getting close.

Key Largo Princess
Mile Marker 100, Holiday Inn Docks ✴ 451-4655
A very comfortable way to view America's most famous, and most frequently viewed reef is to cruise aboard the *Key Largo Princess*. The excursion takes about 2 hours: 45 minutes out, and 45 minutes back, with a half hour stop there while you catch sight of the amazing Molasses Reef. A snack counter (on board, not at the reef!) sells hot dogs and soda; there's a full bar, bathrooms, and the bottom deck, where the glass bottom is located, is enclosed and air-conditioned. You can't do the reef any easier than this! Cost for adults is $22 plus tax; Kids 12 and under go for $12. The boat departs at 10 a.m., 1 p.m., and 4 p.m. Most people enjoy feeding the seabirds, which swoop down for a treat when they see this boat coming.

Spirit of Pennekamp Glass Bottom Boat
Mile Marker 102.5 at John Pennekamp • 451-1621

This fine, big catamaran can carry up to 130 passengers out to the famous and popular Molasses Reef, which has been named by several dive magazines as America's favorite reef. It takes a little under an hour to get there. At Molasses Reef, the boat floats atop the waters of the reef, while passengers gaze at the sealife below through fiberglass plates in the hull. A guide provides excellent narration on what you're looking at and answers your many questions. Then you head back to the park.

The *Spirit of Pennekamp* shoves off every day at 9:15 a.m., 12:15 p.m., and 3 p.m. Set aside two and a half hours total for the trip. When the wind is blowing and the water looks rough, you can be sure that the ride will be a little rough, too. Some people will become quite seasick. (Not you, of course.) If at all possible, take this trip on a calm, clear day when visibility is good; hot, clear summer days are best. Otherwise, we recommend a seasick remedy before the fact. Buy it at any drug store and take it at least a half hour before boarding the boat. The tour is $20, plus tax, for adults; $12 for kids 3 - 11. Babies go free.

A Gambling Cruise

Sun Cruz I
MM 100, Holiday Inn Marina • 451-0000

The SunCruz I is part of a fleet of casino cruise ships operating out of Florida and South Carolina. The 77.8 foot SunCruz motors to just beyond the legal limit, anchors, and bobs on the peaceful waves of the reef while passengers enjoy games of blackjack, roulette, slots, craps, and poker. Your $10 boarding fee (you must be 18 or over to board, and 21 to drink) buys you a welcome-aboard cocktail or beverage, and hors d'oeuvres. There's a full bar and deli style menu of entrees. Departure time is 5 p.m. on Monday, Tuesday, Thursday and Friday. If you miss the boat climb aboard a water taxi and they'll take you out. Taxis sail at 7 p.m. and 9:30 p.m. On Wednesday, Saturday and Sunday the SunCruz I sails at 2 p.m. and water taxis leave the dock at 5, 7, and 9:30. Water taxi is

$10 and you can take it out to the boat, or, if your luck is not good, back to shore. Minimum bet allowed is $5; maximum is $500. Floridans with ID to prove it pay only $3, plus tax, to cruise. Deals for senior citizens. Call for information on corporate rates, specials and new events.

Accommodations

Y OU CAN HAVE IT ALL in Key Largo, of course, but is that what you really want? Stay at a Sheraton, a Marriott, a Holiday Inn or a Howard Johnson's. You know what you'll get in those places. And often the small, funky places are just as much fun as well as considerably less expensive.

A rule of thumb is this: the closer you get to Key West, the more you'll pay for accommodations that are basically the same, with one big exception. In Key West, only the very finest, most expensive rooms are on the water. In Key Largo, most motels and hotels are on the Florida Bay or the Intercostal Waterway. Either way, what's all-important is that waterfront and that amazing sunset every evening. You might be surprised at how soothing the Upper Keys' subtle charms can be.

"No B & B's in Key Largo." At least that's what someone said at the Chamber of Commerce. When I asked why there are none, he explained it this way: "Hurricanes have destroyed all the big Victorian houses, and so there are very few B & B's in this area." In fact, Key Largo's relatively brief history contains few, if any inn-sized, Victorian houses—but nice try. A woman told me a few days later that B & B's are illegal in Key Largo; zoning laws don't permit them. Still, mom and pop joints line the bayside of the Overseas Highway, and the moms and pops who run them know their area well. Staying at one of these is almost as much fun as a B & B. And sometimes you'll find a complimentary continental breakfast.

I don't like to give room rates, because they change so often—from season to season, year to year, from place to place. It's always wise to check on deposit and cancellation policies. Remember when you are quoted a room rate to add on the 11.5% tax. Also, check to see if there are telephones in the rooms—some of the nicest places don't have them. If you have children, say so because some places don't take them either.

Here, in alphabetical order, is an arbitrarily chosen list of some inns, lodges and resorts of Key Largo.

Coconut Palm Inn
MM 92 Bayside,✹ 852-3017 ✹ 800-765-5397
What separates this little waterfront retreat from the others here on the
Florida Bay in Key Largo is its great long beach - 450 feet of waterfront!
Most of the mom and pop places along this lovely stretch of bay are long
and narrow. This property is long and wide. Also, two large docks. Bring
your boat, there's lots of room for it. Or, make use of free kayaks. Fish off
the dock, or snorkel around it. Owners will supply the fishing rods and

simple snorkel gear at no charge. But if you should happen to hook a 20 pound grouper, please let him go. He's a local character, and sort of a mascot. You'll find plenty of hammocks strung between shady palms, as well as standard amenities like ice, phones, heated pool, BBQ facilities, and a free continental breakfast. Kids under 12 years of age stay for free, so this is a terrific and safe place to bring a family for an energetic getaway.

The Coconut Palm Inn was built originally in the 1940s, as a 7 room fishing lodge. Eventually an 11-room inn was built on the property. Then the two buildings were joined together. That's why each of the 16 units face the water. Nice! Also, the ceiling beams in some of the rooms are actually railroad ties from Flagler's Overseas Railroad, which was blown into oblivion by the Labor Day Hurricane of 1935. You can see them still. Patio rooms feature a separate bedroom and screened- in porch, facing the water. The most special unit here is the Coconut Palm Suite, elegant and perfect for a special occasion.

Bay Harbor Lodge
MM 97.7, Bayside ✎ 852-5695
The Bay Harbor Lodge is popular with tourists from Germany and England because the original owners were European and the inn appears in a number of European guides to the Keys. New owners have kept prices very fair for these comfortable, super-clean, air-conditioned and well-equipped efficiencies and cottages. They're adding phones to all the rooms, too. Here you'll find good swimming, sunning, and free use of a paddle boat, canoes and kayaks along a 150-foot-length of bay front. Barbeque grills and tiki huts are well utilized by appreciative guests. There's a lovely, 40-foot-long heated pool. Heated! You'll find lots of places like this along the Florida Bay in Key Largo, and each one of them has its own special personality. Rates vary according to time of year and what's going on. From the Bay Harbor Lodge you can easily walk to some great restaurants.

Holiday Inn
MM 100, Oceanside ✎ 451-2121 ✎ 800-843-5397
You're in the heart of the tourist zone here, in a four-block area of piers, hotel rooms, great bars and restaurants. But...no beach. Two busy pools, though. Some people like the comfort of staying with a known and

trusted host. This is it. If you're planning to do lots of watersports, you won't need to go far to get on a boat. This is THE marina in Key Largo, featuring private fishing charters, a party fishing boat, snorkel tours and diving trips. Also a glass-bottomed boat. And Holiday Inn guests get free passes for the casino boat that docks in the Holiday Inn Marina.

Though Key Largo's history is a very short story, the Holiday Inn pays it homage with endless references and spins on the Bogie and Bacall theme. The Holiday Marina is home to the original *African Queen*, from the film of the same name, the *Thayer*, an outboard that appeared in the film *On Golden Pond*, and Bogie's Cafe, named for actor who starred in the film *Key Largo*. The gift shop sells Bogie and Bacall and Katherine Hepburn-related novelties. Room rates at the Holiday Inn are pretty steep. You pay for the corporate name and reputation, and it really is a nice place.

Jules' Undersea Lodge
MM 103.2 Oceanside, 51 Shoreland Drive ✴ 852-5695

Earn your Aquanaut Certificate! Spend an entire night in this space-age, self-contained habitat five fathoms under the sea, and join an elite army of 10,000 who have slept here too. Several couples have married in this underwater lab-turned-novelty inn. It's a popular nest for honeymooners, too, and with people who were children in the 1950s and remember coming home from school in time for the TV show *Sea Hunt*, featuring Lloyd Bridges as the dauntless diving master of the deep, Mike Nelson.

Like Mike Nelson, you must be in good health and be confident in the water. If you're not certified in SCUBA diving, you're required to take a three-hour diving course ($75 per person) before you enter the hotel. To get to your room, you wear fins and a mask and breathe via a 120-foot-long hookah connected to compressors on the surface. The lodge is located in a mangrove lagoon, birthplace of many species of fish.

You'll want your wits about you, so there's no drinking allowed at Jules' and, certainly, no smoking.

The air-conditioned lodge sleeps four in two bedrooms, with a stereo, telephone, TV and VCR; hot showers and a full galley. The most popular video: *20,000 Leagues Under the Sea*. Lots of portholes keep you from getting claustrophobic. Certified divers are allowed to slip out for a dive whenever they please, but others must schedule buddy dives with a staff member.

Couples or groups may visit Jules' Undersea Lodge for a three-hour mini-adventure during which they have unlimited use of the amenities and opportunity to experience life in an aqua-habitat. The European plan for around $250 per person, however, provides the room, amenities, a prepared gourmet dinner and breakfast supplies. Check-in time is 5 p.m.; check-out is 9 a.m. The most elegant and expensive package is the Ultimate Romantic Getaway, which is $1,050 per couple, per night. The big package includes romantic music, flowers, caviar, and a gourmet dinner prepared by staff.

Lifestyles of the Rich and Famous featured Jules' Undersea Lodge in a program taped in 1987 and has rerun the piece many, many times. Most insomniacs have seen it at least once. Jules does not advertise his bizarre undersea lodge. The world's one and only underwater hotel attracts a lot of attention, though; with all the publicity, Jules doesn't need to buy ads. Call for Manager Rick Ford to learn more or to make a reservation.

Key Largo Bay Beach Resort
MM 103.5, Bayside ✴ 453-0000 ✴ 800-932-9332

This Marriott Beach Resort soars four stories into the sky and features white-washed walls, lots of white wrought iron and coral rock fences. The gorgeous man-made beach is as good as man-made gets. A bayfront pool is in the middle of seventeen majestic acres of finely landscaped waterfront. The gazebo is as big as a house while several tiki huts on the edge of the Florida Bay contain hammocks and tables. What a place to watch the sun go down, and you can do that if you're not booked into a room. Don't miss the blue dolphins statue, another great photo opportunity. Attractive stone tiles take the place of pavement, and a suspension bridge connects restaurants to rooms—Whoa!— one hundred and fifty rooms, suites, or penthouses tropical luxury all the way. Tropical decor. White wood. Bold, flowery prints all over the place. A setting strongly evocative of *Fantasy Island.* Any minute, you expect Ricardo Montelban to step out from behind a royal palm and say "You look maaaar-velous." Naturally, a room in this place will cost you plenty.

Kona Kai
MM 97.8, Bayside ● 852-7200 ● 800-365-7829

In 1994 New Yorkers Joe Harris and Ronnie Farina (now it's Mr. and Mrs. Joe Harris) began renovating this little mom and pop bayside inn. It ain't mom and pop anymore. It's Mother and Father. Very chic. The Harris's have spent over a million dollars turning their inn into a favorite retreat for the rich and famous, in the spirit of the much more expensive and ritzy Little Palm Island, an hour or so further down the road. What makes this retreat more attractive, besides the fact that it's a fraction of the cost, is that not everybody loves the romance of being stranded on a private island. Lots of folks appreciate having that car in the parking lot and the possibility of wandering out for a pizza or a gourmet meal, or a drive on the Overseas Highway.

There are no phones in the units, so bring your cell phone if you must have one. Maids come in every 3 days (although you can ask for all the fresh sheets and towels you like) and rooms are identified by a fruit, not a number, on the key. There's the pineapple suite, the kiwi room, and so on. Joe and Ronnie grow tropical fruits right on the premises, and if you like they'll take you for a tour of their tiny Eden and invite you to pick a banana right off the tree and eat it. Divine! There are fully equipped kitchen units and BBQs outside. Every item at Kona Kai, from the pots and pans in the kitchen to the complimentary Q-tips in the bathrooms, are the very nicest money can buy.

Joe Harris, who used to travel on business 300 days out of every year, says he understands what people mean when they say they want to be left alone. Garbo would love this place. Each unit contains a VCR and videos about the Keys. Magazines. Books. Fat pillows. Cool colors and lots of blonde wood conducive to tropical torpor. The Kona Kai's sandy beach (the sand is imported!) is private and tranquil. The pool is always heated to womb-like warmth. If there's ever a crowd, it's when the guests commune at the beach, for sunset. Nick, the great white heron who hangs around the dock, has become a member of the family and doesn't mind posing for a photo.

The Harris's have a fine knowledge of the entire Keys and direct guests to the best restaurants and activities. They'll even recommend accommodations in Key West, if you want to make a jaunt down there. They live on the premises and maintain a small art gallery, featuring several up and coming European artists. Joe describes the ambiance at the

Kona Kai as "comfortably casual first class." The Kona Kai has been featured in several travel-oriented TV programs, and in a Home and Gardens Network special on Florida Keys gardens. Prices are high, but reasonable for what you get. No kids. Book ahead! And prepare to be left alone.

Largo Lodge
MM 101.5, Bayside ☙ 451-0424

Little has changed here in the nearly 40 years since the Largo Lodge opened for business in the late fifties. The Largo Lodge has got what many people are coming here to find: peace and quiet beneath a canopy of swaying palms. Three duplex cottages containing two units, each with three rooms: living room, bedroom with two beds, and kitchen with whatever equipment you need to cook; private screened-in porches and entrances. No continental breakfast, no phones, no kids under sixteen years. Apartments are all still in the '50s mode—owner Harriet Stokes collects ashtrays and fixtures from the period to keep them that way. They'll remind you of the motor court cabins of your childhood.

Besides the cottages, two rooms with queen-sized beds and color TVs aren't advertised. You might get one of them if you ask nicely. Harriet has tried very hard to keep her prices old-fashioned, too, and she's succeeded. But the secret's out. Harriet gets lots of repeat business so if you want to stay here, call as soon as you know your dates to lock in your reservation.

The grounds at Largo Lodge are wonderful, wild and tropical-lush. You really feel as if you're very far away from the rest of the world. Orchid lovers will go nuts here: brilliantly colored orchids are everywhere. Squirrels scurry up and down the thick trunks of coconut trees. Waterfront is typical bayside: funky, breezy, wondrous at sunset.

And there's something sort of ageless and wonderful about Harriet Stokes, too.

Marina del Mar Resort and Marina
MM 100 Oceanside ☙ 451-4107 ☙ 800-451-3483

Located on a deep-water marina. There's no beach here. There is an excellent dive and snorkel center, a gym, tennis lessons, a giant pool and whirlpool spa. Also, Coconuts Restaurant and Cocktail Lounge with indoor and outdoor dining. After dark, Coconuts is one of the area's hottest night spots. Sharkey's Bar on the water has pool tournaments. At Benny's Galley upstairs you will find reasonably priced indoor and outdoor dining. If you're a sports-minded person in town for a vacation of fishing by day and carousing by night, this is the place for you.

The Marina Del Mar Marina is connected to the Ramada Inn and the Holiday Inn Marina via a long canal-side walkway. Take a stroll along the water and have a look at some of the vessels tied up at the Del Mar docks: grand old wooden yachts from Norfolk, and Philadelphia, and Charleston, that make you think old money; and deluxe fishing boats with flying bridges nearly three stories high. We peeked through the open door of a fishing boat and were amazed to see fat, flowered chintz chairs and dark mahogany—an English sitting room!

You'll see some very serious-looking charter fishing boats, captained by former Navy officers. Should you wish to hire one of them, phone numbers are posted on signs near the boat. And so as to not waste your time or anyone else's, prices are posted, too. A day's fishing on such a splendid vessel as this will cost around $600 - 800 for between one and six people.

Every once in a while the *African Queen* glides down the canal, crying her tremulous steam-engine toot. She looks quite fine from afar— actually quite a bit better than she does tied up at her dockside spot at the Holiday Inn Marina.

Prices for standard rooms, with queen or king-size beds, refrigerators, TVs, and the included continental breakfast are moderate - high. There are also one, two and three bedroom suites, perfect for busy families because you really can have a self-contained family vacation here.

Seafarer Fish & Dive Resort
MM 97.6, Bayside ☎ 852-5349

One Saturday in May we found, after a wearying search, that the Seafarer offered the best deal for one night's accommodations. Our room was small, but very clean and the bed was firm and comfortable. So what else do you need? The Seafarer Beach is absolutely pristine, too, with bright pink accents, a selection of kayaks, paddle boats and sail boats, free to guests. There is a Jacuzzi, BBQs and picnic tables. The owners operate a PADI dive and snorkel boat. Cottages near the water looked splendid, but even ours, just off the highway, inside the motel gates, was fine. Nothing fancy, but cozy, neat and clean. Every unit has a little refrigerator, and there is a laundromat on the premises. Prices are moderate, and probably as good as anything else you will find for comparable lodgings in Key Largo. I liked it well enough, but calling this place a resort is a bit of a stretch.

Sunset Cove Motel
MM 99.5 Bayside ✷ 451-0705

A neat, old-timey joint with very reasonable prices. Many guests reserve rooms from one year to the next, so if you're planning on staying at Sunset Cove, book early. Sunset Cove is also popular with families, and really big families, who rent the entire 23-unit motel for reunions, weddings or anniversaries. The large tiki hut provides protection from the sun, but is open on all sides. Two bars, and the Sunset Cove folks will hook you up with all your party needs. Kids and pets are welcome here.

Sunset Cove is located in that busy something-for-everybody center of Key Largo, near diving, fishing, bars and restaurants, and owned and operated by terrific folks, four local partners, who seem to thoroughly enjoy their mission, which is to keep you happy in the Keys.

No frills bayside cottages are in high demand. All rooms have microwave ovens, refrigerators and TVs. Some units have kitchens and enough beds to sleep a baseball team. No phones in any of them. Also, no pool on the property. Futons are being added in some places to make room for even more guests, a big improvement over pull-out couches and cots. Complimentary continental breakfast.

Two fishing piers, and a couple of fun boats are free to guests. Handwoven Jamaican swings, suspended from the top of thatched chickee huts are perfect nests for napping or watching the sunset. Lockers and dip tanks for divers. Room rates are reasonable, on a par with other mom and pop motels in the area.

Tavernier Hotel
MM 91 Oceanside ✷ 852-4131 ✷ 800-515-4131

In the early '30s a Miami schoolteacher named McKenzie moved to Tavernier and built a movie theater of cinder blocks, a practically unheard of building material in the Upper Keys in those days. The movie theater was a pretty bizarre undertaking, too, considering the tiny population. But the theater operated for a couple of years. McKenzie's cinder block building even survived the Labor Day Hurricane of 1935 and was turned into an emergency hospital by the American Red Cross. McKenzie also built a drugstore, which is now the Copper Kettle Restaurant. In 1938, after the Overseas Highway brought cars full of tourists to the Keys, he added a second story onto the original building and turned it into a hotel.

The eighteen rooms in the Tavernier Hotel are small and very simple: queen or king-sized beds, private bathrooms with showers, TVs and phones. Rooms are moderately priced. It's not the kind of place where you'd spend your entire day: No beach, no pool, just clean, no-nonsense rooms tended by clean, no-nonsense hosts - a good place to choose on a quick layover between Miami and Key West.

Sheraton Key Largo
MM 97 Bayside ✽ 852-5553 ✽ 800-228-3000

Two hundred balconied rooms and forty-four suites with marble vanities, coffeemakers, and fancy hotel fixtures, located in a hardwood hammock where you can wander along footpaths that lead past wild coffee plants and mahogany trees. Dine at three restaurants and lounges. A separate swimming pool for families with kids keeps the quiet, adults-only pool always serene. Also a supervised Kids Club. Other features: a little beach, a jacuzzi, and tennis courts. The well-tended grounds at the Sheraton are home to a lush variety of tropical trees.

This is the very best place in the Keysfor a massage. The table is set up beneath a waterfall, so the only thing you'll hear while you are massaged is the soothing sound of the gushing waterfall. My favorite massage therapist is Joe Markum, AKA Big Daddy, who moonlights as a DJ on the Serendipity Show Sunday mornings on SUN 103.1 FM.

Caribbean Watersports, on the bay in the rear, features waverunners and hobie cats; snorkel, SCUBA and SNUBA diving, guided fishing trips, and parasailing. A snorkel charter leaves from the Westin docks every morning at 10 a.m. and again at 2 p.m. The three-hour trip visits dive sites on the shallow, calm bayside of Key Largo, then cruises through a connecting cut and over to the ocean for some stopovers there. An environmental-awareness tour leaves right from the Westin, too.

On weekdays in season, prices on the Sheraton's basic rooms with two queen-sized beds or one king overlooking the Florida Bay or a tropical hammock start at around $300. There's a buffet breakfast included and two daily complimentary cocktails. When you call for reservations, ask for information on off-season specials and packages.

Camping & RV Parks

There are several camp and RV parks in the Key Largo area. Call the Chamber of Commerce at 800-822-1088 for a list of campsites and RV sites who are members of the Chamber.

Vacation Rentals

Condos, homes, mobile homes, cottages on the Florida Bay or the Atlantic Ocean. Weekly rates go anywhere from $1000 to the sky's the limit a week for a fully equipped home. Don't forget to figure in taxes, cleaning charge and the security deposit.

Bayview Properties
800-226-4577

Century 21 Keysearch Realty
800-210-6246

Florida Keys Rental Store
800-585-0584

Loveland Realty
800-454-5263

Join us on the worldwide web
www.junekeith.com

Dining

Anthony's
MM 92.5 Tavernier Towne Shopping Center ✺ 853-1177
Sometimes, in the midst of a relaxing vacation, all you want for dinner is a nice dish of spaghetti with marinara sauce and a basket steaming garlic bread. At least that's how I feel after a few days of unleashed partying. And I found that dish of pasta at Anthony's. I'd made the mistake for many years of driving past Anthony's believing it was simply a pizza joint. Not so! Anthony's serves steaks, chops, and, of course, native seafood. Thursday is Prime Rib night. Friday and Saturday the special is Ossabucco. Servers in crisp white shirts and ties do their jobs with quiet efficiency, and they know their menu. There's a full bar, too. This is New York style Italian. "The best Italian food north of Key West," one innkeeper told me. It's also reasonably priced. And if you are a pizza lover, or a wandering New Yorker looking for a true taste of home, get yours here. Also calzones. Lunch and dinner.

Ballyhoo's Grille
MM 97.8 (on the median) ✺ 852-0822
Again, a place that treats fish, and the dining experience, with the reverence they deserve. You aren't going to eat fresher fish than this anywhere, so rest assured that this place will treat you right. Service is good, although it's so popular you'll find it busy and bustling at dinner hour. Ballyhoo's used to do breakfast, but they've stopped that and devote themselves totally to lunch and dinner. Truly excellent Keys dining from 11 a.m. till 10 p.m. daily. Happy hour weekdays with great prices on beer, shrimp and chicken wings. Beer and wine only.

Calypso's
MM 100 Oceanside   1 Seagate Blvd.✺ 451-0600
Breezy, outdoor, beer and wine bar on the water. People pull their boats up and even drop a line in the marina while they're eating or drinking. Food is wonderful fish baskets, or plates, featuring several locally caught

fish. Also delicious salads. Hand-cut french fries are worth the visit. If
you're having just a beer, order a basket of those French fries to go with
it. Also, the cole slaw is homemade and much better than the pedestrian
stuff you find in many fish houses. Service is easy. You feel at last you've
found what everybody's talking about when they talk about being laid
back in the Florida Keys.

Menu says: "Yes, we know the music's loud and the food is spicy.
That's the way we like it." We didn't find the music too loud or the food
particularly spicy, so I guess that's the way we like it, too.

Prices are moderate. Dinner becomes a more serious affair, with higher
prices, and excellent local fish entrees. Fishes are priced at market value,
so you might find yourself paying a lot for something superb and local like
mutton snapper. If you're counting your pennies, ask how much that fish
sandwich or saute you just ordered is going to cost you. Closed Tuesdays.
Visa or Mastercard only.

Copper Kettle
MM 91.5 Oceanside ✴ 852-4113
This restaurant adjoins the historic and charmingly plain Plantation
Hotel. The food is good enough to attract a full dining room by 8 p.m., at
least on the night we were there. In fact, the host was turning people
away or asking them to wait at the little bar, which they did. Our waiter
was a very handsome, polite Russian fellow. If he'd understood English,
too, he would have been perfect! The menu is standard fare, with a tiny
bit of exotic flair. Spinach pie in filo dough is delicious and makes you
feel Popeye-powerful; veggies and salad were not out of the ordinary.
They serve only twenty-three diners at a time, so everything runs
smoothly. The full bar seats only a few drinkers. Reservations for this
small, popular cafe are probably a good idea.

The Cracked Conch
Mile Marker 105, Oceanside ✴ 451-0732
Elvis is alive and well and living in Key Largo. A couple of friends of
mine spotted the King, with a wife and two kids, ordering a fried fish
sandwich at the Cracked Conch just last fall. So, like I said, you never
know who you might bump into in Key Largo.

When the people who work in a restaurant are as enthusiastic as the
people in the Cracked Conch, it seems a good sign that the food will be
very good. And it is. But the waitresses, and the beers, are the best thing

about the place. The beer selection must be the largest collection of imported brews in the Keys: pale ales, brown ales, scotch ales, and barley wine; cream stouts, malts, porters, and tap beers; even spiced beers. The beer menu is actually longer than the food menu. You can get the island food you want here, too, stuff like deep-fried fish, excellent cracked conch, good conch chowder. Try the alligator and find out for yourself why this rare delicacy never really got off the ground. Key lime pie is frozen and very refreshing. Dinners are Caribbean, Cajun, and Mexican-influenced with a different menu of specials every night and very reasonable prices.

A note on the menu says, "This establishment is run by a very close staff and family...Close to broke. Close to insanity. Close to killing each other." Guests staple their business cards to the wooden walls. (Makes you wish you had one...well, maybe you do.) Stapled next to my table was the business card of a local realtor. Someone had drawn a mustache and beard on her tiny business-card photo, and then written, in wee, little letters, "Let me sell your house so you can move back up North."

The inside is much bigger than it looks from the outside, which seems to be a trend around here, huh? You can sit outside, too, if you don't mind the traffic on the Overseas Highway a few feet from your table. Open noon till 10 p.m. Closed Wednesdays.

Denny's Latin Cafe
Mile Marker 100, Bayside ✒ 451-3665

The Cubans in the Upper Keys love to hang around talking and drinking strong cafe con leche at Denny's. (By the way, this Denny's is not even remotely related to Denny's, the chain.) Plenty of hardcore Key Westers rave about Denny's, too. It's a favorite stop on the road to, or from, Amerika. They tell you that they wouldn't dream of skipping a trip to Denny's. Cuban food: Do you have any idea what a deal beans and rice is? And we're not just talking money; we're talking nutrition, too. Try Denny's—if you can get near it. Sometimes, if you're not too far away and he's got a man to spare, Denny's will deliver. Open 5 a.m. till midnight, every day.

Key Largo Coffee House and Cyber Cafe
MM 100.2 Oceanside ✺ turn at Holiday 453-0310

It was probably not the best idea to call this place a coffee house. It
serves breakfast, lunch and dinner, as well as terrific coffee. Further, you
can log on to their computers for a small fee. Breakfast is particularly
spectacular, in great part because of the wonderful location. Key Largo
Coffee House is a family business located in a very lush tropical hammock. A wraparound porch is inviting. Service is great. The staff is the
family. Mom and Dad do the breakfast and lunch shift. Their son covers
afternoons and evenings. This place used to be Frank's Keys Cafe. Some
of Frank's kitchen staff is still around, so the food is very good. Saturday
night there is an open mike for poets and musicians. Tuesday night is
Mexican night. Excellent Mexican food nicely priced. Kid's menu is well
thought out. Hours are 7 a.m. till 10 p.m. Closed Wednesdays.

The Fish House
MM 102.4 Oceanside ✺ 451-HOOK

You gotta go to the Fish House because, when you ask where to go for
fresh fish, this is where everyone will send you. It's the hottest seafood
joint in town. So hot, an Encore Fish House has opened two doors down
from the original. Bustling full-time. Lunch from 11:30 a.m. to 4 p.m.,
then dinner till 10 p.m. A full bar. The children's menu is really no bargain—a kid's hamburger is $6.50. All the prices are pretty steep, perhaps
because the food is served on real dishes, not paper. The forks and knives
aren't plastic, and you drink your wine from real glass, but you pay for
elegance like this in a fish house. Chowders, stone crab claw appetizers,
shellfish, and local fish, cooked a dozen different ways. Nice, big, tasty
meals are served with boiled potatoes and corn on the cob; steaks and
pasta for the landlubbers. Lots on this menu is ala carte. Like the bread
basket for $1.50. There's also a sharing charge. Attitude is important at
the Fish House, where owners promote themselves and their employees
as "fun, friendly, and Keysy." Anybody who has eaten here raves about
the food.

Harriette's Restaurant
MM 95.7 ● 852-8689

Lots of folks love Harriette's for breakfast. Some mornings you see them lined up outside the door waiting for one of Harriette's wobbly, worn-out tables. Why? Perhaps it's the gritty atmosphere or the cozy aroma of grill-fried food. The scrambled eggs, pancakes, French toast, grits and coffee at Harriette's are certainly all right, but the service is lightening-fast, maybe too fast... Our waitress was in no mood for questions the Saturday morning we showed up for breakfast. Our meal was a wham-bam deal, in and out. That's Harriette's for breakfast; lunch, too. No dinner. Open 6 a.m. till 2 p.m. every day except Christmas and Thanksgiving. No credit cards.

The Hideout Restaurant
MM 103.5 Oceanside ● 451-0128

Follow Transylvania Ave. to the end. The Hideout is on your right, next door to Jule's Undersea Lodge. People love this place for its local color. A big menu board on the wall announces daily specials, the day's winning lottery numbers, sunset, and the Friday Night Fish Fry. Lots of flower power-type art work, pink walls, and a jumble of mix and match furniture. All very comfortable and funky. No bar and no booze. This is a locals' place, but a favorite with tourists once they find their way to it. Prices are local, not tourist. Breakfast starts at 7 a.m. and the place is full then of boat captains and dive masters, beginning their day by chowing down on steak and eggs, with an eye on the awakening sea and sky just outside the windows. Breakfast and lunch only, except on Fridays, when the famous and traditional All You Can Eat Fish Fry is still only $9.75! If you dine at the Hideout, be sure to check out the underwater hotel and dive lagoon next door.

Mandalay Marina and Tiki Bar
MM 97.5 Oceanside, turn onto E. Second St. ● 852-5450

The Mandalay has recently undergone a very major spiffing up. It's still a little tricky to find, but it is not to be missed. They've got a batter to beat all batters, and everything fried in it is just wonderful, especially when you consume that fried shrimp, conch or fish in that breezy, salty seaside atmosphere. On weekends the Mandalay holds all sorts of fun events for families. There are crab races with proceeds going to charity. Sometimes there's karaoke, a big kick, and there are fishing contests for kids, who drop lines off the fun little dock beyond the bar. It's really funky here, and always full of hungry, happy customers. Call ahead for specials and events. Lunch and dinner. There is also lots happening in the Mandalay Marina in the day time. There are fishing and diving charters, kayak and boat rentals, and waverunner rentals.

Mrs. Mac's Kitchen
MM 99.4 ✺ 451-3722
When the Key Largo well-to-do go slumming, this is where they eat lunch. Mrs. Mac's is the kind of place you came to the Keys to find. From the road it's a shack, but it's quite big once you get inside. Filled with attractive, spunky girls, one of whom reminded me very much of actress Crystal Bernard from television's *Wings*. The menu is long and colorful; the decor is funky. Big fat sandwiches on pita bread, good chili, steaks and different themed specials—Italian, meat, seafood—each night. Frankly, you come here for the atmosphere, not the food, which is nothing to rave about. But it's a lively, friendly, stop with diner prices. Beer and wine only, cash only. Closed Sunday. Call for specials.

Num Thai
MM 103.2 Bayside, in Central Plaza ✺ 451-5955
Ahhh. A soft, serene oasis steeped in Far Eastern tradition. And $1 sushi! It's located in a short, neat strip of shops; just look for the sign. Thai, Japanese, and sushi. Owners are Bangkok natives who lived first in Miami and then in the Keys. Lunch on weekdays only, from 11:30 a.m.–3 p.m. Dinner seven nights from 5 p.m. to 10:30 p.m. Owned and operated by Panyaporn Russmetes ("Num" is his nickname, which means "forever young"), and his wife Tiki. Num's family opened and ran the first Thai restaurant in Miami. Tiki is a Japanese cook so their restaurant Num Thai is a monument to their many years in the food business. Big menu: eighty-three Thai dishes, sixty Japanese dishes, children's meals, curry special each night, and Thai and Japanese beers and wines, also a sushi bar. Grilled chicken with rice and veggies, Key Largo sushi roll, live lobster. Moderate prices for exquisitely prepared food and, what makes it all so wonderful, lovely people doing their best to please their guests. The

people at Num Thai understand good service and fine dining. It's well worth the money and what a find for vegetarian gourmands!

The Old Tavernier
MM 91.8 Oceanside ✶ 852-6012

My friend Thorn Trainer, who owns and operates the Casa Thorn, says we can't write a guidebook to the Florida Keys without mentioning the Old Tavernier Restaurant. "The garlic rolls are wonderful!" Thorn says. Someeone else told me that there is no better rack of lamb, or lamb chops, than what you get at the Old Tavernier. Ilias Kofinas is the Greek owner of the place, so occasionally you'll find a traditional Greek dish among the evening's dinner specials as well as great Italian and American dishes. The Old Tavernier serves dinner only, from 4 p.m.–10:30 p.m. daily. Full bar, and entrees come with soup or salad, and bread: fish, steaks, lamb, chicken, and traditional Italian dishes.

The Pilot House at the Pilot House Marina
MM 100 Oceanside. 13 Seagate Boulevard ✶ 451-3142

Turn onto Seagate Boulevard and drive past a couple of boatyards on your right before you come to the Pilot House's spacious parking lot. Or come in your boat, and pull into the full facility marina for the cheapest fill-up (we're talking gas here . . .) you'll find in the Florida Keys. A full bar inside, air conditioned, and outside a tiki hut, seating up to 150, where you can order some very tasty burgers, seafood and snacks. House speciality is seared yellow fin tuna taco. Award-winning chef Todd Lollis designed the menu. Lunch is modest, but very good. All the seafood sold here is purchased across the street at the Key Largo Fisheries, so you know it's fresh. Menu gets really creative at night.

Snooks
MM 99.9 Bayside ✶ 453-3799

Snooks is difficult to find because their sign, right next to Key Largo Honda, is not the easiest to spot—but the search is well worth the trouble! Press on. This qualifies as one of the most relaxing restaurants in the Keys. The bar inside Snook's boasts a large saltwater aquarium, a unique bartop made of hammered copper to resemble fish scales. You'll meet lots of locals as well as tourists here. Several way-cool boats are always tied up at the dock. A dazzling Sunday brunch, 11 a.m. till 3 p.m., is lazy and wonderful. In a tiki hut down by the water's edge, you'll find Patrick's Waterfront Bar, from where the sunset is splendorous, and you can watch it from a place that is sort of high-scale and laid-back.

Tugboats Restaurant
2 Seagate Boulevard, corner of Oceanside Drive ✶ 453-9010
From the screened dining area you'll see a couple of tropical hardwoods—mahogany trees—that do not grow farther north than South Florida. A little bar, featuring a mesmerizing portrait of Humphrey Bogart, serves beer and wine only. The whole place is small—a full house would be around fifty customers.

Lunch and dinner specials change regularly, but look for fish or crab chowders, roast pork, pan-fried yellowtail or grouper, all served with black beans, rice, and cornbread. Also big salads and open-face sandwiches. Lunch and dinner. Prices at night are a few dollars more, but the food is just as good. Special mention: cracked conch is done just right and priced just right, too. All major credit cards are accepted. Phone for specials of the day.

Big Fish Grill
MM 99, Bayside ✶ 451-3734
Fine dining and a sports bar with live entertainment. Owners are Craig and Caourtney Campbell, both of whom grew up in the area and graduated from Island Christian School. Third partner is Mike Hupka. This is a well regarded local team and business. After-dinner scene features live bands Wednesday - Saturday. TVs. Pool tables, darts, foosball and shuffleboard.

Shops

Phantom Fireworks
MM 106, Gulfside ✹ 451-1198

What? A fireworks warehouse and store in Key Largo, home of eight endangered species, Continental America's only living coral reef, and vacation paradise of millions? Yup. Firecrackers, sparklers, snappers, whistlers, busters, rockets and blast assortments. Red-tagged articles require you to sign a special statement, and for any purchase, you must be 18 years of age and show a valid driver's license.

"Are these legal?" a customer asked.

"I can't tell you that," the store clerk answered. "Because I don't know where you plan to set them off."

"In the parking lot," the young man said.

Phantom Fireworks is a chain, with locations throughout the U.S. Showrooms are open daily, and stay open real late in the weeks before July 4th and New Year's Eve. May the 4th be with you.

Adult VideoOutlet
MM 106, Gulfside ✹ 453-1320

If there's a store like this in your home town you may be understandably reluctant to be seen visiting it. But you're on vacation now so come on in and have your fill of all the toys, creams, naughty outfits, and porny books and videos you've always wondered about. Have you seen the new pyrex dildoes? Store manager is a retired elementary school teacher who says sex is "a normal and natural thing to do." Why hide the helpers?

Cover to Cover Books
MM 91.2, Tavernier Towne ✹ 853-2464

It's a book store, yes, but it'a a whole lot more. Owners Joan Bell and Jenny Bell-Thompson are sisters and graduates of Coral Shores High School, so they know many of the people who frequent their shop and are determined to take good care of them. A third and honorary member of the hometown team is Jill Stevens, writer, educator and store events planner who writes the monthly newsletter and runs the Center 4 Learning (305-522-4869,) a much-appreciated service that prepares local kids for reading and math, FCATs and SATs. They call themselves book babes, women who "can recommend a great book, serve up a latte and blend a Keycino with her beautiful eyes closed." They've stacked the shelves with excellent children's literature and educational games, as well as Florida and Keys special interest books. Also, trendy, booky, gifty things you don't find in other book stores. Regulars at the shop are local writers Carl Hiaasen (*Skinny Dip, Tourist Trap* and *Striptease*) and award-winning children's book writer Eric Carle (*The Hungry Caterpiller, 10 Little Rubber Ducks*).

Island Smoke Shop
MM 103.4, Bayside, in the Pink Plaza ✶ 453-4014

Award-winning Master Blender Santiago Cabana, who spent most of his life in Cuba working in the cigar industry, has created the "El Original", sold here, and named the highest-rated Maduro in the world by SMOKE Magazine. The El Original has received numerous awards for its quality, consistency and flavor. Tobaccos from Nicaragua, Honduras, Dominican Republic, Mexico, Ecuador, and Peru are part of the blend in the El Original. On Saturdays, at the Island Smoke Shop, watch cigar rollers at work rolling cigars just as they did in Key West in the 1800s, when the tiny island city produced an unbelievable 100 million cigars annually! Check out the table, the tools, the way their graceful hands move as they wrap and roll the tobacco. It's so soft and supple, it looks like thin, moist suede. Other prize-winning smokes are the "Torpedo", a tapered cigar, and the "Toro Maduro." It is the goal of Bob Curtis, owner of this shop, to find, and/or create, the world's best tasting cigars.

The Book Nook
MM 103.4, Bayside, in the Pink Plaza ✶ 451-1468

Joel Carmel has moved the Book Nook here to the Pink Plaza from its former long-time location in the Waldorf Plaza. It's the same business, and you'll recognize it by the eclectic exhibit of books and CDs on tables in front of the store, stuff that Joel will sell you real cheap. There are finds here! Check it out. Occasional booksigning parties are good opportunities to meet South Florida's biggest writers, like James T. Hall. Joel's book reviews appear in the *Key Largo Free Press*.

The Book Nook carries sometimes hard to find papers like *Wall Street Journal, New York Times, Barron's, Sun, New York Daily News, London Daily Mail.* Also lots of local music, of course Jimmy Buffett, and other stars you haven't heard of yet. A good selection of audio books. Joel is very well-versed on his local-book section, both about titles and authors.

Key Largo's Strip Malls

Tavernier Towne
MM 92.5 Bayside
Turn at McDonald's. You'll find a whole world back there. When traveling to Miami, or other northern destinations, I make this a pit stop for a good leg-stretching. I can easily spend an hour or two browsing through stores like the new and huge Pier One Import Store, then Family Dollar, where most things are definitely more than a dollar, and then on to Cover to Cover Books coffee bar for a specialty brew or a icey, whipped cream- topped extravaganza and a visit wit whatever local folks or tourists happen to be passing the time there. The movie theater features six films at a time. The Country Gull, the Chinese restaurant, and Anthony's Italian are all great places to eat. I love cruising the Winn Dixie grocery store. I know it's crazy, but whenever I visit a new town I love checking out the groceries, the prices, the produce, the deli and bakery sections, and the non-food stuff. This shiny new store has it all.

Tradewinds Plaza
MM 101, Oceanside
Tastefully hidden behind a thick hammock of trees, if you didn't look for it you might not know this strip of stores is here. K-Mart and Publix are the big stores. Also Arby's, Cheng Garden Chinese Restaurant, Payless

Shoes, Beall's Outlet, and the well worth a visit Key Largo Library. My favorite stop at the Tradewinds Plaza is the Tiffany's Hair Salon where, with a fantastic computer program, you get to try on a variety of hair styles and colors. They scan a photo of your face into the computer, and then you get to see yourself in whatever hair styles you choose form a huge variety of choices. Become a virtual blond or redhead! You get a print-out of yourself modeling 16 different hair-do's, and a video tape with which to dazzle your friends and family back home. They say people change when they come to the Keys. Here's a good place to begin the process.

Key Largo's Secondhand Rows & Fleas

Key Largo Flea Market (Saturdays and Sundays only)
MM 103.5, Bayside

The Pink Juntique
MM 98.2 Oceanside

The Salvation Army Thrift Shop
MM 99.2 on the median

White Rhino Consignment
MM 103.2, Bayside in the Central Plaza

Ashleigh's Attic
MM 99.3 - Northbound median

Keys Castaways
MM 99.2 Bayside

Index

A

Abyss Dive Center, 369
Adderly House, 353
Adventure Snorkel Cruise, 441
African Queen, The, 476-77
Afterdeck Bar, 251
Air Key West, 135
Albury House, 477-78
Alexander's, 212
Alligator Reef Light, 434
Almond Tree Inn, 184
Ambiance Sun Bus Service, 136
Ambrosia Restaurant, 220
Amoray Dive Resort, 489
Annette's Lobster & Steak House, 388
Anthony's Restaurant, 526
Antonia's, 220
Appledore, 131
Aqua, 253-54
Aquarius Underwater Habitat, 488
Artists In Paradise Gallery, 326
Atlantic Shores, 252
Atocha, 113-14
At Your Service Weddings, 273

Athens Cafe & Grill, 455
Audubon House, 31, 80, 96
Audubon, John James, 80
Avalon Guest House, 200

B

B'nai Zion, 36
BP Cargo, 401
Bagatelle, 221
Bahama Mama's, 221-22
Bahia Honda Bridge, 306
Bahia Honda State Park, 310-11
Ballyhoo's Grille, 526
Banana Bay Resort, Marathon, 374-5
Banana Cafe, 222
Bankhead, Tallulah, 106
Banyan Resort, 184-85
Bargain Books, 60
Barnacle Bed and Breakfast, 311-12
Barracuda Grill, 387
Bat Tower, 284-85, 307
Bay Harbor Lodge, 516
Bayview Inn Marina, 375-76
Bayview Park, 177
Beatles, The, 191

Bed and Breakfast of Islamorada, 443-44
Benedict, Debra, 274
Bentley's, 454
Besame Mucho, 261
Best Western Key Ambassador Inn, 184
Beyond Paradise, 59
Big Fish Grill, 533
Big Pine Bicycle Shop, 309
Big Pine Fishing Lodge, 312
Big Pine Flea Market, 329
Big Pine House of Music, 325
Big Pine Kayak Adventures, 301-02
Big Pine Motel, 313-14
Big Pine Seafood Festival, 149
Big Pine Vacation Rentals, 317-18
Bishop, Elizabeth, 50
Blond Giraffe, 400
Blu Room, 259
Blue Heaven, 79, 222-23
Blue Hole, 303-04
Blue Moon Trader, 327
Blume, Judy, 51
B.O.'s Fish Wagon, 45, 223

Bobalu's Southern Cafe, 319

Bocce ball, 163

Bonefish Bay Motel, 376

Borders Express, 60

Book Nook, 535-36

Bougainvillea House, 400

Brinnin, John Malcolm, 50

Bud 'n' Mary's, 430-31

Buffett, Jimmy, 32, 46, 48, 75-79, 171, 233, 319, 400

Bull & Whistle Bar, 33, 252

Burdines Waterfront, 389

Burton, Philip, 37, 52

Burton, Richard, 38, 51

Bush, George H. W., Bonefish Tournament, 428

C

C.B. Harvey Rest Beach Park, 173

Cafe Marquesa, 225

Café Solé, 225-26

Caloosa Cove Resort, 444-45

Calypso's, 526-27

Camille's, 226

Cape Air, 134

Captain Bob's Grill, 226-27

Captain Hook's Marina and Dive Center, 367

Captain Tony's, 48, 82, 252-53

Captain's Corner, 158-59

Caputo, Phil, 52, 405

Caribbean Cobbler, 327

Caribbean Club, 478-79

Caribbean Spa, 164

Carper, Jean, 52

Carson, Johnny, 112

Carey, George, 81-82

Carter, President Jimmy, 31, 113

Carysfort Light, 487-88

Casa Antigua, 34

Casa Morada, 445-6

Casa Marina, 186-87

Casa Thorn, 446-7

Castaway Restaurant, 389-90

Cayo Hueso Y Habana, 102

Center Court, 200-01

Charter Boat Row, 160, 167-68

Chart Room, 78

Cheeca Lodge, 447-8

Cheeca Rocks, 435

Chicken Fest Key West, 147

Chico's Cantina, 227

China Gardens, 321

Christ of the Abyss, 486

Christmas by the Sea, 156

Cinema Shores, 90

Cinema Six Theater, 91

City Cemetery, 97

City Hall Cafe, 454-55

Civil War Days, 140

Clinton Market, 30

Club Body Tech, 164

Coco Plum Beach, 355

Coconut Grove, 212-13

Coconut Palm Inn, 515-6

Coffee Mill Center, 165

Conch Air, 352

Conch Flyer, 253

Conch Republic Cigar Factory, 47

Conch Republic Days, 142-43

Conch Republic Seafood Company, 226-7

Conch Train, 121, 123

Conchs, 25-27, 242

Consigning Adults, 268

Copper Kettle, 527

coral reef spawning, 151

Coral Sea Glass Bottom Boat, 440-41

Coral Tree Inn, 214-15

Corcoran, Tom, 53

Courtney's Place, 202

Cover to Cover Books, 534-35

Cracked Conch Cafe, 390-91

Cracked Conch, The, 527-28

Cramer's Airboat Tours, 509

Crane Point Hammock, 353, 360

Criss Cross, 44, 187

Cuba! Cuba!, 261

Cuban Mix Deli, 248

Cudjoe Key, 285-86

Curry Hammock State Park, 360

Curry Mansion, 33, 99, 202-3

Curves of Key West, 165

Custom House, 30, 100

Cypress House, 34

D

Damn Good food To Go, 240

Deer Run B & B, 314-15

Deli Restaurant, 228

Dennis Pharmacy, 79, 228

Denny's Latin Cafe, 528

Discovery Glass Bottom Boat, 129-30, 166

Dog Beach, 171

Dolphin Care, 496

Dolphin Cove, 496

Dolphin Connection, 498

Dolphin Marina Boat
  Rentals, 299
Dolphin Research Center,
  496-97
Dolphin Marina Boat
  Rentals, 299
Dolphin Watch, 498
Dolphins Plus, 495-06, 500
dolphins, 492-98
Doubletree Grand Key
  Resort, 187
Duffy's Steak & Lobster,
  229
Duval Gardens, 203-4
Duval House, 204

E
Earth Naturals, 464
East Martello, 86, 101
Eaton Lodge, 205
Eden House, 187-88
Eggers, JT, 61
El Siboney, 248
Encore Fish House, 529
Equator Resort, 213
Everglades Ecology Tours,
  509-10
Everglades National Park,
  500-01
Evie's Subs, 319-20

F
Fairvilla Megastore, 267
Fantasy Dan's, 305
Fantasy Fest, 153-54
Faro Blanco, 376-7
Farto, Bum, 37
Fast Buck Freddie's, 262
Faulkner, Henry, 43, 82
ferry ruins, 308
Finnegan's Wake, 229
Fish Bowl, 437
Fish Tales, 391-92
Fishhouse, The, 529

Five Brothers, 248-49
Five Brothers II, 322
Flagler, Henry, 186, 338-49
Flagler Station, 104
Flagler's Restaurant, 254
Flamingo Crossing, 263
Flamingo Inn, 377-78
Florida Bay Kayak Tours,
  510
Florida Keys Fishing
  Tournaments, 429
Florida Keys Fly Fishing
  School, 430
Florida Keys Poker Run,
  152-53
Food For Thought, 401-2
Fort Jefferson, 104-06
Fort Taylor, 106-07,
  169-70
Frances Street Bottle Inn,
  206
French Reef, 486
Friday, Nancy, 53
Frost, Robert, 32, 50, 53,
  108
Full Moon Saloon, 256
Fury, 157
Fury Flyer Parasailing, 127

G
Galley Grill, 320
Gardens Hotel, 206-07
Geiger Key Marina, 320-1
Gellhorn, Martha, 48, 252
George Dolezal Library,
  351
Gingerbread House, 18,
  39
Gingerbread Square
  Gallery, 87
Goldman's Bagel & Deli,
  229-30
golf, 162, 363

Good Food Conspiracy,
  327-8
Green Parrot Bar, 256
Green Turtle Cay, 455
Greenville, S.C., 78
Greyhound Airport
  Shuttle, 136
Guild Hall Gallery, 87
Gulf Stream Airlines, 134

H
Haitian Art Gallery, 87
Half Shell Raw Bar, 230
Hard Rock Cafe, 230-31
Harriette's, 530
Harrison Gallery, 88
Harrison, Ben, 278
Harry Harris County Park,
  499
Havana Docks, 78, 256-57
Hawk's Cay, 378-9, 498
Hawn, Goldie, 44, 187
Heartbreak Hotel, 213
Helen Wadley Library, 421
Hemingway Days, 71, 150
Hemingway House, 69-70,
  107-08
Hemingway, Ernest, 48,
  50, 62-71, 108, 253
Hemingway, Pauline, 33,
  81, 108
Herbie's, 392
Heritage House Museum,
  32, 108-10
Herlihy, James Leo, 39, 43,
  53, 82,
Herman, Jerry, 41
Hersey, John, 50, 53
Hideaway Restaurant, 394
Hideout Restaurant, 530
Hilton Resort and Marina,
  188-89
Hog Heaven, 456
Hog's Breath Saloon, 257

Holiday Inn (Key Largo),
    516-17
Holiday Isle Resorts and
    Marina, 432, 436, 448-
    49, 457
Homer, Winslow, 80, 83
Hooked on Books, 464
Horizon Club, 457
Horseshoe Reef, 435
Housman, Jacob, 410-12
Hoyos, Elena, 276-78
Hungry Tarpon Cafe,
    457-58
Hurricane Monument,
    417-18
Hurricane, 1935 Labor
    Day, 414-17

I
Impromptu Concert
    Series, 94
Indian Key, 409-14, 422
Indigenous Park, 179
Irish Kevin's, 254
Irvine, Anne, 83
Islamorada Chamber of
    Commerce, 406-07
Islamorada County Park,
    426-27
Islamorada Fish Company
    458
Islamorada Founders Park,
    427
Islamorada Motel, 450
Islamorada Tennis Club,
    437
Islamorada,
    accommodations in,
        443-53
    beaches of, 426-27
    dining in, 454-63
    fishing in, 428-33
    history of, 408-16

Island Aeroplane Tours,
    134-35
Island Arts, 86
Island City House, 42, 189
Island City Strolls, 123
Island Food and Music
    Festival, 137-38
Island Grill, 456
Island Smoke Shop, 535
Islander Motel, 449-50
It's a Dive, 490

J
Jackson Square, 107-08
Jig's Bait and Tackle, 301
Jose's Cantina, 249
Jules' Undersea Lodge,
    517
July 4th Hospice Picnic,
    149-50

K
Kaiyo, 458
Kaufelt, David, 53
Kelly's Caribbean
    Restaurant, 32, 231
Key Ambassador, 185
Key Colony Beach Golf
    Course, 363
Key Colony Beach Marina,
    367
Key Colony Beach Motel,
    380
Key Colony Inn, 393
Key Deer Protection
    Alliance, 293
Key deer, 290-93
Key Dives, 436
Key Encounter Theatre &
    Museum, 91
Key Lantern Motel, 451
Key Largo Bay Beach
    Resort, 518

Key Largo Chamber of
    Commerce, 471
Key Largo Dry Rocks, 486
Key Largo Library, 505,
    536-37
Key Largo Princess, 511-
    12
Key Largo, the movie, 475
Key Largo, the song, 475
Key Lime Inn, 190-91
Keys Fisheries, 393
Keys Fitness Center, 364
Keys Shuttle Airport
    Shuttle, 136
Key West Aloe, 47, 263
Key West Aquarium, 28,
    95
Key West Art and
    Historical Society, 30,
    101, 110
Key West Art Center, 88
Key West Bed and
    Breakfast, 42, 207
Key West Bight, 45
Key West Botanical
    Garden, 175-77
Key West Butterfly and
    Nature Conservancy, 97
Key West Business Guild,
    217
Key West Chamber of
    Commerce, 28
Key West Cigar Factory,
    263-64
Key West City Hall, 37
Key West Craft Show, 138
Key West Express, 125
Key West Fishcutters, 324
Key West Hand Print
    Fabrics, 47, 264
Key West International
    Airport, 133
Key West Island Books, 59

Key West Lighthouse Museum, 110-11
Key West Literary Seminar, 138
Key West Nature Bike Tours, 121
Key West Poetry Guild, 61
Key West Pub Crawl Walking Tour, 251
Key West Reader, The, 59
Key West Seaplane Service, 135
Key West Songwriters Festival, 145
Key West Symphony Orchestra, 93
Key West Women's Club, 156
Key West Women's Flag Football Tourney, 139
Key West,
    accommodations in, 181-214
    annual events in, 137-156
    architecture of, 16-21
    bars in, 251-60
    beaches of, 169-74
    diving in, 157-59
    fishing in, 159-62
    history of, 5-15
    walking tour of, 28-49
    Keys Fisheries Market & Marina, 393-94
Keys weather, 24-25
Kingsail Resort Motel, 380-81
Kino Sandal Factory, 49, 265
Kiraly, John, 83-84
Kirkwood, James, 50, 54-55
Klein, Calvin, 42-43

Kona Kai Resort, 519-20
Kozuchi Restaurant, 47
KWest, 254

L

La Concha Hotel, 192-93
La Dichosa, 249
La Mer, 208
La Pensione, 208-09
La Te Da, 231-32
La Trattoria Venezia, 232
Lands End Marina, 46
Largo Lodge, 520
Lash, Joseph, 50
Layton Nature Trail, 359
Lazy Days Restaurant, 459
Lazy Way Shops, 46
Leathermaster, 267
Leslie, John, 55
Liberty Schooner, 131
Liberty Clipper, 131
Lignumvitae Key, 423-25
Lime Tree Resort, 381
Little Hamaca Park, 178-79
Little Italy, 394-5
Little Palm Island, 315-16
Little White House, 111-13
Long Key State Recreation Area, 356-58, 373-74
Long Key, 337-38
Looe Key Dive Center, 299-300
Looe Key Reef Resort, 316
Lorelei, 460
Louie's Backyard, 78, 232-33
Lower Keys Chamber of Commerce, 289
Lower Keys,
    accommodations in, 310-18
    dining in, 319-26

history of, 283-88
Lucky Street Gallery, 88-89
Luknis, Capt. Karen, 127
Lurie, Allison, 50, 55

M

Mallory Square, 28
Mandalay Marina and Tiki Bar, 530-31
Mangoes, 233
Mangrove Mama's, 321
Mangrove Mike's Cafe, 455-56
Marathon Airport, 351
Marathon Chamber of Commerce, 350
Marathon Community Cinema, 354
Marathon Community Theatre, 354
Marathon Guides Association, 366
Marathon Jeff's Boat Rentals, 371
Marathon Kayaks, 371
Marathon Lady, 366
Marathon Skate Park, 364
Margaritaville, 77, 234
Marina del Mar Resort and Marina, 520-21
Marker 88, 460-61
Marquesa Hotel, 36, 196
Marrying Sam, 273
Martin's Cafe, 234-5
Martha's Steak and Seafood, 234
Martin Luther King Community Pool, 163, 167
McGuane, Tom, 55
Merlinn Inn, 209
Mermaid and the Alligator, 209-10

Merrill, James, 50, 55

Meteor Smokehouse, 235

Middle Keys:

accommodations in, 373-86

biking in, 361-62

dining in, 387-99

diving in, 368-70

fishing in, 365-67

history of, 336-49

Midnight Cowboy, 39, 82

Mini Lobster Season, 151

Minimal Regatta, 149

Molasses Reef, 486

Monroe County Library (Key West), 167

Mosquito Coast, 127-29

Mrs. Mac's Kitchen, 531

Ms. Cellaneous, 465

Mudd, Dr. Samuel, 104

Museums of Crane Point Hammock, 352-53

N

Nancy's Secret Garden, 36, 177-78

Nautilimo Tours, 441

Nine One Five, 219

No Name Key, 304

No Name Pub, 322-23

Num Thai, 531-32

Nut House, 328

O

Oasis, 214

Ocean Beach Club Resort, 382

Offshore Powerboat Race Week, 155

Old City Hall, 47

Old Island Days, 137, 140

Old Town Mexican Cafe, 236

Old Road Cafe, 323

Old Seven Mile Bridge, 359-60

Old Stone Church, 35

Old Tavernier Restaurant, 532

Old Town Trolley, 30, 122

Old Wooden Bridge Fishing Camp, 316-17

Once Upon An Island, 59

Our Lady of Lourdes Shrine, 114-15

Out of the Blue Gallery, 327

Overseas Railroad, 338-44

P

PADI, 158, 485

Papa Joe's Landmark Restaurant, 461

Papa Joe's Marina, 432

Papa's Hideaway, 210

Papio, Stanley, 84

Paradise Inn, 193-94

Paradise Tattoo, 265-66

Parawest Parasailing, 126-27

Park & Ride, 22

Parrotdise, 324

ParrotHeads, 15, 155

Peaches, 261-62

Pearl's Rainbow, 215

Pelican Cove Resort, 438, 441-42

Pennekamp Coral Reef State Park, 480-84

Pepe's Cafe, 45, 236

Perrine, Henry, 412-13

Phantom Fireworks, 534

Pickles Reef, 434

Pier House, 194, 237

Pigeon Key, 346-49

Pilot House Restaurant, 532

Pinewood Nature Trail, 304

Pink Juntique, 537

Pioneer Cemetery, 418-20

Pirate Soul, 120

Pirates in Paradise, 155

Pisces, 224

Pitts, Susan, 78

Porky's BBQ, 395

Presidential Gates, 31, 32

Pro Fitness Center, 165

PT's, 45, 237

Q

Queen Mother Pageant, 146

R

Ragged Edge Resort, 452-53

Rain Barrel Village, 466

Rainbow Bend Resort, 382-83

Reach Hotel, 195

Red Barn Theatre, 92

Reef Relief, 150

Reserve America, 311, 483

Rhodes, Evan, 56

Rick's / Durty Harry's / Rumrunners, 257

Ripley's Believe it or Not Odditorium, 115

Rob's Island Grill, 323-24

Robbie's Marina, 440

Russell, Kurt, 44

Rusty Anchor, 237-38

Rutledge, Leigh, 56

S

sailboat races, 138

Sailor's Choice II, 508

Saltwater Angler, 162

San Carlos Institute, 92

Sanchez, Mario, 84-85

Schooner Wharf Bar, 46, 258

Sculpture Key West, 138

Sea Dwellers, 490

Seacoast Airlines, 134

Seafarer Fish and Dive Resort, 521-22

Sea Isle Resort, 216

Sea Store, 46, 266

Seascape Ocean Resort, 383-84

Sebago, The, 158

Seven Fish, 238

Seven Mile Bridge Run, 142

Seven Mile Grill, 395-96

Shape U Fitness Center, 164

Sharkey's Dive Center, 491

Shell Warehouse, 28, 30

Sheraton Key West, 197

Shields, Brooke, 42

Shipwreck Historeum, 30, 115-16

Shula's on the Beach, 238

Siesta Motel, 384-85

Sign of Sandford, 35, 88-89

Silverstein, Shel, 56, 202

Simonton Street Beach, 171

Skydive Key West, 305

Sloppy Joe's, 48, 258-59

Smathers Beach, 173-74

Snooks, 532-33

SNUBA, 507

Sombrero Beach, 355-56

Sombrero Country Club, 363

Sombrero Marina and Dockside Lounge, 399

Sombrero Reef, 368

South Beach, 170-71

South Beach Motel, 198

Southernmost Motel, 198

Southernmost Point, 116-17

Southpoint Divers, 159

Spirit Snorkel Trips, 370

Spirit of Pennekamp, 512

Sponge Market, 30, 266-67,

Spring Break, 141

Square One Restaurant, 239

St. Paul's Episcopal Church, 117-18, 156

Stevens, Wallace, 57

Strabel, Thelma, 57-58

Studio Alan Maltz, 89

Strike Zone Charters, 300-01

Sugarloaf Key, 283-84

Sugarloaf Lodge, 317

SunCruz I, 512-13

sunset celebration, 119-20

Sunset Cove Motel, 522

Sunset inn, 459

Survivor's Party, 146

Swim Around the Island, 148

T

Tavern by the Sea, 396-97

Tavernier Bicycle and Hobby, 506

Tavernier Hotel, 522-23

Tavernier Towne Cinema, 507

Tavernier Towne, 536

Taylor, Elizabeth, 37-38, 262

Thai Cuisine, 48, 239

Thayer IV, 476-77

Theatre of the Sea, 438-39, 497

The Cafe, 219

Tradewinds Plaza, 536-7

Traveler's Palm Garden Cottages, 199

Treasure Island Village, 465-66

Tropic Cinema, 90

Tru Art Bakery and Bookstore, 329

Truman, Harry S, 31, 34, 111-13,

Truman, Harry S, Legacy Symposium, 145

Tugboats, 533

Turtle Hospital, 353

Turtle Kraals, 259

U

U.S. Fish and Wildlife Key Deer Refuge, 290

Ultralight Tours, 305

Underwater Music Festival, 148-49

V

Valhalla Beach Motel, 385-86

Valladares and Son, 60-61

Venus Charters, 127

Veterans Memorial Park and Beach, 358

Village Cafe, 397-98

Von Cosel, Carl 190-91, 276-78

W

Waterfront Market, 45

Waterfront Playhouse, 93

Waverunner tour, 129

Weddings Without Worry, 274

Wellspring Medicine Garden, 179-80

Wesley House Valentine's Party, 139

West Martello Tower, 180

Whale Harbor Inn and
    Marina, 433, 461-2
Wilbur, Richard, 50, 58
Wild Bird Rehab Center,
    501-04
Williams, Tennessee, 50,
    72-74, 82, 118
Tennessee Williams Fine
    Arts Center, 92-93
Windley Key Fossil Site,
    420-21
Wine Galley, 259
Womenfest, 152
Wooden Spoon, 397
Woody's, 462
World Wide Sportsman,
    466
Wreck and Gally Grill,
    397-98
Wreckers Museum, 118-19
Wright, William, 58
Wyland Wall, 45, 46

Y

Yankee Freedom, 126
Yellowtail Inn, 386
Yoga College of India, Key
    West, 165

Z

Zane Grey Lounge, 463
Zorsky, Joe, 190-91

Order Form

Palm Island Press
411 Truman Avenue ⋆ Key West, FL 33040 USA
305-296-3102

Send _____ copies of *June Keith's Key West and The Florida Keys* at $18.95 each

Send _____ copies of *Postcards From Paradise* at $14.95 each

I understand that I may return any books for a full refund—for any reason, no questions asked.

Add $4.50 Priority Mail postage and handling for the first book and 75¢ for each additional book. For books shipped to Florida addresses, please add 7.5% sales tax per book.

Enclosed is my check for: _____

Name: _____

Address: _____

City, State, ZIP: _____

☐ This is a gift. Please send directly to:

Name: _____

Address: _____

City, State, ZIP: _____

☐ Autographed by the author
   Autographed to: _____